*Cultural Revolution
and Revolutionary Culture*

Cultural Revolution and Revolutionary Culture

Alessandro Russo

Duke University Press   *Durham and London*   2020

© 2020 Duke University Press All rights reserved
Designed by Drew Sisk
Typeset in Portrait Text by Westchester Publishing Services

Library of Congress Cataloging-in-Publication Data

Names: Russo, Alessandro, [date] author.
Title: Cultural Revolution and revolutionary culture
  / Alessandro Russo.
Description: Durham : Duke University Press, 2020.
  | Includes bibliographical references and index.
Identifiers: LCCN 2019054783 (print) | LCCN 2019054784 (ebook)
ISBN 9781478008590 (hardcover)
ISBN 9781478009528 (paperback)
ISBN 9781478012184 (ebook)
Subjects: LCSH: Political culture—China—History.| Communism
  and culture—China. | China—History—Cultural Revolution,
  1966-1976.
Classification: LCC DS778.7 .R87 2020 (print) | LCC DS778.7 (ebook)
  | DDC 951.05/6—dc23
LC record available at https:/ /lccn.loc.gov/2019054783
LC ebook rec ord available at https:/ /lccn.loc.gov/2019054784

Cover art: Claudia Pozzana, *Veiled Mao*. Shanghai, 2009.

CONTENTS

Acknowledgments vii
Introduction 1

PART I   *A Theatrical Prologue*

    1 Afterlives of an "Upright Official" 11
    2 Political and Historical Dilemmas 26
    3 An Unresolved Controversy 48

PART II *Mao's Anxiety and Resolve*

    4 A Probable Defeat and Revisionism 91
    5 Shrinking the Cultural Superego 104

PART III *A Political Test for Class Politics*

    6 Testing the Organization 141
    7 A Subjective Split in the Working Class 167
    8 Facing a Self-Defeat 204

PART IV *At the Edge of an Epochal Turning Point*

    9 Intellectual Conditions for a Political Assessment 239
    10 Foundations of Deng Xiaoping's Strategy 263

Notes 285
Bibliography 323
Index 343

ACKNOWLEDGMENTS

A special motivation for this work came from having shared much of my intellectual journey with Claudia Pozzana, including our long study sojourns, field research, and teaching in China. Her research into the origins of Chinese Marxism and contemporary Chinese poetry, and her critical attention to the development of my research, have been a source of warm and constant inspiration.

I have discussed theoretical issues and hypotheses that have enriched the intellectual horizon of this work with Alain Badiou, the founder of the contemporary rebirth of philosophy, friend and comrade since the 1970s. Some years ago, Badiou asked if the Cultural Revolution was "the last revolution." Many of my arguments in this volume try to answer this question.

Friends and colleagues, whom I thank for their criticisms and suggestions, have read various chapters of this book's previous versions: Judith Balso, Tani Barlow, Chris Connery, Mobo Gao, Gail Hershatter, Rebecca Karl, Fabio Lanza, Rosalind Morris, Patricia Thornton, Frank Ruda, Wang Bang, Wang Hui, and Wang Xiaoming.

I am especially grateful to Ken Wissoker of Duke University Press, who has warmly supported the project that gave rise to this volume. Four anonymous reviewers have made, some with passion, others with impatience, remarkable contributions to the development of this version.

The late David Verzoni, a faithful friend whose recent loss is a great sorrow for me, contributed decisively to restoring to the English language a prose inevitably marked by my "neo-Latin" linguistic habits.

Previous versions of chapters 4 and 8 were published respectively in *Crisis and Critique* 3, no. 1 (2016) and in *positions* 13, no. 3 (2005). Chapters 9 and 10 include parts of essays published in *Modern China* 39, no. 3 (2013), *The China Quarterly* 227 (September 2016), and in the volume *Afterlives of Chinese Communism: Political Concepts from Mao to Xi*, ed. C. Sorace, N. Loubere, and I. Franceschini (London: Verso, 2019).

INTRODUCTION

This book proposes a new way to understand global political turmoil in the innovative 1960s and 1970s. The Cultural Revolution was a crucial turning point for China, but also the moment when a much longer and truly global "revolutionary" era ended. At the same time, it was an attempt to make sense of that history and to find new possibilities within it. That is why at that particular time the event in question had global resonance, and why we should still concern ourselves with it today, since those questions remain unsolved.

To look for a new egalitarian mass politics it is necessary to come to terms with the Cultural Revolution and the 1960s in general. It is actually impossible to find a new path without new ideas about that last great political period, a persistent tendency as regards modern revolutions. A fundamental challenge of every great political cycle is how to reassess the previous great political cycle. For the October Revolution, it was how to reassess the Paris Commune, and for the Cultural Revolution it was how to reassess all the historical experience of socialism from the October Revolution onward. Even for Marx and Engels, a crucial issue was how to evaluate the French Revolution, which they interpreted as the great bourgeois revolution preceding the proletarian revolution that was to come.

The main hypothesis of this book is that China's Cultural Revolution was a communist movement whose aim was to undertake a thorough reexamination of communism. In essence, it was a radical scrutiny of the existing alternatives to capitalism. As such, the study of the Cultural Revolution must take into account two historical periods: events that began as far back as 1848, when the *Communist Manifesto* heralded the long search for a way out of capitalism, and the unique worldwide political phenomenon of the 1960s, and its Chinese hotbed, one of whose main projects was to rethink the foundations of modern communism.

The mass movements of the 1960s placed at the head of the communist agenda an urgency to reexamine the essentials of modern egalitarian politics by searching for a new beginning and not mere dissolution. Those events are not to be confused with the disintegration of the Soviet bloc, which occurred two decades later. Indeed, the collapse of the USSR and its satellites was ultimately the aftereffect of the mass movements that had radically criticized and finally discredited the political value of state communism.

For their part, the USSR and its satellites violently opposed that critical uprising, labeling as anticommunist the mass movements that criticized the socialist states' claim to be the indisputable alternative to capitalism. However, it was precisely while indignantly rejecting any doubts about the validity of "their" communism that those very party-states were racing toward a radical crisis, about which they remained in steadfast denial. When they finally started to perceive the danger, it was too late.

Between the late 1980s and the early 1990s, when the Soviet bloc collapsed overnight, all those parties disintegrated and their fragments enthusiastically declared that there was no alternative to capitalism. The bureaucrats of state communism, the polemical target throughout the 1960s, were nihilistically driven to neoliberalism, but not before they had vilified and finally annihilated the mass movements that had criticized them. The self-dissolution of twentieth-century state communism is in fact one of the main obstacles to the study not only of the 1960s, but also of the entire historical experience of modern communism.

The other huge obstacle to the study of the 1960s is that in the Chinese epicenter of the decade there is still the largest communist party that has ever existed, and so far the most stable and powerful. Obviously, it exists at the price of unprecedented paradoxes that further obscure the issue. For the CCP has embraced capitalism with conviction and extreme rigor, while maintaining a substantial organizational continuity with the past, to the point of declaring itself the "vanguard of the working class" and proclaiming communism as its maximum political ideal. The "socialism with Chinese characteristics" label adds a bit of nationalist veneer, part and parcel of which has been a "thorough negation" of the Cultural Revolution, and with it the 1960s, for having hindered not only state communism but also the advent of "capitalist communism."

The official government narrative that, immediately after Mao's death, the arrest of Maoist leaders rescued China from chaos and misery was a mere pretext. In fact, the issues at stake were intensely political and the situation was one of neither anarchy nor economic collapse. However, the passage from a mass political laboratory for reassessing communism to unabashed capitalism in the end went exceptionally smoothly and calls for close examination.

Mao repeatedly foresaw that "in China it [was] quite easy to build capitalism."[1] The main reason was that capitalism is the rule of the modern social world, and socialism was an exception that could exist only if renewed by repeated movements of mass experimentation. The Cultural Revolution was the latest such movement, in its turn exceptional, since its main target was to reassess the nature of the socialist exception. The most farsighted revolutionary leaders were fully aware that a brutal termination of the experiment and a return to the rule of wage slavery was all too likely, yet they were fully convinced of the need to persevere on the path of the exception. As Zhang Chunqiao, one of the main Maoist leaders, said at the trial of the Gang of Four in 1981, "In accordance with the rules of this world, I have long thought that such a day would come."[2] This volume will undertake a political reexamination of that exception to the rule of this world.

There are two possible approaches to studying the Cultural Revolution. One, which prevails today, starts from the assumption (often tacitly understood) of a definitive political judgment as the yardstick for assessing those events. In fact, this perspective, being limited to the criteria of the more or less fatalistic contemporary consensus regarding the rule of capitalism, studies the Cultural Revolution inevitably as "thorough negation"—that is, just what it was not, or rather, what it should not have been. This is the tone of most of the studies that have been done in the last decades.[3] The present volume explores another path, affirmative but still largely in development, which starts from the idea of a very incomplete knowledge of what the politics of today could be, and studies the Chinese events of the 1960s and 1970s as a possible resource for rebuilding an intellectual horizon of egalitarian politics.

The Cultural Revolution compels us to rethink the conceptual coordinates and fundamental paradigms of modern political theories and constitutes a decisive test case. The Cultural Revolution traces paths of thought whose uniqueness needs to be examined because those paths did not fully fit the framework of political knowledge in force in the mid-1960s, but in fact, from the beginning posed the urgency to subject that framework to a mass political test.

To study that immense ten-year political process, we need categories appropriate to its singularity, many of which must be built during the analysis itself. We need to build a track to proceed upon. This also explains why in this book there are rigorous analytical parts in which the reader is invited to follow even minute details, and other parts that are attempts to formulate theoretical hypotheses.

This study is based on a detailed examination of declarations made by the protagonists, linked to the time they were made. They are the fundamental units of analysis for all the processes examined. I hope readers will bear with me for the superabundance of quotations I have placed in this book. They are cited in order to yield the floor to the variety of voices that spoke up at that decisive moment in modern Chinese political and intellectual history.

On the other hand, since the analytical categories are calibrated on those same political statements, the theoretical perspective constitutes a work in progress. At some points it will be necessary to dwell minutely on nuances, while at others it will be necessary to consider the general horizon and the specific categories in order to examine a single passage. These two registers are integral parts of the project itself.

The volume explores some key passages of the decade, four of them in particular: the historical-theatrical "prologue" of 1965; Mao's original attitude; the mass phase of 1966-68; and the Maoists' unfinished attempts to make a political assessment of the decade.

These are relatively short passages, between which, even when there is a temporal contiguity, there are essential discontinuities due to the political stakes, the extent and conditions of the mass involvement, and the balance of power at the summit of the party-state. But what links these different passages is that in each of them the thrust, the political novelties, the hesitations, the oppositions, the obstacles (most often internal), and the efforts to overcome them were essentially about the problem of how to reevaluate what had been in the twentieth century the way out of capitalism, its subsequent impasse, and how to find a new path—in other words, how to rethink the experience of the socialist states, which had been transformed into a bureaucratic machinery that mirrored those of the capitalist regimes, and ultimately how to find a new meaning in communism.

This volume will examine these passages in terms of a general hypothesis about China's revolutionary decade. They constitute the stages of an immense mass political laboratory, whose problematic nucleus takes on different aspects in its various phases, each of which entails from the beginning a peculiar confrontation between the new political subjectivities involved in the experimentation and the framework of political culture available to the revolutionaries. In this sense, the general topic of this book is the relationship between the

Cultural Revolution, understood as the set of those subjective multiplicities, and the revolutionary culture, understood as the cultural framework of politics through which the revolutionaries acted and declared their intentions.

I will start by studying the historical-theatrical prologue (part I, chapters 1-3), namely the controversy over the historical drama *Hai Rui Dismissed from Office* in the months preceding the beginning of the mass phase. That controversy, which was supported by widespread involvement of the intellectual public, with thousands of risky, first-person press interventions, has generally been neglected in studies of the Cultural Revolution.

In fact, the controversy was infused with real intellectual and political stakes, namely the urgency for a theoretical clarification about whether "historical materialism" could deal with both the peasant revolts in the history of imperial China and the political role of the peasants under socialism. Although the specific terms of the historical-political-theatrical polemic have remained unresolved, it played a decisive role at the start of the revolutionary decade.

I will then discuss, from two converging perspectives, Mao's original intentions, one of the trickiest themes in any study of the Cultural Revolution (part II). The last twenty years of Mao's revolutionary enterprise (1956-76) were marked by a peculiar anxiety about the destiny of socialism, which also propelled his obstinate quest for a new political path (chapter 4). I will argue that his interventions between the end of 1965 and mid-1966 aimed at removing obstacles to the participation of the masses in a critical reexamination of the revolutionary culture and its institutional space (chapter 5).

While the mass phase of the Cultural Revolution, between 1966 and 1968, is certainly the most studied and best documented in scholarly research, its most enigmatic aspects remain opaque and need to be explored from new perspectives (part III). Two problems in particular require thorough rethinking. One concerns the processes by which the creation of an unlimited plurality of independent political organizations was overturned in the space of two years in a powerful self-destructive drive that deprived those political inventions of value (chapters 6 and 8). The other problem concerns the culmination of this phase, namely the foundation, in the aftermath of the Shanghai January Storm (1967), of the Shanghai Commune and its shutdown after a few weeks with the foundation of the Revolutionary Committee (chapter 7).

The political stakes of the first two years, and the experimentation with new forms of mass organization beyond the horizon of the party-state, radically superseded the space of existing political culture by questioning the value of key concepts. The revolutionaries had to face—within themselves, clearly— the ambiguities with which concepts such as "class" and even "working class" were used to hinder and suppress ongoing political experimentation. The point I argue is that the new subjective intentions met a decisive impasse in the face of a key concept of revolutionary culture, that of "seizure of power."

This concept, so central to the revolutionary culture of twentieth-century communism, soon ended by becoming for the revolutionaries a substitute for yet unelaborated new concepts that could enable an intellectual assessment of their political activism. In examining their freshness and courage, as well as their hesitations, backslides, and self-destructive moves, we need to take into account the discontinuities that were opened up by that political novelty in the general framework of political culture and the feedback of that culture on the political inventions.

All those events drove the revolutionaries to reexamine the entire cultural horizon of their own politics. That need appeared most explicitly in the latter part of the revolutionary decade. In the fourth part of this volume (chapters 9 and 10) I will analyze aspects of the large mass study campaigns that took place between mid-1973 and 1976. This final phase of the decade, though in fact marked by strong theoretical intent, has also been, overall, poorly explored. The topics discussed then included not only Marxist-Leninist political theory, in particular the concept of the dictatorship of the proletariat, but also the main currents of ancient Chinese political thought, above all the polemics between Confucians and Legalists.

These study movements intended to lay the groundwork for a mass-scale assessment of events. Mao tried in vain to propose it in the last year of his life, when he stressed the need for a thorough rethinking of the extent to which the Cultural Revolution had fallen short of its aims. An insurmountable obstacle came with the rejection by Deng Xiaoping, then the actual head of government, who mounted a counterattack against the theoretical study movements launched by Mao, especially the one on the dictatorship of the proletariat, and categorically quashed Mao's proposal for a vast campaign of self-critical reflection on the decade.

Deng's early victory consisted essentially in his preventing a political assessment of the Cultural Revolution and at the same time interrupting the theoretical evaluation of twentieth-century communism. Thus, he achieved a decisive result, whose effectiveness continues in China's present-day governmental stability. Impeding the revolutionaries from taking stock of their enterprise was the prerequisite for breaking their subjective determination, sowing political disorientation among the masses, and placing all political decisions firmly in the hands of a government elite that wished to settle accounts with whatever mass political experimentation it labeled as mere chaos and anarchy.

The revolutionary decade ended with the effort toward a vast political assessment the Maoists tried to make, but which remained unfinished, no doubt due to the political and theoretical limits they themselves were trying to overcome. The interdiction to conclude that assessment exercised leverage on these "internal causes." The coalition led by Deng, in its turn, drew essential resources for its reactive energy from the capacity to impose that prohibition.

The fundamental themes of that unfinished assessment, as well as the long-term consequences of its interdiction, constitute the starting point for the theoretical and analytical perspectives of this book.

PART I

A Theatrical Prologue

I

Afterlives of an "Upright Official"

The prologue to the Cultural Revolution is crowded with multifarious figures: mandarins, peasants, famous historiographers and radical critics, higher ministers of culture, loyalists, opponents, centrist politicians, and even false "leftist" polemicists. The curtain opens on a scene set in the Ming era. An irreproachable imperial governor, at the beginning definitely a positive hero, sings in the style of the traditional Beijing opera:

> I must strengthen law and order
>
> And redress grievances for the masses.
>
> The people have suffered more than they can bear,
>
> Because the evil officials are cruel and lawless.
>
> To kill dragons and tigers is a man's duty;
>
> And I need no monument to serve my country.

The character, however, first *coup de théâtre*, will soon become a negative hero and the target of a bitter controversy—a prologue decidedly unusual for a revolution, from which in any case it is essential to start in order to find a political reading track of the Cultural Revolution. Theater, politics, and history were intertwined in a controversy over a historical drama that was the first spark of the revolutionary decade.

Our task in the first three chapters of this volume is to scrutinize the political nature of this prologue, one of the least explored stages of the Cultural Revolution. It will be necessary to consider first the sides that were staked out in initially framing the debate over the content of the play and its critique in November 1965. A second step will examine some major political and historical dilemmas of China in the early sixties that provided the background to the controversy. Then we shall proceed to a close reading of the debate, from late 1965 through the first months of 1966, and to a reflection of its vast scale.

Hai Rui the Upright

The preamble to the revolutionary decade, as recalled in all texts on the history of contemporary China, was the publication in November 1965 of Yao Wenyuan's critique of the historical drama *Hai Rui Dismissed from Office* (海瑞罢官 *Hai Rui ba guan*). The play had been written a few years earlier by the eminent historical scholar Wu Han, and the ensuing controversy the critical appreciation aroused was altogether unexpected. Although usually labeled a mere pretext used by Mao Zedong to purge literary circles, this episode cannot but be cited as at least the immediate antecedent to the momentous events that followed.[1] In effect, almost all specialist observers still maintain that it was nothing but a conspiracy of the old "Red Emperor" seeking to restore the grandeur of his own personality cult and rid himself of his opponents. This narrative has it that he found the excuse for dealing with both in the essay written by Yao, at that time a literary journalist in Shanghai.[2]

While the study of the Cultural Revolution as a whole is dominated by the motif of "thorough negation" (彻底否定 *chedi fouding*)—this has been for decades the official verdict issued by the postrevolutionary government—what is seen as its initial phase is almost totally ignored save mention only in passing. Even considering the power of the "virus of the present," against which Marc Bloch warned historians[3] (in our case the blanket of intellectual bewilderment that dominates questions of politics and the state), it is not clear why such an extraordinary episode has not attracted much more attention on the part of historians.[4]

Admittedly, never before had a controversy over a historical play, which was in fact a full Beijing opera staged in classical style with all its attendant elaborate theatrical rules, classical music, traditional costumes, and highly formalized gestures and intonations, set off such intense and prolonged political turbulence. While historians are often attracted by the unrepeatable and the extraordinary, not only does a stereotypical narration of such a unique episode continue to prevail, with firsthand studies being extremely rare, but seldom are the terms of the controversy and, less common still, the content of the play itself directly cited. Even a voluminous biography of Wu Han refrains from any specific analysis of the play.[5]

What, then, is one to think about this theatrical prologue to the Cultural Revolution, so richly embossed with operatic characters, mandarins and peasants, eminent historians engaged in dramaturgy, bitter controversies about the theater, history, and politics, and even philological disputes over sources in the archives?

The author of the play, Wu Han, notably remembered as the "first target" of the Cultural Revolution, was an eminent Chinese historian and renowned specialist in the Ming Dynasty. He was a pioneer in the field, having been since the 1930s one of the first scholars to engage in historical research into the Ming era, which had been a taboo topic during the following Qing Dynasty until its fall in 1911.[6] Incidentally, the typical bureaucratic practice of Chinese imperial governments in forbidding independent scholarly research on the previous dynastic era is still recognizable in the palimpsest of the "thorough negation" cloaking the Cultural Revolution.

Wu Han also held an official post very close to the elite leadership of the state as deputy mayor of Beijing. He was also a representative in the People's Assembly and a prominent figure in important national cultural institutions and editorial boards of academic journals and publishing houses. By the late fifties Wu Han had cultivated a special interest in Hai Rui. We will later examine in detail the motives and the development of his peculiar involvement with this real historical personage (chapter 3). He wrote articles about him, edited his collected works, and published *Hai Rui Dismissed from Office* in 1961. The play ran for a few months the same year and received enthusiastic reviews in authoritative Chinese newspapers.

Wu had expressly meant to portray Hai Rui as a model of "morality" (好品德 *hao pinde*) and to show his current significance (现实意义 *xianshi yiyi*). The play was initially welcomed in the press as an example of "using the past to serve the present" (古为今用 *gu wei jin yong*) and of the "integration of historical research with participation in the real struggle." It had been particularly praised, Yao recalled in his critique, for the high educational value that such a model of an "upright official" (清官 *qing guan*) could still exert.[7]

Hai Rui Dismissed from Office is set in the second half of the sixteenth century, during the last period of the Ming Dynasty in Suzhou, southern China. Hai Rui, the "incorruptible imperial official," had recently been appointed governor but soon came into conflict with rapacious local despots who were abusively seizing land. When he finally forces them to return the land to the legitimate owners, his enemies slander him until the Court, influenced by this defamatory campaign, orders Hai Rui's dismissal from office.[8]

Hai Rui shines with the qualities of traditional virtues and modesty befitting a lifestyle "at the people's service." He is even depicted as having some of the traits of the heroism found in socialist propaganda.[9] The governor, his enemies complain, cannot find the time to receive other officials, but "goes every day to the river to supervise work there and talks only to poor peasants, workers, and small traders." Hai Rui diligently oversees the execution of these "classic" water works, of which the imperial bureaucracy was so proud, but does so with a benevolent care for the people. At times, he even wears civilian clothes, so that the other functionaries do not recognize him in the street, and he does not indulge in ceremonies. He has thoughts only for the well-being of the people, or more precisely for the ills that afflict them.

The reading of some passages of the drama, besides being essential to get an idea of what sparked the controversy, provides a perspective that we shall adopt in examining some key political moments of the decade. As our focus will be on analysis of the statements of the protagonists, we shall begin with Wu's drama. The lines of the actors can be read as political statements, as in fact they were read by all the participants in the controversy of 1965–66. Emphasizing the subjective intentions in the declarations of characters is the essence of theater, and in this case the political stakes were present at every turn of the play. The following scenes from act VI, entitled "Judgment" (断案 Duan'an), the same as the initial quote, condense the underlying tone of the work and also constitute a key passage in the plot.

This is where Hai Rui makes his stage entrance attired in official mandarin hat and long scarlet silk robe. As the supreme legal authority of the district, he has summoned to his official residence (衙门 yamen) both the corrupt xiangguan (乡官 local despots, frequently former officials who still enjoy certain privileges) and the peasants, who complain about the wrongs they have suffered, for judgment. The latter have come to beg for justice, while the former anxiously await the arrival of the "incorruptible Hai," who enters the scene with the following monologue.

> ADJUTANT: The governor has given orders to open the yamen doors and hold court.
>
> *(Exit all officials)*
> *(Music plays. Army officers, soldiers, yamen runners enter. Hai Rui also enters, wearing an official silk hat and scarlet robe)*
> . . .

HAI RUI (*speaks*): I am Hai Rui, Governor of Yingtian. Since I took office, I have learned that the xiangguan and the rich people are despotic and lawless. The officials are corrupt and oppressive. Positive criminal evidence has been found concerning all those involved. The law clearly prescribes that all evil men must be eliminated. In today's court trial, I definitely must uphold this ideal, wipe out the blot of evil, and protect the people. Men, summon the officials.

(The functionaries enter, heads bowed, increasingly worried and trembling with fear when the governor thus harangues them:)

HAI RUI: My lords.

OFFICIALS: Your Highness.

HAI RUI: How have you performed your official duties?

OFFICIALS: We have always been honest and careful, serving the Imperial Court on the one hand, and sharing the worries of the common people on the other.

HAI RUI: Is that really so? Have you really been serving the Imperial Court on the one hand and sharing the worries of the common people on the other?

OFFICIALS: Yes.

HAI RUI: Ha, ha! Since you are all honest officials, then, I will request your participation in the trial of this case. Who's the magistrate of Huating County?

The magistrate of Huating prefecture states that he is present and the trial begins. Hai Rui unveils point by point the plot by which this magistrate had masked the evildoings of a powerful xiangguan, who had unlawfully appropriated lands and brutally terrorized the peasants. At the end of his harangue, Hai Rui sings of his firm determination to punish the wicked:

HAI RUI (*sings*):

You heartless creatures, so corrupt and filthy,

You have soiled your official robes with infamy.

Heavy as the mountain, the law cannot be lenient.

To punish your crimes, I will not relent.

The corrupt officials and xiangguan can do nothing but plead for clemency. The peasants, on the contrary, having finally obtained justice, exult in a chorus and promise to worship the upright official, both day and night.

VILLAGER A: My great lord, your sentences are the fairest. But our lands have been seized by the Xu family and other xiangguan. And yet we still have had to pay taxes. The people's lives are extremely hard. We hope Your Honor will do something.

VILLAGERS B AND C: My great lord, you must please do something.

HAI RUI: Adjutant, make a written announcement ordering all xiangguan to return to the people, within ten days, all the land they have seized. There must be no delay. Those who refuse to obey the order shall be punished in accordance with the law.

ADJUTANT: Yes, Your Highness.

VILLAGERS: (*kowtowing*) Your Highness has acted on our behalf. The common people of Jiangnan will have a better life from now on. We are deeply grateful. When we return home, we shall paint your portrait and worship it morning and night.

(*Sing*):

Today we've seen the cloudless "blue sky";[10]

To rebuild our homes, we shall work diligently.

Having land, we shall lack neither clothes nor food,

In the near future, we shall find a better livelihood.

(*Speak*):

We thank your great lordship!

HAI RUI: There is no need. You may go home now.[11]

The act ends with the governor's assistant, surrounded by a group of soldiers, who reads out an official proclamation to the sounding of a gong.

ADJUTANT: Listen carefully, everyone, especially the xiangguan:
Hai Rui, Third-Class Censor of the Censor General's Office and Governor of the ten prefectures of Yingtian, makes the following announcement to all regarding the question of giving back the land to its lawful owners: the xiangguan and other ferocious despots have, in the past, seized many people's land. Consequently, the peasants have become unemployed and live miserable lives. The law demands that all the land thus seized must be returned to its lawful owners. Anyone who dares to disobey this order will be duly punished.

(The common people listen quietly, then leave the stage happily. Adjutants and soldiers also depart.)

With all the precautions one must bear in mind when evaluating the peculiar forms of the Beijing opera, as well as considering losses in translation, one might wonder whether what sounds like a pretext in this episode is rather an artistic convention of the quoted dialogue. This may depend on the fact that, due to the extreme formality of the scenic devices in the Beijing opera, the effect is somewhat stereotypical when there is no penetrating creative intention.

In fact, *Hai Rui Dismissed from Office* had exclusively didactic purposes. The theater was a medium to popularize history, an educational bent widespread in Chinese historical circles in those years and one that Wu himself actively promoted.[12] However, the author repeatedly declared, even in the preface to the play, that he was not a connoisseur of the Beijing opera and rarely went to see it. His lack of interest in the theater did not seem a serious problem to him.[13] On the formal level, *Hai Rui* was mostly a lesson in historical-political morality conveyed through a popular medium. That Wu rarely went to see the Beijing opera may not have been for lack of time, but for the fact that in the fifties and early sixties cultured Chinese did not consider it a very commendable spectacle, at best suitable for popular enjoyment.[14] It was probably also for this reason that the state's central cultural apparatus used the Beijing opera to disseminate historical knowledge.

Finally, what Wu had staged was not a historical character but a typical self-celebratory figure of Chinese bureaucratic imagery. Hai Rui was the virtuous official, surrounded by wicked officials against whom he does not hesitate to act even if he is obliged to endure unjust punishment from the monarch because of slander and intrigue, and despite his unconditional loyalty to the Court. The program of a seventeenth-century faction of scholar-officials, the Donglin Party (东林 党), as summarized by Etienne Balasz, provides an element of comparison: "The enemy is absolutism, meaning badly advised emperors encircled by abject eunuchs, who are the worst enemies. We have good emperors who, in a purified atmosphere, under the guidance of morally irreprehensible persons—that is, persons from our group of virtuous scholar officials—will lead the country toward a glorious renewal."[15]

Besides a conventional portrait of the irreprehensible official, Wu also portrays the peasants as innocent victims waiting for the grace of a savior, and finally joyful in venerating him. The return of this topos, greeted as a model for Chinese communists, was significant. For forty years, the Chinese communists had explored radically different possibilities for the style of a political cadre and his relationships with the peasants. If the complacent image of the reassuringly benevolent official surrounded by kowtowing plebeians could be so authoritatively propagandized in the China of the early sixties, it meant that crucial political divergences were at stake.

The Stage and the Archive

As the criticism of *Hai Rui* played such a seminal role, one should ask if Yao's essay had some intrinsic qualities, and what its arguments were. In fact, Yao's essay was a noteworthy, very well-written text. It developed three main argumentative lines that deserve to be considered in detail: one properly theatrical, one historical, and one directly political.[16]

While Wu did not defend his theatrical criteria with much conviction, the theater being for him little more than a didactic device, Yao on his part directly discussed the artistic structure of the play. First, he raised an essentially theatrical question: the functions of the characters. The structure of the drama, Yao observed, pivoted around three types of characters. There was a single positive figure, Hai Rui, the sole savior of the oppressed. Besides him, a series of negative figures, the other officials, nearly all of whom were wicked, opposed him but trembled at his name. Finally, there was the mass of imploring peasants who sang hymns of gratitude in praise of the benevolent mandarin and who swore to behave as obedient subjects.

A close reading of Yao's criticism gives a sense of how much attention he paid to theatrical details. Moreover, since this episode is generally portrayed as a pretext whose content is irrelevant, some attention to the specific arguments and to style is helpful for reflecting on its developments. Here is a passage of Yao's criticism that also contains a synopsis of the plot.

> In this historical play—Yao wrote—Comrade Wu Han has portrayed Hai Rui as a perfect and noble figure, "who had the people in his mind in everything" and who "was the savior of the oppressed, the bullied, and the wronged at that time." You can hardly find any shortcomings in him. He seems to be the ideal figure for the author. Not only was he the savior of the poor peasants in the Ming Dynasty, he is also an example for the Chinese people and cadres to emulate in the socialist era.
>
> The author has taken great care to delineate his hero. To prepare for the appearance of this honorable official, he has reserved three complete acts of the nine acts in the play. In the first and second acts Hai Rui does

not appear at all, and much ink is spilled to portray the House of Xu—the family of Xu Jie [the main negative character, a corrupt official enemy of Hai Rui]. The script describes how this family encroaches upon the land of the peasants, carries off by force the daughters of common people, and bribes the officials into beating the poor peasant Chao Yushan to death. When the peasant woman Hong Alan, "full of anguish, appeals to heaven for justice," an urgent dispatch brings the order that Hai Rui will be the governor for the Ten Prefectures of Yingtian. To the officials, who are beside themselves with self-satisfaction, this is a bolt from the blue. They cry out in alarm, "What are we going to do?" Even the yamen underlings exclaim "the Honest Hai is coming! This is terrible!" In the third act, Hai Rui appears incognito. The playwright describes how Hai Rui personally listens to the "villagers who feel as if they were in the frying pan" and express in the most respectful terms their expectations of Hai Rui, praising him for his "impartiality," "wise judgments," "high repute," and "good record." Although in a feudal society "the world is controlled by officials from top to bottom, and justice is denied even to those who are in the right but have no money," the peasants who voice their maltreatment all believe that "the Honest Hai" is an exception and think that "he will make decisions for us."

This technique of strong contrast seeks to make the impression on the audience that only Hai Rui can alleviate the miseries of the peasants. It tries to delineate in every conceivable way for today's audience a hero who determines the destiny of the peasants. In this play, only Hai Rui appears as a positive heroic figure. The peasants can merely air their grievances passively to their lord and beseech "their lord to decide for them," entrusting their destiny to the "Honest Hai."[17]

Note the accuracy of the theatrical analysis and the role that it played in Yao's criticism. From this first angle of attack, the critique did not concern historical verisimilitude, but the subjective capacities of the theatrical characters as such. What Yao discussed first was not what the characters represented historically, but what they were capable of saying and doing on the stage. It was by this wholly subjective means that the heart of the divergence emerged as intrinsically political: Is it conceivable that peasants might have political capacities? Or are they only able to sing praises to the glory of "Honest Hai"? Further, Yao asked, what should our attitude, as communists, be toward the matter?

One should not forget that all the critiques in this controversy qualified their authors as political militants, or "revolutionary professionals," according to the famous Leninist definition, and that precisely for this reason such questions appear extremely remote today. Political sociology would at best classify the episode in a typology of "intra-elite cleavages." In neither China nor elsewhere today is it self-evident what a political militant or a revolutionary might be, still less a communist. Moreover, it is definitely obscure to current Chinese public opinion, or intentionally subject to denial, why in the mid-sixties the issue of the political subjectivity of the peasants was so hotly disputed.

For decades, the recurring issues in official Chinese government pronouncements concerning the destinies of the countryside have been rather the price that must be paid in order to conform to the "laws of the economy," as the extension of inequalities, the dislocation of a hundred million peasants, and the abdication of the state in educational and health policies in rural areas. Disdain of peasants, a structural element in the Chinese cultural identity, has resurfaced: in spoken Chinese, "peasant" (农民 *nongmin*) is today one of the most widespread synonyms for "stupid."

Therefore, some effort will be required in order to appreciate the fervor of that debate and its nexus of political-cultural references. The question of the possible political capacities of peasants had been decisive, and always highly controversial, in all the major political situations in which the CCP had been involved since its foundation. This is especially true of the Great Leap Forward of 1958–59, which had been at the core of fundamental and unresolved political divergences that *Hai Rui* brought fully to the fore, as we shall see in detail in the next chapter.

Yao's second angle of attack was properly historical and involved the problem of the representation of period personages. With the necessary scholarship, the author, who was not himself a professional historian but had consulted specialists, pursued his critique of Wu on strictly documentary terrain.[18] Yao proved, on the basis of the available sources and modern techniques of historical research (he even cited local archives, so highly praised by China scholars), that there was a series of incongruities, not simply of detail, in a play written with the intention of rigorously respecting historical truth, as Wu had repeatedly declared as a major criterion for historical plays. Of Yao's historiographical arguments, all of them well documented, the most relevant were the following.[19]

First, as a historical figure, Hai Rui could not plausibly be represented as the central figure of a situation concerning all peasants in general. In the scene described above, Hai Rui acts against a typical abuse of his time: the forcible surrender of land by small and medium owners to rapacious local officials (xiangguan). Actually, the situation involved a series of contradictions within the narrow social group of landowners, who at that time, in the district and throughout the whole region, did not exceed one-tenth of households, as local archives document. The peasants represented in the drama were, therefore, a tiny segment of rural society since the overwhelming majority of peasants had no land.

Moreover, Yao argued, Hai Rui was not, as depicted in Wu's play, an exceptional case in censuring those abuses. As was widely attested, many other officials in the same position had adopted, with greater or lesser conviction, similar measures (sometimes due only to contradictions and envy among the local gentry), including those in the same district who are portrayed as corrupt officials and Hai's deadly enemies. The Ming governments, which did not ignore the problem, had issued laws and decrees to counteract the abuses, which not only aggravated social instability in the countryside but also reduced the empire's income from taxes.

The xiangguan enjoyed tax exemptions, privileges that also extended to illegally acquired lands. In many cases, they were able to force small landowners to yield their holdings and to become their employees in exchange for the promise, not always kept, of avoiding taxation and *corvées*. Relying on available documentation, Yao also proved that Hai Rui could do very little about this abuse: restitution never exceeded 10 percent of the lands acquired illegally in a given district.

Finally, in spite of the "dismissal" cited in the title of the drama, and of some previous friction with the central government, the Court later fully reinstated Hai Rui and always praised him as an example of loyalty to the Court, although a man with a "difficult temperament." It was impossible, Yao argued, to extend the scope of the decisions taken by Hai Rui to the problems of the oppression of peasants in general. For the historically documented Hai Rui, the peasants were ignorant and treacherous plebeians, a potential hotbed of rebellion to be policed and firmly repressed if necessary.

The subjective traces of the historical figure of Hai Rui found in reports, administrative acts, and so on are very explicit in this regard. One of his earliest such memos concerned the suppression of a peasant rebellion on the island of Hainan, a measure that he systematically advocated throughout his career. When he was the local governor at the time described in the drama, he was in fact extremely suspicious of the grievances of peasants about the surrendering of land: in most cases, he declared them unfounded and punished the plaintiffs. In the introduction to a selection of Hai Rui's writings by Michel Cartier, a philological work that deliberately refrains from any judgment on the criticism of 1965, we find the following synthesis of Hai Rui's "social theories": "The society is [for Hai Rui] naturally divided into two classes: the scholars (*shi* 士) who constitute the conscious aristocracy and, because they received a Confucian education, are vested with the responsibility of maintaining order and harmony in the world; the people by nature ignorant (to the word 民 *min*, 'people' is usually attached the qualifier 愚 *yu*, 'stupid'), whose fate is to obey and to engage in productive activities."[20]

In Chinese, as in many other languages, insults referring to the stupidity of peasants have a long pedigree. In any event, Hai Rui's declared objective, Yao observed, despite all the conflicts he encountered with other factions of officials, was always the stability of the imperial regime: his administrative acts did not reach down to the roots of peasant dissatisfaction. Moreover, uprisings exploded in the area not long after the facts narrated in the drama.

Yao even noted that Hai Rui had repeatedly declared, "It is a proper principle to make the lower serve the upper. I have tried to adjust advantages and disadvantages *so that the system may last*" (emphasis added by Yao), and often urged the peasants to observe "propriety and morality" and "not to become bandits." As to peasant uprisings, he proposed that "the use of arms and pacification of the people be carried out simultaneously." His opposition to the most reactionary big landlords was not intended, Yao argued, to weaken the system of land ownership but merely to fortify it and consolidate the political power and long-term interests of the Ming Dynasty.

"To portray Hai Rui as the representative of the peasants' interests," wrote Yao, "is to confuse the enemy with ourselves, to obliterate the essence of the dictatorship of the landlord class." Hai Rui, who "always expressed his unshaken loyalty to the Emperor," wrote in a letter to another powerful local official, "I have exhausted my energy and wisdom for no other purpose than to establish a long-lasting foundation of rule here in Jiangnan, in order to repay the kindness and confidence bestowed on me by the Emperor." How then could Hai Rui, concluded Yao, do anything that might jeopardize the "foundation of this lasting enterprise"?

The third level of criticism concerned contemporary politics. The praise of Hai Rui, Yao remarked, focused on a specific issue: he acted in defense of the peasants because he "reversed unjust verdicts" (平冤獄 *ping yuanyu*) and imposed the "restitution of land" (退田 *tui tian*). However, having clarified that the restitution of land narrated in the drama concerned only a series of specific abuses produced within the bureaucratic and fiscal structure of the imperial system, the problem was, Yao argued, what the analogy was that the spectators were to learn from the play in the "present times." In other words, which unjust verdicts were supposed to have been reversed and which contemporary abuses were supposed to have been corrected with the restitution of land?

Because the play was aimed at providing an "example" of political morality from which contemporary spectators were supposed to learn, Yao asked first, what did Wu Han try to convey for present audiences by so central a plot theme as the return of land? Given that in China at the time land was under the collective ownership of people's communes, who had to return the land and to whom was it to be returned?

While Yao expressed clearly the criticism on the fate of the communes, much more indirect and encrypted was his criticism of the other political theme of the plot, "to reverse wrongful verdicts." Here Yao proposed first a classic argument. "The most thoroughgoing reversal of wrongful verdicts in human history" has been "the breaking out from the darkest human hell by the proletariat, as well as by the oppressed and exploited classes, and their smashing of the yoke of the landlords and bourgeoisie to become the masters of society." Finally, Yao discussed the "actual significance" of the play with respect to the conditions surrounding its composition in 1961.

It was a time, Yao wrote, quoting the official stance of the CCP in 1965, "when our country suffered temporary economic difficulties owing to natural disasters that lasted for three successive years." At that moment, "the attacks on China instigated again and again by the imperialists, the reactionary parties of various countries, and the modern revisionists, reached their climax." In the same years in China, "the landlords, rich peasants, counterrevolutionaries, and rightists" stirred the "wind of individual farming" (单干风 *dan gan feng*) and the "wind of verdict reversal" (反案风 *fan an feng*), seeking to "return the occupied land" and "to destroy the people's communes and their evil rule."

Yao did not elaborate further about the role of Wu's play in that moment, but wrote only that "class enemies" at that time clamored vociferously for a reversal of wrongful verdicts, "hoping for the emergence of someone who represented their interests," and to "reverse those verdicts [so that] they might return to power." The return of occupied land and reversal of wrongful verdicts, he concluded, were "the focal point of contention in the bourgeois opposition to the dictatorship of the proletariat and to the socialist revolution."[21]

It is evident that the controversy over *Hai Rui* involved inflammatory political issues and was not, as is often depicted in current narratives, a pretext for "purging literary spheres." Moreover, on the cultural level it mainly concerned not literature but history in its relationships with politics and, albeit in a somewhat twisted manner, with the theater. However, on the plane of the political present, Yao's arguments were indirect and incomplete, besides being couched in the recondite jargon of Chinese political prose of the time.

Some of the most frequently cryptic passages in Yao's text therefore need some translation. The Chinese government had indeed shown a tendency in the early sixties to roll back to a considerable extent the people's agricultural communes and collective land ownership in the name of a need to return to production on a family basis. This was the meaning of the expression *dan gan*, literally "to work on one's own." Yao polemically maintained that this downsizing was aimed at a return to private land ownership.[22] He claimed that in Wu's play the whole motif of land restitution, which apparently concerned the reasons and results of Hai's acting in favor of the peasants by restricting the authority of corrupt officials, in actual fact reflected the strong policy urgings among the CCP leadership to abolish the people's communes.[23]

The economic situation that obtained in rural China toward 1961 was extremely difficult. (We shall discuss in the next chapter the political nub of the impasse of the Great Leap Forward by exploring new assumptions.) Yao's reference to the issue is framed in terms of the political controversies of the moment. According to critics of Maoist policies, the causes were the "excesses of the Great Leap Forward," whereas for supporters of these political experiments, the hardship had been the effect of a series of natural calamities (droughts and extraordinary floods), together with the international stranglehold over the country.[24] When Yao speaks of attacks by "imperialism" and "modern revisionism," he is referring to the almost total hostility on the diplomatic-military plane, not to mention the economic and ideological, which surrounded China by the end of the 1950s.

The most allusive argument concerning contemporary politics was the issue of overturning the verdicts. A knowledgeable Chinese reader would undoubtedly have understood that "verdict" meant that a drastic decision about a political conflict was at stake. Yao, however, restricted mention to "unjust verdicts," which the play credited Hai Rui with having "overturned," and in actual fact alluded to a certain contemporary political verdict. Briefly, Yao held that the play concerned a bitter and unresolved political dispute but did not mention any specific episode.

The imbalance between the fully argued historical critique and the convoluted political polemic in Yao's essay is manifest. This point anticipates, moreover, a key feature of the controversy that the essay ignited in the following months and became its main point of impasse. The latter coincided, as we shall see, with the opening of a divide between the political and historiographical discourses that was destined to deepen in the following debate.

It is, however, significant how passionate and detailed Yao's critique was on the theatrical issues proper. I assume here that the theatrical dimension played a decisive role in the controversy by tightening the tensors linking politics and history. In other words, thanks to the peculiarities of the theatrical form per se as a ground of analysis of subjective statements, and beyond any judgment on the artistic value of the play, the political issues emerged as vital. Ultimately, the question was whether the peasants were capable of existing politically, or whether it was their fate merely to obey and to engage in productive activities under the rule of benevolent mandarins.

Yao's article concluded with the hope that the issues raised could be satisfactorily addressed through proper use of "historical materialism" and, more particularly, "class analysis." Yet, by examining several major background motifs of Yao's polemics in the following chapter, we'll see that his article brought to the fore thorny and unresolved political and historiographical issues of China in the early sixties.

2

Political and Historical Dilemmas

The Nub of the Dismissal

In late December 1965, several weeks after the publication of Yao's essay, Mao stated it was an excellent text that was having "an enormous impact in theatrical, historical, and philosophical circles" but "had not grasped the crucial point." The "nub" (要害 *yaohai*) of *Hai Rui*, Mao maintained, was precisely the dismissal (罢官 *ba guan*). "Emperor Jiaqing had dismissed Hai, we have dismissed Peng Dehuai in 1959, and Peng Dehuai is Hai Rui."[1] Originally a rather secondary passage in a speech given in Hangzhou, Mao's remarks would obviously come to play an essential role in the dispute, as we will discuss in more detail in the next two chapters, though for several months only indirectly because other central party leaders vigorously contested it.

At first sight, one might say Mao was countering with an allegorical interpretation the equally allegorical reading that Wu Han and his supporters were proposing in those weeks. For his part in the course of the dispute, Wu firmly declared that *Hai Rui* contained no allusion to contemporary politics but was merely a theatrical representation of the figure of an honest official who had acted in favor of the peasants and, above all, had acted in favor of the "progress of history." This specific argument played an important role as the dispute unfolded. By contrast, Mao maintained that Hai's dismissal was in the final analysis the "dismissal of Peng Dehuai," which had occurred in the wake of the pronounced political discord that surfaced at the Lushan Conference.

However, there was far more than the unveiling of a hidden allegory in Mao's statement. In recalling the outcome of the Lushan Conference, he was citing the gravest political impasse the Communist Party faced after 1949. Yet, from this point of view, the allegorical interpretation was not exactly the nub of the question. The analogy between the dismissal of Hai Rui on the part of Emperor Jiaqing and the dismissal of Peng Dehuai on the part of the Party Central Committee was quite formal: two functionaries removed from office. Furthermore, Mao, who was familiar with Ming history, could not have had any particular respect for Emperor Jiaqing; if anything, he himself had spoken positively of Hai Rui as a historical personage (as we shall see in chapter 3).[2] The key question was what intrinsically political element there was in the contrast with Peng Dehuai apart from just the shuffling of leading posts in the state apparatus. The problem that Mao's statement raised, far more than the question of the dismissal of Peng Dehuai, was that of the nub of the Lushan Conference and the unresolved dilemmas that the theatrical dispute brought to the surface six years later.

The conference was undoubtedly the most critical moment in Chinese politics before the Cultural Revolution. The very name in Chinese of Lushan (Mount Lu), one of the most picturesque and famous places in China, situated north of Jiangxi, evokes a landscape that is hard to decipher, as in the well-known saying "the true face of Mount Lu" (庐山真面目 *Lushan zhen mianmu*). This means that it is difficult to see its richly varied scenery if you are on Mount Lu itself, since clouds often envelop it. In other words, in observing a situation merely from within its own outlook, you risk coming up against a whole series of prejudices that obscure your view.

The clouds that today obscure Lushan's "true face" depend on the fact that, although six decades have passed, that event still plays a peculiar consensual role in contemporary Chinese ideology. In governmental discourse, the Lushan Conference is a sort of "primal trauma" marking the onset of an irreconcilable fracture in the leading group of the CCP that led to the Cultural Revolution. It is also a founding reference to Deng Xiaoping's strategy, which established a cult of Peng Dehuai as the forerunner of the abolition of people's communes and of an uncompromising criticism of Mao's policies after 1958. A special atmosphere of ritual reverence thus surrounds the topic.

The current version of the Lushan Conference, based on the verdict formulated by the Chinese government after the Cultural Revolution, is essentially the following: Since the Great Leap Forward had been a total failure, and Mao did not want to admit the catastrophe, the entire party apparatus, from the top echelons to the roots, being composed mostly of courtiers, had hidden the tragic reality from the emperor. The one exception was the brave minister of defense, Peng Dehuai, who during the Lushan Conference had dared to oppose Mao and had been cruelly humiliated and finally dismissed from office.

This is the picture of the Lushan Conference that one will find, with minimal variations, almost every time the subject is mentioned. Marie Claire Bergère, for example, adds a well-known corollary about the long-term significance of that political contrast. She writes that at Lushan, "Mao uses his personal power to defeat the one who dares criticize him openly. It is precisely at this moment that the symptoms of a tyranny appear, against which a docile and fearful apparatus gives up any opposition, abandoning Peng Dehuai to his downfall. China will dearly pay the price of the silence held by its foremost leaders."[3] The success of such a stereotypic image of the Lushan Conference cannot simply be due to the efficacy of post–Cultural Revolution government pronouncements. There must be some unusual difficulty if even specialist historians uncritically accept this version, whereas the extensive documentation of the event, which has been available for years, enables a very different view of the stakes and content of the disagreement.

Current narrative casts Peng as a protomartyr, the victim of one of Mao's sudden despotic whims. Yet the documentation available is quite detailed and confirmed by various sources. It reveals that the Lushan Conference was nothing like that. The relationships among the protagonists were in no way similar to those between an emperor and his servile ministers, only one of whom had dared tell the truth. Lushan was the seat of a bitter political conflict over crucial issues, a conflict, moreover, quite open and protracted. Almost all the leaders of the party and the Chinese government took part in it for over six weeks, and the dispute with Peng lasted for over half of that time. The fulcrum of the contrast was whether the Chinese Communist Party would be able to promote the peasants' *political* existence.

The Original Agenda of the Lushan Conference

Paradoxically, one of the works that best clarifies the content and tone of the political tensions at Lushan comes from Li Rui, one of the very few who openly supported Peng.[4] Li had previously worked in one of the offices of Mao's secretariat and took part in the conference as recorder of the minutes of the main debates. In the late 1980s, he published a "diary" of those weeks, written in a style that does not lack literary merit and provides extensive documentation based on his personal notes. From the detailed transcription of the positions taken at the main meetings (assuming they are as accurate as they seem to be), including considerable subjective shades of meaning in the face-to-face discussions among the participants, it is possible to see how intensely political the divergence was. Despite the fact that the author's intentions are in any case still very much on the side of Peng and very hostile to Mao, the political stakes of the contrast appear in clear relief.[5] From Li's book, as well as from all the available documentation,[6] one can see that both Mao and all the other participants were fully aware of the specific difficulties of the situation. Lushan was in fact convened to decide how to consolidate political experimentation and to rectify some trends that were turning out to be disastrous.

Serious research on the causes of the failure of the Great Leap is now hampered by the general execration, in some respects even more "integral" than that of the Cultural Revolution, which it raises both in the judgment of the Chinese government and among the majority of specialist foreigners. The version that has been repeated for decades is that the mad extremist adventurism imposed personally by Mao had finally produced a famine with tens of millions of deaths. Recent studies have begun to dismantle this version with a systematic rereading of the available documentation and a questioning of the validity of the alleged statistical data on the demographic catastrophe.[7] It can be expected that much effort will still be needed to reorganize research on this topic, but these studies are valuable contributions to reopening the dossier on one of the most critical moments of the entire Maoist era.

It is unquestionable that, after the divergences arose during the Lushan Conference, the Great Leap ended with a sharp setback, and that in the years immediately following a serious famine hit the country. The key problem is how to investigate the political root of a series of organizational malfunctions. As Mobo Gao rightly observes, among the major factors of the imbalance was the effect of decentralization, which had been a key point of the Great Leap's policies, on the highly centralized and hierarchical structure of state authority. The hierarchy was in turn the result of the bureaucratic structure of the Soviet model, largely imported during the first decade of the PRC, and on the other hand it fed on the hierarchical tradition of the imperial state. Decentralization allowed each administrative level great margins of autonomy in deciding its own priorities, but on the other hand, the hierarchy meant that the expectations of the higher level became the main referent of the decisions taken at a lower level.[8] In short, decentralization, which should have been a major lever to stimulate local initiative, turned into an obstacle.

The problem of decentralization was actually the subject of debate and protracted controversy even in the years following the Great Leap. However, the specific issue that in Lushan the leaders of the party-state were committed to rectify was a specific distortion constituted by false reports on production, which aggravated and exacerbated the conflict between centralism and decentralization. Not only did the lower levels take care to respond exclusively to the higher ones, ignoring the conditions of the lower levels, where they were asked to reach unrealistic production goals, but they came to declare that those imaginary production goals had been achieved.

The problem of false statistics, which was one of the sensitive points on the agenda at the Lushan Conference, not only was a problem of administrative discipline, but was the symptom of a profound political predicament. On this point the contradictions that emerged in Lushan and the peculiar "afterlife" of Hai Rui were knotted, and he ended up becoming the catalyst for tensions that certainly exceeded the evaluation of his historical figure. As we shall see, the first to mention Hai Rui had been Mao himself in previous months, intending to incite the lower levels of the party not to comply without discussing unrealistic orders and expectations coming from the higher levels.

For some months, many party officials at various levels had been carrying out a grotesque competition of bureaucratic emulation by issuing false reports on production, which obviously impeded any central coordination of the economy. In the situation of notable mass political enthusiasm that accompanied the first year of the Great Leap Forward, many cadres at the time had started to fantasize about their own role, seeing themselves as propagandists of a purely economic ideal of "communism."

The root of the phenomenon, which seems to be simple administrative malfeasance, in fact touched on the political essence of the Great Leap Forward. What the problem of false statistics revealed, and the developments at the Lushan Conference shed full light on, was something unexpected: the radical difficulty that the Chinese Communist Party had had since 1949 in organizing peasants politically. Ten years after conquering state power and, hence, apparently in a most favorable condition to carry out any political project, the same party that had skillfully organized the political capacity of Chinese peasants in the People's War now found itself facing an obstacle on the very issue of peasant politics. What appeared to be a hurdle turned out to be an insurmountable impasse.

The current image of the Lushan Conference obviously rests on the "thoroughly negative verdict" that the Chinese government pronounced after the Cultural Revolution on the Great Leap Forward. The latter is labeled as the onset of "left-wing extremist" deviation, which was responsible for a total failure on the economic plane, and for an unbridgeable rift that supposedly convulsed the normal functioning of the party on the political plane. For over four decades, the Great Leap has acted as a negative "founding myth," the beginning of a radical disorder that only Deng Xiaoping's "reforms" finally ended.

This is not the place to discuss the Great Leap Forward in terms of economic history. However, the foundations of China's productive structure, which has remained essential even for the celebrated economic performance of recent decades, trace back to those years. This is particularly true of industry, but the seeds of several key elements of the rural economy, from managing hydraulic infrastructure works to local industrialization, were sown in the years 1958–59. The Great Leap's current image of an economic strategy that was purely utopian and lacking all realism reflects today's intellectual and political disorientation and the consequent difficulty of historiography and sociology in rethinking the nature of that political moment with new tools. It would be worthwhile to reread today the analyses that the great sociologist Franz Schurmann carried out in the mid-sixties, which point out the subtleties and meticulousness of the options discussed in the economic debate in the China of the mid-fifties.[9]

The true failure of the Great Leap, whose legacy was to last longest and whose consequences became increasingly onerous, was not economic but political. The difficulties in the economic field were temporary and far more limited than many of the "horror stories" circulating on the topic have it, but they were above all the consequences of a political impasse. The version that narrates the political disagreements of Lushan as resting on divergent evaluations of economic performance, extremely poor for "realists" like Peng but excellent for "utopians" like Mao, is very misleading. On the contrary, the disagreements were thoroughly political and severely conditioned the effective pursuit of a series of readjustments necessary to guide an experiment of such proportions as the Great Leap Forward.

The Great Leap Forward's Political Impasse

The Great Leap Forward undoubtedly marked the beginning of a political fissure in the CCP that became unbridgeable. However, Mao's alleged despotism says nothing about the political stakes involved. What is true is that he stubbornly maintained his standpoint. The Great Leap was a vast political experiment that had to stimulate the political capacities of the peasants and be based on their activism. It initially aroused enormous popular enthusiasm but very soon encountered decisive political obstacles. The people's agricultural communes, which were launched in a national campaign by the Communist Party, were initially created by the peasants in one of the poorest areas of China. The Great Leap was experimenting with a set of egalitarian political inventions supported directly by peasants within a socialist type of state. It is on this plane that the terms of the political conflict that held the floor at Lushan are to be discussed.

The impasse in the way of the Great Leap Forward arose when the criteria for assessing the peasantry's political enfranchisement were based exclusively—one might say almost automatically—on productivity, a view that became the predominant attitude in the party-state. The tendency to exaggerate production reports and even to falsify data rested above all on this basic ambiguity. There was certainly a pattern of minor and major bureaucrats boasting irresponsibly over invented production results for fear of spoiling their careers. This would not have occurred if the political experiment being carried out had not been distorted toward criteria that merely measured productivity. Briefly, the idea that spread through the various echelons of the party-state was that the value of the new political existence of the peasants consisted in their ability to produce more.

The antecedent to this viewpoint was obviously Stakhanovism. In the tradition of states of the Soviet type, all governmental propaganda rituals proclaimed the political value of the worker, but definitive proof of such coin lay in his presumed superior economic productivity. The rhetoric of "labor heroes" from the 1930s reduced the figure of the socialist worker to a pathetic "man of marble," as in Andrzej Wajda's tragic film,[10] one meekly disciplined by the bureaucracy of the party-state.

A similar attitude induced many Chinese communist officials to address the peasants during the Great Leap Forward as if they were "rural Stakhanovs," and then to fabricate production records to prove it. The outcome was a highly chaotic situation. On the one hand, the false production figures then circulating obviously impeded any coordinated management of the country's economy. On the other hand, there was pressure in many cases from the upper to the lower echelons of the party-state, and from the latter to the peasants, to meet these imaginary output targets.

At the Lushan Conference there had initially been considerable optimism concerning the possibility of rectifying this phenomenon. The general outlook of the participants was that, at lower party levels, it would have sufficed to carry out a campaign of political education aimed at convincing the basic party cadres that conveying false information about production was a grave error that needed to be corrected as soon as possible. At higher party levels, the conference envisaged more articulated campaigns for investigating fundamental theoretical themes, such as the nature of socialist political economics, political assessment of the theory and practice of Soviet planning, and so forth.

In the preparatory documents for the conference that Mao had meticulously drawn up, one major issue on the agenda was that it should be an occasion of collective study for the Chinese Communist Party in order to correct errors by raising—educating—theoretical awareness. The program relied on a tradition of the CCP that had been consolidated in practice ever since the years of the People's War: theoretical study was one of the cadres' main tasks and was particularly needed at the most critical moments.

The Lushan Conference had decided to publish a series of handbooks for the political education of grassroots cadres that focused on the need to be realistic when writing reports on production. The higher up the party ladder the members were, the more demanding their theoretical study was to be.[11] The central government levels were even required to study the *Manual of Soviet Political Economics*. Mao dedicated himself in the following months, together with a study group, to reading it systematically and critically.[12]

Reestablish the Normal Situation of 1957

After about two weeks of meetings, the Lushan Conference seemed to be drawing to a close when Peng Dehuai intervened in the forum. He wrote a letter addressed to Mao, who then forwarded it to all the participants. It brought about a sudden change in the meeting. In effect, it revealed that the situation was very different from the one the participants had imagined, given the particularly relaxed atmosphere of the discussions up to that point. Until that moment, there had been an almost unreal calm compared to the storms of the following weeks.[13]

Peng's letter dispelled in an instant all the optimism about the possibility of continuing the political experiment by means of fine-tuning details and of promoting a common effort at raising the theoretical level. The letter showed, to the contrary, that there was a fundamental disagreement about the essence of the Great Leap. Peng did not discuss specific problems. For him there was nothing to experiment on politically, and no adjustments to make. It was necessary only to reestablish the status quo ante. "Petit bourgeois fanaticism," he wrote, dominated the situation.[14] The Communist Party's biggest quandary was "not having yet found for problems of economic construction" methods "at hand" (得心应手 *dexin yingshou*) as effective as those adopted "in the bombing of Quemoy and the crushing of disorders in Tibet."[15]

Peng's sanctification rarely mentions these points of a letter that was so central to his view of the situation, since it merely represents him as one high minister attempting to be the spokesperson for peasants before the "emperor."

The latter for his part is supposed to have quashed all dissent, being blinded by the "mad" aims of his "utopia." Yet Peng spoke only about a "disorder" that had to be rectified, openly and precisely advocating such military methods as bombing and crushing as means for governing the situation. Above all, he did not acknowledge any merit in the ongoing political experimentation. This was the essence of his disagreement with Mao.

The minutes that Li Rui made during the key moments in the dispute, despite his own strong resentment toward Mao, show that Mao's so-called despotism was essentially his commitment to overcoming an impasse the experiment had run up against and of which Peng was well aware. However, Peng's attitude did much to determine the tone of the political conflict. He first launched an attack on all sides, throwing the weight of his position into a head-on collision, but he could not then defend the content of his letter and soon capitulated in the face of the first objections raised by Mao.

Mao did not reply immediately to Peng, leaving the task up to the defense minister for several days. Yet the latter had no other substantive arguments in the end but the immediate, unconditional withdrawal of the Communist Party from all political initiatives in rural areas. What he proposed was interrupting from one day to the next a mass mobilization of hundreds of millions of people. All experiments of the Great Leap Forward were to be ended, and it was necessary to dedicate all available strength for "at least two years" to policies aimed at a return to the "normal situation" (正常情况 *zhengchang qingkuang*) of 1957.[16]

However, making such a U-turn and effectively draining away the political dynamism that the CCP had stimulated and then acclaimed the year before, in an appeal for calm couched in a request for everyone to go home as if nothing had happened, would hardly have been enough. Indeed, to put an end to what Peng called "petty bourgeois fanaticism," what was needed were the same methods he called "at hand" that were adopted in "crushing the tumults in Tibet." Even if Peng did not go so far as to formulate a detailed plan in such terms, it is clear that the whole idea behind his letter would have meant, as the sole operational response, recourse to heavy-handed tactics to "reinstate the normal situation of 1957." Nor could the CCP have done otherwise: if it had approved Peng's line, it would inevitably have had to adopt violent repressive measures against the peasants and rural cadres, thereby producing a disastrously chaotic situation.

Indeed, the defense minister did not find any support among the other leaders attending the conference. We can assume that their attitude was dictated not by any "courtier cowardice" before the "emperor" but by the fact that Peng was proposing the political suicide of the Chinese Communist Party. In the face of Peng's position, silent connivance was not an option. Various participants raised highly polemical voices, and not just those of the "left." Even Zhou Enlai, usually depicted as the untiring mediator between divergent standpoints, used an extremely critical tone toward Peng.[17]

While Mao was forthrightly opposed to Peng, he carefully argued all his responses at his most polemical. His dissent was particularly strong concerning "petit bourgeois fanaticism," a formula that accorded no value to the political enthusiasm of that mass movement. What the Lushan Conference was discussing, and what Mao strenuously defended, was on the contrary a rectification capable of dealing realistically with the then current subjective processes.

In effect, Mao's stance can be readily summarized. Enthusiasm was positive because there could be no political invention without mass momentum. It was, however, necessary to make the specific objectives more realistic and above all to put a halt to the absurd bureaucratic boasting. Taking several steps backward was inevitable, but such experimental initiatives as self-organization of agricultural tasks, collective canteens, self-managed schools, and cooperative medical services should remain operative wherever possible. In all fields, Mao believed, the experiment of an original political role for the peasants should be kept alive.

By that time, however, even international factors were making themselves felt, exacerbating the discord. The Communist Party of the Soviet Union's interference in CCP affairs (there had been an open ideological and political disagreement between the two parties for at least three years) became much stronger during those very weeks. At the same time as Peng intervened at Lushan, Nikita Khrushchev made several public pronouncements that were very hostile to the Great Leap Forward and that were picked up and emphasized by the international press. Khrushchev's statements were not necessarily the result of a prior agreement with Peng. Indeed, they were most likely made on his personal initiative, rather typical in fact of his style. It is clear, however, that the coincidence of timing between such a head-on attack coming at the most controversial moments of the Lushan Conference appeared deliberate.

Mao had been trying since 1956 to find an original, independent path in both domestic and foreign policy that would keep a distance from the USSR and from the very logic of the Cold War. It was this very independence of policy choice and decision promotion that became the object of the growing hostility on the part of the CPSU. The Great Leap Forward was certainly one of the factors that deepened the rift between the two parties. In the event, Peng's standpoint entailed de facto realignment with Soviet positions, which aggravated the harshness of the clash at Lushan. However, despite the external pressure, the true stakes were internal and concerned the political essence of the Great Leap. While Peng represented a very skeptical viewpoint on the question of whether it was possible to experiment with a new political existence for the peasants, Mao represented the political determination to continue the search for an experimental course at Lushan.

Was a New Political Existence for Peasants Possible under Socialism?

The nub of the clash at Lushan thus concerned the political existence of the peasants. The crux of the issue was that the political role the peasants had played during the protracted People's War could not merely be extended under the circumstances of socialism, and would thus have to be thoroughly reinvented. It was no accident that the discord involved two great military commanders of the People's War—Mao and Peng. The discontinuity with the previous phase was irreversible and bore the marks of a radical divide.

For almost two decades, from the latter half of the 1920s to the end of the 1940s, the political activism of the peasants had been the novelty that had changed the destiny of the country and made it possible to break a long chain of destruction and humiliation that had lasted for over a century. The Chinese people had "risen to their feet," as Mao said in 1949, and this had been possible precisely thanks to the political existence of the peasants. The People's War had been above all an inventive form of egalitarian organization, not merely a matter of military tactics. The military plane had been an experimental terrain and even succeeded in developing a nonmilitaristic view and practice of war. It had brought to an end an age of militarization that had lasted since the decline of the Qing Dynasty. In any case, the efficacy of the People's War was the result of a singular egalitarian invention.

The peasants, people who counted for nothing in Chinese society, particularly those of the poorest strata, were the true political protagonists. The People's Liberation Army, consisting to an overwhelming extent of peasants, created profoundly egalitarian relationships as much between officers and soldiers as between the army and the civilian population in rural areas. Chinese peasants widely participated in the war not so much out of a process of patriotic identification (in some cases the enemy was also Chinese, such as the Guomindang army), but because they recognized in it an exceptional existential condition.

The People's War was in fact a terrain for organizing the political existence of a vast mass that was socially *inexistent*. I quote here a philosophical term, a key point of precise logical thought in the philosophical outlook of Alain Badiou.[18] It helps to clarify the singularity of what, in the final analysis, the stakes are in any great egalitarian invention: *to organize the political existence of the socially inexistent*. The ordinary "social value" of the Chinese peasant was restricted to conforming to the rituals that guaranteed their inexistence. In his famous *Inquiry into the Peasant Movement in Hunan*, Mao described those rituals with the subtlety of an anthropologist in the field, and above all with the intentions of a revolutionary organizer. He showed that they consisted in a triple subordination: to the dominance of the authority of the clan, of landowners, and of the "spirits," to which one had to add marital authority for women.[19] In no way was the political existence of the peasantry in the People's War a continuum with their station in society. It was a radical exception compared to the rules of Chinese society of the time. The Red Army overturned the strict traditional ritual hierarchies in unprecedented forms of egalitarianism: those who in ordinary social relations had no control over their own lives became the backbone of a political invention.

However, the People's War, despite being conceived as strategically "protracted," which was one of the reasons for its originality, was a form of political organization destined in any case to terminate once the objectives of the reconstruction of independence and national dignity had been attained. The ensuing victory thus inevitably also marked the end of the organizational prerequisite that had permitted peasants to exist politically for two decades. The paradox of the Liberation (as the foundation of the People's Republic is called in China) was therefore that, while it had been possible only thanks to the peasants' activism, it irreversibly concluded the political figure of the peasant as it had existed in the two previous decades.

The alternative since 1949 has thus been either to reinvent the political existence of the peasants or to keep it as mere celebratory rhetoric. The end of decades of militarization had undoubtedly removed enormous obstacles from the lives of China's peasants, but they were inevitably destined to return to their ordinary condition of social inexistence without new, extraordinary political inventions.

It is well known that even before the Great Leap there had been profound differences in agricultural policies. The most well known, if the collectivization were to have mechanization as a condition, implied that peasants could grow politically only by developing industry. Following the Soviet model, the first five-year plan (1953–58) had favored the development of industry, and of heavy industry in particular, over agriculture, and in fact had strongly subordinated the latter to the former.

For his part, Mao, since 1956, had pushed toward a profound rethinking of the priorities of the first five-year plan, supporting in his famous *On the Ten Major Relationships* the need to reorganize in a balanced and nonhierarchical way the relationships between heavy and light industry, and between industry and agriculture.[20] Furthermore, Mao already in previous years had promoted a vast movement of creating forms of cooperative organization in agriculture based on the initiative of the peasants, by avoiding the distortions of forced collectivization. The Great Leap was conceived as a further decisive terrain of mobilization of the peasants' subjective energies. All Mao's initiatives concerning the Chinese countryside after 1949 were attempts to experiment with new forms of an egalitarian organization of peasants. So it was that at the Lushan Conference a "Great Leap Forward" in this novel set of political inventions was at stake.

However, after the Liberation, and despite being pursued tenaciously for almost thirty years, such attempts never reached the heights of the theoretical and practical plateau they had gained during the protracted People's War. In fact, they repeatedly ran into one formidable obstacle after another pointedly thrown up by the system of the new state itself. Yet it would be more precise to say that the experiments themselves were serious obstacles to the regular functioning of the Chinese state. One can consider Peng Dehuai as a forerunner of Deng Xiaoping, though not exactly because he had proposed *in nuce* a plan at Lushan that the latter would have implemented in his policies twenty years later. In fact, that Peng had no realistic plan was why he remained isolated in 1959. He did, however, come to represent the knee-jerk reaction on the part of a socialist state for suppressing those experiments in order to defend its own "normal" functioning. In the late 1970s, one of the first crucial decisions adopted in the name of governmental order was to dismantle the people's agricultural communes, that is, to quash any attempt at organizing the peasantry politically.

Peasant Wars in Chinese History

Another line of divergence that flowed into the dispute over *Hai Rui* was properly historiographical, but on a terrain that was deeply intertwined with the political differences that came to light unequivocally in Lushan. If the latter concerned the political role of the peasants under socialism, the historiographical controversies concerned the political role of peasants in imperial history. The stakes of these historiographical controversies ultimately concerned the very coherence of historical materialism in defining the process of constituting Chinese political and cultural singularity.

On the other hand, the historiographical divergences on how to evaluate the meaning of the peasant wars of imperial history inevitably involved the problem of how to conceive the political role of the peasants under socialism. The politicization of the matter had been latent since 1949, but it became more evident in the early 1960s, as a result of the impasse that emerged in Lushan. It can be said that the controversy surrounding *Hai Rui* fully brought to light controversial issues that had already been ready to surface for fifteen years.

Nevertheless, in evaluating these antecedents in the historiographical field, it must be borne in mind that the dispute over *Hai Rui* did not involve, as we shall see in the next chapter, a solution to all the questions of the political role of peasants both in imperial history and in the present one under socialism. The question remained essentially unresolved.

Therefore, these two terrains, the political and the historiographical, did not form a single framework, and while it is essential to consider both, they must be examined separately. Indeed, the controversy initiated by Yao's essay developed according to its own logic and was not merely an extension of previous historiographical debates. However, since key standpoints in Chinese historiography of those years inevitably converged in the dispute, it is useful to recall the most salient.

By the early sixties, a debate had grown more heated around the question of how to study the peasant wars that have marked much of Chinese history.[21] The most authoritative scholar in this field at the time, and in many ways more influential than Wu Han, was Jian Bozan, the head of the Department of History at Beijing University (Beida). He was renowned as the author of a theoretical perspective called "policies of concessions" (让步政策 *rangbu zhengce*) that from the early fifties constituted the prevailing viewpoint in historiographical research on imperial China. The prestige Jian enjoyed was so widespread that the school under his direction compiled in the early 1960s a short history of China. The book was translated into English by the Beijing Foreign Languages Publishing House and became the main historiographical "visiting card" of Chinese cultural diplomacy before the Cultural Revolution.[22]

Jian too became involved in the *Hai Rui* controversy, at first indirectly and then more openly. The respective standpoints of Jian and of Wu are distinct. Jian was a scholar who also cultivated a theoretical model endowed with its own originality, even if it was indicative of a radical political and historiographical predicament. Wu, on the other hand, had little propensity for theory. He rather leaned to a sort of Marxist-Confucian view that was quite fashionable at the time. Moreover, after 1949, he had mainly been a high-level official in the cultural apparatus of the state.

A major difference between Jian and Wu concerned peasant revolts in Chinese history. Wu was not much interested in the issue, and in *Hai Rui* he portrayed peasants as merely passive plebeian masses. Jian had come instead to a complex vision of peasant wars in imperial China based on his policy of concessions theory, which moreover was entangled with the canonical conceptualization of historical materialism and rested on the classical dialectics of productive forces versus relationships of production.[23] While subscribing to the idea that historical progress was the result of class struggle, he specified that only the "progressive classes," those really representing the "new productive forces," were able to reverse the "old relationships of production" and the corresponding forms of the state as "superstructure" through "revolution." The peasants, Jian argued, had never represented the new productive forces. Their rebellions against the exploitation and tyranny of feudal rulers therefore "did not and could not" (没有, 也不可能 *mei you, ye bu keneng*)—this was one of his favorite expressions on the topic[24]—constitute them as a class capable of overturning, or even really opposing, the feudal system.

However, peasant rebellions did occur throughout the whole period of imperial China, a fact that Jian did not (and could not) deny. Tumultuous uprisings had marked all dynastic changes. In Jian's theory, though, the peasants did not and could not become a true progressive class. In other words, they did not correspond to the characteristics of productive forces at the economic base, and even less could they since they were not endowed with an ideology or a political program.

The problem was thus: How could one fit the concept of peasant rebellion into the theory that the history of class struggle had shaped China in a course that developed such a major contradiction as that between the ruling feudal class and the peasants? Although they existed, Jian argued, peasant revolts did not represent the new productive forces and, hence, could not have been direct factors in historical development. The main factor, he maintained instead, was that after the peasant uprisings, the ruling classes were more inclined to implement a set of policies of concessions, measures that would ease contradictory social tensions while producing the convergent results of consolidating the long-term interests of feudal rule and of meeting certain immediate interests of the masses.

As Jian's critics remarked in 1966, according to the theory of concessions, only after their suppression did peasant rebellions attain what they had been unable to achieve during their active phase.[25] The sarcasm obviously leaned on the argument that the suppression of peasant revolts was a task performed with meticulous brutality, whether in imperial China or anywhere else. However, if we try to explore the issue from new perspectives, the problem can be reformulated. What "debt" does a particular form of government, established after a major event of egalitarian mass organizational invention, owe toward the latter, despite having labeled it as inadmissible disorder and finally destroyed it?

The hypothesis I would suggest is that, after a political mass uprising, no new governmental circumstances can be established without eliminating some elements of the old forms of government that the political moment had revealed to be particularly inconsistent, as well as particularly odious to the masses. The new governmental stability is not merely the result of the annihilation of the political existence of inventively organized masses. It is also indebted to the latter for having indicated the points of inconsistency in the previous form of government.

What Jian conceptualized under the "benevolent" name of concessions, I would argue, alludes to a more twisted process. Undoubtedly, after a mass political event, the stabilization of a new government rests primarily on the suppression of the egalitarian mass subjectivities. However, such repression can never be complete—"thorough negation" does not exist or is ineffective— since no new government can establish itself without internalizing to some extent the discontinuity that the political event caused in the previous governing order. The whole process cannot give rise to any ultimate stability, as "all history" shows with examples.

Jian developed a true theoretical option, although its aporias were rooted in an unresolved political dilemma of Chinese communist ideology after 1949. Did peasant rebellions have both a historical significance and a political value? Paradoxically, in Jian's view, what peasant subjective agency lacked most was historical value (they did not represent new productive forces). Their political value was, in the final analysis, undeniable as large peasant rebellions even made dynasties collapse. But their revolts could not directly promote historical development since they did not represent new productive forces. The argument is twisted, but reflects nonetheless a real difficulty inherent in historical knowledge of peasant wars, particularly in regard to historical materialism.

It is noteworthy that Jian had been shaping his theories since the early fifties,[26] a sign that the end of the People's War in 1949 immediately, even inevitably, led to the reopening of the issue of the political value of the peasants. Equally significant is the fact that Jian's theories were highly influential in the historiographical debate of the early 1960s. And the political deadlock that emerged at the Lushan Conference undoubtedly aggravated the problem of the political value of peasant revolts in Chinese history.

In the debate of the early sixties, the influence of Jian's views was dominant, playing the role of a sort of "centrist" historiographical ideology. The theory of concessions also played a similar role in the *Hai Rui* dispute, as we shall see in chapter 3. One could say that Jian's theories became so influential in Chinese historiographical circles because of their intermediary function between opposing camps, although none of these managed to gain full currency at the time.

On the one hand, let us say on the right wing, there was the position that negated, more or less openly, the political value of peasant revolts, considering them a hodgepodge of feudal superstition, cultural backwardness, and despotism. The main argumentation, one must remember, was strongly class-based: given their class status, peasants could have had no systematic knowledge of living in a feudal system, let alone oppose it with any positive consequences.

On the part of those who supported the political value of the peasants, the left wing, the main argument was, on the contrary, that the peasants had in any case a systematic ideology, as in their aspirations for "equality." The right wing replied in turn that that equality did not have the characteristic of the "proletarian" class; that is, it was not projected toward "historical progress." It was, therefore, a utopian aspiration, essentially founded on the ideology of small producers. At best, it was a form of "absolute egalitarianism," which could never be attained but had the effect of slowing down the development of the productive forces on the economic plane and of leading to the most brutal despotism on the political.

Jian's concessions theory was conciliatory compared to the two opposing positions. For, while not completely denying the political value of peasant revolts in Chinese history, it excluded any capacity on their part to promote the progress of history and the development of productive forces. The peasants had repeatedly rebelled, it is true, but history had "developed" thanks to the concessions by which the ruling classes, once the revolts had been suppressed, had managed to stabilize feudal domination on the one hand and attenuate the burden of the exploitation of peasants on the other. One can say that Jian's theory made a series of concessions to both the right and the left, to both imperial government and peasants, it being understood that truly efficient historical progress was restricted only to the former.

They Had Not, nor Could Have Had

Let us make a short digression of a rather "doctrinal" nature that is connected nonetheless to the dilemmas of Chinese politics in the 1960s. Jian's views included all the conceptual devices of historical materialism, such as productive forces versus productive relationships, base versus superstructure, advanced classes versus backward classes, and so forth. The theory of concessions respected much of the Marxist-Leninist orthodoxy and, although labeled in 1966 as anti-Marxist and antisocialist, it led to the emergence, if anything, of a predicament within historical materialism.

Take, for example, the above-quoted expression, "they had not, nor could have had," which recurs in Jian's arguments concerning the key thesis of his theory, that is, that rebel peasants "had not, nor could have had" a "class" position in opposition to the feudal system.

> The peasants opposed feudal oppression and exploitation, but they did not have, nor could have had any awareness [没有, 也不可能意识到 *mei you, ye bu keneng yishidao*] [allowing them] to oppose feudalism as a system.
>
> The peasants opposed the feudal landlords, but did not have, nor could have had, any awareness [allowing them] to oppose the landlords as a class.
>
> The peasants opposed the feudal emperor but they did not have, nor could have had any awareness that the imperial power they opposed constituted an ideology. (60)

Jian's formula, repeated so insistently, undoubtedly echoes, without citing it directly, a famous expression in Lenin's *What Is to Be Done?*, though in a way that was not only different but also essentially the opposite. Let us try, by means of comparison, to capture better both Lenin's and Jian's positions, but also to pinpoint the theoretical perspective necessary to examine the highly complex stage of Chinese political thought in the 1960s and 1970s.

In *What Is to Be Done?* Lenin emphasizes that the workers, as both individuals and as a class, "did not have and *could not have had*" (Lenin's emphasis) "spontaneously" any "consciousness" of their antagonism toward "the entire contemporary political and social order."[27] While well-known theory, it is also a particularly thorny issue because it is the premise of the equally well-known, and controversial, theory that "consciousness" can come to the working class only "from outside." To keep to the bare minimum, ignoring all the objections that the theory has aroused, Lenin's problem in this key passage is that the workers do not have and cannot have any spontaneous political awareness because their "social condition," their place in the modern historical-political order, has no existential value. Workers' "social value" is worth no more than that of commodities exchangeable on the labor market. For Lenin, therefore, workers rooted in their "spontaneous ideology," which is the reflection of their class position, are at best able to negotiate some details of their inexistence. They can spontaneously negotiate the sale of their labor as a workforce just like any other commodity, but in no way can they spontaneously organize themselves to achieve a true politics of liberation; more precisely, they cannot do so without first attaining a theoretical leap.

The political "disposition" of workers, which for Lenin as for Marx is above all a *theoretical* capacity, can only come from outside. This is attainable, however, only if they are able to elevate themselves theoretically outside their own social condition and to make a political leap beyond their ordinary inexistence. This is the crux of the polemics against spontaneity and trade unionism. For Lenin, the political existence of workers, their "revolutionary consciousness," is in no way a reflection of their class station. Rather, it is literally a "deviation"—Lenin's term—the discontinuity that they manage to establish with their spontaneous social inexistence.

Thus, the difference between the *"and could not"* in Lenin and in Jian. Lenin's problem was how to succeed in turning social impotence ("they could not have") into political existence. Based on the dominant governmental discourses in the modern social world, the political existence of workers is unquestionably impossible. However, it could become real provided that the inexistent could organize themselves independently of the fundamental system of values that decides the degrees of existence in that world.

For Jian, instead, "they could not and could not have" meant that any attempt by peasants at political existence, whether in revolt, war, or the tumults that marked dynastic changes, was inevitably destined to end up in the same baseline impotence that marks their basic historical nonexistence. The progress of history thus depended merely on what the ruling elites were prepared to concede to the insubordinate plebeians once a revolt had been subdued. For Lenin, workers' political subjectivity was not the consequence of social class. Rather, workers must break away from the spontaneous ideology that derives from this condition in order to overcome their impotence and organize themselves in an independent way. For Jian, on the contrary, the peasants' social class is a historical condition that remains insurmountable; nothing makes it possible to deviate from it, and thus nothing permits the peasants to organize an independent political existence.

Anyway, That's How Matters Stood

The historiographical divergences of the early sixties over the study of peasant revolts in imperial China entailed issues that were unequivocally political. The debate originated in a fundamental political question that emerged directly at Lushan: Was a political existence possible for the peasants under socialism? The fact that the difficulty of giving a positive answer to this question would likely set off such an extensive historiographical debate that a panoply of theoretical references to historical materialism would ensue generally resulted in a destabilization of the political value of those references.

Take, for example, the criticisms aimed in the early months of 1966 at Jian Bozan's "they had not and could not have" theory coauthored by Qi Benyu, who was one of the main radical theorists of the time and author of another critical essay in December. The latter's articles, written with considerable polemical ability and theoretical vivacity, undoubtedly captured some basic weaknesses in the theory of concessions. He was the author of the sarcastic comment quoted above that, according to Jian, only after having been defeated did the peasants manage to attain something.

Qi's critique captured above all the fact that the assessment of peasant revolts in ancient China concerned the thorny questions of the CCP's peasant politics. His stance, however, shared the same limitations of the historical materialist perspective as Jian's. While it is true that he opposed to it a more radical and revolutionary view, he reached the same impasse; indeed, he exacerbated it. To Jian's "could not have had" position—that is, that the peasants were unable to achieve a complete awareness of the feudal system and of the classist nature of the oppression they rebelled against—Qi repeatedly objected that "even if the peasants did not know it, that is how matters stood anyway."

> The fact that peasant revolts and wars railed against the feudal system and the class nature of the landlords depended in a decisive way on the main contradiction of feudal society—that between those two classes—and was not founded on the fact that the peasants of that era were aware or not aware of it (当时农民是不是认识到这一点 *dangshi nongmin shi bu shi renshidao zhe yi dian*). In feudal society, peasant struggles against the landowners became revolts and wars; whether the peasants of the time knew it or not, it was like that anyway (当时农民认识到这一点是这样，认识不到这一点也是这样 *dangshi nongmnin renshidao zhe yi dian shi zheyang, renshibudao zhe yi dian ye shi zheyang*). Opposition to feudal oppression and exploitation was opposition to the feudal system; opposition to landowners was opposition to the class of landowners; whether the peasants knew this or not, it was like that anyway (农民认识到这一点是这样，认识不到这一点也是这样 *nongmin renshidao zhe yi dian shi zheyang, renshibudao zhe yi dian ye shi zheyang*).[28]

These two conflicting stylistic tics were too insistent not to be revealing of a theoretical stalemate. To Jian's 没有, 也不可能 *mei you, ye bu keneng* (they had not, nor could have had), Qi responded 也是这样 *ye shi zheyang* (that's how matters stood anyway) with equal insistence. Yet if matters stood like that anyway, in all his effort to formulate a radical reply to Jian, there is in his response the echo of another famous phrase, Ranke's hyper-objectivist *wie es "eigentlich" gewesen ist* (as it has "actually" been), although Qi criticizes the German historian for his pro-Bismarckian stand masked by academic neutrality.

Yet the formulas Jian and Qi were so intent on reiterating were symmetrical because they stemmed in the end from the same conceptual framework. Albeit in more radical or more moderate version, both authors shared the idea that the logic of history decided the day over politics. History determines the existence, or the inexistence, of peasants' political subjectivities; what the peasants are able or not able to know and to think is secondary. For one, peasant political cognizance remains impossible; for the other it is at best unconscious.

Though it may seem merely doctrinal, the contrast between Qi and Jian is not far from the critiques of *Hai Rui*. As we shall see in the next chapter, all the sides in the controversy that erupted following Yao's article cast their views in emphatically theoretical terms. The positions taken by Qi and Jian can serve as an introduction to the issue of peasant revolts in history within the cultural framework—historical materialism—of Chinese politics in the mid-sixties. That symmetry was an indicator signaling that the issue of how to place peasant revolts politically within that framework was insoluble. In the end, it was to be History itself that decided the political worth or worthlessness of peasant rebellions.

Historical materialism[29] was a philosophy of history grounded in the principle of the development of productive forces. It calls upon the "advanced classes" representing the "new productive forces" to overthrow the "reactionary classes" representing the "old" as roadblocks to the development of productive forces per se. It was in this context that the controversy over *Hai Rui* brought to the fore a conceptual void in historical materialism. The latter had, in fact, been simmering for a long while in Chinese socialism and became more conflictual at Lushan. Historical materialism proved incapable of dealing with the dilemma posed by the political role of the peasants under socialism as it did with the political significance of—the value judgment to be accorded to—peasant revolts in the history of China proper.

The issue revolved around the question of whether such rebellions were to be seen as promoting the development of productive forces and, hence, the progress of history. Hardening the contour lines of that stalemate was the point-counterpoint of Jian and Qi. The former advocated resolving the dilemma by seeing the revolts as positive, receiving a "refractive" response in the concessions granted by the imperial regime's dominant classes. The latter argued that the positive attribute was independent of any active consciousness the rebellions might have raised in the role the development of history assigned them.

As we have seen, finding a way that led beyond capitalism meant involving most of the peasant masses in the country's political life. Yet historical materialism offered no solution to the problem of what their political role should be under socialism. On the one hand, the peasants as a class did not represent the development of productive forces—a position that will be argued often during the course of the *Hai Rui* controversy. On the other hand, how was it possible to think that the contemporary political role of the peasants could be assigned by history independently of their own actively raised awareness?

3

An Unresolved Controversy

Chance and Necessity

Yao Wenyuan's essay marked the beginning of events, but it was neither the first move in a strategic plan, nor merely the consequence of long-term controversies. By its own intrinsic logic, the criticism of *Hai Rui Dismissed from Office* set a new political stage with particular issues at stake. In examining the debate, we shall obviously find many elements of the historiographical climate of the mid-sixties in China that we discussed in the previous chapter, as well as the dilemmas the Lushan Conference left unresolved. However, the controversy was not a continuation of the previous situation. Rather, it was shaped and developed by the behavior and reactions of the actors, which were far more unexpected than predetermined.

From November 1965 to May 1966, the fierce controversy over *Hai Rui* put the intellectual milieu, cultural circles, and upper echelons of the party-state center stage. Mao later stated that it had been a "matter of necessity" (必然的事 *biran de shi*), although only "chance had brought [it] about" (从偶然性中暴露出来 *cong ouranxing zhong baoluchulai*).[1] How, then, did the singular logic of that political dispute arise, and what were the key elements that drove it from chance to necessity?

Specialist historiographers today, usually unanimous in ascribing those events to the intrigues of despotism, appear somewhat undecided about the first months of the Cultural Revolution. Marie Claire Bergère, for example, writes of a "shadow area" in the Cultural Revolution, as in this case, "Mao's victory over the apparatus seems strangely easy." One cannot understand, she writes, why the leaders of the party-state, who in the past had so often been able to create trouble for Mao, in this case "opposed to him muffled, scattered and indirect resistance, while the issue at stake was essential for them as well as for the country."[2]

Chinese historians are equally hesitant. Despite their obligation to recount those events as the result of Mao's personality cult and court intrigues, they are not able to describe in such terms alone the swiftness and depth of the institutional crisis of those months, much less the subjective intensity of the political struggle. They usually solve the problem by quoting a statement by Deng Xiaoping in the early eighties, claiming, "In those circumstances, given the real situation, it was difficult to oppose [Mao]."[3] This was, however, a retrospective justification. If one considers the declarations and behavior that constituted the real situation, one would be hard-pressed to find Mao suddenly without enemies, or facing weaker opponents. On the contrary, he met with an opposition that was even more intransigent than he might have expected. Moreover, the controversy soon involved the public at large because it touched upon highly sensitive political and ideological issues, and central leaders had to tackle widespread subjective involvement.

Although the criticism of *Hai Rui* is usually referred to as merely the result of Mao's despotic willfulness, he in fact played a discontinuous and initially quite marginal role. Yao's essay was not written directly on Mao's initiative, but was suggested and sponsored by Jiang Qing and Zhang Chunqiao. Zhang, whose theoretical skills Mao had appreciated since the 1950s, was a leading cadre of the Shanghai party, where he had been editor of *Jiefang ribao*. Jiang Qing, as is known, was Mao's wife—an intense story of love and political passion that blossomed in the Yan'an period—and from the early 1960s she had led the reform of the Beijing opera. So both were very close to Mao, but they did not have a leading position in the cultural apparatus of the party-state, whose powerful leadership groups were immediately very hostile to their initiative.

While Mao certainly supported them, at first he confined his involvement to discussions and revisions of Yao's article. The text was published in the 文汇报 *Wenhui bao*, one of the most important Shanghai newspapers, which was also widely read in other cities for its articles on cultural topics but was not formally a party organ and thus was less subject to preemptive controls.[4] This detail reveals the balance of forces at that time: despite Mao's support, the text could not be published directly in Beijing, where the power of the cultural authorities was concentrated. The latter did not hesitate to impose strong restrictions and finally resorted to strict censorship over the debate, which is exactly contrary to what Deng recalled about the difficulty of opposing Mao at that moment. "In Beijing, in this red city," Mao later commented sarcastically, "not a single pin, not a drop of water may fall."[5]

Reactions beyond Our Expectations

Two highly unexpected factors were decisive in igniting the dispute. First came the wide split in opinions among intellectual circles, as expressed by an increasing number of letters and articles submitted to newspapers and the firm opposition to any such dispute on the part of the central cultural authorities that ensued. The Central Department of Propaganda and the powerful Beijing Party Committee reacted with irritation to what they considered an act of insubordination that had to be brought back under their control quickly. The most intransigent was Peng Zhen, the mayor of Beijing (Wu was a deputy mayor). He was a core leader of the party-state with special powers in cultural and ideological fields. He headed a top-level commission of the Political Bureau of the Central Committee in charge of cultural policies called the "Group of Five"; it soon became one of the main characters in the opening scene.[6] Caught off guard by a publication that had bypassed preemptive controls, Peng Zhen reacted by using all the power at his command. For the first three weeks, he prevented other newspapers from republishing Yao's essay. Then, having had to consent to its being reprinted, he did his best to censor any contemporary political implication of the dispute and then succeeded in having the Central Committee adopt a formal decision to that effect.

The lively responses from the intellectual community and the stubborn opposition at the top levels of the state's cultural apparatus created a tension that went far beyond the expectations of those who had promoted Yao's article. As Zhang Chunqiao stated later: "Only after [Yao Wenyuan's] essay was published did we understand how serious the problem was. We had thought that it could be a shock, but at the beginning, we did not foresee that it would be so big. . . . We did not know that it would stir up such deep feelings [触动这么深 *chudong zheme shen*]; even less did we know that Peng Zhen would oppose it so firmly."[7]

As Zhang was himself surprised by the intensity of the reactions to Yao's article, he took the remarkable initiative of a systematic inquiry into the debate. From the first days of publication, he organized a group of journalists of the *Wenhui bao* to carry out interviews in Shanghai and Beijing, the main centers of the debate, with university teachers, journalists, and editors of newspapers and academic journals to gather their opinions about the dispute. The results of the survey were published in a bulletin that also recorded articles and letters sent to newspapers on topics related to Yao's critique.[8] The bulletin was published until May 1966 under limited circulation and for "internal use." One of its first readers was Zhou Enlai, who wanted it to be sent regularly to the Politburo of the Central Committee; another, of course, was Mao, who made it something he read daily.[9]

These details come from a well-documented book by Zhang Zhanbin on the first months of the Cultural Revolution that is entitled, in compliance with the obligation to describe these events as court conspiracies, *The First Literary Inquisition of the Cultural Revolution*. He thus writes that this was a "typical, secret, and even mysterious" intrigue by means of which Zhang Chunqiao and Jiang Qing created a "privileged channel" that allowed them "to keep the tendencies of the intellectual world under control [控制 *kongzhi*]." Specters still haunting Chinese historiography today, Jiang and Zhang at the time had in fact very little weight in the state's central cultural institutions, their influence being in no way comparable to the powers wielded by Peng Zhen and his group.

The bulletin was an instrument created to sound out opinions in intellectual circles, and it became its promoters' strong point. The fact that the bulletin circulated regularly among the central party leaders shows that it was not secret, though it was addressed to a restricted readership.[10] This systematic reporting of the varying views among intellectuals in the controversy very likely played an important role in central party arguments and in the decision making of the following months.

Zhang Chunqiao later reported that readers sent more than ten thousand articles and letters to various newspapers on the questions raised by Yao's critique of *Hai Rui* until early May of the following year.[11] The newspapers received contributions that were even more critical than Yao's essay, and in the following weeks they became increasingly radical about the political issues the dispute was raising. The book on the "literary inquisition" notes that "most of the articles were written by intellectuals" and comments that this is "a tragic and painful truth."[12] It would be much safer, warns the author implicitly, for intellectuals not to get involved in matters political, especially as they lack proper authorization from the government.

The response of readers increased the intransigence of Peng Zhen, who imposed rigid control over the press. Although Yao's critique of *Hai Rui* was already known and discussed outside Shanghai, for nearly three weeks no other newspaper agreed to reprint it. Even a personal request by Mao was rejected. He proposed the publication of the essay as a pamphlet in Shanghai but met with the firm opposition of the Beijing authorities. The Xinhua Shudian (New China Bookstore), the central organ of book distribution, categorically refused to distribute it. This is yet another sign that it was not really too difficult to "oppose Mao." In fact, only after mediation by Zhou Enlai did Peng Zhen finally permit *Renmin ribao* [People's Daily] to reprint Yao's essay. It appeared on November 29, accompanied by an editor's note announcing that its columns would carry a "debate on Wu Han's historical drama" and "connected issues."

> We think [the note stated] the evaluation of Hai Rui and of the drama *Hai Rui Dismissed from Office* involves the problem of how to deal with historical personages and historical dramas, of which view to adopt in the study of history, and of what artistic form to use to reflect historical personages and events. On this problem in the Chinese intellectual world, there are disparate opinions, since it has not been systematically discussed yet and for many years has not been properly resolved.[13]

The note, likely the result of a compromise, was rather bland. It admitted that such fundamental issues as history, historical dramas, historical events, and personages were at stake but carefully avoided contemporary political issues. Between late November and early December, even the most important local and national newspapers reprinted Yao's essay.[14] The editor's notes that introduced the reprints emphasized different aspects, the nuances probably reflecting the attitudes of the various groups in the central leadership. The 北京日报 *Beijing ribao* for example, which was obviously close to Peng Zhen's view as mayor, on November 29, wrote that the principle of a "hundred flowers and hundred schools" should be followed in order to open a debate in which "everybody could distinguish right from wrong through the search for the truth in the facts [实事求是 *shi shi qiu shi*] on the basis of the views of dialectical materialism and class analysis." The 光明日报 *Guangming ribao*, the newspaper most often read in intellectual circles, on December 2, wrote that although there were different opinions, "Yao Wenyuan's essay raised the problem as to whether the viewpoint of dialectical materialism deserved everybody's attention and whether class analysis should be used in evaluating historical personages and in studying historical facts."

Remarkably different was the style of the editor's note in the *People's Liberation Army Daily*, the 解放军报 *Jiefangjun bao*. On November 29 it declared that "[*Hai Rui Dismissed from Office*] is a great poisonous weed [大毒草 *da du cao*]. Through methods of distorting historical reality and 'in using the past to satirize the present,' the author makes every effort to embellish the feudal ruling classes, propagandizing, carrying out not the revolution but class conciliation." The newspaper of the People's Liberation Army highlighted the class criterion in this way:

Chairman Mao taught us that we must never forget class and class struggle. The appearance of *Hai Rui Dismissed from Office* is a reflection of the class struggle in the sphere of ideology. Class struggle is the highest form of politics. . . . In the face of any sort of facts [遇到什么事情 *yudao shenme shiqing*] we must always sniff out with our nose [都要用鼻子嗅一嗅 *dou yao yong bizi xiu yi xiu*], to evaluate, in the last analysis, in whose interest it is, of which class, of which sort of person.

Despite its resolute tone, the military newspaper immediately hit on the thorniest issue of the dispute. The problem was that the reference to class categories was shared, despite various nuances, by all the actors on the scene, but with opposing intentions. For instance, although a basic dividing line in the dispute was between those who linked *Hai Rui* to contemporary political issues and those who excluded any political implications, both camps referred equally to the same classist conceptual framework.

As mentioned, Peng Zhen had a hand in drafting the *Renmin ribao*'s editor's note and then acted to set the limits of the debate. Under his leadership, the central cultural authorities countered articles whose arguments eluded present-day political implications while highlighting specific historiographical issues to keep the debate within "apolitical" boundaries. This use of "history against politics," so to speak, with overstated adherence to class arguments, would also come to characterize the "orthodox" positions of the cultural apparatus of the state in the early stage of the Cultural Revolution.

Moreover, the leading groups of that apparatus resorted to rather contorted tactics during the dispute over *Hai Rui* in order to preserve their authority while defending Wu Han. They even fabricated virulent texts of scholarly and doctrinal class criticism against Wu written by his closest supporters and aimed at limiting political implications. These tactical maneuvers eventually turned against the cultural powers and resulted in a serious weakening of their ideological authority.

In analyzing the debate as it appeared in the press, we should take into consideration the process of filtering and editing that the texts underwent. In any case, the phenomenon was quite limited: most of the articles published reflected real attitudes and were in fact distinct. Apart from a few "fakes" mentioned below, they are significant and reliable traces of that ideological conjuncture. The prologue to the Cultural Revolution, probably the best documented and at the same time the most neglected moment of the decade, was crowded by a chorus of discrete voices.

The Left, the Center, the Right

Yao's article prompted strong feedback by professional historians from the very first days of its publication, in the form of letters, articles, and records of scholarly discussions held in various universities. This was presumably the main reason that Zhou Enlai decided to exert mediation in moderating Peng Zhen's opposition to reprinting the article in the *People's Daily*. Yao's critique soon became a nationwide intellectual affair that could not simply be quashed as a local infraction of party discipline.

The first report was published as a "Letter from Four Comrades in the History Department of Fudan University" on November 23, less than two weeks after Yao's article appeared. It was a summary of more extensive discussions that had been going on for several days.[15] Its publication, not by chance, was possible only on the 29th, the same day that the *Renmin ribao* finally allowed the reprint of Yao's article and was taken off preemptive censorship. The letter, from one of the key Shanghai universities and published in the same newspaper that had first published Yao's essay, the *Wenhui bao*,[16] can be cited as an introduction to the style and content of the dispute. Since the Fudan letter contains in embryonic form virtually the complete range of positions expressed on the subject in the early weeks, it provides a helpful overview of the debate's onset.

The letter summarizes a series of "widely different opinions" expressed during a meeting of faculty members and students in the department; some agreed with Yao's critique, some were more doubtful, and others disagreed.

> Those who supported it noted that it not only analyzed the historical personalities in the play from the class viewpoint; it also linked them closely with present realities. Some comrades said: "In the past, class analysis was often neglected in evaluating historical personalities, and Lenin's theory on the state was often overlooked in the study of feudal society. Yao Wenyuan's article has been inspiring to us in these respects.
>
> Those who disagreed argued that Yao's article actually panned the play and the way Hai Rui was portrayed. It lacked concrete analysis of the plot and of the character Hai Rui, made no distinction between good and bad historical personalities by oversimplifying them, and is unconvincing in the end. Some comrades contended that if Comrade Yao's method were followed, nothing in history would be worthwhile.
>
> Still others held that Yao's viewpoint was clearly defined, his stand basically correct, but, because of insufficient historical evidence, he is not convincing on certain issues—for instance, when he says that no peasants ever "surrendered land."

This three-way split of opinions continued in the following weeks. Although positions varied somewhat depending on the specific issue, it is not unfair to group them after a sort of "parliamentarian" typology into basic left, right, and center aisles: those who agreed, disagreed, or held doubts about Yao's critique. Put briefly, some reviews were pro-Yao, advocating the value of his class analysis, others against him, criticizing the lack of concrete historical analysis, and a number of middle-of-the-road positions.

The burning issue from the beginning was the implications for contemporary politics. In the early weeks Wu Han's supporters, who shunned connections with present-day disputes, were the most vocal. They argued that Yao had "dragged political issues into academic questions" and advocated a "distinction between scholarship and politics," otherwise it would have been "highly difficult to express any opinions." They thus tended to play down any link between the play and discord in the CCP over peasant politics. If *Hai Rui* had exerted some influence on political issues, they maintained, it was not "deliberate" but an unintended consequence of an "ethical" perspective that Wu wanted to propagandize through his drama.

Most of the views reported in the Fudan letter tended to exclude or minimize the play's contemporary implications. Wu's critics, on the other hand, who were quite a minority in the early days, were cautious in connecting the play to current political divergences. After all, even in Yao's essay the issues concerning contemporary political implications of *Hai Rui* were much less direct than the detailed criticisms of the historical and theatrical aspects. Then, too, the most debated issues in those first weeks focused on the political evaluation of Hai Rui as a historical figure, although they inevitably revealed very different attitudes toward controversial contemporary issues.

The most critical argued that the play embellished Hai Rui as savior of the people and thus violated "the principle of historical materialism, which holds that it is the masses who make history." Many of the episodes praising Hai as dramatic character, they wrote, were not in conformity with historical fact. They viewed Yao's argument that Hai's motive in ruling against the surrender of land and for the return of occupied land was to "solve the financial difficulties of the Imperial Court" as well founded. It was therefore not the peasants but the landlords and feudal system that benefited from these measures.

Most of the early opinions were "centrist"—neither fully con nor pro in evaluation of *Hai Rui*. They often advocated an "impartial" judgment based on "historical" criteria. One of those recurrent arguments was that in appraising Hai Rui's political stance one should consider whether it had "promoted or hindered the progress of history." The progress of history, which Wu Han used in his self-defense some weeks later, was obviously an issue related to historical materialism and to be treated with the utmost prudence ("no absolute rule," "neither confirm nor condemn"). In this line of argument, the criterion for judging the progressive role of a historical character was whether he had promoted the development of productive forces and, consequently, historical development.

The opinions of the third cohort even more openly maintained that "Hai Rui should be totally upheld." These "reviewers" also mentioned a historical criterion but in exclusively moral terms: virtue, benevolence, uprightness. Hai was an altogether positive character, they argued, unlike corrupt officials, and beneficial to the people for his unshakable morality. "Upright and practical," they noted, Hai truly wanted to mitigate the exploitation of the peasants and enable them to live a better life. His struggle against corruption was still worth learning. "Are we today not against corruption and wastefulness? Hence, *Hai Rui Dismissed from Office* has a certain practical educational value."

The arguments partially favorable to Hai in the name of historical progress and those fully favorable in the name of morality and benevolence were not mutually exclusive, and they were often combined. They essentially held that Hai was upright and benevolent while promoting the development of productive forces. A perfect combination, one might say, of a historical materialist and a Confucian official.

Yet the moral criterion was far from being unanimously accepted. Fiercely critical opinions about the virtues of incorruptible officials also appeared, as the Fudan letter recorded. However, an essential feature of the entire dispute was that both the critical arguments and the counterarguments over Hai's "virtue" shared the same conceptual framework. The critics inevitably referred to the "class status of incorruptible officials," but were rebuked with arguments of no less a historical-materialistic bent. For instance, some sarcastically remarked that the only difference between a corrupt and an honest official in the imperial regime was that the former "took the egg by killing the chicken" and the latter "took the egg by raising the chicken," since both equally represented the class interests of the feudal system. Others argued, instead, that this view was "unilateral." They held that, given a more completely developed "historical" criterion, it would be more correct to say that in eras shaped by the rule of strong dynasties, which represented advanced productive forces and the progress of history, incorruptible officials were progressive, whereas in eras of declining dynasties they were reactionaries.

In the early weeks the debate unfolded mostly in the terms expressed in the letter, including endless discussions about historical materialist criteria for evaluating the progressive or regressive view of imperial officials. In any case, from early on Yao's criticism aroused an extraordinary subjective involvement of predominantly historical scholars. The issues were so compelling as to prompt articles as diversified as they were strongly felt.

Even more remarkable was the fact that the party-state's propaganda apparatus did very little to promote the debate, and not merely at the beginning. On the contrary, these authorities were openly disdainful of it. All the participants were quite aware they were personally responsible for the views being aired on a topic that the cultural authorities would have preferred to avoid. Indeed, there is a clear perception in the great majority of the comments of a sense of intellectual generosity and of personal risk, as well as of theoretical anxiety over issues that perhaps exceeded both the political and the historiographical conceptual coordinates available to the contributors.

After the reprint of Yao's article on November 29 and the publication of the Fudan letter on the same day, an increasing number of articles on the topic were sent to the main national and even local newspapers.[17] Those defending the play's import were notably numerous and pointedly vigorous in the first few weeks. Some even attacked Yao as "reactionary"[18] for having invoked the class criterion but then not using it to distinguish honest from corrupt officials.[19] A recurrent argument of this type was that Hai was a "model of virtue," a source of pride for the Chinese cultural tradition where honest officials like him were "at the service of the people" and "fought against corrupt officials." The defense of Wu Han was in this case unconditional even in political terms. The play had nothing to do with the political tendencies that in the early sixties were aimed at dissolving agricultural cooperatives. On the contrary, it showed "a great enthusiasm for Socialism."[20]

The contrarian critics, on the other hand, who were a minority at the outset, saw Hai as merely an instrument of feudal rule, and Wu had portrayed a fictitious characterization of him.[21] *Hai Rui*, several articles noted, was "a hymn to the feudal law [that] covered class contradictions," whereas in fact the historical Hai could not have taken any decision "in favor of the peasants."[22] As far as the contemporary political implications were concerned, Yao's supporters were rather cautious in the first weeks and somewhat understated the issue. "To say that *Hai Rui Dismissed from Office* is just an academic problem that must not be linked to politics is not very serious," wrote the literary historian Liu Dajie, who later expressed more openly critical views.[23]

Between these positions was a broad center swath. Since Yao had brought strong historiographical arguments to bear, even those most favorable to Wu could not exclude the idea that the praise of Hai had been "perhaps excessive." On the other hand, most of the centrists argued that Hai should be evaluated as a historical figure. His "positive aspects" were related to the "historical conditions of his epoch" and could not be "judged under present-day criteria." "History taught" (a frequently used expression in those months) that while the honest officials favored the stability of feudal rule, under certain conditions they had also been favorable to the peasants. The centrists, too, excluded any present-day political relevance, although some conceded the play could have "perhaps reflected," albeit "unconsciously," certain currents that in the early sixties were opposed to the agricultural cooperatives. In any case, both moderate and full supporters of Wu Han maintained that the dispute should not involve political arguments that would perturb serene scholarly debate.[24]

It is remarkable that throughout the controversy the comments critical of Yao not only emphasized the historical terrain so as to exclude political issues but also defended the apolitical boundaries with categories drawn from Marxist-Leninist philosophy. For example, some articles criticized Yao as "mechanistic" for arguing Wu's portrayal of the peasants was far too passive to have contemporary political implications.[25] The philosophical-political lexicon of the time held "mechanistic" as the equivalent of "nondialectical," "metaphysical." In Marxist-Leninist philosophy, metaphysics was the contrary of dialectics, and a good Marxist-Leninist should, of course, be materialist *and* dialectical.

This was the sense of the accusation of "metaphysical materialism" (or "mechanistic materialism") often leveled at Yao by his critics. The link established with present-day politics was labeled as "purely metaphysical," the charge being that it failed to grasp "historical dialectics."[26] Wu, they wrote, had been somewhat "one-sided" but was acting in good faith. It was not Wu but rather Yao who should change his attitude and firmly assume a "historical materialist" view.[27] The strongest of Wu's supporters even marshaled dialectical materialism to argue that there was nothing wrong with portraying peasants as passive, and Hai's benevolence toward victims and his rebuke of corrupt officials were still important lessons to learn.[28]

Jian Bozan's "policies of concessions" theory was also often quoted in defense of Wu Han. While Jian publicly engaged in the debate only marginally at a later moment, a certain number of articles picked it up and applied it to *Hai Rui*. (See the full discussion of his theory in the previous chapter.) These articles thus drew a line between an "erroneous representation" of the passive portrayal of peasants and a "basically faithful description" of Hai's actions, remarking too that his motives resulted from the concessions compelled by peasant revolts. Hence, their authors concluded, "from the point of view of historical materialism," *Hai Rui* "has a certain significance for our times."[29]

Given our tripartite grouping, these articles were as much centrist as those that expressed moderate support of Wu.

The "Left"

Our partition into left, center, and right, however, is not quite accurate enough. The Chinese ideological scene at the time featured another important character type: the "left in appearance and right in reality," or simply the "left" in quotation marks. This pointedly incisive definition shines light on figures who played an important role in the controversy and in contemporary Chinese politics. To be sure, the "true face" of "leftists" could not be easily detected under "appearances," as was often pointed out in the political tangle of those years.

The situation was considerably more complicated by the publication of some very critical articles against the "grave errors of Wu Han." While the arguments they espoused were inflexibly doctrinal, they were actually written by Wu's closest supporters in order to defend him by pointing criticism toward innocuous targets. These fake critiques, though quite limited in number, were very influential in the dispute and were fabricated at the top of the propaganda apparatus under Peng Zhen to create a smokescreen to prevent the debate from touching political divergences. Not by chance, one typical issue concerned the class criterion for evaluating "morality," the most slippery terrain of the entire class-based conceptual framework. The immediate result the authorities of the central cultural apparatus deliberately pursued was to muddy the waters of the dispute. Within a few months, however, these maneuvers became one of the major factors in the discredit and loss of authority the apparatus and its leading cadres suffered.

It was not easy to distinguish immediately the true from the false criticism. For example, an article reporting developments in the debate, written in mid-December by the *Renmin ribao* editorial board, was drafted in a way similar to the Fudan letter published in the *Wenhui bao*. It stressed the two most divergent options, apparently reporting the opposition between an even more radical left fiercely opposed to Wu's inclination toward "reformism" and "class reconciliation" on one hand, and a typical unconditional defense by Wu's supporters on the other.

The latter "school of opinion," the article noted, "holds that *Hai Rui Dismissed from Office* has sung praise through the image of Hai to the upright spirit of daring to take action and fight evil forces, expressed the hopes of the people, and reflected by twists and turns the class struggle of that time." The play had therefore a realistic educational significance since it had displayed "Hai's spirit of wholeheartedly serving the poor peasants, opposing corruption and waste, reducing exorbitant taxes and levies, evenly spreading official press-gangs of the poor, and favoring the establishment of an honest, incorrupt, and intelligent government." This view was realistically portrayed since the articles fully favorable to Wu were often more forceful than his own.

Equally incisive was the presentation of the opposite view:

> Some comrades are of the opinion that the play *Hai Rui Dismissed from Office* frenetically publicized and extolled the feudal superstructure, the theory of class reconciliation and reformism, and the out-and-out bourgeois viewpoint on the problem of state and law.... [According to these comrades] the ideological foundation of *Hai Rui Dismissed from Office* is the "theory of moral inheritance" of comrade Wu Han. Comrade Wu Han tries his utmost to publicize and extol a set of feudal ethics—loyalty, sincerity, filial piety, and brotherly subordination; propriety, morality, integrity, and sense of shame—with historical characters, stories, and episodes which he has processed and molded for the stage. He wants people of today to study, promote, and glorify fully such ethics, and arbitrarily wants people to believe that the moral code of the feudal ruling class is in agreement with the interests of the people and can be inherited.[30]

However, such harsh criticism of the "theory of moral inheritance" was not exactly an example of an uncompromising critique of "comrade Wu Han's bourgeois outlook on history in the sphere of literature and art." It referred in fact to an article written by one of Wu's closest friends and longtime coauthor, Deng Tuo. Deng was then the person responsible for cultural affairs in Beijing Municipality (a very strong position nationally) and the closest collaborator of Peng Zhen, who had directly requested and personally revised the "severe criticism" of Wu's ideological mistakes. The article, signed with the pseudonym 向阳生 Xiang Yangsheng, had appeared a few days earlier in the *Beijing ribao* as a "discussion" of the theory of moral inheritance erroneously "propagated by Comrade Wu Han" and permeating *Hai Rui Dismissed from Office*.[31]

Xiang first apologized for not having "had time to study all the works of comrade Wu Han." Nevertheless, he found it "extremely difficult to understand" why Wu demanded that we, "the men of the present time, living in the age of Socialism under the leadership of the great Communist Party," should be inspired by the moral qualities of and exalt an honest official of the Ming Dynasty. The explanation, he argued, lay in a theory of moral inheritance forming the "basis" of the views expressed in the drama constructed by Wu from various texts, of which Xiang provided a detailed list. Some of the most relevant were articles published between 1961 and 1962 in the journal 前线 *Qianxian* [Frontline], the official organ of the Beijing Party Committee, as independent essays or as parts of the series 三家村 *San jia cun* [The village of the three families].

What was Wu's gravest mistake? The fact that, although he had often claimed that the morality of the past "should be inherited" only "in a critical way," he did not actually carry out any "class analysis"—an attitude "completely opposed," the author argued, "to historical materialism." Marxism-Leninism has always stressed, Deng wrote, that "morality has a class character" and that different social classes have different morals.

The omissions were far more significant, especially given the fact that both Deng and Wu had long been the promoters of a cohesive group of propaganda officials who were as highly influential in the political life of Beijing as they were nationwide. Deng did not mention that only a few years earlier and under another pseudonym he had coauthored with Wu (and 廖沫沙 Liao Mosha[32]) "The Village of the Three Families." This was a series of articles well known for the veiled sarcasm aimed at Maoist politics and that ridiculed the Great Leap experiments as "great empty words." Nor did he mention that the editor-in-chief of *Qianxian*, the journal that had welcomed the essays of Wu he was criticizing in the *Beijing ribao* article, was none other than himself.

Even less did Deng link *Hai Rui* to any possible contemporary political controversy: all the problems were to be presented as strictly doctrinal, a terrain that he had fully mastered. Not by chance had Deng been editor-in-chief of the *People's Daily* in the fifties, and by the mid-sixties was a key figure in the ideological field. A sample of Deng's prose can give an idea of the "gravity" of Wu Han's doctrinal mistakes: "What we need is a new communist moral. Today the Chinese people, under the great guide of the glorious and just Communist Party and under the red flag of Mao Zedong's thought, is marching forward in the unprecedented enterprise of the Socialist revolution and construction. Socialism is the initial phase of Communism; our ideal is to realize Communism in the future and to carry out the most glorious and arduous historical task that constitutes the necessary responsibility of the proletariat."[33]

The premise corresponded to the standard version of historical materialism in the socialist states of the time and is still a vital component of current Chinese government discourse. The CCP has never ceased to proclaim it as its "historical task." Much more in the style of the mid-sixties political lexicon was the "left" pitch of Deng Tuo's criticism about class conflict and the "life and death struggle" between two antagonistic worldviews of the "moral." The socialist and communist moral conceptions, Deng wrote, "arise from the antagonistic struggle between the bourgeoisie and the proletariat . . . [and] . . . must necessarily proclaim the death sentence for all the old bourgeois and feudal morals." Here was the crux of Wu Han's ideological mistake.

> Comrade Wu Han does not want to proclaim this death sentence. Therefore, in *Hai Rui Dismissed from Office*, besides in his text "On Morals" and in several academic writings, he has propagandized feudal . . . and bourgeois morals, and has argued that they are "components of the socialist and communist moral." Is all this not ridiculous? . . . I do not understand why at this very moment [in the early sixties] comrade Wu Han has propagandized the theory of moral inheritance, has propagandized historical idealism, dimming the difference between dictatorship of the proletariat and dictatorship of the bourgeoisie.

The last sentence, however, more in tune with the routine litany, implied that the political issues at stake in the early sixties were not the main topic of the criticism. Despite the severe reproach to Wu for not having subscribed to "the proclamation of the death sentence," the author finally hoped that through "the discussion and the radical criticism of the moral conceptions" of all the exploiting classes, "the proletarian moral [can] achieve advances and development" and that "the Socialist revolution on the ideological and political front could progress." Xiang's "inflexible" doctrinal criticism, though aiming at delimiting the issues to an ideological-moral terrain, later became a major weakness of Peng Zhen's group once it openly emerged that under the pseudonym the author was one of Wu Han's active supporters.

In late December, the central press published other texts with similar fierce criticisms of Wu, aiming in fact at keeping the situation under control and confining the dispute to the doctrinal terrain. One was even written under the direction of Zhou Yang, a renowned senior cultural official and a member of the Group of Five. Published under the pseudonym Fang Qiu, the article, which purported to expose "what kind of social currents of thought" Wu's drama represented,[34] was apparently so virulent in tone that it caused a shock, and not only among Chinese readers.[35] An indignant American scholar even cited it as an example of the "reigning orthodoxy" inspiring Wu's enemies, who denied the existence of honest officials in the imperial ages.[36]

The main point of the article was, it is true, the question of honest officials, but beneath the surface of heated rhetoric Fang Qiu's argument was not a frantic attack leveled at Wu Han or at the honest officials of the imperial tradition. The latter, wrote Fang Qiu, "represented the long-term interests of the feudal system," but "in certain historical conditions, besides strengthening the feudal rule, some of them could within certain limits attenuate the burden of a part of the people and reduce the despotic violence of some corrupt officials." As we shall soon see, Wu adopted these arguments—the "long-term interests of feudalism" and "short-term interests of peasants"—in his "Self-Criticism." Fang argued that only by relying on a "fundamental line of demarcation of class," and not on moral criteria alone, could an impartial "historical judgment" of the honest officials be expressed.

Unlike Xiang Yangsheng, the alias of Deng Tuo, who avoided mentioning any political issue, Fang Qiu admitted, albeit with provisos, that the play "reflected" or "echoed, voluntarily or involuntarily, consciously or unconsciously," some political issues. In any case, the "social current of thought" represented in *Hai Rui*, which the article declared it expounded, was essentially a scholarly issue. The play, Fang wrote, was an expression of the phenomenon of an "immoderate admiration for the ancient" in vogue at that time among some "bourgeois historians." Despite some deceptive overtones, Fang's article was very mild and sympathetic toward Wu on the political plane. The point was to keep the dispute within the terms of a controversy among historiographical ideologies. Wu, on his part, was ready to admit having exaggerated his praise of Hai as a moral figure and to declare his firm will to rectify his stand and assume a class viewpoint.

I Forgot Class Struggle

On the same day Fang's article appeared, December 29, the *Beijing ribao* [Beijing Daily] published Wu Han's long "Self-Criticism." Reprinted the following day in the national press, it signaled that a major moment in the dispute was at hand.[37] Following the advice of Peng Zhen to write a text to "rectify the mistakes and confirm the right things,"[38] Wu had included some doctrinal self-criticisms, although they ended in a basic reassertion of his previous positions. Wu first pleaded his good faith as an old-fashioned scholar who was too detached from present reality.

> What was my purpose in writing this play? It was rather undefined and unclear at that time, although I thought I was writing about the internal struggle of the feudal class in those days. Historical research and historical plays should serve contemporary politics. What is the relationship between this play and the actual conditions in 1959 and 1960?
>
> I completely forgot the principles of using the past to serve the contemporary, deemphasizing the ancient, and stressing the contemporary.

It was entirely ancient for ancient's sake, writing the play for the sake of writing a play. I was divorced from both politics and reality. I was directed by bourgeois ideology, not by proletarian ideology. I completely forgot the unshakable principle that the literature and art of the proletariat must serve contemporary politics.

Hai Rui Dismissed from Office was completed one year after my article "On Hai Rui." During that year, all the people of our country had been moving forward; yet I remained behind and did not advance a single step. Furthermore, if there were a tiny trace of political significance for our times in "On Hai Rui," there was not even a faint breath of the times in *Hai Rui Dismissed from Office*. I had not only lagged behind, but I had regressed.

In a word, I forgot class struggle!

Wu admitted that he had "overestimated the role of Hai Rui" and had given him "too imposing" an image. The problem, he wrote, was that "all in all [he] failed to use the method of class analysis," but now, thanks to the criticism received, he had finally realized that Hai was only a "reformist." Hai had "attempted to ease fierce class contradictions and class struggles by employing reformist measures under his official powers to compel the local gentry to return the land that had been illegally seized from the peasants."

The admission sounded suitably self-critical. Yet, for one thing, to be a mere "reformist" and not a true "revolutionary" was a cardinal political sin in the Marxist-Leninist liturgy, at least in its radical version. For another, the conceptual touchstones, as is well known, history and class struggle were identical. In this sense, the gravity of the *mea culpa* was soon extenuated since the petitions for the restitution of surrendered land, Wu wrote, should be considered as a "lower form of class struggle" (阶级斗争的一种低级形式 *jieji douzheng de yi zhong diji xingshi*). The "class analysis" was therefore to be taken as incomplete rather than "lacking."

Yet the key point in Wu's historical-political arguments was whether the situations portrayed in the play were higher or lower forms of class struggle. In any case, Hai Rui's policies, as well as those adopted by honest officials of the imperial regimes, should be praised for having promoted historical progress. Their "good deeds" were "compatible with the long-term interests of the feudal ruling class" on the one hand, and with the "immediate interests of the broad masses" of oppressed and exploited peasants on the other. The acts of honest officials, though intended to "preserve the feudal system," were also "beneficial to the peasants," who therefore "praised such good officials and called them Blue Sky."

Because of their personal background and for other reasons, they [the honest officials] were closer to the people and understood their sufferings. They were relatively upright and farsighted.... [Their] good deeds ... were also advantageous to the development of production [生产的发展 *shengchande fazhan*] and to the progress of history [历史的进展 *lishi de jinzhan*]. Therefore, people honored them as Blue Sky, and they should be acknowledged and commemorated in history. In some respects, they were figures whom we should learn from today.

The reference to the development of production was important, but that to the progress of history was decisive. Since class struggle was the "motive power of history," if the benevolence of the honest officials had also promoted historical development, did it not play a role comparable to class struggle? Once the interchangeability had been ensured, Hai could be venerated as Blue Sky even by the strictest revolutionary orthodoxy. The above-cited passage was originally written for Wu's "On Hai Rui" article and is reproduced here to evince his basic views on the matter.

Yet Wu Han added a self-critical remark as to the contemporary emulation of Hai Rui's virtues that he had advocated earlier. As Comrade Xiang Yangsheng had pointed out, and Wu could not but thank him for the immense ideological help, it was a mistake to have encouraged the emulation of Hai's moral virtues because of the "radical difference" between proletarian and feudal morals. Full acknowledgment of the "class character of the moral" was meant in the end as the seal of approval guaranteeing Wu's doctrinal correctness.[39]

Fully aware of the fulcrum of the dispute, Wu was still somewhat on the defensive as far as the contemporary political implications were concerned. The "Self-Criticism" started with a detailed chronology of his writings on Hai—the play and articles written between 1959 and 1960. He intended implicitly to demonstrate that there was no connection with the Lushan Conference. Yet, besides the fact that such a preamble sounded like an unnecessary apology since Yao had not directly mentioned the issue, the chronological specification was hardly convincing. In effect, the dates of his Hai Rui articles were actually very close to those of the conference, as they were published just before and after it.

In fact, even Wu himself seemed less than convinced by his denial of any connection with the political conflicts of the late fifties. He then admitted that perhaps he had over-glorified Hai but had had no intention of justifying the "rightist opportunists criticized at Lushan" (a circumlocution indicating Peng Dehuai).[40] Quite the contrary: he aimed exclusively at "unmasking" the "false Hai Ruis," the real "opportunists." Had he not concluded his 1959

"On Hai Rui" article, which appeared immediately after Peng Dehuai's ouster, with an entire paragraph extensively quoting his "Self-Criticism," wherein he exhorted people "to learn from Hai Rui" the spirit of fighting the "rightist opportunists"?[41] The "right opportunism" quote from the 1959 article reads: "Some people claim to be Hai Rui and call themselves 'the Opposition.' . . . The large masses certainly will single out such persons, expose them under the open sky, and shout at them: Stop your pretense of passing yourselves off as [Hai Rui]! Let the popular masses clearly see the true face of rightist opportunists [for] they are definitely not Hai Rui. In this perspective, to study Hai Rui, to learn from him, and to oppose any distortion of him are useful and necessary and have a real significance for the present."

To make Hai a champion of the development of history and a savior of the peasants was questionable. But to make him also a model of the struggle against rightist opportunism was an excess of bureaucratic virtuosity, as several critical articles remarked in the following days. The above-cited paragraph, they objected, had been clearly tacked on to the rest just in case of trouble, which is precisely what happened six years later.[42]

Wu was particularly anxious to exclude contemporary political implications. All the subtleties about class analysis and historical progress were secondary. In the conclusion to the text, he raised the distinction that was the key argument of his supporters throughout the dispute. He had lacked "ideological vigilance," but his mistakes were merely academic, involving as they did historical and scholarly issues; that his political position was steadfast and his loyalty to the party unshakable was never in question: "Why should I have made such mistakes? I now realize that, on the one hand, under the party's continual education, nurture, and care, my political stand has been firm during the past twenty years. However, on the other hand, my class stand in academic thinking is still antiquated, old, and bourgeois, and there are even feudal elements in it. I have not been careful and alert. I thought there was no problem and relaxed my self-reform. Here was the problem, and here came trouble."

The Construction of the Character Hai Rui

The aspects of Wu Han's "Self-Criticism" that appeared least convincing and aroused the most controversy were the self-portrait as scholar lost in admiration for antiquity and the arguments that excluded any connection between the play and Lushan. Wu, who was surely aware of Mao's "Peng Dehuai is Hai Rui" remark on December 21, published the "Self-Criticism" just a week later. While it was essentially aimed at refuting that equation, he could not mention it directly.

In fact, the events of 1959 had profoundly shaped the composition of *Hai Rui Dismissed from Office*. While Mao's statement hit the mark, it would on closer inspection be more precise to say "Peng Dehuai *became* Hai Rui." In other words, the equation linking the Ming official and the minister of defense was the result of a shifting, somewhat tortuous, but finally coherent rendering of the character. A flashback to the process of the play's development can help to clarify some of the circumstances Wu refers to, albeit indirectly and with reticence on key points.

There were at least three stages in the portrayal of a historical character that was so decisive in the prologue to the Cultural Revolution. The first was a short article on a specific episode of Hai's life that Wu Han published immediately before Lushan. The second was the lengthy essay evaluating the historical personage that Wu wrote and published during and immediately after the conference. The third was the play itself, which Wu started in the following months and published after revisions in 1961.

Hai Rui Scolds the Emperor

To complicate matters, the first person to mention Hai Rui in positive terms was Mao himself in 1959. He did so in a talk at one of the preparatory meetings for Lushan held in Shanghai in the spring. Mao was closely monitoring the developments and difficulties of the Great Leap and was particularly concerned about how to counteract the phenomenon of false statistics. He saw the problem mainly as the effect of the submissiveness of the grassroots cadres in the countryside to unrealistic productive targets established by higher echelons. At one point in his Shanghai talk, Mao cited Hai Rui as an example of an official who had challenged authority by writing a "Memorandum to the Emperor" in which he criticized him "very sharply and without any compliments." "How many of our comrades today," he concluded, "have Hai Rui's courage?"[43]

Some reconstructions of this episode recall that Hu Qiaomu, who was then Mao's secretary,[44] had taken the initiative of seeking out Wu to ask him to write on Hai Rui. Hu's intention was presumably to spread Mao's indication, and the contact was in line with the then quite widespread tendency to promote the popularization of historical knowledge as a tool for raising the level of political consciousness. While there is only indirect evidence that Mao himself had solicited Hu about contacting Wu,[45] one may assume that he did not object to it. The episode is usually cited as further proof of Mao's tyranny, since he had earlier mentioned Hai as a model to be emulated but some years later fully supported the attack on Wu.

Upon closer inspection, Mao's first mention of Hai Rui was as an exemplum used to make his thoughts clear without resorting to any particular historiographical details. In effect, and apart from historical facts, Hai was a figure who occupied a specific place in China's popular cultural imagination. Besides being one of the Blue Sky figures typical of imperial ideology, his image was even more proverbial for some rather unusually provocative attitudes toward the imperial court, views that cost him the famous, albeit temporary, dismissal. As Mao's remarks in the Shanghai speech indicate, Hai Rui was the more or less legendary topos of someone who did not try to please his superiors and had even written a memorandum whose intent was to criticize the emperor.

The sense of the train of thought was clear. Mao had good reason to believe that the spate of false statistics was aggravated by the fact that the higher bureaucratic echelons demanded spectacular harvest figures from the lower levels, and the latter bowed to these demands in order to curry favor, even to the extent of officially declaring targets that were never attained or attainable. One of the most deleterious effects was that the grassroots cadres exerted very strong pressure on the peasants to deliver the planned harvests. Paradoxically, it was the collective enthusiasm for the Great Leap that made room for these arbitrary decisions since most peasants had confidence in the cadres' judgment in the beginning. Yet that same mass momentum vitiated the political essence of the experiment by merely turning it into an exhibition of superior production figures that proved a sham in the end. Mao realized it was indispensable to stop the books being cooked and to "correct" those doing it as soon as possible while safeguarding mass political activism.

Briefly put, the lower cadres must be able to report things to their superiors that the latter would prefer not to hear. Hai Rui was thus a "proverbial" example from the Chinese cultural tradition, irrespective of any philological exactitude. Mao quoted him in 1959 as an appeal to the grassroots cadres to take a firm stand when faced with erroneous decisions by their leaders in an effort to interrupt the perverse mechanism of bureaucratic one-upmanship and infighting carried out using fictitious statistics.

At this point Wu Han entered the fray at Hu Qiaomu's prompting and began writing on Hai Rui. His initial foray was a brief article entitled "Hai Rui Scolds the Emperor" (海瑞骂皇帝 *Hai Rui ma huangdi*).[46] Yet, in his coached "Self-Criticism" during the dispute in late 1965, Wu could not explicitly remark on the issue at hand. Indeed, his line of defense turned out to be contradictory since he portrayed himself as an old-fashioned academic detached from reality and entirely oblivious to all matters political. While it is true that the article was published in mid-June 1959, about two weeks before the Lushan

Conference and, hence, at a date supporting his estrangement from any political issue, it had in fact been requested in the broad context of the preparatory work for the conference itself.

The article looks quite neutral at first glance. It simply summarizes the petition quoted by Mao that Hai Rui sent to Emperor Jiaqing in 1566. It is a famous memo even if it did not concern any specific government decision, despite a polemical tone that sounded a bit over the top for a minister complaining to his sovereign. Hai Rui was duly castigated and then dismissed for having sent the petition, and was only reinstated after Emperor Jiaqing's death.

A closer reading, however, shows that instead the memorandum sums up a kind of ideal model for criticizing the decadence of the sovereign's virtues, a practice that was typical in the Confucian tradition from ancient times. The upbraiding of the emperor really takes issue with that sovereign's historically notable disinterest in governmental affairs. The latter's brusque and arrogant replies to the discontents reported by his ministers were the result of his assiduous dedication to occult practices in the pursuit of immortality. While Hai's memorandum requested that the sovereign repent and renounce his mania for the occult, the true essence of the criticism is rather vague. The key passage is probably the following: "The main problems today are that the Way of the sovereign is not straight and the ministers' tasks not well-defined [目前的问题是君道不正, 臣职不明 *muqian de wenti shi jun dao bu zheng, chen zhi bu ming*]."[47]

This is the kind of critique that can be found elsewhere in the imperial tradition. The accusation regarding the emperor's wholehearted dedication to magic potions in a quest for immortality, for example, is the same as the charge the Confucians had leveled from the time in the Han era at their favorite polemical target, the first Legalist emperor, Qin Shi Huangdi.

Wu's 1959 article was later sharply criticized for having exaggerated and distorted the content of Hai's memorandum. For, it was noted, far from being a reprimand to the sovereign, the memorandum should rather be taken as a sign of mere submission to the imperial regime. Wu, the critics argued, praised the "scolding" only insofar as it concerned the "bad emperor," not the legitimacy of the emperor as such. Moreover, given the situation in 1959, the critics contended that Wu's article would have been an invitation to rightist opportunists to upbraid the correct political line of the party itself.[48] The first argument is obvious; the second seemingly overestimates Wu's political influence. However, the key point is that there was no trace in the article of what political import Hai's example held for Mao vis-à-vis his appeal to the lower rural cadres not to give in to their superiors when the latter set unrealistic crop targets. "Hai Rui Scolds the Emperor" ignores the main political motive for quoting Hai at the time. Indeed, it highlights a staple parable of the Confucian tradition—the honest functionary in conflict with the emperor who lacks virtue. For Confucianism, when the sovereign's *Dao* was not "upright" (君道不正 *jun dao bu zheng*), it was the beginning of all evils.

Wu's article on the memorandum may be considered the first brushstrokes in the portrayal of his play's leading character. Hai Rui is depicted from the outset as entirely dissociated from the contemporary political scene. In fact, however, Hai was an inevitable participant: Mao mentioned him on purpose, and Wu the historian was tapped to contribute a piece intended to enhance the significance of that reference at an extremely tense political moment. Wu's initial attempt was to "depoliticize" Hai, a broad stroke he retained in the subsequent steps of his portrayal.

"On Hai Rui"

Wu Han did not make much mention in the "Self-Criticism" of "Hai Rui Scolds the Emperor," probably because he could not explain his sudden interest in the personage in the spring of 1959 without giving details of his actual proximity to the highest political spheres of the party-state. He did quote another, longer essay of his entitled "On Hai Rui," published in September 1959, albeit in this case, too, omitting anything that would have contradicted his self-portrait as "apolitical" scholar. This was the article that contained the above-mentioned passage against right-wing opportunism, which Wu cited as proof of his fidelity to the party. The passage was visibly inserted in the text in case the situation worsened, as happened in late 1965. Indeed, it was added on Hu Qiaomu's advice immediately after the Lushan Conference and its dismissal of Peng Dehuai for "right-wing opportunism."[49]

It can be assumed, however, that while Hu had solicited the first article, "On Hai Rui" was likely written on Wu's own initiative, and that Hu's prompting was limited only to suggesting the addendum. The third and final stage in character construction—the play itself—seems to be more directly attributable to Wu. These details further complicate the issue of Wu's relationship to Lushan, which is certainly the thorniest part of the story.

There can be no question that Wu was aware of the ongoing political confrontation in 1959. While not entitled to take part in the conference, he was certainly soon informed that Hai's name had come up several times during the contest between Peng Dehuai and Mao.[50] He also likely knew that Mao was quite surprised at seeing his exemplum quoted to a completely different purpose from what he had imagined, and did not leave unanswered the reference to the "spirit of Hai Rui" by the opponents of the political experiments that were the Great Leap Forward.

Incidentally, as noted in chapter 2, if one reads the transcripts of the Lushan Conference, which have been available for many years, the situation appears very different from the image of brute despotic censorship exercised by Mao against Peng Dehuai, which goes all but unquestioned when the issue is mentioned today. As a small example in this connection, here is Mao's reaction to the Hai Rui episode, which occurred at one of the tensest moments of the controversy. "Hai Rui has moved house [搬家 了 banjia le]; in the Ming Dynasty Hai Rui was on the left . . . now Hai Rui is on the right. I have selective listening [偏听偏信 pian ting pian xin], I only listen to one side. Hai Rui was left-wing; I like the left-wing Hai Rui. Today, to criticize our shortcomings based on a Marxist position is correct; I support the left-wing Hai Rui."[51]

We can suppose that the notably political implications of his allusion to Hai during the conference would have been more disturbing than reassuring to Wu. The character he had so apolitically praised a few weeks earlier had become the subject of heated controversy at Lushan. In "Hai Rui Scolds the Emperor," Wu Han had "sterilized" the political reference to contemporary issues, eschewing even the faintest allusion to freedom of spirit on the part of grassroots cadres toward the upper echelons. Now, however, Hai Rui unexpectedly reappeared even more dramatically as a touchstone in the most serious political confrontation at the apex of the CCP's leadership after 1949.

"On Hai Rui" should be read, like the previous article, by considering what it says as well as what it omits, namely the fact that in those same weeks Hai Rui had become a highly politicized name that played a direct role in the confrontation between Mao and Peng Dehuai. Wu reacted with a further depoliticizing step. In his first article Wu had brought the character back to the stereotypical image of the Confucian official who laments the sovereign's loss of virtue. Now, faced with the fact that a new and far more turbulent political implication had emerged—a split between a "right-wing" and a "left-wing" Hai Rui—Wu hastened to adjust by distancing the character even further from contemporary politics. The personage in "On Hai Rui" was neither right nor left, being beyond any possible contemporary political division. He was merely, Wu wrote, a champion of the development of history.

The length of the essay, published immediately after the conference, very likely points to its being written during or toward the end of the conference. Obviously, the tirade against the "right-wing opportunism" of the "false Hai Rui" was written afterward. Wu had gone too far in depicting a character fully dissociated from contemporary political controversy, and Hu Qiaomu had probably remarked that he risked being associated with the "right-wing Hai Rui." He therefore prudently suggested that Wu add the passage noted above. The result was that a higher, more authoritative hand, something that Wu alone would likely never have thought of writing, was clearly recognizable in the praising of Hai as a champion of the "fight against right opportunism."

The character traits clearly and directly attributable to Wu in the long September 1959 article portray an altogether different Hai Rui from the original that Mao mentioned in spring. Hai is no longer even remotely the paradigm of the official who dares to tell his superiors something they do not wish to hear. He is now a "benevolent governor" acting in favor of peasants and history. If one major concern in the previous article was to remove the political reason for quoting the memorandum, or the exhortation to the lower cadres not to be submissive to the arbitrary targets imposed from above, the omission in "On Hai Rui" of any possible contemporary political implication is much more systematic.

The Dismissal as Adjunct

The urgency that drove Wu Han to work on the subject is supported by the dates of the third and final step of the character's composition. Wu supposedly started writing *Hai Rui Dismissed from Office* shortly after Lushan, and had already completed a first draft by March of the following year and a second in June. The final text was published in August 1961 and staged in early 1962. The variations among the three versions were carefully and polemically examined at the time of the controversy of 1965–66.

The main difference is that the title of the final version has 罢官 *ba guan*, *Dismissed from Office*, while the two previous versions carried only *Hai Rui* as the title. Critics writing during 1965–66 remarked on the temporal distance between the drafts and the final version. They concluded that the addition to the title was only possible in 1961 because only then was support strong enough at the top of the CCP for Peng Dehuai's rehabilitation. This fact, they argued, attests to the active participation of Wu in the ongoing political conflicts.

Yet I suggest that the title was rather the final step in the process of stripping the character Hai of any possible political implications. The thrust to depict an apolitical Hai is inversely proportional to the political tension that was palpable at Lushan. Given the political controversy it had aroused, there is no trace of rebuking the emperor in *Hai Rui Dismissed from Office*. Gone too is any allusion to the development of history, which, in spite of every precaution to limit it to the development of productive forces, had one vague political reference. And, of course, there no longer was any trace of Hai as a banner of the struggle against rightist opportunists, which Wu had been authoritatively advised to introduce in the previous article.

The Hai of the play is finally portrayed as Blue Sky, the scourge of wicked officials and benefactor of grateful peasants to whom the latter swear perpetual devotion. The prerequisite of the character is no longer Confucian sorrow for the sovereign's lack of virtue or the historical promotion of productive forces; here it is simply the political impotence of the peasants. Thus, stripped of political allusions, the staged Hai is fully consistent with the view that the experiments of the Great Leap are devoid of value. In this respect, the play reflects not only the views of Peng Dehuai but, more essentially, the deadlock in the search for a new political existence for the peasants that was manifest in the CCP at the end of the fifties.

But why in his final version did Wu Han feel the need to add the theme of dismissal to the title but omit it from the plot? In the event, the disappearing dismissal would only increase its symbolic weight. After managing so effectively to strip any political allusion the character Hai might embody by omitting any mention of dismissal in the plot, was the new title not signposting that Wu was likely once again to bring a *political* nuance back to the fore? In fact, that is precisely what occurred in the controversy of 1965-66.

We can only resort to conjecture. If, for example, the Lushan confrontation pivoted on the possibility of inventing a new political existence for the peasants, and if the motive force that induced Wu to strip the character Hai Rui of political significance was fully consistent with the denial of any such potentiality, the character construction would have been incomplete had it not also touched upon the dramatic outcome of the conference. Or better, it would have been ultimately ineffectual had the political significance of Peng Dehuai's dismissal not been eschewed and reduced to a court intrigue in which an honest official had been unduly punished.

For it is at this point that Peng Dehuai fully *becomes* Hai Rui. Yet the adding of dismissal to the title also, and inevitably, had a retroactive effect. As Mao's remark cogently underscored, it turned Peng Dehuai into Blue Sky from the moment he entered the stage in the Lushan dispute. While the addition of dismissal to the title was a coherent move, its absence from the plot also reveals that Wu was aware of the risk of a blowback if too much emphasis was put on it. In the event, he decided to take the risk, though without going too far by openly arguing the issue. This final brushstroke brings to light a sort of indecision, if not reluctance, on Wu's part. In effect, his involvement in the "Hai Rui affair" was not of his own initiative from the very start, and we've seen that his first reaction was to keep *Hai Rui* and himself as far as possible from the political fray.

Comrade Wu Han Is Too Modest

Our overview of the character's composition allows a closer look at the subsequent trajectory of the dispute, since most of the above developments were well known to the participants even if only indirectly mentioned. While the "Self-Criticism" was coordinated at the highest levels in an effort to dampen, if not to end, the critiques of *Hai Rui*, it had in fact the opposite effect by rendering the discord acute. Wu's attempt to exclude any contemporary implication from the play magnified the Lushan controversy and, hence, markedly pointed attention to the thorniest aspect of the polemics. The arguments of his "Self-Criticism" did not convince the critics, who increased in number and became even more polemical in tone. Nor could they be of much help to Wu's supporters, who found it frequently contradictory even if they continued to defend the play in tones even more forceful than those of its author.

By the time of its publication in late December 1965, Wu's "Self-Criticism" marked a turning point. For by January the subjective involvement of the intellectual public was even more pronounced than in the previous weeks, driven as it was by the awareness that the issues at stake were of a fundamental political nature. Moreover, the numerous signs that the authorities presiding over the party-state's central cultural apparatus were often exerting twisted influence on a dispute they wished had never happened made the critics more stubborn while inevitably eliciting more obstinate counterarguments from Wu's supporters.

Among the newspaper accounts were articles carrying detailed reports of discussion forums and seminars held in various Chinese cities by some of the most prominent Chinese historians. These meetings focused on and summarized the most significant and influential views concerning Wu's "Self-Criticism." Given the large number of articles and letters on the topic by January authored by the participants at the seminars, to rely on those reports, as we have for the December onset of the critiques, is again helpful in delineating a concise, coherent picture of the situation.

One of the first of these discussion groups was held in Shanghai on December 31, the day after the "Self-Criticism" appeared, and reveals the intensity of the debate. It was convened on the initiative of the *Wenhui bao*,[52] the daily that had started the dispute by publishing Yao Wenyuan's article and undoubtedly reflected the most critical positions. Wu's supporters in attendance were in considerable difficulty with his arguments, especially that of Hai Rui's portrayal as the epitome of an "anti-rightist" militant.

The speaker of the opening address at the Shanghai forum exclaimed at one point, "How is it that Wu Han has associated the campaign against rightists with Hai Rui?" This was Zhou Yutong, deputy director of the Institute of History of the Shanghai Academy of Social Sciences and one of Wu's most friendly and understanding supporters.[53] Some observed that "mechanically arranging a chronological table while sidestepping the ideological essence of the issue cannot solve the problems."[54] Yet even those most well-disposed toward Wu admitted that they were "at a loss as to what connection there is between Hai Rui and opposition to rightists."[55]

Much more openly polemical were the remarks of almost all the other participants at Shanghai, most of whom were senior historians. Many contested Wu's article as a mixture of self-assurance, doctrinal litany, sophistries, and limited concessions on minor points that avoided all the major, above all political, issues. The main points discussed were the claim that Hai symbolized a hero of the "struggle against right-wing opportunism," the timetable of Wu's writings, and the apology for being "divorced from present reality" by pursuing "the ancient for the sake of the ancient" and "the theater for the sake of the theater."

Liu Dajie remarked that while the timetable of his works included at the beginning of the "Self-Criticism" was intended to prove that his play had nothing to do with politics, Wu also stated he wrote the "On Hai Rui" article to "oppose right opportunism." It was unlikely, Liu noted, that the play, written from the template of "On Hai Rui," should have as "ambiguous" and "confused" a purpose as the author would have us believe. Liu also noted that some years earlier in his article "On Some Questions Regarding the Historical Play," Wu had maintained that writing historical plays "in short, is not to serve the dead, but to serve the living." Wu had stressed that the main objective of such a play should be "to inherit our ancestors' experience and lessons in struggles so as to make them serve the socialist construction of today, thereby achieving the use of the ancient in the service of the present." However, Wu stated in his "Self-Criticism" that in writing *Hai Rui Dismissed from Office* the principles of "making the ancient serve the present" and "stressing the present and deemphasizing the ancient" never occurred to him. He was only "studying the ancient for the ancient's sake, writing the play for playwriting's sake." Liu concluded, "How could this convince people?"[56]

Another critic observed that not only was it unlikely the play had been written to oppose the right opportunists who claimed to be like Hai, but that Wu's argument also showed that "such people needed Hai Rui after all, even if they were incapable of fully representing themselves in that guise." Thus, "the articles on Hai Rui and the play met the needs of the rightist opportunists who likened themselves to Hai Rui, thereby functioning where the people were unable to function."[57] Here we find a trace noted above that the participants in the dispute were aware that the rightist opportunists finally "became" Hai. However, the critics did not elaborate further, nor did they explore in detail the process of the character's composition as a series of steps in reaction to developments at the Lushan Conference. The exact references were mostly cryptic or enveloped in circumlocutions (Peng Dehuai's name was never mentioned), mainly because it was known that the divergence at Lushan was still unresolved.

The point that most of the participants considered both unlikely and politically unreliable was the divorce between historical scholarship and politics, or the claim of an inner contrast between a "firm political stand" and "backward academic thinking."[58] As for Wu Han's regret over the "apolitical defect" of the play, some observed that there are in fact scholars of ancient history who study "antiquity for antiquity's sake." However, this could not be the case where Wu was concerned, since he had long ago advocated that the writing of a historical play should lay emphasis on "its instructive impact on the next generation."[59]

Finally, the argument of having forgotten class struggle posited by an author who had repeatedly stressed the contemporary value of historical research was seen as a pretext for circumventing the political stakes on the table. As several speakers pointed out, "not only had Wu Han not forgotten class struggle, but he also had absolutely taken part in it, except that he was on the side of the bourgeoisie."[60] Wu, said another at the meeting, "was just being modest . . . he has not forgotten it for a single moment."[61] The note of sarcasm was evident. An article in the following days noted, "Comrade Wu Han, rather than being divorced from politics and reality, is in fact a person with a keen political sensibility and good knowledge of what political struggle really is."[62]

Poisonous Weed or Fragrant Flower?

By January 1966, the polemical winds over the "Self Criticism" fanned the controversy, spreading it to other issues of the play and the character Hai. While there were not many new arguments either pro or con in this connection, the positions became increasingly polarized. While the moderate centrists manifested little enthusiasm for the "Self-Criticism," the critical barbs from both wings became sharper on the political and historical issues, and Wu's most ardent supporters became more intransigent. Thus, the center thinned and the left and right became more pungently vocal. To put it in the political idiom of those years, those who criticized *Hai Rui Dismissed from Office* as a "poisonous weed" and those who praised it as a "fragrant flower" stood head to head.

The minutes of two discussion forums held in Wuhan and Guangzhou and attended by historians and other scholars from the most important local universities and research institutions were published in mid-January. They provide a reliable summary of the positions aired, along with various nuances in many articles that then appeared in the national press. Given the multitude of participants, the remarks in both reports are grouped into pros and cons, an arrangement reflecting and emphasizing the depth of the divide on the dispute's political, theatrical, and historical planes.

A look at the strictly political shows that the Wuhan scholars all referred their remarks in transparent jargon to the controversies concerning the destinies of agricultural cooperatives and the results of the Lushan Conference. Wu's supporters denied any connection to specific political controversies and vigorously stressed the patriotic value of the moral qualities of Hai Rui. In the difficult situation and international isolation of China in the early sixties, they said, "when the imperialists and modern revisionists joined in a great anti-China chorus a few years ago, the attributes of uprightness, impartiality, and undauntedness praised by *Hai Rui Dismissed from Office* did play an inspiring role in the actual struggles of that time."[63] The critics, by contrast, contended that the play was representative of a political project for the suppression of the people's communes and was fully in tune with the "anti-China chorus." They noted that "The play appeared at a time when the imperialists and modern revisionists were churning up an anti-China high tide and when the feudal forces and the bourgeoisie in the country were launching a frenzied attack and fanning the winds of 'going it alone' and 'verdict reversal.'"[64]

A recurrent argument among Wu's supporters was the policy of concessions, the only truly theoretical touchstone available. In their view, "Hai Rui implemented a reformist policy of concessions that were in fact by-products of revolution, a kind of refracted reflection of the role of the masses of people in history."[65] The critics, however, countered that the historical record of Hai Rui's attitude toward peasants proved the imaginary nature of the character in the play. For them, the idea that Hai could be portrayed as a feudal reformist was mere fantasy.[66]

The polemic in January over the historical issue of honest officials was more radicalized than in December but also marked a stalemate along the main fault lines. While articles favorable to Wu insisted that Hai was a "paradigm of morality" and a promoter of "historical progress,"[67] the supporters of Yao argued that the very concept of the honest official was a "curtain of fog" disguising the real class relationship in the imperial ages.[68]

Yet the divergences over the issue of class analysis in the play were significantly more ambiguous and hard to distinguish in the end. The critics, who by now were in the majority, contended that Wu's was a "theory of class reconciliation" and that the complaints of peasants could not be considered as forms of class struggle.[69] Articles favorable to Wu Han maintained instead that he had used a class criterion and that there was not in principle any divergence with his critics.[70]

Significantly, the plane on which the divergences were most sharply defined was the theatrical. Wu's supporters admitted that the portrayal of the character Hai was "somewhat exaggerated" but nonetheless considered it "permissible in writing a historical play." The educational function of historical plays, they noted, "does not lie in compelling people to learn directly from the particular behavior of a historical figure but aims rather at arousing a kind of associated idea in the audience." The critics, by contrast, maintained that "while it is permissible in a historical play to portray the development and magnification of a historical character," in this case there was no trace of real life, and the struggles on stage had no political content, merely being "struggles between good and evil." Hai and the wicked officials were representatives of good and evil.[71]

The contrasts at the Guangzhou forum were as marked as at Wuhan. The three planes of debate were here more entangled, but the different positions were even more sharply defined. For Wu Han's supporters, "Hai Rui possessed many good qualities worthy of emulation . . . he was not a sham moralist," and his "incorruptibility was genuine." Like all honest officials, "although serving the interests of the feudal class as a whole," Hai was "also objectively beneficial to the development of production at that time and was welcomed by the people."[72]

The critics, however, focused on the inconsistency of Hai's portrait as a historical figure. The idea that "when a prince violates the law, he should be punished just like a commoner," which Wu had presented as the main motive for Hai's actions, blurred "the basic nature of the state apparatus of the landlord class."[73] On the other hand, Hai's readiness to meet death when the emperor wanted to execute him was not, as Wu claimed, a virtue of "uprightness and straightforwardness" and worthy of emulation, but mere "subservience to the feudal imperial court." "To die in order to safeguard the feudal system is an utterly unworthy death." Wu was "even worse than a historian of the feudal age," one remarked, "for he not only has described Hai Rui as an honest official but has even portrayed him as the people's savior."

The sharpest critiques at the Guangzhou meeting addressed the theatrical issue. The area under Hai Rui's jurisdiction, said a participant, was described not as an imperial prefecture but "as something similar to a liberated area during the People's War" and the "return of occupied land . . . as something similar to agrarian reform." In the play, observed another more sarcastically, some traits of the protagonist even transformed "an orthodox feudal moralist" into a "parliamentary statesman. In a scene of the play Hai Rui convenes a sort of a family conference in which the three factions in his family—the left (mother), the center (wife), and the right (servant)—exercised freedom of speech." It was thus an action that could never be expected by the head of a feudal family who "measured everything by the criteria of the three bonds and five relationships of human society."

History, Politics, and Party Discipline

The critical articles in response to Wu Han's "Self-Criticism" had intensified to a peak by January. While the number and vigor of those pro and con writings were remarkable in themselves, the contrasts on the historiographical plane proper only confirmed the previous positions, despite some new details. However, the issues on which the controversy reached a stalemate were more political than historiographical, or better, they concerned the coherence between them.

Yao Wenyuan had concluded his critique of *Hai Rui* hoping that both the historiographical and the political questions would be discussed and resolved via the concept of class struggle. As the polemics peaked and positions polarized, however, the most problematic point emerged. Was it possible to employ the same conceptual framework on both historical and political grounds? Wu's critics had become increasingly radical in this connection, but none had been able to argue convincingly that his historical views had the same class nature as his political, or vice versa.

Wu Han had tried to separate the two, claiming his unshakable political rectitude and loyalty to the party while admitting some shortcomings on the historiographical plane (having partially "forgotten class struggle"), which in the event he was fully prepared to rectify. This argument had caused the most critical comments, but even some of his supporters did not find it fully convincing. On the other hand, although the historiographical issues of *Hai Rui* had been hotly debated, none of the critics had actually proved via classist arguments that depicting the peasants as politically inert and the honest officials of the Ming period as highly charitable was tantamount to a specific class position in contemporary politics. Indeed, Wu's supporters had mustered class arguments to point out the political inability of the peasants and the historical value of benevolent officials in imperial China while underscoring the author's political loyalty to the party.

As this framework began configuring the theoretical deadlock, a spate of markedly critical articles on Wu published in January introduced a new argument intended to decide the issue: the "antiparty" nature of Wu's views. However, this tack immediately unleashed a strong backlash in Wu's defense that eventuated in a breakthrough that brought the historical-political controversy to a close. This turn of events deserves a close reading.

An article signed by Shi Shaobin, for instance, took sharp issue with Wu's "Self-Criticism" for excluding any political implications in the play and stated that its main theme was the dismissal. The argument obviously echoed Mao's statement in December about the "nub" of *Hai Rui ba guan*, which had remained an unpublished spoken remark but had circulated to a certain degree, more so in Shanghai than in the rest of the country.[74] The dismissal theme, argued Shi, was the glorification of "those antiparty, antipeople 'heroes' who claimed they were dismissed for 'pleading for the people' by complaining about the injustices done them and then making plans on their behalf."[75]

An inflammatory article some days later went even further, proclaiming the urgency of accepting the "challenge launched by Comrade Wu Han" to the party line.[76] Other articles the following day stated that Wu's attitude was a "trial of strength with the proletariat,"[77] and another ended by branding the character Hai as an "antiparty and antisocialist political tool."[78] It is not easy to pinpoint the exact source of these articles, which were often signed not by individuals like the great majority of the texts examined here but by pen names or groups of writers.[79] These articles were presumably the expression of more or less organized radical groups in the party who were trying to gain traction in the controversy.

Most of these articles were initially published in national newspapers, not in the *Wenhui bao*, which had started the debate. It is also difficult to ascertain any direct support from Mao, despite the clear echo of his statement on the dismissal issue. As we shall see below, Mao too will use the same argument in the clash with Peng Zhen, though it will prove a very weak one in those conditions. In fact, Peng Zhen was able to ignore it for months and to keep his position. Chapter 5 will provide a discussion of Mao's and Peng Zhen's respective positions on the issue and the complex shifting of their weak and strong points.

Let us keep our focus on the radicalizing January articles. The crucial point here is that the antiparty label used as the deciding argument at the peak of the dispute hit an impasse. Why did it seek to be decisive at just that moment? The party, the "class party of the proletariat," embodied the historical guarantee of and for politics. Under historical materialism, the Communist Party was the political consequence of the historical development of class struggle. Therefore, to label Wu Han as antiparty appeared to be the solution to the dispute's conceptual stalemate. It stigmatized a grave historiographical and political mistake. It claimed to prove that Wu's class view was equally wrong, both as specialist of Ming history and as party member, and that *Hai Rui* was a "challenge" that should be accepted and counterattacked "in defense of the proletariat and socialism." However, such a solution only short-circuited the controversy's aporias by increasing the ambiguities inherent in the vision of the political consequences of historical development.

More essentially, the antiparty label was a disciplinary issue in the radical articles of January 1966. Wu's challenge to the proletariat and socialism was referred to, albeit in a more or less cryptic manner, as the breakdown of party discipline concerning the final decision of the Lushan Conference. Wu denied any connection to that controversy and strenuously proclaimed his unshakable fidelity to the party and, of course, to its discipline, which some minor academic shortcomings could not disprove. Under those conditions, who could then distinguish between the right and wrong of the matter? In other words, what authority could decide an issue that, from the point of view of the critical January articles, ultimately concerned the cultural discipline of the party-state?

An organ of the CCP's top leadership did exist at the time to exercise that authority. Set up a couple of years earlier, it was the Group of Five we briefly mentioned earlier. Officially called the "Group for the Cultural Revolution,"[80] it was headed by Peng Zhen and had played a major role in the debate since the publication of Yao Wenyuan's article.[81] By early February it assumed an even more important role and managed to impart a decisive turn to the situation by imposing a strict "apolitical" constraint on the dispute.

Peng Zhen had become increasingly concerned the previous November about the criticism of Wu and had both formally and informally intervened, first to quash the dispute and then to keep it under control. Early in February, after the publication of articles raising the antiparty argument, Peng Zhen activated the Group of Five to draft a formal disciplinary code of criteria to confine the polemics. The group issued a document, usually referred to as the "February Outline" (the full title was "Outline Report on the Current Academic Discussion"), that soon became the officially adopted position of the Central Committee and strictly regulated the debate over the next two months.[82] The Outline was intended to quash publication of articles in the press mentioning present-day political issues in connection with the *Hai Rui* debate.

The official version of Peng Zhen's downfall in May 1966 was that he had arbitrarily used his power to protect Wu and hastily forced through approval of the formal procedures for imposing strict censorship on all political criticism.[83] By contrast, the story current in the Chinese government today is that the main motive for this document was the urgent need to respond to a wave of revulsion among public opinion over the criticism of Wu Han.[84] We have seen, however, that the reactions to Yao's critique were far from unanimously indignant, and that intellectual opinion was deeply split on the issue. The most irritated was Peng Zhen, as well as the leading circles of the cultural ministries of the party-state, who had been opposed to the airing of any such polemics right from the beginning. While it is likely that Peng Zhen used rather heavy-handed tactics in getting the Outline approved, he succeeded only by his timely intervention at that peculiar juncture, which also explains why he insisted the Outline be approved with such haste.

Peng Zhen had moved in response to the most radical critics, who by January were attempting to force the theoretical impasse of the dispute by attacking Wu's antiparty political-cum-historiographical stand—an essentially disciplinary argument, as noted above. More to the point, Peng Zhen was essentially seizing the moment to settle the score with the entire dispute over *Hai Rui*, which he had considered an unprecedented breakdown in party discipline since November. Now that the radical critics had openly raised a disciplinary issue against Wu, Peng Zhen did not hesitate to counterattack.

At the time, in fact, it was the fully institutionalized Group of Five that dictated the disciplinary rules for the behavior of party members in the cultural sphere. Peng Zhen was the highest authority regarding the party's cultural code of discipline and, when the radical critics trespassed into disciplinary terrain, he exercised his full powers without meeting any serious obstacle. The Central Committee quickly and unanimously approved the Outline, and even Mao, although he personally expressed his disagreement to Peng Zhen, was unable to thwart the document's approval, as evinced by the details in chapter 5.

Yet Peng Zhen's strong-arm tactics also belied a decisive weakness that emerged in less than a couple of months. While the Outline managed to neutralize the antiparty argument by asserting its own higher authority regarding disciplinary criteria, to do so effectively it also had to quash the controversy completely by banning all political arguments. One of the major and most effective criticisms Mao later brought to bear against the Outline was that it was censorship in disguise.

Acting under the Leadership of the Party

A key document of the prologue to the Cultural Revolution, the February Outline was initially submitted to the highest party organ, the Central Committee, which approved it on February 12 and issued it as the basic guidelines to be followed at all party levels. It should be implemented especially by the "comrades responsible for the work of academic debate" and, naturally, by "the comrades engaged in scholarly research." It remained formally in force until the approval of the May 16 Circular, but, as we shall see in chapter 4, Mao raised a polemical storm against it in mid-March.

The Outline opened with a preliminary definition of "the situation and the nature of current academic criticism." The topics it specified concerned "moral heritage, honest officials, polices of concession, appraisal of historical figures, and the outlook and methods of historical research." The Outline stated that discussions had "enlivened the public ideologically, opened the lid, and achieved great results." However, it avoided any reference to contemporary political issues and, significantly, never mentioned Yao's essay. On the other hand, the general tone of the document was ideologically intransigent, even bellicose at some points. A Chinese researcher who has appraised the text according to the criteria of the CCP's current prose style has even reproached its use of "leftist" expressions. It was an understandable choice, he argued, given the general atmosphere of those months, when the main problem was how to deal with the dangerous true leftists on their own ground.[85] We have already seen how such a "left" was active in the *Hai Rui* debate and, hence, in reading this text we must take into account what the leftist intonation aimed to achieve. Here, for instance, we find the Outline has dramatic stress as a life-and-death struggle: "The nature of this great controversy is a struggle between Marxism-Leninism and Mao Zedong's thought and the thought of the bourgeoisie in the ideological domain, a struggle to liquidate bourgeois and other reactionary or erroneous thinking in the academic sphere under the conditions of the proletarian dictatorship and the practice of socialist revolution. This is a life-and-death struggle between the proletariat and the bourgeoisie, which is a component of the struggle between the two lines of socialism and capitalism. This great debate is bound to be expanded to other academic spheres."

While doctrinal references were peremptory, the key point was the strict delimitation of the questions to academic spheres. More explicit is the prescription in the following paragraph: "We must conduct this struggle under direction, with prudence, seriousness, and energy to hit at bourgeois ideology and consolidate and expand the ideological front of the proletariat." Here the key words were "under direction" (有领导的 *you lingdao de*), which meant of course within the boundaries of the ideological jurisdiction of the party-state. The main issue was exactly how to bring back under official control a debate that had spread largely beyond the reins of the party-state and its cultural machinery.

The document was thus conceived as a guideline addressing the four-month-old, ongoing debate over *Hai Rui*. All the prescriptions should therefore be read as indicating the directions in which the debate *was not* allowed to continue and the correct path that *was* to be followed. So, except for some doctrinal references, the document was a list of prohibitions and prescriptions. A lack of "prudence" (谨慎 *jinshen*), for instance, was clearly a serious shortcoming (that could well be exemplified by Yao's article, albeit unmentioned) to be overcome with a more moderate attitude, which on the other hand could greatly benefit from a responsible and rigorous direction. Less obvious were the problems of "seriousness" and "energy," given the quality and vigor of the arguments in the dispute, though the Outline indicated the need for greater self-restraint.

The Outline noted that it concerned nothing less than the "thorough liquidation of bourgeois ideas in the realm of academic work—a question which remains unsolved in the Soviet Union and other socialist countries." Such a struggle should obviously be conducted "under the guidance of Mao Zedong's thought." However, impatience and imprudence would jeopardize that strategic plan. These issues needed to be resolved "gradually and systematically," given "the chronic, complicated, and difficult nature of this struggle and the need not only to pay attention to the enemy strategically but even to take full account of him tactically."

Therefore, another important prescription was that "this task" could not "be fulfilled merely after several months of struggle by publishing a number of conclusive articles or formulating political conclusions about certain people who have been criticized." Short-term political conclusions were neither possible nor desirable. On the contrary, a "policy of opening wide" was necessary because "scholarly dispute is an intricate question and comprises matters which cannot be clearly understood within a short period." At any event, the discussions "must grasp major political problems, and first trace a demarcating line between the two classes (the proletariat and the bourgeoisie), two roads (the socialist road and the capitalist road), and two 'isms' (Marxism-Leninism and anti-Marxism-Leninism) and clarify controversial problems of fundamental nature in the academic field."

Here also, beyond such liturgical references as classes, roads, and isms, the key point was to assert that the controversies were exclusively academic. Even concerning issues involving possible political aspects, such as "Wu Han's treatment of history with a bourgeois world outlook," or the case of "people who have made political errors," the Outline made it clear that "the discussion in the press should not be confined to political questions but should go fully into the various academic and theoretical issues involved." It was highly recommended to "take hold of large quantities of materials for scientific analysis so as to push academic work forward." The preparation of "articles of comparatively high quality" was also announced, tacitly lamenting that the articles already published were deemed of poor quality.

The main task was "to form a revolutionary and fighting force that is red and expert and that surpasses bourgeois intellectuals not only politically but academically as well." Only by doing so was it possible to "promote proletarian ideas, to gradually remold old intellectuals, to raise the level of revolutionary intellectuals, [and] truly isolate the extremely few who obstinately cling to mistakes or reactionary viewpoints and, hence, to gradually destroy reactionary academic opinions." However, besides the forceful appeals to recast the *Hai Rui* debate as a grand design of ideological struggle, the real prescription-prohibition was: "Criticism and repudiation by name-calling in the press should be conducted with caution and with the approval of the leading bodies concerned."

The first addressee, albeit implicitly and retrospectively, was Yao Wenyuan. His essay had mentioned Wu "incautiously" and without the "approval of the leading bodies concerned." Similar aberrations of conduct would no longer be tolerated. The Outline reserved special attention in its last few sections for the "staunch Left" (坚定的左派 *jianding de zuopai*), as it was repeatedly called, issuing warnings to change direction as soon as possible. The admonition was unequivocal despite being barely disguised as an offer to "help" in correcting ideological and political mistakes; it added a hint as menacing as it was sarcastic.

One of the final sections was in fact entitled "The Left Needs to Help Each Other." It included curious prescriptions of "mutual help" and even ideological "cooperatives" that "Left academic workers" should form to correct their waywardness. Otherwise, it warned, external help would become indispensable. "Considering the long-term performance [从长期表现来看 *cong changqi biaoxian lai kan*] [of the] staunch left," a "rectification" (整风 *zhengfeng*, a word that made no clear distinction between conviction and coercion in that political context) might be required:

> Large numbers of mutual help groups and cooperatives should be formed among Left academic workers. Mutual criticism and mutual help in an appropriate manner should be promoted on the basis of cooperation and collective discussion. Arrogance should be opposed and precautions taken by Left academic workers against becoming bourgeois experts and scholar-tyrants. Outstanding young writers emerging in the struggle should be highly regarded and trained and help should be given to them.
>
> Even among the staunch Left (judging from long-term performance) there are people who have not thoroughly examined their old ideas or, due to a lack of understanding of problems, have aired erroneous opinions

on certain occasions and committed mistakes, big and small, on certain questions, and therefore need to get it straight at the proper time with the learning and rectification method used by a handful of persons so as to increase their power of immunity and resistance. It is all right if those in error can correct or are determined to correct their mistakes. Don't pick on each other too much, which will only interfere with the academic criticism and repudiation of the bourgeoisie as well as one's own future.

The "one's own future" warning could not have been more explicit. Another paragraph became famous since it was the object of a detailed confutation by Mao a few months later. As we will see in the next chapter, it contained not only the basic evaluation of the way the dispute had been conducted in previous months (Wu's critics had behaved like scholar-tyrants), but even two theoretical theses. We have already seen one ("everyone is equal in front of the truth") in Deng Tuo's article:

> We must insist on searching for truth in the facts [实事求是 *shishi qiushi*] and the principle that everyone is equal before the truth [在真理面前人人平等 *zai zhenli mianqian renren pingdeng*].
>
> We must deal with people by reasoning and must not behave like scholar-tyrants [学阀 *xue fa*] who are always acting arbitrarily and trying to overwhelm people with their power. We must persevere in the truth and correct mistakes whenever they occur.
>
> We must have both destruction and construction [要又破又立 *yao you po you li*]. Without construction, there can be no real and thorough destruction [没有立, 就不可能达到真正的, 彻底的破 *Mei you li, jiu bu keneng dadao zhenzheng, chedi de po*].

We shall see Mao's reaction in chapter 5. Note the remarkable level of theoretical abstraction that political battles then tended to assume in China.

The Outline concludes by announcing the establishment of an Office for Academic Criticism (学术批判的办公室 *xueshu pipan de bangongshi*) charged with implementing the desired policies. And it was indeed efficient: articles airing allusions to contemporary political issues went unpublished. That most of the articles published in February and March 1966 were quite supportive of Wu, and that the critical ones were often limited to such doctrinal issues as the "moral inheritance," was thus hardly surprising. In effect, too, the scholarly topics the Outline had stressed were merely the repetition of those already discussed at length: the favorite was still which line of demarcation should be drawn between imperial China's honest and wicked officials. The articles dealing with Wu's "Self-Criticism" all but disappeared from the press in those same months.

While the Outline temporarily froze the controversy, it made even more acute a predicament that obviously did not concern simple disciplinary issues but ultimately did affect a key pillar of the CCP's ideological and organizational structure. The stalemate the polemics had reached over how to resolve the play's historiographical and political dilemmas revealed looming clouds, for it disclosed a gap in a crucial area of revolutionary culture's fabric. Indeed, this was why such an unusual intellectual controversy had prompted a chorus of so many voices, even to the point of becoming a cause célèbre of state whose consequences were to prove so turbulent.

All the participants, I suggest, were motivated by the anxiety of facing a destabilization of historical materialism. Wu's defenders sought to restore an equilibrium that in the event had been shaken by the blow of Yao's essay. Most of them sought to reconstitute the moral consistency of historical materialism. However, even the critical barbs his detractors aimed at Wu's play were also indicative of a desire to find a way out of the deadlock by intensifying the class-based view even as they too failed to fully assess the historical and political issues.

In concluding this review of the main positions expressed in the dispute over *Hai Rui*, I should note that the specific issues did not continue into the next decade. The problem of how to rethink a communist politics among the peasants was much less prominent in the Chinese political debates of the Cultural Revolution than were problems such as the political relationship between workers and factories, or the "revolution in education," along with long-term consequences that we will discuss in the final chapter of this volume. The political role of the peasantry in socialism remained in fact the greatest unresolved question of Maoist politics, which in turn became a strong point of the "reforms." In the countryside, the latter meant, first of all, abolishing the popular communes in the 1980s as a precondition for the formation of an immense reservoir of cheap, flexible labor for industry.

In the short term, however, it was precisely the failure to resolve the dispute over *Hai Rui* that brought about decisive consequences. The February Outline blocked the controversy but failed to recompose the conceptual void that it had revealed in historical materialism. The Group of Five, and with it the entire summit of the cultural apparatus of the party-state, aimed exclusively at peremptory reaffirmation of its disciplinary supremacy. However, this severely weakened the institutional authority of the Group of Five, which, as we have seen, it proclaimed to be based on its undisputed capacity for ideological leadership in the cultural field, but actually hindered the pressures that came from that controversy for a critical rethinking of key themes of revolutionary culture.

It is in this context that we will interpret Mao's subsequent political initiatives. He strongly hoped that those critical potentialities could fully manifest themselves, but the main obstacle came precisely from the top of the cultural institutions of the party-state. As we will see in chapter 5, within a few months, as soon as it appeared that the moves for hindering the controversy were in fact weakening the leadership of the cultural apparatus, Mao made a series of countermoves aimed at reducing their authority. It was for him a prerequisite for undertaking a vast mass reexamination of the political culture of socialism.

PART II

Mao's Anxiety and Resolve

4

A Probable Defeat and Revisionism

The manifold documentary evidence clearly shows Mao playing a major role in the *Hai Rui* controversy, including nearly every step he took. Yet, in recounting those months that were the preamble to the revolutionary decade, the body of this literature to date portrays his political aims and polemical targets in the most confusing and finally derogatory terms. Mao's "despotism" is in fact the only interpretation proposed. I shall frame a clearer picture in this second part by taking our bearings along two angles of view. The pages of this chapter offer a close reading of key statements on two parallel issues—the likelihood of the revolution ending in imminent defeat and a critique of revisionism—that Mao reiterated throughout the Cultural Revolution. The next chapter will follow the main steps Mao took regarding the polemics the play aroused from autumn 1965 to spring 1966.

The Probability of Defeat

Mao's pronouncements on the topic are most problematic. They were noticeably amplified by his repeated clarion calls for a mass movement, urging all citizens to participate in the country's political life. Yet these appeals were aired in a chiaroscuro light cast by his repeated declaration that the outcome of the struggle between capitalism and socialism was not to be taken for granted. Indeed, he never ceased to maintain that the former was likely to triumph over the latter.[1]

However paradoxical this view may appear, Mao's remarks bore the marks neither of premature capitulation nor of an appeal to martyrdom in the name of the faith. Mao was counting on the vast numbers of a truly mass movement to provide the thrust needed to jettison capitalism. Yet, as reiterated, his remarks also underscored that in the event the most likely outcome, or what he called the "possibility" that he placed "first" in his mind's eye, was defeat.

It is worth recalling that socialism was the exception, the only alternative, to capitalism in the political landscape of the twentieth century. Looming on the former's horizon, however, Mao saw the likelihood of the latter's restoration as the rule of wage slavery in China. It was a prediction that proved to be as prescient as it was far from the current narrative's depicting him as an aging despot altogether out of touch with the modern world. It was also something Mao had been pondering since at least the early sixties, for it was bound up with what he saw as the main mission of communist politics—to break through the roadblock posed by capitalism.

In effect, those statements composed a refrain that would accompany the last phase of Mao's political career, imparting as well a key insight into the politics he preached and practiced throughout that revolutionary decade. One of his most explicit iterations occurred in May 1966 as events were moving toward a turning point. The *Hai Rui* controversy as prelude to the Cultural Revolution was all but over, and Mao stood on the threshold of a policy victory. The context was a meeting with a delegation of the Albanian Workers' Party, which then governed one of China's few international allied countries. Mao was talking about the current situation in China. We can only imagine how perplexed his listeners must have been when his thoughts abruptly changed course:

> My health is quite good but Marx will eventually invite me to visit him. Things develop independently of man's will. . . . Do you know when revisionism will likely occupy Beijing? Those who now support us will suddenly, as if by magic [摇身一变 *yao shen yi bian*], become revisionists. This is the possibility I place first. . . . When those of our generation die, it is very likely that revisionism will come about. . . . We're at dusk, so now, taking advantage of the fact that we still have some breath, let us give a bit of a hard time [整一整 *zheng yi zheng*] to the restoration of capitalism. . . . In short, we should have in mind two possibilities: the first is that there is a counterrevolutionary dictatorship, a counterrevolutionary restoration. Putting this probability as the first to take place, we are a bit worried. I too am sometimes distressed. To say that I do not think it so and do not

feel anxiety would be false. However, I woke up, I called some friends to a meeting, we've discussed it a bit and are looking for a solution.[2]

It was also between April and May 1966 that the party leadership was about to disavow the February Outline, as noted in chapter 3; it will again be taken up in the next chapter. It was the culmination of daring maneuvers Mao had undertaken to regain the political highground. At the heart of Mao's political "anxiety"—he repeatedly called it so—was surely his probable defeat. Yet his more immediate concern was how to find the momentum to turn the insight of the impending end of an entire political and cultural era into a set of positive political propositions.

What Mao ironically called the imminent "invitation by Marx to visit him" added an element of pathos. So too did the prediction in a famous July 1966 letter to Jiang Qing in which he stated, "At my death the right will seize power."[3] Nonetheless, this anxious anticipation was much less important than the question of how, while there was still some breath, to give "a bit of a hard time" to capitalism and to those who "now support us" but would suddenly turn, "as if by magic," into successful "revisionists."

Incidentally, it is surprising how often Mao raised the issue of probable defeat at other meetings with Albanian envoys between 1966 and 1967. Coincidentally, it may even have been that Mao wanted to air his concerns regarding essential issues then confronting communist politics generally, and not solely those bearing on China itself. In 1967, for instance, Mao clarified his position to a visiting military delegation from Tirana. While he struck a quite optimistic note when he said that with the Cultural Revolution a form had finally been found to fully mobilize the masses "to reveal our dark sides," Mao also stated, "There are two possibilities: [either] revisionism will overthrow us or we will overthrow revisionism. Why do I put defeat as the first possibility? Seeing the issue in this way is beneficial; it allows us not to underestimate the enemy."[4] Meeting with another Albanian delegation, he insisted that "Most probably revisionism will win out, and we will be defeated. Through the probable defeat, we will arouse everyone's attention [用 可能 失败 去 提醒 大家 *yong keneng shibai qu tixing dajia*]."[5]

The Uncertain Fate of Socialism

Mao was saying that we can't see the real situation, the forest for the trees, if we see victory as the most likely outcome. In order to deal with the crucial issues facing us now, thinking that we can proceed from political victory to victory is misleading without first removing the illusions impeding our assessment of the situation—"arousing everyone's attention." Conversely, the time had come when it was especially important to think in terms of the likelihood of being defeated; maybe it would be a rout of the vastest scale. Nor was it merely a matter of tactical import. It was, indeed, a strategic question concerning revolutionary politics itself that Mao had been posing for at least the past decade. The starting point was the censure of Stalin aired by the new Soviet leadership in 1956; it was the first formidable crisis to engulf the twentieth century's bloc of socialist countries.

It is also common knowledge that the Stalin question precipitated a series of increasingly bitter, divisive exchanges between the CCP and the CPSU. While Mao had sought to keep a substantive independence from the positions of the CPSU since the thirties, Khrushchev's "secret speech" denouncing "Stalin's crimes" was a particular bone of contention for him. In the last analysis, for Mao it didn't go far enough. Mao had by then begun to see that the most pressing task for all the socialist governments was a critical rethinking of the entire communist enterprise to date. And a crucial ideological fulcrum in such a reckoning was the notion of victory and defeat; it was to be an issue that occupied a central place in his political thinking throughout the last two decades of his life.

During the last decades of the past century, we were so accustomed to seeing most of the communist parties founded in the twentieth century—especially in Europe—overwhelmed by a self-destructive drive that we might underestimate how crucial the issue of victory was in their ideological outlook and organizational imprint from the 1950s to the 1970s. Then, "as if by magic," as Mao foresaw, they changed from "victorious" communist bureaucrats to extremist apologists of capitalism.[6]

The most striking aspect of probable defeat provides a jarring dissonance with the certainty of victory, a conceptual pillar of historical materialism whose full affirmation dates to the consolidation of the Soviet Union's government in the thirties. In 1936, Stalin said with indisputable optimism, "The complete victory of the Socialist system in all spheres of the national economy is now a fact."[7] The great purges, however, were soon a sinister sign of the tragic ambiguity of that complete victory.

For Stalin's immediate successors, despite various adjustments and large doses of rhetoric, the main rationale of the socialist states was still measurable in the last analysis by the standard of the historical guarantee of victory. The *supplément d'âme* of "humanism," which from the latter fifties was appended to the ideology of most communist parties, did not change the essence of that position. Despite the crisis that emerged with Khrushchev's report—or rather, as a way of denying the political essence of that crisis—the then official ideology of the communist parties took for granted that socialism was in any case the historical antecedent of communism.

In the immediate aftermath of the Twentieth Congress of the CPSU, Mao began to chart an altogether different course. Since that watershed in the history of the twentieth century's communist parties, he had been scrutinizing, as lucidly as much as anxiously, the depth of the international political crisis while simultaneously expressing discordant statements and assessments with respect to any "victory" rhetoric. He made a point of not giving credit to any definitive victory of socialism. Indeed, he did not even consider it the "necessary" historical premise of communism.

Ever since his 1957 *On the Correct Handling of Contradictions among the People*, Mao maintained that the question of "which will win," whether socialism or capitalism, "has not been really resolved yet."[8] A new road map would be needed to determine the destiny of socialism. For Mao the idea that the latter was the necessary historical antecedent of communism was a dangerous illusion. After the Great Leap Forward, Mao insistently focused attention on the fate of revolutionary politics and the socialist state. In the early sixties, he remarked on several occasions that "a socialist society can generate a new bourgeoisie";[9] the "danger of a bourgeois restoration" remained.[10] Even "bourgeois revolutions," he noted, had met several reversals of fortune and, hence, a socialist China too could "go in the opposite direction."[11]

Although the formula "restoration of capitalism" seems fully compatible with the historical materialist vision of progress that harbors the risk of "regression," the crux of this controversy, I suggest, exceeded the peculiar historicism that dominated the ideology of the communist parties of the time. In fact, almost all the others invariably repeated that Mao's statements were ludicrous. The very idea that a socialist state could become capitalist, even do so peacefully (another point stressed in the controversy with the CPSU), and that the communist parties were about to become part of a "bourgeois government" was prima facie evidence—intoned both *Pravda* and *L'Unità*—of insane extremism.

When in the sixties the CCP declared—surely under Mao's unrelenting pressure—that the restoration of capitalism in the Soviet Union had *already* taken place, the CPSU and its satellites thundered against such a "divisive" attitude. This stance, they maintained, was irresponsibly harming the "unity of the international communist movement" and its "victorious march" toward communism. Even more amazing, however, was the accuracy of the forecast, especially considering that, compared to today, almost none of the requisite conditions for the full "restoration of capitalism" in the USSR, not to mention in China, obtained at the time.

In the doctrine of historical materialism, victory—more accurately, the victorious seizure of power—was much more than the overthrow of a government. It was above all the converging point of historical contradictions between advanced and retrograde classes, new productive forces and old modes of production, counterpoised ideologies, and even between worldviews. Revolutionary culture carried the historical guarantee that socialism, which had led the way to complete victory over capitalism, would triumphantly march on to communism.

Mao, however, was not a believer. For he persisted in pointing out that not certain victory but the likelihood of defeat loomed on the horizon and needed to be addressed. In his view, it was time to rally forces to mass political activism. The strident, dissonant clash Mao's remarks struck over revolutionary culture's tenet of assured victory was perceived as insidious. It inevitably cast a harsh yet penetrating light on the coherence of a common political mind-set and symptomatically pressed for the necessity of a thorough reevaluation of its entire theoretical matrix.

Illusions of Victory

During his last score of years, Mao's reflections on the subject of victory clearly stemmed from close reconsideration of the 1949 triumph in the protracted People's War and ultimately focused on the fate of socialism in the twentieth century. The "ethics of politics"—the convictions, hopes, and attitudes of the revolutionaries vis-à-vis their achievements—was also a concern. A well-known interview with André Malraux (recounted in *Anti-Memoirs*) in summer 1965—a few months before the prologue—reveals much about Mao's state of mind on the issue.

"Victory is the mother of many illusions," Mao said. He considered victory anything but a point of stabilization. Rather, it was a subjectively ambiguous terrain, a source of great disquiet for him. He had long maintained and often noted that victory implied the risk of "complacency, arrogance," and a loss of political realism. It had been, as we've seen, one bone of contention in his disagreement with the CPSU and the assessment of Stalin since 1956. Stalin had committed egregious errors, some even more grievous still because he had been unable to correct them owing to his "arrogance and complacency."[12] Furthermore, Stalin believed in the certainty of victory, that there would be a definitive consolidation. Mao thought that nothing in the world could be definitively consolidated.[13]

The connection to overconfidence in the certainty of victory better emerges in a 1963 text on the issue of presumption and modesty. It is focused on the close relationship between victory and complacency. The following excerpt reveals much of his attitude and intentions in the years preceding the Cultural Revolution.

> Arrogance and complacency [骄傲自满 *jiao'ao ziman*] are produced and develop in highly diverse forms and circumstances, but in general this is more likely to happen in the case of a victory. This is because when one finds oneself in difficulty, it is easier to see one's own defects and thus be prudent. In the face of objective difficulties, one cannot but be modest and prudent. But with victory, so many come forward to express gratitude and praise; even enemies can change their minds and come to render homage and adulate. In conditions of victory, it is easy to lose one's head, to feel as light as air, and think: "From now on, the empire will be stable." We must fully comprehend that the more we are in a situation of victory, the more the party is exposed to the assault of arrogance and complacency.[14]

The disadvantage of victory is that it produces presumption; it leads to feeling "full of oneself" (自满 *ziman*), conceited, to thinking one has attained the definitive realization of the very image of one's own identity. Mao considered it a problem so urgent and important as to dedicate an entire party document to it. It is remarkable that warnings such as this should circulate in the Chinese Communist Party. The presumption resulting from victory means the loss of political realism, and hence one must be on one's guard against the illusions of victory, against the hypertrophy of the ego that victory engenders.

Mao returned in that conversation with Malraux to the subject of the illusions of victory, his thoughts this time focusing on the circumstantial condition of politics and the state in China after 1949. The victory over the Guomindang, he said, had been a basic turning point, but to consider it decisive was illusory. It had made reconstruction of the state possible after decades of violent, postimperial disintegration of its institutions amid the destruction of warlords, the Japanese invasion, and the corrupt and ferocious Guomindang military dictatorship.

On the other hand, Mao said in his typically dialectical style, the victory had brought "new contradictions." "The truth is this: if the contradictions that we owe to victory are—fortunately!—less painful for the people than the old ones were, they are, however, just as profound."[15] Mao spoke of this with a mixture of fatalism and impatience. Malraux's version, while perhaps not a literal transcription, fully grasps Mao's anxiety and the accuracy of his vision.

> Corruption, crime, the arrogance of university graduates with their desire to honor the family by becoming officials while keeping their hands clean: all these stupidities are mere symptoms, both within and outside the party. The cause lies in the historical conditions. But even in the political conditions, the forces that thrust toward inequality are powerful. They cannot obtain what they want unless they take it from the masses. They will perhaps not necessarily restore the private ownership of the means of production, but they will reestablish inequalities.[16]

The Urgent Need for Theoretical Clarification

On a subjective level, predicting likely defeat while fostering political mobilization of the masses to combat is a good summation of a core component of Mao's attitude even during the Cultural Revolution; it applied as much to China as to the century's communist enterprise in general. In the shadow of imminent demise, what the decades-long experiment of the socialist states searching for a way to break free of capitalism implicated for Mao was the question. His reply was that the most pressing issue was a radical reappraisal of that entire political endeavor. It was to be an "experiment within the experiment," both at the theoretical level and in organizational practice.

The Cultural Revolution attempted to pursue it as a laboratory of a truly mass movement that would test by reappraisal the intellectual and political mettle of the socialist "exception" in the expectation of a probable restoration of capitalist rule. To Mao there could be no way out of capitalism's grip without a thorough critique of that political experience. It was what Mao had hoped to achieve in that last revolutionary decade. As Mao noted in late 1974, and as we shall see in the last part of this volume, the focal point of the "study theory" campaign—the last political campaign he launched—was to be the dictatorship of the proletariat, and it would involve the "entire country."

The polemics with the CPSU after the latter's 1956 Congress saw a run of editorials, beginning in April, prompted and edited by Mao in *Renmin ribao* under the title "On the Historical Experience of the Dictatorship of the Proletariat." That even as the revolutionary decade came to a close twenty years later the need for a theoretical review of this conceptual pillar of twentieth-century communism still held primary focus in Mao's political preoccupations is significant. Indeed, he maintained not only that dictatorship of the proletariat as a model of governance did not per se ensure the transition from socialism to communism; he even noted that "failure to clarify" (不搞清楚 *bu gao qingchu*) it would theoretically become a main factor prompting the resurgence of capitalism in China.

Anti-Revisionism

Mao's reiterations of socialism's probable defeat and the attendant challenges for revolutionaries provide the necessary background for a close reading of "combating and preventing revisionism" (反修防修 *fanxiu fangxiu*), his other major preoccupation of the Cultural Revolution's decade. Whereas probable defeat signaled the pressing need for a mass movement to reappraise twentieth-century socialism, anti-revisionism pointed to the obstacles in its path to be overcome.

While "combating and preventing revisionism" may at first sight seem like a mere formulaic rallying cry, it deserves a second look. Revisionism for Mao indicated twin phenomena: socialism's likely defeat without root-and-branch political reappraisal of its merit and the hurdles to overcome in order to achieve that reckoning. It also acquired a double face during the revolutionary decade. It appeared as a synonym for the "capitalist road" (资本主义道路 *zibenzhuyi daolu*) as indicator of the socialist exception falling under the latter's sway. And it stood for what within communist state organizations impeded a mass movement for the political reappraisal of the singularity of the "socialist road" as a preventive measure against capitalist normalization. That new paths had to be found via mass political experiment to overcome the hurdles while combating the very forces that had laid them and wanted a clear "road back to capitalism" was implicit in the slogan.

A more expansive view of the concept of revisionism will help to bring Mao's intent into sharper relief. Revisionism, or better its critique, occupied a specific niche in the history of twentieth-century communism. It was especially prominent in its second decade in Europe and in the sixties in China.[17] If we look at just these two epochs without going into the attendant philological details, it was a prominent target for criticism within the revolutionary camp itself. Lenin's barbs against it were directed at Kautsky's "opportunism" and Mao's against the "new revisionists," first in the USSR and then in China. The polemics in each case concerned specific issues and outcomes on convergent planes of revolutionary politics: reappraisal of preceding turning points of political invention and specific tasks elicited by the current situation.

Given the experimental nature of communist politics, for Lenin as for Mao, assessing acquired experiences was an ineluctable task for identifying and pursuing their political objectives. What was newly acquired that had to be kept and developed? What were the mistakes not to be repeated? What obstacles stood in the way of new opportunities? Perhaps the hardest question to answer was what in capitalism's nature gained advantage from the limits shown by revolutionaries and their difficulty in learning a lesson from them? An unblinking appraisal was necessary for the most pressing political decisions. Comparing Lenin's anti-revisionism can show the continuity and novelties vis-à-vis Mao's.

Lenin

Lenin's polemical clash with Kautsky chiefly concerned their differing views of World War I.[18] Though in a notably roundabout manner, Kautsky essentially justified it, as did the overwhelming majority of workers' parties at the time. Lenin instead was vehemently opposed to the imperialist war and saw it as the prerequisite for political action. Notable here is the fact that one of Lenin's key arguments turned on a reappraisal of the Paris Commune. Following in the footsteps of Marx and Engels, Lenin culled their analysis of and scattered references to it in their writings. He then fashioned a set of fundamental theories on the transformations of governmental ways and means that had led to the slaughter in Europe and on the tasks facing revolutionaries in such circumstances.

For Lenin the argument that summed up Marx and Engels's view of the Commune was that its fundamental yet unachieved objective was to "smash [*zerbrechen*] the bureaucratic-military machine [of the state]." Marx had enthusiastically hailed the fact that "The first decree of the Commune ... was the suppression of the standing army, and the substitution for it of the armed people." Lenin emphasized that Marx came to his view not so much from a general theory of the state as from specific analysis of changes in mostly late-nineteenth-century forms of government as "reactions" to revolutionary events.

In his *Civil War in France*, Marx had noted, for instance, that after prior revolutionary movements "the purely repressive nature of state power became even more evident." State power after 1848–49 had "assumed more and more the character of the national power of capital over labor." The need to smash the bureaucratic-military machine was thus a "prerequisite of every popular revolution." Lenin found its full confirmation in the "filthy and bloody morass" of the war, wherein the bureaucratic-military apparatus of all the European states had sunk.

For Lenin, Kautsky's view of Marx's theories was a distortion. It was all the more execrable because of the political and intellectual prestige Kautsky enjoyed among revolutionaries, and because his reasoning exhibited connivance with the "social-chauvinist" prowar stance then prevalent among the socialist parties. Kautsky "forgot" Marx's arguments and fantasized about the advent of an "ultra-imperialism"—unhesitatingly called "ultra-stupidity" by Lenin—capable of exerting pacific global domination. All were positions Lenin viewed as even more abhorrent still since Kautsky and all the others who had "reduced socialism to the outrageous shame of justifying and concealing the nature of the imperialist war" disguised it under the concept of "national defense" in a "Marxist" language.

Lenin instead saw reprising and developing the original objective of the Paris Commune as the task of revolutionaries—they were to "break up" the state's bureaucratic-military machinery. That apparatus had become even stronger in the decades immediately leading up to the great imperialist war, and with it, in Lenin's view, war had become the real government of Europe. Bureaucratic-military institutions characterized all of its nations at the time: they "subordinate everything to themselves, and suppress everything." For Lenin, the fundamental task of revolution was as much the seizure of state power as the evisceration of its bureaucratic-military machinery. Only once that was accomplished was it possible to organize a revolutionary movement capable of interdicting the absolutist militarization of the governing regime imposed by the ongoing war and initiate experiments with completely new forms of government. The original momentum of the Soviets aimed at breaking up the state's apparatus as a separate entity of society and dispersing via a vast popular movement the affairs and functions of the state among the most common people.

Mao

Half a century later, Mao's critique of revisionism arose in the same theoretical horizon as did Lenin's; it developed along similar lines and also against an internal obstacle. The specifics at stake, however, were different. By the latter half of the fifties the basic grounds of Lenin's arguments—analysis of past revolutionary experiences and the political tasks called forth by the Great War—had shifted and now were inextricably overlapping. The most pressing stock-taking after the Twentieth CPSU Congress involved all the post–October Revolution socialist states. The latter were the then governing circumstances in which revolutionary organizations operated. In effect, the main political task they viewed through their party ideology and organization had become maintaining a new, separate, machinery of state power—a far cry from any thought of "smashing" it.

A common ground that Lenin and Mao shared in their critiques of revisionism is their notably theoretical motif, even striking doctrinaire chords. Revisionism is entangled with the intellectual repertoire of revolutionary politics; it plays upon the same theoretical concepts in the same keys, the same idiom, the same refrains, and the same tempos of the same political culture. That's why for both leaders it thus had a strong theoretical bent and was seen as a political roadblock that must be theoretically eliminated. It also explains the doctrinaire pitch. Revisionism very much resembles its target and has a more than orthodox structure. A keen observer of nuances, Lenin once quipped that "All social-chauvinists are Marxists."

Essential to the critique of revisionism, on the other hand, was the "distorting" of revolutionary theoretical arguments and correcting revisionism's errant ways—in polemic with what the latter says or what it ignores. For both Lenin and Mao, it was not a matter of "defending the faith" against apostasy. It was an urgent, immediate political task. Indispensable to meeting that challenge was a proper reckoning with the last momentous political invention. For the October Revolution, that meant the Paris Commune; for the Cultural Revolution, it meant the October Revolution and its consequences vis-à-vis the establishment of a governing dictatorship of the proletariat.

Stock-taking is in order here too. In the two decades since his initial dispute with the USSR in 1956, by 1976 Mao regarded the concept of revisionism as both an analytical prediction and a target for mass political mobilization. In the tug of war between socialism and capitalism, the former could take nothing for granted in its favor. In effect, capitalism loomed as the "probable" winner. Thus, only a critical reassessment of socialism and deployment of new political inventions through mobilization of the masses could counteract such a likelihood.

The first step was deciding what political organization was to lead the reappraisal and guide the necessary subsequent experiments. The Communist Party was the only legal tender. Yet it was part and parcel of socialism's governing circumstances whose epoch-making transformation was forecast as imminent and whose party leadership vehemently denied any such change was on the horizon. Thus, the question that preoccupied Mao, as well as the source of his anxiety, boiled down to whether new forms of political organization could be found beyond the horizon to combat capitalism's probable defeat of the exception that was socialism.

Yet Mao found a standoff instead of the answers he urgently sought. The party blocked the road to reappraisal. It had assumed the state's governing functions, and its top leadership either refused to countenance a reckoning of the socialist experience or shunted the urgency of the matter onto purely formalist sidings. That's why Mao insisted in his last two decades that revisionism resided in the party-state's elite. The main obstacle within communism was thus its own organizing principle. What Mao needed for the tasks at hand was new roads.

5

Shrinking the Cultural Superego

If facing probable defeat and combating and preventing revisionism were Mao's main concerns on the eve of the Cultural Revolution, it is not obvious why he gave his full support to a dispute such as that initiated by Yao Wenyuan's article. Speculation of behind-the-scenes plots on this point is rampant. Some say, for example, that Wu Han was a suitable polemical target since he was not high enough up in the nomenclature to elicit a reaction to any strong defense of the institutions, even if he was not exactly a minor professor of history.[1] Others claim that Peng Zhen had fallen into a trap because he had not realized that the true objective was really to overthrow *him*.[2]

As we have seen in part I, however, the top echelons of the party-state staunchly defended Wu Han for months; Peng Zhen had immediately realized that the stakes were of supreme political importance. Today's official story narrates that in the name of despotic orthodoxy the Cultural Revolution had initially targeted the intellectuals. In fact, the first targets were the highest authorities of the state's cultural apparatus, and the criticisms against them came precisely from the intellectual milieu at the grassroots, as most of the participants in the dispute were history teachers.

We have already mentioned the importance of the cultural machinery in China's party-state of the time and how effective its power was in the *Hai Rui* dispute. It is in the very offices of the state cultural apparatus (education, journalism, publishing, etc.) that Mao encountered the strongest, and the most equivocal, opposition to what he considered crucial political issues, which he summarized in his symptomatic "probable defeat" statements.

Mao and the Central Cultural Apparatus of the Socialist State

Mao was certainly obstinate, and the choice of the first targets was consistent with his preoccupations. Yet the development of the situation depended on the statements and responses of all the many actors who had been active in the first scene. On the other hand, Mao's views on the political matters he considered crucial met dull hostility from the party-state's top echelon.

A scene that André Malraux portrays in his famous meeting with Mao, no doubt with some recourse to poetic license, captures much of the atmosphere. It was the summer of 1965, and the eve of those momentous events was fast approaching. In the official hall where the conversation was held, several other top-level Chinese leaders were sitting around in stony silence like Buddhist statues. At a certain point, Mao said, "I am alone." "Mr. President," replied Malraux, "you have often been alone."[3] "Yes, I am alone with the masses." Yet how can one be held to be a sort of divinity under tutelage in the Heaven of the party-state and at the same time be "with the masses"?

By mid-1965 Mao had quite a few means at his disposal to find a way to do so. Yao was certainly no great authority, and the criticism of Wu per se was not a decisive factor. However, his sights pointed in one evident direction: the ideological, and repressive, authority of the state's top cultural apparatus. At the outset of the Cultural Revolution Mao's aim was to drastically restrict its authority by initiating a radically new forum to discuss the fundamental orientation of politics and the state under socialism. He therefore was attempting a hazardous but for him an indispensable reconsideration of basic political issues. It was a project that under the circumstances could never have emerged from the (apparent) stability and compactness of the state's institutionally embedded cultural framework. The cultural levers that set in motion the machinery of the socialist state were forged in the historical materialist steel that was the certainty of victory.

Mao never missed a chance to express his dissatisfaction with that cultural setup. Virtually all his remarks concerning the matter in those years were highly polemical. He was irritated with the schools and with education in general, with publishing houses and the press. As a young man, he had been a progressive educationalist in the New Culture Movement of 1919 and viewed the

Chinese educational system of the sixties as stifled by a pedagogical formalism that wasted young people's intellectual talents.[4] By at least 1964 he suggested that school programs and curricula, all of them copied almost to the letter from the Soviet system of the early fifties, should be thoroughly reformed.

Mao further proposed a radical reduction in the number of school years so that education would combine teaching with various types of social activities, say, in agriculture, industry, military service, politics. As we shall see below, he suggested opening up each of the socially structured activities to the others, thus overcoming the limitations of specialization and its entrained social hierarchies. The Chinese educational system in the mid-sixties was, in his opinion, anything but oriented toward these changes. When in his conversation with Malraux the French ambassador praised the success of the Chinese school system in glowing terms, Mao diplomatically replied that he had perhaps seen "only part of the situation."

In supporting the publication of Yao's article, Mao persevered in his critical attitude toward the cultural situation. This time, however, the polemic brought the debate around the compactness of the cultural machinery of the party-state into the open. Within a few months the dispute ended up by publicly discrediting the ideological authority of the apparatus. Thus, as we have seen in chapter 3, an unexpected involvement of intellectual public opinion, and the perhaps more predictable rigid line of self-defense advocated by Peng Zhen, revealed the intrinsic weakness of the apparatus and, naturally, of its top leadership.

Mao's Initial Reaction to the Hai Rui Controversy

In the early stages Mao did not succeed in obtaining much. The published critiques of *Hai Rui* opened a fissure in a supposedly solid institutional edifice. One of its leading exponents was being criticized on matters of principle, and the image of the political and ideological infallibility of the state's cultural apparatus was smeared. Yet a reaction of self-defense was immediately set in motion. The controversy, the high cultural authorities of the party-state proclaimed, was merely a disagreement over historiographical viewpoints. They were careful to stress that these viewpoints did not exclude each other categorically and above all had no contemporary political implications.

Despite all appearances, Mao could fully rely only on those whose institutional authority was minimal. As mentioned above, those who had suggested initiating criticism of Wu's play, and who in actual fact had taken it upon themselves to approach Yao to write the piece, were Jiang Qing and Zhang Chunqiao. Mao read Yao's draft carefully and presumably suggested revisions but left it up to the promoters to find a way of publishing it, something that one could not take for granted. From the reconstructions of Chinese historians, one infers that Mao moved cautiously, even rather hesitantly, but quite directly. He advised Jiang to have such senior leaders as Kang Sheng and Zhou Enlai read the text. She objected that if she did so, then she would also have to ask Deng Xiaoping and Liu Shaoqi to read it, and they would have prevented its publication. In short, the essay could only be published by managing to avoid asking for prior authorization.

Mao did respect, however, a series of more or less formal procedures that regulated the relationships among the party-state's top leaders. During a work conference of the Central Committee convened in September 1965, Mao, who likely had read the first drafts of Yao's essay, personally asked Peng Zhen whether Wu could be criticized. Peng Zhen replied, "Wu Han can be criticized in some matters" (吴含有些问题可以批判 *Wu Han you xie wenti keyi pipan*). Chinese historians have often reported the episode to praise the tactical skill of Beijing's mayor. His reply, they explain, meant "about other matters Wu Han could *not* be criticized."[5] However, this bureaucratic savoir-faire, usually one of Peng Zhen's strong points, turned out to have the opposite effect. The greater the subjective tension is, the more the coherence between what one says and what one does becomes paramount.

Mao then intervened toward mid-November, a few days after the publication of Yao's essay in the *Wenhui bao*. He sought to lift the veto against its publication in other newspapers. The publication had already put the central cultural authorities on maximum alert. But it was only when Mao intervened that they realized he supported the initiative. When faced with Peng Zhen's categorical refusal to let other newspapers reprint Yao's essay, Mao suggested that at least one publishing house might reprint it as a pamphlet. However, the party's central editorial bureau, the New China News Agency, utterly opposed its distribution. As we have seen, the deadlock was resolved only through the mediation of Zhou Enlai, who obtained permission to reprint Yao's article in the *People's Daily*. The issue had thus become a matter of state even if Mao's direct influence was still minimal.

Mao's first important statement in the dispute was "Peng Dehuai is Hai Rui." We have already discussed the famous equation and its consequences; we shall now consider context and time line. Mao made the remark during a work conference of the Central Committee held in Hangzhou.[6] (These were ad hoc conferences convened several times a year for party leaders to discuss specific issues of important political measures and theoretical questions.) Here, on December 21, over six weeks after the publication of Yao's essay, Mao expounded at length in his usual style, intermingling themes of the country's contemporary cultural-political scene with a discussion of theoretical questions he believed to be vital.

His speech dealt with Yao's essay only marginally, but, as we have seen, as a specific topic. While the article was very good, he said, it had not gone to the nub of the question, "dismissal." One might wonder why from the outset Mao, who had read and revised Yao's draft before its publication, did not suggest highlighting dismissal. Yao did mention the play's connection with the divergent views of the late fifties and early sixties on peasant policies, but not the specific outcome of the Lushan Conference—Peng Dehuai's dismissal.

Probably at the beginning neither Yao nor Mao focused their attention on dismissal; it was in the title but absent from the plot. If so, that would make the nub a later "discovery," for which Mao jokingly credited the copyright to Kang Sheng, who had not read the draft, as can be deduced by the exchange between Mao and Jiang Qing quoted above. It is best, however, once again to keep our distance from any backstage narrative in evaluating the political consequences of Mao's statement on the "nub of dismissal." We should read it in light of the developments in the dispute over Yao's article by late December 1965. Clearly, the exact timing of a statement is essential at moments of peak political tension; its meaning completely changes if pronounced a week, or even a day, earlier or later.

As we have seen in chapter 3, the main phenomenon in those weeks was the "historiographical depoliticization" of the debate. This was the tendency, sponsored by the heads of the cultural ministries, to present the issue as a matter of divergent historical ideologies that dealt with "moral issues" while having no contemporary political relevance except as a violation of an orthodoxy as strict as it was vacuous. We have discussed above "authority-prompted" articles that posed the divergence in terms inflexibly doctrinaire, proclaiming it as a "struggle to the death" between "bourgeois and proletarian morals," while excluding any real political issue. Xiang Yangsheng had published his article on "moral inheritance" just a week before Mao's speech in Hangzhou. Mao was surely aware that under the pseudonym the author was Deng Tuo, Peng Zhen's closest collaborator.

Considering the circumstances of those weeks, one can assume that Mao stressed the nub of the divergence as altogether political. For it played on the contrast between the antipolitical use of history and the vacuous doctrinaire arguments the cultural apparatus was promoting by every means at its disposal. Openly mentioning the then thorniest unresolved issue in Chinese politics, Mao recalled that the judgment on the 1959 clash at Lushan was still highly controversial. He noted that the decisions taken there had not settled the issue. In fact, they had worsened it, breeding greater disorientation in the political landscape and, despite all appearances, greater disagreements. It was against these background conditions that, as we have seen, Peng Dehuai "became" Hai Rui at Lushan. Had there been no clash at that conference, there would have been no dismissal, no unresolved tensions over it, and no reason for Wu Han to write such a play.

Mao's nub remark also pointed up, though indirectly, a weakness in Yao's article. The development of the controversy was proving that the same historical-political conceptual network, first and foremost the class-based argument, could be used in very antithetical and even in antipolitical ways. Mao, of course, could not argue the point in such a manner; indeed, class struggle remained a key concept for him. Nonetheless, it is significant that he did not posit any historical-political argument to emphasize the political nature of the divergence, even taking pains to mention the equation between the two dismissals without reference to class.

Although intended to repoliticize the debate over *Hai Rui*, Mao's remarks nonetheless produced the tortuous effects, which we started to examine in chapter 3, vis-à-vis Peng Zhen's reaction—he openly mentioned dismissal—to the first critical articles in early January 1966. As noted above, any reference to the Lushan dismissal against the background of the *Hai Rui* controversy immediately turned into a disciplinary issue, as the central cultural ministries were quick to claim. Dismissal, Peng Zhen argued, could not be the subject of any freewheeling debate since it was a matter of adherence to party discipline in the field of cultural affairs. It was therefore an issue that the Group of Five he presided over had full authority to deal with. This was the bone of increasing contention between Mao and Peng Zhen; it explains the complex, shifting balance of strengths and weaknesses in the span of less than two months.

Peng Zhen's Response

Peng Zhen soon reacted with notable resolve to Mao's "Peng Dehuai is Hai Rui." On December 22, the day after Mao's speech in Hangzhou, the two met. Peng Zhen objected that there was no reason to consider the dismissal as the nub of the issue since no organizational ties between Wu Han and Peng Dehuai had ever been proved. He also confirmed the defense of Wu in a further private conversation with Mao. Yet not only was it unlikely that Wu had acted directly on behalf of Peng Dehuai; it was also unnecessary, as we noted above.

Early in January 1966 Peng Zhen convened a meeting of the Shanghai Party Committee. He strenuously argued that Wu was "left-wing" and that the debate should "remain within academic limits."[7] This posture was then formalized in the February Outline analyzed in chapter 3. At the beginning of February, Mao received the draft of the Outline. It had already been approved by the Group of Five and was ready to be ratified by the Central Committee. He tried to express his disagreement in a face-to-face meeting with Peng Zhen but was unable to make any changes.

Official Chinese books on the subject, which state in chorus that everything depended on Mao's wishes, do nothing but increase the misperception at a time when Mao was clearly in the minority. Nonetheless, the Chinese authors of the lengthiest Mao biography, while having to record what the relationship between Mao and Peng Zhen was really like, describe the situation in those months as follows: "Since Chairman Mao enjoyed very considerable prestige both in the Party and throughout the country, and since democratic centralism had been seriously damaged, life within the Party had become very irregular, and Chairman Mao's personal leadership had gradually replaced collective leadership."[8]

The way the central organs of the CCP approved the Outline demonstrates yet again that Mao met open resistance and effective opposition. If anything, the problem was how he managed to reverse such an unfavorable position in the following months. His presumed "considerable prestige" had thus far counted for very little, and the so-called personal leadership (the formula generally used to mean despotic rule) had not managed to convince even one publisher to print and distribute a pamphlet when he had tried to get Yao's essay reprinted in November 1965. By early February 1966, Mao had even less of a chance to change a document like Peng Zhen's Outline that the Central Committee fully supported and was ready to approve.

The meeting between Mao and Peng Zhen to discuss the Outline deserves some comment. Here, too, the current Chinese historical narrative is rather contorted. In one of the best-known books on the Cultural Revolution, for instance, Gao Gao and Yan Jiaqi report that after the Outline had been telegraphed to Mao in Wuhan, a delegation of the Group of Five led by Peng Zhen went to discuss the document with him. Here is the likely mood at the meeting:

> Mao Zedong once again clearly said, "The nub of *Hai Rui Dismissed from Office* is the 'dismissal.' This concerns the Lushan Conference and Peng Dehuai's right-wing opportunism." Turning to Peng Zhen, he asked twice, "Was Wu Han not perhaps against the Party and against Socialism?" Peng Zhen gave no direct answer. As can be seen, the meeting was carried out in a far from friendly atmosphere.

Besides the fact that in this and other Chinese books about the subject, the documentary sources are rarely quoted, the authors, having thus described the ambiance of the meeting, go on to remark without hesitation:

> Peng Zhen, in the wake of what Mao Zedong had said, and based on his own understanding of the content of the meeting, charged the vice-minister of the Department of Propaganda, Xu Liqun, and Hu Sheng [a member of the secretariat of the Group of Five and, not by chance, a renowned historian] with drawing up an accompanying Note to the Outline.... The following morning Peng Zhen telegraphed the Note to Beijing, and on the same day, after the Standing Committee of the Political Bureau had approved it, the Outline became an official document of the Central Committee [and was] sent to the whole Party.[9]

Accounts by other Chinese historians concerning the details of this meeting are equally vague. In any event, Peng Zhen did what he had intended to do. In fact, he was fully able to contradict Mao, and could easily have done so because, for the motives discussed above, the chairman's position was at that moment quite weak. As far as Wu Han's "antiparty" posture was concerned, it was not Mao but Peng Zhen and his Group of Five who embodied the supreme authority over the cultural discipline of party members, including Mao himself. Peng Zhen was therefore able not to take into the least consideration the nub of dismissal, as he had done in fact since late December, and Mao was obliged to comply, at least temporarily.

Peng Zhen also turned a deaf ear to Mao's disagreement on another key point, the "rectification" of the left wing. The Outline clearly stated the need to "rectify the obstinate Left," bearing in mind its "long-term behavior." In other words, it explicitly threatened to call the left-wing members to account in the near future. Peng Zhen later said that he had believed the chairman was not opposed to the Outline. Mao said, on the contrary, that he had never formally approved it. Whatever the procedural details of the matter might be, either way Mao could have done nothing to counter Peng Zhen. For Peng Zhen and the Group of Five were then the highest, indisputable authority, and, hence, the Outline was quickly endorsed by the Central Committee and circulated as the established party line.

Peng Zhen was convinced of having won a decisive battle. In the following two months, the central organs of the party-state's cultural apparatus worked full-time to see that the terms prescribed by the Outline were enforced. The Group of Five's offices began a series of verifications of the "long-term behavior" of the "obstinate Left" in view of the foreseen rectification. Even an inquiry into who in Shanghai had made it possible to publish Yao's essay in November without first asking for the Department of Propaganda's permission was begun.

At the height of his success, Peng Zhen even tried to enlist Peng Dehuai in the effort, going to see him in March. He asked him to declare that Wu Han had had no organizational ties to him, presumably offering in exchange his support for full rehabilitation. Although it was something Peng Dehuai dearly wanted, he obviously understood the gravity of the ongoing clash and refused to get involved.[10] The episode also gives an indication of the extent to which Mao's opponents were at liberty to maneuver and how much stronger they were at the time.

Down with the King of Hell

Mao regained the initiative several weeks after the promulgation of the Outline. One cannot say that he brought any pressure to bear, as the situation was in any case still under Peng Zhen's control.[11] By the latter half of March, however, Mao started to express his total disagreement with the Outline and finally succeeded in reopening the discussion among the top leaders. While he certainly brought to bear all his prestige and resolve, the power to convince and the efficacy of his persuasiveness were due to developments in the situation itself. The flash point of his intervention was the real effects of the Outline on the *Hai Rui* dispute.

For the controversy had not died down. Local and national newspapers were still receiving articles and letters dealing with its political issues, which were censored following Peng Zhen's directives. Indeed, no articles either mentioning dismissal or discussing political differences ever appeared in print. As it turned out, the Outline proved to serve the opposite of its declared purpose. Peng Zhen had said it was intended to promote "open debate," but it actually suppressed any piece that had not first been authorized by the "competent organs." Thus, only approved articles appeared in the press. The unpublished others, however, circulated in the central offices. Party leadership had access to systematic accounts of the debate; those promoted from November by Zhang Chunqiao with the journalists of the *Wenhui bao* are just one example.

By late March, the Outline's claim to being a key document for coordinating a strategic ideological struggle against the bourgeoisie "under the Party's leadership" was no longer tenable. Mao's criticism was that, far from guaranteeing the wide-open forum it had announced, the Outline was exerting heavy-handed censorship. That was not a minor shortcoming for an official document proclaiming itself to be the spearhead of a "struggle to the death against the bourgeois worldview."

Mao argued that it was necessary to put an end to restrictions on the dispute and to allow complete freedom of speech. This is evident from the transcripts of addresses given at a meeting of the Politburo in Hangzhou from March 17 to 20. Although touching upon a wide range of issues unconnected to the *Hai Rui* controversy, Mao directly confronted Peng Zhen's censorship.[12] "One should not fear," he argued, "young people's transgressions of 'imperial decrees' [王法 *wang fa*]. Their manuscripts should not be prevented being published.[13] The Department of Propaganda has not done good things.... It has repressed others' activism; it has not permitted the revolution to be carried out."[14] Addressing the top leaders, he noted: "When you of the Politburo of the Central Committee, of the provinces and municipalities return [to your posts], you have to encourage the free expression of opinions. In the months of April, May, June, and July there must be great freedom of speech everywhere.... This great Cultural Revolution must be carried out and revisionism opposed. When we have departed [我们走了 *women zoule*], I doubt whether the next generation will be able to stop revisionism."[15]

The latter, of course, was one of Mao's greatest preoccupations. Probable defeat loomed, but despite, or rather because of it, the most broad-based freedom of speech had to be allowed. Between March 28 and 30, Mao called other meetings during which he again expressed his criticism of the Outline and of the way in which Peng Zhen was dealing with the problems.[16] The content of Mao's statements was soon reported at his request at larger meetings of central leaders. His aim was to reopen the discussion of the Outline.

Mao took particular issue with the Group of Five's "inquiries" into the unauthorized publication of Yao Wenyuan's article in Shanghai. Peng Zhen maintained that, since the competent organs had not been informed before its printing, the Central Department of Propaganda had ordered a check on responsibility for the error. Mao cut him short:

> Wu Han has published many essays without it being necessary to ask [the Central Department of Propaganda] for approval. Why then should Yao Wenyuan's essay have had to ask for prior authorization? ... Those who prevent the publication of left-wing essays and protect the right are great scholar tyrants [大学阀 *da xue fa*]. The Central Department of Propaganda is the King of Hell's Palace [阎王殿 *yan wang dian*]. The King of Hell's Palace has to be overthrown and the imps set free: overthrow the cliques, set free the Left.[17]

The image, which was to become quite famous, has a literary background. The King of Hell was a figure of Buddhist inspiration, a synonym for absolute terror and the supreme judgment of human actions. It was represented, however, in a tragicomic key in traditional Chinese stories. Besides slightly tormenting everyone, the King of Hell exerted a special tyranny over intellectuals—Confucian scholars—in classical China, on whom he inflicted grotesque torments during the imperial system's grueling exams for the selection of civil servants (科举制度 *keju zhidu*). As portrayed with subtle humor by a great specialist in the subject, Miyazaki Ichisada, the keju zhidu was a true "examination hell."[18]

The image of the King of Hell, a sort of bizarre cultural superego, thus evoked an iron ideological and bureaucratic disciplining of the intellectuals. Mao here mentioned it in the "literary-popular" register that he often favored in his polemical statements. The palace bore in any case a precise contemporary institutional reference to the Central Department of Propaganda (中宣部 *Zhong xuan bu*), the fulcrum of the state's cultural apparatuses—the press, publishing, the mass media, education, and so on—all of which were crucial to the socialist system.

The clique of great scholar tyrants installed in the palace was the manifestation of the special institutional privilege of "university discourse" in socialism. The fact that the next scene in the Cultural Revolution, that of the first mass movements in the spring and summer of 1966, should take place precisely in the universities was closely connected to the crisis that the prologue caused in a nerve center of the Chinese state in the sixties. The cultural machinery, the role of the university, and the privileged position of history in that political culture structured, even in organizational terms, the socialist state system. The efficacy of the Outline had in fact increased its disciplinary role.

The Outline Suspended

By late March Mao's efforts had succeeded in reopening the discussion about the Outline's validity. Since the Central Committee had formally adopted the document, however, it was there that the issue had to be addressed once again. A series of formal meetings of the party's central organs were held from early April to mid-May, presided over by the top leadership.[19] The political consensus reached at these meetings—the Circular of 16 May, examined below—is well known. However, not much is known about the details of the discussions leading up to it. For several reasons the period from mid-March to mid-May 1966 is the less well documented. The participants' speeches have only been reported indirectly, and the accounts of Chinese historians are fragmentary at best.[20]

The main available "source" so far is a sort of historical novel entitled *The Earliest Resistance: Peng Zhen on the Eve of the Great Cultural Revolution*.[21] Published in the early nineties by the Party School of the Central Committee, it is a "hagiography" with no precise indication of sources, as is the case with most Chinese books on the subject. The dialogues of the characters are reported in quotation marks but cannot be taken as literal transcripts. Rather, what emerges is a portrait based on the official government narrative that the party-school writers draw of a venerable ancestor and his entourage. No literary masterpiece by any measure, the story can be read as reflecting something of the style of the personal relationships existing at the time within the political elite, or better, of the style that the present-day propaganda officials propose as a positive example to praise.

By all accounts of the episode, Peng Zhen's initial response to Mao's objections was to keep steadfastly to his position. He argued that, despite its defects, the Outline was only intended to encourage a liberal, open forum. The small group of Maoists took a very active part in the discussion. Early in April, Zhang Chunqiao published his essay "Some Opinions about the Group of Five's Outline," and had it circulated. He criticized the restrictions imposed by Peng Zhen, basing his arguments on direct, personal knowledge of the controversy's developments he had been following and documenting for over four months.[22] The subsequent discussions, from April 9 to 12, were held in meetings of the Secretariat of the Central Committee. Peng Zhen once again maintained the Outline was basically sound and shortcomings could be corrected. Kang Sheng and Chen Boda, two leaders very close to Mao's position, criticized Peng Zhen's reasoning at length. Their speeches, of which no direct texts are known, respectively concerned the policies of the Group of Five (Kang was a member, but in the minority) and Peng Zhen's previous political positions, likely his activities as Beijing's mayor.

Apparently, there were no significant rebuttals in favor of Peng Zhen. It may well have been that the arguments he marshaled in his stubborn defense of the Outline left little maneuvering room for his supporters, who were also among the most influential party leaders. Indeed, the latter included Liu Shaoqi and Deng Xiaoping. They likely thought along the same lines as Peng Zhen and even chaired some meetings. Yet within a few weeks the upshot of these proceedings was the revocation of the Outline and the ouster of Peng Zhen. While Deng later stated that the outcome was a concession to Mao because it was "difficult to oppose him," it is hard to credit such a scenario. Liu and Deng had all the political authority they needed to defend Peng Zhen. That they did not manage to do so would indicate they apparently had no persuasive grounds for mediation. Peng Zhen's obstinate line of defense had likely left them with no leg to stand on.

In effect, it soon became clear as the meetings proceeded that Peng Zhen's obdurate defense of the Outline was proving ineffective. Although the content of the speeches at the Central Committee meetings is not directly known, much can be inferred from further developments in the internecine clashes and Peng Zhen's subsequent maneuvering. As we've seen, the criticisms had touched the Outline's authorial Group of Five and, seemingly, the policies of the Beijing mayoralty. The two issues were obviously interlaced since Peng Zhen headed both bodies. The criticisms involved the fact that the Party Committee of Beijing Municipality had been the main institutional grounding of the authorial group, and that some years earlier the latter had published "The Village of the Three Families." As mentioned in chapter 3, this was a well-known series of articles coauthored by Wu Han, Deng Tuo, and Liao Mosha satirizing the Great Leap experiments. As a matter of course, the role of Deng Tuo in the *Hai Rui* affair was also sharply criticized.

In the Outline Peng Zhen had threatened to settle the score with the "staunch Left" for its "long-term performances." Now, however, he was in a difficult situation, coming in for criticism both on his recent leadership of the Group of Five and for his own "long-term" activities as Beijing's mayor. Wu Han was one of Beijing's vice-mayors, and the criticism of Peng Zhen for having protected him from the beginning of the dispute was well grounded. Deng Tuo, alias Xiang Yangsheng, as we have seen, had been the author of the "uncompromising class criticism" of the "theory of moral inheritance" in December 1965, one of the most patent fakes fabricated to protect Wu. He was also head of the Beijing Party Committee for Cultural Affairs, the closest collaborator of Peng Zhen, and responsible for implementing many of the Group of Five's ploys in defense of Wu in the preceding months.

When staunch defense of the Outline became untenable under the pressure of these attacks, Peng Zhen suddenly changed tactics—a U-turn, indeed. He convened a meeting of the Beijing Party Committee where he announced that enforcement of the Outline was to be suspended. He even decided that the committee should initiate criticism of "The Village of the Three Families" and formally enjoined Deng Tuo to write a self-criticism and submit it to the Central Committee. Below are passages from the "novel" regarding Peng Zhen's "earliest resistance." The criticism of "The Village of the Three Families," Peng Zhen said in the meeting, was inevitable, "otherwise the losses would be much greater." He then charged his office to write critiques that would keep the political issue within bounds so as to "pitch the tune" to public opinion. Equally urgent was Deng's self-criticism. This supposedly was the tenor of Peng Zhen's speech during the key meeting concerning the destiny of his number two, as narrated in *The Earliest Resistance*:

> Comrade Deng Tuo [said Peng Zhen in his presence] in the last years has done much work for the party, but since on every matter "one divides into two"

he also has several shortcomings and [made] mistakes. He has not followed the directives of the Central Committee and of Chairman Mao, and has not propagandized well Mao Zedong's thought. Are not these evident mistakes? I hope that comrade Deng Tuo can make a thorough self-examination on these issues and send a high-level self-criticism to the Central Committee.

Peng Zhen then called his secretary and said: "Before tonight you and the comrades of the office will write one report expounding Comrade Deng Tuo's mistakes, and the help, the criticism, and the attention the Secretariat of the Municipal Party Committee is giving to him. You should pay the greatest attention not to deal with political matters, absolutely do not use words such as 'antiparty and antisocialist.'"[23]

The novel portrays Deng Tuo as lying in complete silence on a sofa at the back of the meeting room listening to Peng Zhen's words. The same night, Peng Zhen asked his secretary:

"Has comrade Deng Tuo written his self-criticism?"

"No," answered the secretary. "I have asked him several times, but he said he has not written it yet."

Peng Zhen was visibly upset, but kept a tolerant attitude and loudly retorted, "Probably you do not remember well, Deng Tuo is deeply aware of his own mistakes. I would advise everybody not to be confused on this matter. If we actively criticize them it is to help them. We must criticize to help."[24]

"Them" referred to Deng Tuo, Wu Han, and Liao Mosha.[25] Presumably, by abandoning his closest protégés, Peng Zhen sought to establish a stronger line of self-defense. Yet the tactic fully contradicted his behavior and statements of the previous six months, not to mention his long-term alliance with those to be "helped." On the other hand, Peng Zhen charged his offices to prepare dossiers against his Maoist critics, a move that the historical novel recalls as a sign of his resolve to resist the left. In fact, however, it made his tactics look even more contradictory and definitively weakened his position. The Central Committee thus decided in the latter part of April to disavow his handling of the situation, to revoke the Outline in light of all the criticism, and to disband the Group of Five and the Beijing Party Committee Peng Zhen headed.

The committee's decisions were formulated in the Circular (通知 tongzhi), also called the Circular of May 16. It was the first wide-ranging political declaration of the Cultural Revolution. The title, which sounded so dryly administrative, was chosen by Mao and perplexed nearly everyone at the meeting.[26] In fact, the Circular was a lengthy summary for a political document that weighed up the controversies following the publication of Yao's article and opened a new phase in the affair. Chen Boda drew up the initial draft and submitted it for what would be many revisions. Mao contributed his own at the end of April, later saying he only "added oil and vinegar" (加油加醋 *jia you jia cu*). In fact, however, his editorial changes covered all the key points and amounted to about a third of the text. The final draft, therefore, largely reflected his thoughts at the time.

Liberate the Imps

Before examining this famous document, we should dwell a little longer on Mao's speeches in those weeks for a better grasp of the Circular's intended purposes. After his revision of the Circular, Mao voiced this summary of the situation:

> Peng Zhen wanted to transform the Party according to his own view of the world, but things developed to the contrary, and he himself created the conditions for his overthrow. It is a fact of the order of necessity, which was manifested in chance and step by step [it] sank deeper. . . .
>
> If on the Central level [中央 *zhongyang*] there are people plotting, I appeal to local levels [地方 *difang*] to rise up, to Sun Wukong to bring upheaval within the Celestial Palace among those who protect the Jade Emperor. . . .
>
> The phenomenon is visible, the essence hidden. The essence can reveal itself through the phenomenon. Peng Zhen's essence was hidden for thirty years.[27]

Mao's polemical attacks were argued on two planes. He employed both a philosophical touch ("things" that are dialectically transformed into their "contrary," the "necessity" manifested within "chance," the "essence" of Peng Zhen, and the "phenomenon" of its appearance) and once again literary quotations that were well known. The Celestial Palace and Jade Emperor come from the great classic novel by 吴承恩 Wu Cheng'en, *Journey to the West* (西游记 *Xi you ji*). The fantasy-cast hero is 孙悟空 Sun Wukong, to whom Mao had dedicated a poem in the early sixties. He is the "magic monkey" who brings confusion to Heaven and is able to dispel the "miasmal mist" that obstructs the view of the real political obstacles.

In March and April, Mao had invoked the "overthrow" of the King of Hell's Palace and that of the Jade Emperor. The message also called for the liberation of the imps, the magic monkeys and grassroots cadres, so they could rise up, "bring disorder to the Celestial Palace," and put an end to the "plots of the Center." The intentions and expectations these literary allusions conveyed were quite clear. Mao's statements in these months can be summed up as focusing on two pressing themes: it was necessary to dismiss certain authorities and open to an unlimited plurality of political voices in China. We shall discuss pluralization and dismissal in chapter 6.

The two issues were then closely linked for Mao. The double set of parallel metaphors showed his conviction that the two processes could, and should, be complementary: overthrowing the King of Hell and setting free the imps were dependent one on the other. Mao had evidently become convinced that if one really wanted an open discussion in a mass-movement forum on the most urgent political issue—the destiny of the revolutionary party—it was necessary to dismantle the unconditional oversight authority of the state's cultural machinery. In fact, the climax of the prologue to the Cultural Revolution was the overthrow of the King of Hell's Palace.

This undoubtedly led to ousting certain kings, viceroys, princes, ministers, and other dignitaries of the Celestial Palace. Yet, even before leadership changes, dismissal concerned above all the authority of a key institution of state in China. The King of Hell's Palace indicated the apparatus of ministries that oversaw and enforced strict ideological discipline. Those in charge preempted what Mao considered a decisive revolutionary task: an unrestricted mass movement for assessing the CCP's political merit in the face of an impending general defeat of socialism itself.

Which is why Mao thought it indispensable to allow the imps—in theory, everyone in China was subject to disciplinary compliance—complete freedom of speech even if that might sometimes entail a display of disorderly conduct. All of this would inevitably lead to mixed signals and conflict with the authority of the palace. In any case, the imps could not make their voices heard unless they kept their distance from the very seat of that authority. "If you are [in] the King of Hell's Palace," Mao said, "the imps will not come to visit you [你们是阎王殿, 小鬼不上门 *nimen shi yanwangdian, xiao gui bu shang men*]."[28] Yao Wenyuan, Mao said, was also an imp, and indeed the Celestial Palace did not intend to listen to what he had to say. "Liberating the imps" thus involved opening the door to an infinite number of political subjectivities organized outside the party-state's control.

A Circular

An overview of some of Mao's main statements in spring 1966 provides more elements for reading the finale of the prelude to the Cultural Revolution. The Circular was the "minimalist" name for the first political salvo of the Cultural

Revolution. Issued on May 16, 1966, it was the outcome of the party's top-echelon meetings initiated by Mao in late March.[29] If the title was deliberately understated, the intention of the document was clear enough: to restrict the authority of the Celestial Palace and to offer unrestricted freedom of speech at a critical time.

The Circular's tenor was sharply critical and made no concessions to the "enemy," an aspect that Chinese historians often ascribe to Mao's despotic and adventurist attitude. Yet, while the same historians did not hesitate to describe the Outline's language as "extremist," they also did not hesitate to justify it as needed in order to counter the left. Peng Zhen had in fact exhibited a most inflexible doctrinal rigor, as did many articles coming from the King of Hell's Palace, in order to restrict the scope of the dispute in terms purely formalistic and to tighten the reins of ideological discipline.

One goal of the Circular was therefore to redefine the terrain of political controversy by necessarily refuting opponents' moves in detail. Mao and the small group of supporters around him aimed at exposing the Outline's obsessively disciplinary nature couched in ultrarevolutionary language. That the party's central bodies clearly recognize the ideological and organizational stalemate the state's cultural apparatus had created was even more essential for Mao. It might even be conjectured that he considered reaching such a consensus a prerequisite for any mass political experiment.

The Circular, which then became a document of the Central Committee—that is, an official guideline for the whole party—dealt in detail with the crucial issues of those months: the criticism of *Hai Rui*, the controversy that followed, and Peng Zhen's initiatives that culminated in the February Outline. Mao made significant additions to the document on key points, which we shall cite extensively, as they constitute the real structure of the Circular's arguments.[30]

The Circular's reversal of the Outline's positions was evident from the very first lines. Officially approved as a document of the Central Committee, it started with the declaration of a double dismissal. First and foremost, it "voided" (撤消 *chexiao*) the validity of the Outline the same Central Committee had approved barely four months before. Moreover, a point added by Mao, it announced the "dissolution" (again *chexiao*) of the Group of Five, the organ presided over by Peng Zhen that had drawn up the Outline and enforced its application. In a word, the order of the day was "dismissal" (as we can roughly translate *chexiao*). It vitiated the top cultural authority of the party-state and revoked its last political machination.

Among Peng Zhen's political errors, which the Circular analyzed minutely in its ten paragraphs, the first was overturning the "relationships between the enemy and ourselves"—he defended Wu Han and prevented discussion of any political aspect of the criticism of *Hai Rui*. "Instead of encouraging the whole Party," the Circular reads, "to mobilize courageously the great masses of workers, peasants, soldiers, and fighters for proletarian culture so they might continue to progress, the Outline does its best to lead the movement toward the right." The Outline had adopted "a confused, contradictory, and hypocritical language ... [for] obfuscating ... the bitter class struggle that is being waged in culture and ideology." More succinctly, it obscured the fact that "the objective of this great struggle [is] to criticize and repudiate Wu Han."

A second important revision by Mao was that while the criticism concerned first the cultural apparatus, it was not restricted to any one particular sector of the party-state. We can read in Mao's own handwriting, immediately following the passage quoted above, the sentence "The objective of this great struggle is to criticize and repudiate Wu Han and the numerous other representatives of the anti-Party and anti-Socialist bourgeoisie (some of whom can be found in the Party's Central Committee, in the government, and in other departments of the central, provincial, municipal, and autonomous regions level)."

It is remarkable that this passage in the Circular deliberately presents the dismissal as indeterminate. It concerned not only "numerous" individuals but, in theory, *anyone* (Wu Han was not a definitive example) in a position of authority at any level of the party or state. The horizonless scope of dismissal thus constituted a crucial subjective theme of the Circular. Anyone in a position of authority was subject to it, including Mao. In his letter to Jiang Qing of July 1966, he even considered his own authority as destined to be pulverized by events, despite or rather because of the personality cult that surrounded him, as happened not many years later. In the following sections of the Circular, the indeterminacy of dismissal is increasingly accentuated and reaches its climax on the last page. In other words, the Circular declared that nobody in a position of power at any level of the party-state apparatus could deal with that political situation based on established authority. This aspect of the Circular, as we shall see below, elicited anxious reactions as much among Mao's closest allies as among his adversaries.

One crucial error in the Outline had been to "channel the political struggle in the cultural field into a purely academic discussion." As we have seen, Peng Zhen's strong point, but also his weak one, had been the antipolitical use of historiography. The Circular contained the Outline's "wide opening" (放 *fang*) promulgation. Yet it was in fact a "treacherous trick" to restrict the dispute to purely historiographical arguments and, hence, to censor political criticism. "Wide opening," the Circular read, citing an earlier statement by Mao, "means permitting all the people to express freely their opinions so that they should have the courage to speak, criticize, and discuss." In effect, however, Peng Zhen's wide opening was restricted to the Jade Palace.

The Circular objected that the Outline, having made assessment of political criticism subordinate to the evaluation of its academic standard, had in fact presumed to set the bar of scholarship high as a tool of censorship. The Outline had prescribed that only those articles showing they could "truly and extensively surpass [the adversary] from the professional, academic point of view" might be published. In actual fact, the scholarly standard of the critiques of Wu was not at all low, beginning with Yao Wenyuan's initial salvo.

Connected to the latter issue was the question of who was oppressing whom. The Outline had declared that in the *Hai Rui* dispute "the academic workers of the Left" criticizing Wu were behaving like "scholarly tyrants" (学阀 *xuefa*). As we have seen in chapter 4, labeling the imps as academic warlords who were "acting arbitrarily and trying to overwhelm others through their power" while announcing a rectification in order to prevent them from acquiring the pernicious habits of bourgeois experts sounded like a sarcastically worded warning shot that swift retaliation awaited untamed subordinates.

The Circular's rebuttal was another of Mao's additions. Who was acting with "tyrannical arbitrariness"? Where were the "potentates"? Mao overturned the accusations in a polemical crescendo that involved both the King of Hell and the Jade Palace. It concerned "those who have authority in the Party and follow the capitalist road" (党内走资本主义道路的当权派 *dangnei zou zibenzhuyi daolu de dangquanpai*). This formula would gain wide currency over the next ten years.

> In actual fact, those who obtain authority in the party and follow the capitalist road, and those representatives of the bourgeoisie who have infiltrated the party and protect the bourgeois tyrants of culture, are in truth the great tyrants of the party who have usurped the name of the party. They do not study (不看书不看报 *bu kan shu bu kan bao*), literally "[they] read neither books nor journals [incidentally, there is a political polemic for attacking adversaries because they 'do not study'], have no contact with the masses, and know nothing, relying solely on the fact that they 'act arbitrarily' and try to overwhelm the people with their power."

While the Outline had labeled Wu's critics as scholarly tyrants and prescribed a series of disciplinary measures to deal with them, the Group of Five and staffers were also busy collecting documents for dossiers to be used in an imminent settling of scores with the left. The Circular retorted that the authors "had attempted all sorts of pretexts to attack left-wing elements and intended to launch further attacks against them by means of a 'campaign of rectification' in the vain attempt to scatter their ranks." They had even "conferred on the bourgeois representatives, revisionists, and renegades that have infiltrated the Party the title of 'consequent Left' and protected them. In this way, they are trying to boost the arrogance of the bourgeois and right-wing elements and suffocate the spirit of the proletarian Left."

The Outline had prescribed that the *Hai Rui* controversy should be carried out "under direction . . . with prudence . . . caution . . . [and] the approval of the leading bodies concerned." The Circular would have none of it, rebutting that it all aimed to "impose restrictions on the proletarian Left" and enacted "taboos and commandments with the purpose of tying the Left's hands." Mao added that while the Outline's authors imposed a whole series of preemptive prohibitions on the imps, they instead "accord full freedom of action to all the various evil spirits that have for many years permeated the press, radio, magazines, novels, textbooks, conferences, works of literature, cinema, theater, ballads, short stories, music, dance, and so on. In doing so they never consulted the proletarian leadership nor felt the need for approval. This contrast shows which side the authors of the Outline are really on."

The Circular was a full-scale counterattack. Its polemical emphasis depended on the fact that the "evil spirits" [牛鬼蛇神 *niu gui she shen*, literally "demons of oxen and spirits of snakes"] were not writers in general, as the current version says, but the highest cultural authorities of the party-state.[31] The bourgeois academic authorities the Circular attacked were the leading elite of the cultural machinery of the party-state, and the evil spirits were the lordly dignitaries in the King of Hell's Palace.

Politics and Philosophy

We must examine two points of the Circular separately because of their philosophical and political entanglement: the relationship between truth and equality in politics (point 4) and between destruction and construction (point 6). Mao made significant additions to both in reply to two of Peng Zhen's arguments in the Outline. Remarkable too is that such philosophical issues are enmeshed in a heated political conflict. Yet this very web of politics and philosophy is worth reexamining.

Here is Peng Zhen on truth: "Everyone is equal in the face of truth" (真理对面人人平等 *zhenli duimian renren pingdeng*). So he had been arguing for some months, and, as we have seen, had been quoted by close allies like Deng Tuo, alias Xiang Yangsheng. The Circular's rejoinder was that the Outline was mistaken: it rejected the "class nature of truth" (真理的阶级性 *zhenli de jiejixing*) so as to "protect the bourgeoisie and oppose the proletariat."

A thorny issue indeed. Yet how can one say Peng Zhen was wrong? How can we believe in the "class character of truth"? This tangle of philosophy and politics requires much more than usual scrutiny. For several years, scholarly debate has virtually banished the philosophical issue of truth and reduced it to mere word play.[32]

Both the Outline and the Circular had a specific political objective. Peng Zhen's was to circumscribe any such contemporary implication in the *Hai Rui* dispute; Mao's was to explicitly underline its political nature. However, in both the philosophical aspect was not simply superimposed on political intentions, as much of the historiography of the Cultural Revolution has it, seeing ideological disputes as so much smoke and mirrors. In fact, the way in which the two positions were articulated and conflicted with each other on the strictly theoretical plane played an essential role in the development of events.

A close look at Peng Zhen's argument that "each is equal before [对面 *duimian*] the truth" makes truth an "object"—*Gegenstand*, as German philosophers would say. It stands right "in front of" human subjects whose mutual "equality" consists in adapting themselves to the "objective" character of truth. In fact, objectivity rather than the truth advocated by the Outline concerned above all historiographical knowledge purified of any political implications.

We have already seen how the defense of an apolitical history aggravated the predicament of the King of Hell's Palace. "Everyone is equal in front of the truth" was the equivalent of saying "everyone has to adapt themselves to the same degree of history's objectivity," irrespective of differing political persuasions, especially contemporary ones. However, more than a few participants had repeatedly criticized the historiographical objectivity of Wu's position as unadulterated and indisputable erudition.

By noting the class nature of truth, the Circular's reply constituted a political-philosophical tangle that led to an irresolvable impasse. We have seen that class struggle was a synonym for politics in the political language and culture of the time. However, it inevitably led back to a vision that placed the truth of politics within history, the history of class struggle. Mao was intent on reinvigorating the intellectual merit of politics and turned to philosophy for help. But every time an argument was grounded in a philosophical-cum-political argument, the effect of intellectual revitalization eventuated in erasing the singular stakes at play in the political situation. The relationship that Mao established between philosophy and politics wavered between a properly philosophical thesis and one that "sutured" together philosophy and politics. In a famous conversation about philosophical questions a couple of years before, Mao had said something that this passage in the Circular undoubtedly echoed: "Only if there is class struggle is there philosophy [有阶级斗争才有哲学 *you jieji douzheng cai you zhexue*].... Those who study philosophy think that philosophy comes first [以为哲学第一 *yiwei zhexue diyi*]. This is wrong: first comes class struggle [阶级斗争第一 *jieji douzheng diyi*]."[33]

There are two notable aspects to this thesis. Arguing that philosophy cannot come before politics (class struggle), its antecedent (one of its "conditions," Badiou would say), is healthy for philosophy itself. However, the problem for which Mao could not find a solution was how to avoid the fusion, the suturing, of philosophy and politics, with all its antiphilosophical and, in the end, antipolitical consequences. In other words, Mao's advocating the primacy of politics over philosophy opens the door to a contemporary intellectual need—the "political condition of philosophy." Yet it inexorably leads to a suture of philosophy with politics that is one and the same as the Stalinist worldview of dialectical and historical materialism. Thus, the category of class struggle fuses together philosophy, politics, and history in an inextricable web.

Mao's editorial accretions mainly concerned confuting Peng Zhen's argument that equality should conform to the objectivity of truth. Mao considered this to be sophistry, an attempt to conceal a political divide. He thus opposed Peng Zhen's "everyone is equal in front of the truth" by equating truth with political subjectivity, or class struggle. The classes that are struggling, Mao said, are not equal; even less equal in front of the truth were revisionists and revolutionaries.

> Can we perhaps permit that there is some equality on basic issues such as the proletarian struggle against the bourgeoisie? ... For several decades the old social democratic parties and for a few years [now] the new revisionists have conceded no equality with the bourgeoisie to the proletariat.... They are a set of counterrevolutionary, anticommunist, and antipopular elements. Their struggle against us is a life-or-death struggle and certainly not a matter of equality. Thus, our struggle against them, too, cannot but be a life-or-death struggle, and our relationship with them can in no way be one of equality.... Between exploiting classes and exploited classes there can be no other type of relationship, such as a so-called relationship of equality, of peaceful coexistence, benevolence, and morality [仁义道德 *renyi daode*].

While this emphatic reminder that class is the nature of political subjectivity undoubtedly reanimated the political debate, it also produced a series of side effects in the very tortuous course of events that we shall discuss in detail in the next part of this volume. We have already seen the ambivalence of the reference to class struggle in the prologue, and even its use against the politicization of the controversy. As we shall see in the next chapters, class as the main political criterion engendered even more confusing antipolitical results.

The other political-philosophical knot in the Circular was another of Mao's editorial additions: destruction and construction. As he had been arguing for several months, Peng Zhen had written in the Outline that "there can be no true, full destruction without construction." The rebuttal in the Circular was that Marxism had indeed been constructed through the "struggle to destroy bourgeois ideology." Accordingly, Peng Zhen's thesis was equivalent to "forbidding the proletariat to carry out the revolution." Mao added a theoretical argument: "Without destruction, there cannot be construction [不破不立 *bu po bu li*]. Destruction means criticism [批判 *pipan*], it means revolution. In order to destroy, it is necessary to argue one's own point [讲道理 *jiang daoli*], and this implies construction. By placing destruction first, there will also be construction within it [破字当头, 立也在其中了 *po zi dang tou, li ye jiu zai qizhong le*]."

Here, too, the philosophical and political planes intersect. Yet we should note that, unlike the "truth" thesis, there is no historical-political category suturing the arguments. The contrast was certainly one of principle, but the question of what to place first revolved around specific, radical differences directly pertinent to the prologue: which destruction and which construction were in the Outline–Circular contrast? Peng Zhen put construction first. He argued that the safeguard of the existing socialist governmental order was the precondition of any potential political subjectivity. Mao, however, wanted to promote new forms of thought and political organization capable of confronting an epochal, cataclysmic crisis he considered imminent. Specific destruction was thus necessary. The task was to take down by more than a few pegs the ideological and organizational obstacles, the roots of the problem, that prevented people from thinking politically of that crisis. This is what he meant by releasing the imps so they might think of it, and, hence, it also entailed construction.

Destruction thus had the same targets as the dismissal of the King of Hell, the Jade Emperor, and the demons of oxen and spirits of snakes in the rooms of the Celestial Palace. Without calling into question their ideological authority or diminishing their prestige, those cultural phantoms of politics would continue to thwart any reexamination of the ideological and institutional horizon of socialism that Mao considered an urgent priority. As discussed above, for Mao the issue at stake was therefore how to counter revisionism. The Circular had declared that the struggle against the "revisionist line" was a "problem of fundamental importance which would exercise a vital influence on the fate of our Party and of our State, on the future shape of our Party and of our State and on world revolution." Far from a violation of orthodoxy, revisionism designated the main impediment for envisioning an imminent, epochal change concerning the fate of socialism in China and the world and, hence, for experimenting with new possibilities of egalitarian politics.

Dismissal in the Circular

The Circular's last item concerned the issue of dismissal. Mao revised it at length, lending full support to the criticism of both the academic authorities and the "people in a position of power who follow the road to capitalism." It was urgent to "remove or transfer them to other posts" and above all "not give them the task of leading the Cultural Revolution." The reference was clearly to Peng Zhen, but not only: "The representatives of the bourgeoisie [exclaimed Mao] who have infiltrated the Party, the government, the army, and various cultural sectors are a group of counterrevolutionary revisionists. Once the conditions are ripe, they will seize power and transform the proletarian dictatorship into a bourgeois dictatorship. Some of them we have already identified, but not others. Others, for example individuals like Khrushchev who still enjoy our trust, are being trained as our successors and can be found at present among us [睡在我们的旁边 *shui zai women de pangbian*, literally 'they sleep by our side']."

Who was this "Khrushchev," besides being the personification of revisionism? One of the few details known about the atmosphere of this meeting is that this paragraph that Mao added made an enormous impression on all the participants, especially those closest to him. Lin Biao, for example, said that he found this statement "extremely disturbing" (惊心动魄 *jing xin dong po*).[34] Later, Zhang Chunqiao said that at the time he did not know at all to whom the sentence might refer.[35] The shock, as it were, was the result of the indeterminacy of dismissal in the Circular. None of the eighty members present at that Central Committee meeting had any idea who the "individuals like Khrushchev who sleep by our side" were, because Mao's statement left this key issue deliberately vague, undetermined.

In the *Hai Rui* controversy, we have seen at least three facets of dismissal. In the early contrasts between Mao and Peng Zhen about the nub of *Hai Rui*, dismissal was directly attached to the political divergence at Lushan about peasants' subjectivity; it was also a disciplinary act regarding the relations within the party-state. In April 1966, Mao's polemical barbs against the King of Hell's Palace were aimed at the dismissal of the state's cultural apparatus so as to curtail in no uncertain terms its ideological authority.

The main novelty of dismissal in the opening scene was its relation to pluralization. For Mao, overthrowing the King of Hell's Palace was a prerequisite for the multiplication of the voices of politics. Revisionism could thus be countered only if the functions of the party were drastically restricted and the authorities in the offices of its cultural apparatus dismissed. Mao also realized, however, that releasing a multitude of imps whose voices were not subject to the King of Hell's prior control would inevitably have wrought disorder in the Jade Palace.

Yao Wenyuan and all those who intervened to make the dispute political were imps. They were arguing a thesis from their position on the periphery of the party-state and, hence, were not wholly dependent on the latter's ideological and organizational authority. Peng Zhen defended to the bitter end the principle that the party was the only seat authorized to formulate declarations of a political nature and that a suitable "rectification" of anyone who insisted on thinking and doing otherwise was required.

Dismissal in the opening scene of the Cultural Revolution thus mainly concerned the party as the sole venue of organization and the only place for the enunciation of political declarations. It must be remembered that this had been an incontrovertible "truth" in the political culture of twentieth-century socialism. However the party in each country might be structured, only within it could proclamations, meaning, arguments, theses, analyses, and prescriptions have any political merit. Outside of the party, there were at best apolitical opinions, or opinions whose political character could only be legitimized if based on the ideological and organizational grounding of the party.

In parliamentary regimes the only form of political declaration permitted by those who do not play any part in the exercise of power was, and is still, a tick on the ballot. In socialist regimes, on the other hand, the party-state imposed not so much electoral consensus, which where it existed was negligible, as the confident recognition of the cultural, even "scholarly" supremacy of the King of Hell's Palace. The overthrowing of the King of the Hell's Palace that concluded the prologue had a singular political significance—the urgency of pluralization.

However, by the end of the prologue, dismissal also remained a structural invariance, a phenomenon intrinsic to all forms of state power. By itself this presented no novelty. Nor was there anything new in removing and transferring ministers and leaders to other offices; it has always existed in all recorded forms of government.[36] What was new was promoting unrestricted political voices beyond the reach of the party in twentieth-century socialist political culture.

Can any distinction be made between a dismissal internal to governmental circumstances and dismissal external to them as related to mass political inventions? A tightly drawn knot, to be sure, but the question obviously concerns how to individuate any discontinuity between egalitarian politics and the structural operation of government. Is there a logical difference, one of governmental subjectivities and one of egalitarian inventions? A possible answer may be found in the details distinguishing between pluralization and dismissal, to which we shall return in part III.

History as History of Coups d'État and Mao's Absolute Authority

If we focus exclusively on intragovernmental dismissal, one such tendency did emerge immediately following the May 16 Circular. Indeed, it did so in its most dramatic appearance—the coup d'état. A mere two days after the approval of the Circular, Lin Biao gave a long speech at the same series of meetings of the Central Committee. He did not refer to any liberation of the imps, nor did he mention the controversy over *Hai Rui*. Lin offered instead a view of the situation based on two essential urgent tasks: to "forestall a counterrevolutionary plot"— an imminent coup—and to establish the absolute authority of "Mao's thought."[37]

Lin's view was symptomatic of a radical problem and his attempt to find a solution. He was, however, heading in the worst direction by obscuring the issues raised by the situation. Lin read the content of the Circular as intended to "forestall counterrevolutionary subversion," but then compounded the issue by expounding his own philosophy of history—the coup d'état as the crucial issue for politics. Lin did not restrict his remarks to the then current circumstances. Instead, he spoke at length, with examples taken from the whole of Chinese history and from the contemporary worldwide situation. To sum his speech up as a light parody, one could say "all history is the history of coups d'état." Lin's reasoning was a further sign of the predicament that viewed politics as based on presumed laws of history. Equally symptomatic of a radical impasse was the other key argument he posited—"Chairman Mao's genius." The words of Chairman Mao, he said, "will continue to be the touchstone of our action ... with Mao Zedong's thought ... there will be no problem that cannot be solved.... Every sentence of Chairman Mao is a truth; one of his sentences is better than ten thousand of ours."

It is well known that a series of disagreements with Mao that later deteriorated and led to the catastrophic outcome five years later go back to Lin's speech. We cannot deal with this issue here except to observe that there was some coherence to Lin's arguments. As noted, his reaction to the Circular was shock. What drew his response were the very points where the indeterminacy of dismissal was most stressed ("individuals such as Khrushchev"). It may be that in his speech Lin was placating his anxiety. In effect, he placed it within the peculiar view of history as one of coups d'état and then relied on Mao's supreme authority to make up for all the institutional uncertainty.

Mao, however, could not find Lin's view acceptable. He believed there was no absolute authority anywhere, let alone his own, capable of stabilizing the inconstancy of the human condition. A now famous letter to Jiang Qing of July 1966, which circulated after Lin's death in 1971, is instructive. Mao wrote that in "that speech of [our] friend" there were ideas that "deeply disturbed" him. He did not subscribe to the idea that the main problem was to forestall an attempted coup; that was not what Mao meant by the "struggle against revisionism." If anything, one novelty in Mao's analysis was the possibility of a "peaceful restoration" of capitalism.

Moreover, he found the extolling of the supreme authority of his genius ridiculous. "I have never thought that the pamphlets I have written had such magic power. Now that he has taken to inflating them, the whole country will follow suit. It seems to be exactly like the scene of the marrow-monger wife Wang who boasts of the quality of her goods." Such exaltation, Mao dialectically commented, would inexorably be transformed into its opposite. "They flatter me by praising me to the stars, [but] things turn into their contrary: the higher one is driven, the harder his fall. I am prepared to fall, shattering all my flesh and bones. It does not matter; matter is not destroyed, it only falls to pieces."

These are undoubtedly materialistic convictions, albeit suffused with a peculiar sadness because Mao also stated that he could not find any effective way of countering such worship: "I am forced to let them do so . . . and I say so for the effects they have on me." Unfortunately, soon "all the Left are speaking in this way." Yet to reveal his criticisms to the public "would mean dousing them with cold water and helping the Right." Although he therefore assented to the circulation of Lin's speech as one of the Central Committee meeting's official documents, he was to no extent convinced by it. "This is the first time in my life that, on an important point, I have given way to another against my better judgment; let us say independently of my will."

That Mao felt compelled to go against his better judgment was a decision, or rather a nondecision, that was to cost him dearly. He was to wage an acrimoniously devastating political battle against Lin in 1970–71. The endorsement that Mao was forced to give in 1966 to Lin's positions was not simply a result of power politics. To be sure, the episode reveals more clearly Mao's isolation on the "right and the left." It also shows that on this as on other occasions Lin had acted autonomously and could do so without Mao's consent. This despite— or rather thanks to—his declarations on the chairman's absolute authority. However, there was likely something more basic leading Mao to yield, albeit "regardless of my will." In that speech, Lin dealt only with dismissal. Yet Mao was especially interested in the experimental possibilities of pluralization, thinking that ultimately the two were compatible. In other words, Mao may have considered "our friend" as one-sided but not antagonistic.[38]

A Great School

A couple of weeks earlier, at the time of his May 1966 meeting with the Albanian diplomats, Mao outlined an ambitious political experiment in a letter to Lin. It would become famous in the following months and years as the May 7 Directive. Its addressee also signaled how important Mao held their friendship, hoped it would be reciprocal on crucial issues, and why some days later he was so disturbed by Lin's speech.

Although written at the same time as the meetings that brought about Peng Zhen's downfall, Mao's letter did not refer to relations between the King of Hell and the imps. Rather, it was a draft blueprint concerning the potential role of the People's Liberation Army in reinventing "school." It was a grand design for narrowing the great gap in social differences between manual and intellectual work and for rethinking the concept of school.

The very idea that the army had something to do with an educational experiment is so remote from our thinking at a time of hypermilitarization and the decline of state school systems that it is very easy to equivocate. It is almost inevitable to dismiss the issue as yet another sign of Mao's obscure despotism. That it could also have eventuated in a nationwide military mobilization that would supposedly have dominated China in the sixties is taken as given in the current official narrative. However, a document that inspired extensive experimentation deserves a much closer reading. It shows that the issues at stake were both farsighted and closely connected to the situation that actually prevailed at the time.

The starting point was what the army's role should be in the event of a world war. It is worth recalling how high tensions ran during that peak moment in the Cold War. Yet, even as US military aggression in Vietnam was brutally escalating, Mao persevered in a nonmilitaristic vision. Inevitably, influential CCP leaders likely saw a rapprochement with the CPSU for joint intervention in

Vietnam as desirable. Mao defiantly opposed such an option. Indeed, he continued to criticize CPSU revisionism while advocating independent support for Vietnam's War of Liberation. The issue of adapting to the new military situation by professionalization of the PLA was also a major point of disagreement among the top leadership.[39]

There was a markedly nonmilitaristic side to Mao's view of the issue. Even in the case of a third world war, he wrote, "our army can become a great school." The army he envisioned should not merely be a military institution. It was to be a corps engaged in various civic activities. Recapturing the political tradition of the People's War, Mao argued that the combination of specialized and nonspecialized roles in the army should be a model extension-service task force for key national work projects. "Besides fighting," he wrote, "the PLA should carry out various other activities as it did during the eight years of the Second World War against the Japanese." Significantly, Mao uses the term *school*, or rather "great school" (大学校 *da xuexiao*) to indicate the change: "In this great school politics, military problems and culture must be studied. Soldiers can also be engaged in subsidiary agricultural production. Medium to small workshops can be built in which goods are produced not only for their own needs but also goods to be sold back to the State on the basis of an exchange of goods at equal value."

Note the exactitude of the remark: the experiment was audacious but not purposed to some kind of "primitive communism," a criticism often leveled against Maoist politics. "Exchange at equal value" designated in the Marxist lexicon the trade of commodities in the market. We shall see in chapter 10 how Mao intended to deal with the inevitability of commodity exchange under socialism. Suffice it to note here that he did not underestimate the issue.

The soldiers should also be engaged in "mass work"—participate in political movements, work on farms and in factories, and "in the revolutionary struggle to criticize bourgeois culture" so that "the army may become one with the people." Soldiers were to "carry out at the same time their military duties and study subjects military, agricultural, industrial, and of the masses [politics]." While persevering in the containment of militarism intrinsic to every army by means of a program involving millions of soldiers in all sorts of civilian activities, Mao thus made this interchange of military-civilian activities a model for all other socially useful tasks.

The letter to Lin continued:

> Similarly [to the soldiers], workers, besides mainly carrying out industrial work, should also study military questions, politics, and culture; they

should participate in the movement for socialist education [the main political movement before the Cultural Revolution] and the criticism of the bourgeoisie. Where local conditions permit, they should also dedicate themselves to agricultural work, as well as in the oil fields at Daqing [at that time a model of integration of industry and agriculture].

In the people's communes, too, besides carrying out agricultural work (including silviculture, fish farming, herding, and subsidiary activities) they must also study military questions, politics, and culture. When circumstances and time permit, they should open small collective factories, and they should criticize the bourgeoisie.

Nor are students to be overlooked. Studying is their main job, but they must also learn other things. This means they must learn not only culture but also industry, agriculture, and military issues, and must criticize the bourgeoisie. The length of the period of study must be reduced, education must be revolutionised, and we must not permit our schools to continue to be dominated by bourgeois intellectuals. Where conditions are suitable, those who work in commerce, in services, and in the Party and government offices should also do the same.

Remarkable here is the perceptiveness of the plan, audacious but not naïvely utopian, even less a blueprint for what was later alleged to be anarchy. Mao specified that the interchange "should be coordinated appropriately, and a distinction must be made between main and secondary tasks. Among agricultural, industrial, and mass work every unit of the army can choose one or two activities, but not all three together."

In sum, even in the event of a world war, Mao outlined a "great school" for overcoming social barriers and hierarchies. The idea of a multitasking army was the jump-off for setting in motion a similar process for overcoming the barriers among specializations in socially important civic tasks. For a few months each year, everyone had to engage in work they had never done before. Factory workers had to become farmers and farmers factory workers; soldiers had to work both in factories and on farms; students, teachers, and state functionaries had to do likewise. Most importantly, those engaged in manual labor had to have time to study, even those employed in forestry, herding, and fish farming. Mao had a penchant for details.

Yet one might well wonder why this experiment went by the name "great school." It was not merely a metaphor. Mao had studied as an educator in his youth and pondered over the very meaning of the word *school*. Ever since he had been a student at the Teacher Training College in Changsha, school had been the name for a series of inventions that needed to be tested; it was far more than that of an institution purposed to the development of the modern nation-state. Mao did not have a scholastic view of school. He saw it not as a subsidiary system of state machinery endowed with its own "bureaucratic rationality." Rather, it constituted a circuit of places for didactic creativity whose specific forms were to be found by means of repeated experimentation.

Obviously, school also meant an organized body for the transmission of knowledge. Yet he always considered such transmission as the condition for opening the mind. As is well known, he advocated that education be placed under politics, "proletarian politics," which is something that may not naturally be self-evident today. Mao's "great school" had to be equal to the grand new design that had been germinating in modern politics since Marx. Placing education under the guidance of politics would open its doors to dismantling the divisions of labor and social hierarchies.

So what kind of a school was it supposed to be? A reference, in many aspects unconnected with this enterprise, may help to clarify its proper pedagogical and even didactic side, because it indicates that the category "school" is not to be taken in the slightest for granted. As Durkheim's extraordinary *L'évolution pédagogique en France* shows, the school has never been the outcome of spontaneous development in educational systems. It has existed historically in very different situations under the fillip of certain political and intellectual inventions. Charlemagne's Palatine School, the medieval university, or the *Écoles centrales* of the French Revolution, despite all their obvious differences in content, method, and institutional duration, were for Durkheim forms of "unprecedented" scholastic invention. As he showed, the form of teaching and its organization in each were the result of finding themselves at the precarious crossroads between the systematic transmission of knowledge and opening this very knowledge up to hitherto unknown areas of thought. In every epoch, this crossroads for transmitting the "encyclopedic" unity of knowledge and movement toward the unknown—toward "truth," as Durkheim philosophically termed it—became articulated in peculiar, unrepeatable forms. Every school had a specific role in the intellectual issues of the day. It was certainly not classrooms, examinations, or grades that made the category of school coherent, as Durkheim emphatically argued.[40]

What Mao proposed in May 1966 was precisely the reinvention of school as a category and equal to the creation of a politics designed to reduce inequalities and social hierarchies. The classroom, exams, marks, diplomas, and even codes of discipline did not constitute its fundamental criteria. The core criterion of an intellectual invention designed to promote and shape the very existence of "school" was first and foremost politics. It is thus purposed to dismantling social barriers between occupations, thereby providing everyone with any number of egalitarian potentialities. All this, it should be remembered, occurred on the eve of what was to be a worldwide crisis in modern educational systems.

We must reappraise that project of a "Great School" in a new light, one cast beyond today's disorientation in matters of politics and the state that impedes any serious research on the Cultural Revolution. Lest we forget, it took a century to initiate detailed study of the French Revolution. To remain solely within the field of education, it took the perspicacity of a Durkheim to realize that the Écoles centrales created by the Convention, although they lasted for very few years and were considered for a century thereafter the height of educational disorder, were in fact the true seeds of twentieth-century schools. It is to be hoped that we shall not have to wait as long before reconsidering today the worth of the "great school" in the years of the Cultural Revolution.

Did Mao Have a Plan?

Chinese historiographers, though firmly endorsing the official version of the Cultural Revolution as a great disaster and the outcome an enormous mistake on the part of Mao, are in fact far from definitive arbiters in assessing his role in the prologue. For neither straightforward predetermination nor, even less, a strategically conceived plot can be attributed to him. For example, Wang Nianyi, the author of one of the most popular "official" histories of the Cultural Revolution, *The Years of Great Disorder*, writes that Mao's goal was to "overthrow revisionism among party leaders," but that he had no precise strategy.

For Wang as for most of Chinese historiographers, Mao had not evaluated the consequences of his actions. Indeed, he did not want to weigh them. The portrait of Mao they paint is ultimately that of an adventurist despot. "Mao had not thought out a plan clearly," notes Wang, "nor could he have done so. He even considered that it was not necessary to think about a plan clearly . . . because he had always maintained that class struggle . . . 'can be conducted solely on the basis of the given situation' [因势利导 *yin shi li dao*]."⁴¹

In his conclusions, Wang sees that by the spring of 1966 Mao was moving toward what he judged as constituting "a political program of the extreme Left," which became the Circular of 16 May. Yet Mao "did not clearly say what the necessary requisites for carrying it out were . . . and thus it was not a fully detailed political program." Wang takes this lacuna as a sign of programmatic adventurism upstream of the "ten years of disorder." Ultimately, for official

Chinese historians, the absence of an elaborate program readily fits into the portrait of Mao as at once an aged, unpredictable tyrant and a childish extremist who pulled hundreds of millions of people into a decade of unalloyed irrationalism.

We have followed another course, which incidentally Wang himself, quoting Mao's view (albeit to dismiss it as leftist adventurism), has suggested: the necessity of "conducting politics on the basis of the singularity of the given situation." In fact, only by focusing on the subjective singularities of a specific sociohistorical situation is it possible to make its inherent logic politically cognizable. In other words, it is a matter of identifying the structural elements that hinder egalitarian politics and turning them into positive resources.

This perspective has enabled our close reading of the *Hai Rui* controversy and provided elements for exploring the articulation of chance and necessity in the prelude to the Cultural Revolution. We have seen, on the one hand, the uncertainty and unpredictability of those events and, on the other, how Mao's thoughts and actions regarding key points of the unfolding situation revealed his internal logic. The publication of Yao's article in November and its unexpected consequences soon brought to the fore significant structural elements of that situation. The controversy's rapid spread and the impasse it reached in January revealed the intrinsic instability of the historical-political fulcrum of the ideological framework of the socialist state and soon shook the authority of its central cultural apparatus. Mao intervened at first from the margins. Yet this tentative step met strong resistance even before he managed to express his reasoned opinion of the matter. The February Outline dealt with the dispute by merely blocking it, a step that resulted in a tense stalemate and later would also discredit the Group of Five and, more importantly, the King of Hell's Palace.

By late March, Mao saw the incipient wavering of the cultural leadership apparatus and clearly decided to restrain its authority. It may not have been a plan in the premeditated sense of the term. Rather, his was a response to the developments in the *Hai Rui* controversy and its impasse. Thus did "overthrowing the King of Hell's Palace" become one of Mao's crucial goals. He was increasingly convinced that curtailing the authority of the central cultural apparatus was a prerequisite for prompting a mass movement to examine vital issues concerning nothing less than the fate of socialism in general and the political merits of the party in particular. We have seen that the controversy had not had (and could not have had) a political-cum-historiographical conclusion. But, given the vicissitudes examined in the previous chapters, it culminated in the Circular and the ousting of the highest officials responsible for the party-state's cultural policies, which essentially meant resizing the ideological infallibility of the Celestial Palace.

We have also observed how the controversy laid bare the vital role of the cultural apparatus in the overall stability of the socialist state. In order to explore the following acts, namely the bursting upon the scene of the Cultural Revolution's mass movements, we must also consider another peculiar feature. Unlike those that Althusser called the "Ideological State Apparatuses" (ISAs), which he theorized as polycentric and convergent in a unified command only in the last instance, the party-state's cultural apparatus under socialism was highly centralized.[42] It was no coincidence that the official name of the King of Hell's Palace was the Central Department of Propaganda (中央 宣传 部). Moreover, while for Althusser the ISAs have functions distinct from the Repressive Apparatuses of the State (RSAs), what we can call socialism's cultural apparatuses enforced ideological discipline with means similar to those of RSAs. The party-state thus exerted an authority both ideological and repressive. The image of the socialist cultural apparatuses as specialized in policing thought, to which Mao's metaphor of the King of Hell obviously referred, was well grounded.

The political activism of students in the early mass phase of the Cultural Revolution was a result of "chance and necessity." The disbanding of the Group of Five and the disavowal of the policies of the Central Department of Propaganda affected the authority of all the offices of the central cultural apparatus. In the weeks immediately following the Circular, the weakening of their repressive capacity was one factor that favored, or rather did not hinder, the liberation of the imps, schools, and universities. It was something that Mao had hoped for, though without any precise foresight or specific expectations as to the role of the students. As we have seen, he even confided to Albanian diplomats in early May that he doubted the next generation would be able to halt revisionism.

However, student activism soon exceeded educational matters. The political movements on the campuses and in the high schools starting in the summer of 1966 were not merely the implementation of the May 7 Directive. As we will see in the next chapter the crucial issue immediately arose of how to experiment with new forms of political organization.

PART III

A Political Test for Class Politics

6

Testing the Organization

Mao's interventions examined in chapter 5 aimed to highlight the internal weaknesses of the summits of the central state cultural apparatus, starting from the ambiguous and fundamentally censorial nature of their initiatives in those months. Mao wanted to keep open a field of political possibilities that had formed during that historical-theatrical controversy, or better, to mitigate a major obstacle by downsizing the claims of the cultural superego incarnated by the King of Hell.

The appearance of the imps in turn originated from a specific event, the famous "first *dazibao* of Beida" of May 25, 1966, in which a dispute over principle was created on an essential point of the revolutionary culture, namely the possibility of political initiatives outside the exclusive organizational primacy of the Communist Party. Mao immediately attributed a decisive importance to this episode.

Converging Anxieties

The rapid rise and explosion from mid-1966 to early 1967 of independent groups known as the Red Guards (a shorthand umbrella designation that does not fit all, as we shall see) is as much of a conundrum as their equally rapid subsequent self-destructive implosion. The impetus and unfolding of these events were without precedent. The question is, what pushed hundreds of thousands at first, and then millions of China's citizens to turn to direct forms of political activism that would eventuate in the rise of such a vast number of self-organizing groups independent of the party-state? The complementary question is, of course, what led to their self-destruction?

The most common version propounded in explanation is in terms of "charisma." Masses of ingenuous students were drawn in and carried away by the enormous prestige of Mao, that prestige waned, and factionalism ensued. However, the Maoist "personality cult" had been a fixture for years; nor is it accurate to say that it was weakening in mid-1966, or that Mao did everything he could to shore it up. As we noted in discussing *Hai Rui*, the "Maoist" rhetoric was already established—ritual kowtowing to Mao Zedong's thought, to the "shining sun," and so on. Indeed, it was exploited by the official propaganda apparatus to support positions utterly at odds with Mao's. But that litany did not produce, nor was it intended to produce, mass political activism of any sort whatsoever.

In the rapid onset of independent organizations set up by Chinese university students by mid-1966, Mao's prestige inevitably played a certain part, but the real nexus between the vast student movement and Mao's own view is to be sought, rather than in his charisma, in the political anxiety over the probable defeat Mao expressed on a number of occasions at the time. As I've already pointed out, these utterances, far from being a sign of capitulation, were symptomatic of a rationalistic view of the situation, prompted by what he saw as the need for a political movement that would "awaken the attention of everyone."

It was this "mobilizing anxiety" that provided the grounds enabling the mass movement of university students to converge with Mao's own positions. Note that initially Mao made no direct appeal to the students. In fact, he had voiced rather strong doubts in the preceding months that anything of political import could come from China's existing system of schools and universities. He even told the Albanian diplomats in their early May conversations (see chapter 5) that he doubted that the younger generation would be capable of stemming the tide of revisionism.

By mid-1966, however, a spark had ignited the students, and, even though unexpected even by himself, Mao unreservedly supported them. In any event, the spark was as unforeseen as it was unpremeditated by any order of Mao. It is my contention that the anxiety prompted by Mao's warning of a probable defeat found extremely fertile soil among the university students, for several reasons.

Those students were anything but naïve kids in search of some hero to venerate. They were intellectually caught up in the political tensions and disputes of the day. They not only possessed a fairly knowledgeable political culture but were even well versed in what were then the Chinese Communist Party's ideological vicissitudes. In all likelihood, many had followed the *Hai Rui* controversy—most certainly those in the humanities had—and all knew that the May 16 Circular had dismissed the contents of the February Outline and declared the ideological and political authority of the party-state's cultural apparatus unreliable.

Formative too for the political and cultural education of those students were the ever-diverging paths of China and the USSR. Many had read the polemical articles of increasingly shrill tone that the party news organs had been prominently publishing in the decade-long dispute the CCP had engaged in with the CPSU and its satellite parties. The major theme of those articles was that revisionism was the order of the day in the USSR and that it was in the ascendant in the communist parties linked to Moscow. The probable advent of revisionism in China, a threat the May 16 Circular emphasized ("persons like Khrushchev . . . sleep beside us") was thus tantamount to putting paid to the CCP's political existence and to the entire communist enterprise of the twentieth century.

What was new after the Circular was the mass deployment of the "mobilizing anxiety" vis-à-vis the fate of the Chinese Revolution that had prompted Mao's view of the situation. Mao did not order the creation of the Red Guards, nor was he in any position to do so. True, he immediately gave them his unconditional support. Yet the anxiety fomented by the perceived advent of revisionism and the ensuing fallout that would engulf the revolutionary undertaking of communism in China as elsewhere was a major source of political mobilization. It released the main propulsive force driving the movement of student groups. It propelled their rise and provided the political thrust to experiment with independent forms of self-organization capable of putting to the test the leadership role of the CCP in the face of this potentially epoch-making challenge.

I suggest that in mid-1966 a further element of the "political anguish" that was at the source of the Chinese students' activism was the perception that the country's modern cultural and political foundation was in crisis. The communist revolutionary enterprise had intended to reestablish the very idea of "China," destroyed by the ruin of the empire just over half a century earlier. The famous slogan "without the Communist Party there would be no new China" (没有 共产党 没有 新 中国 *meiyou gongchandang meiyou xin Zhongguo*) implied that the revisionist transformation of the CCP, the ruin of the international communist movement, and the undoing of revolutionary culture involved the possible disintegration of that "newness" of China.[1]

The probable defeat thus acted as a motive force conveying energy at various levels simultaneously. China's university students could hardly be indifferent to such an authoritative political aperçu—here Mao's prestige clearly counted a great deal—that focused on the fate of the CCP, international communism, and even of "modern China." The mass student activism was clearly a demonstrative sign of that angst and the determination to deal with it politically. Since the immediate issue at hand was the impending fate of communist politics, experimenting with new forms of political organization was imperative for coming to grips with it. Even so, however, it remains unclear how such a subjective thrust eventuated in a nearly endless proliferation of independent organizations.

The developments of the situation pursuant to the May 16 Circular are to be seen, as in the case of the controversy over *Hai Rui*, as the result of a "necessity" born of "chance." The random factor, the new event, was the first manifesto at Beida and the appearance of the first Red Guards organizations on the campuses in the city. The necessary factor in the situation was the resolve with which the ideological-disciplinary apparatus of the party-state intervened to impede and repress those independent organizations.

The student movement also gained momentum from another quarter. Among the students on the one hand were the "rebels" who confronted the officials the party dispatched to quash the unrest in the universities, and on the other the "loyalists" who supported the party officials. In actual fact, the independent student groups arose not by some specific design but by an unexpected spark, and they continued to spread in response to the repressive measures unleashed by the authorities of the party-state.

When the first dazibao appeared at Beida in early June, a few weeks after the Circular, Mao gave it his approval. Note that this initial manifesto was still an isolated spark. Mao realized its import, however, seeing something at work that he had hoped for but could not have foreseen in the event. And his wholehearted support added fuel to it. When he said it was the "declaration of China's twentieth-century Paris Commune," his statement emphasized the unprecedented nature of that dazibao.

Mao's stance vis-à-vis the Beida dazibao underscores what he saw as something altogether new in the manifesto. Just as the establishment of the Paris Commune in 1871 signaled for the first time the will of workers to take over the levers of the state's governing machinery, the appearance of the Beida dazibao in June signaled for the first time the will of a small group of teachers and students to take a political stance that in the current situation was independent of the party-state. In terms Mao had used previously, what had happened was that the King of Hell's Palace was being overthrown and the little devils, now unfettered, raised their liberated voices to declare their political convictions and determination to retain their independence.

Two Political Processes and Their Entanglement

In chapter 5, I remarked that Mao's statements on overthrowing the King of Hell's Palace and liberating imps outlined the copresence of two registers of politics, *dismissal* and *pluralization*, which he considered fully compatible. I will try to clarify this distinction—a path I have followed for some years[2]—in order to formulate the theoretical pertinence to the study of the Cultural Revolution. "Politics" as commonly accepted today encompasses the exercise of all the actions, declarations, and intentions of those who pursue a particular satisfaction in governing others. This "enjoyment of power" corresponds to Weber's definition of "politics as vocation,"[3] understood as the drive to occupy superordinate positions at various levels in the collective life.[4]

Yet, apart from being a response to a "transcendent vocation," a calling to exercise power over subordinates, politics can assume other immanent forms. There are, in effect, discontinuous moments in the social world, which can unexpectedly bring to the fore egalitarian inventions, experiments seeking new relations among people of notably different persuasions. Politics as vocation is clearly the rule and politics as egalitarian invention the exception. The former is the enjoyment of deciding the fate of others, the latter a set of peculiar experiments since no one knows a priori what "equality" is in the human condition. So my working hypothesis is that pluralization pertains to the exception as dismissal does to the rule. Over the Cultural Revolution's decade, and especially in its first two years, the egalitarian exception and the governmental rule experienced particularly controversial, tumultuous relations.

Dismissal

This descriptor is in a sense the less problematic of the two since it is also quite consistent with a classic conceptualization of political sociology. One typical outcome of competition between rulers and/or would-be rulers, dismissal is the subjective automatism that is omnipresent in every course of action that results in overthrowing, more or less violently, those who govern the life of others from their positions of authority at every level. The same automatism commands the resistance of established authorities to new competitors, as well as all sorts of rivalry among the latter to establish their supremacy in a bureaucratic hierarchy.

This perspective is adjacent to the view that Weber defines as the essence of *Politik als Beruf* (politics as vocation)—the "striving to share power or to influence the distribution of power." The dismissal process is consistent with Weber's politics as vocation since it concerns the claims, acts, and ambitions of those who are, or want to be, in a position to govern others. Dismissal is at once a typical goal of every governmental subjectivity and one of its main results. It is a structural phenomenon: the actors change, but the dismissal remains a general operating rule of thumb in any form of governmental circumstances. Moreover, the higher up the level is, the more violent the conflicts of "striving for power" tend to be.

Dismissal played an intricate role during the Cultural Revolution. It involved the crucial issue of the seizure of power, which in revolutionary culture was seen as the result of class struggle and therefore claimed a higher historical legitimacy. Moreover, dismissal, especially in China at that time, touched upon the question of leadership in revolutionary organizations, conceived of as the result of a struggle between ideological and political lines. These elements added a more "scientific" rationale to the rather fatalistic Weberian *Beruf*, but, as we shall see, the entire historical-political conceptual framework of revolutionary classism played an ambiguous and finally contrasting role. The class-based vision of politics managed to conceptually formulate the progression of events only within the strict limits of the established political discourse: "class enemies" should be "dismissed." However, not only did the subjective novelties of the situation exceed revolutionary classism, but the latter even turned out to be a major political obstacle.

Pluralization

This category leans much less on sociological conceptualization and more on a necessary, albeit tentative, new theoretical approach. While dismissal is the rule, a kind of "recurrent compulsion" in the sphere of governmental subjectivity, namely the desire to compete for supremacy in ruling others, there are also egalitarian exceptions. Those who are usually in the position of being governed, more or less meekly resigned to and even complicit in maintaining the network of social hierarchies, are at times capable of self-organizing their political existence and inventing egalitarian forms of relations, keeping at a distance both the ordinary practices of hierarchic subordination and intragovernmental structural dynamics.

Though it is always tenuous and has to be reinvented in the social condition at any given time, the distance between egalitarian invention and governmental automatisms was particularly intricate in the Cultural Revolution. Even if every egalitarian invention involves a pluralization of political groups, the unprecedented magnitude of a phenomenon that, during the onset of the events, spawned tens of thousands of political organizations—what we might call hyperpluralization—needs to be explained. Indeed, too, just how did these independent mass organizations experiment with equality in the political sense of the term?

There is a distinct trail marker that can provide initial insight for explaining the singularity of this phenomenon. It was laid down in a classic historical locus that is a cornerstone of the modern conception of equality. Saint-Just pointedly argued that equality does not mean that an individual can lay claim "to having the same power" (*puissance*) as any other, in that there is no such thing as "legitimate power" (*puissance légitime*). Rather, "the spirit of equality" means that "every individual is an equal portion of sovereignty" (*une portion égale de la souveraineté*).[5]

This sharing of sovereignty in "equal portions" leads to the radical idea that any individual has the possibility to initiate inventive forms of collective organization. The multiplicity of organizational inventions is therefore a major criterion of any egalitarian invention, or rather its unmeasurable measure. Since political equality cannot but be a set of inventive processes, and nobody has prior knowledge of how to establish it, such an invention should result from countless initiatives for experimenting with organizational forms capable of curbing the ordinary hierarchical rituals of the social condition.

By late spring 1966, the driving force in the creation of an unlimited plurality of independent organizations in China was the urgency to test the very nature of the established political organization, namely the crucial leadership role at the organizational core of revolutionary endeavor, the Communist Party, which for its part was the very paradigm of every egalitarian politics at the time. The Red Guards sprang up as forms of egalitarian experimentation for reexperimenting with equality. This is as much the hard core of their novelty as of their intrinsic fragility.

A crucial issue, especially in the first two years of the revolutionary decade, was the relationship of egalitarian inventions to governmental circumstances. The former cannot, in any event, derive from the latter, which are essentially the escalating network of ritual hierarchy in a given social condition. Egalitarian subjectivities involve a radical dispersal of sovereignty in a multiplicity of political subjectivities that are heterogeneous to the tasks of the "acquisition and distribution of power" in the Weberian sense. Each governmental subjectivity remains, in fact, regulated by the imperative of asserting the superiority of one's "legitimate power," whereas egalitarian subjectivities dissolve any "legitimacy of power."

Indeed, a key issue in this perspective is the difficulty the new egalitarian experiments met in distancing from the intrinsic automatisms of governmental subjectivities. Such an automatism not only inevitably consists of toppling those who occupy, or seek to occupy, the same position of power, but also requires quashing any egalitarian invention not compatible with the dismissal process.

Hypotheses of Periodization

The distinction between the two processes allows us to distinguish dates. Like all mass political events, the Cultural Revolution was marked by a series of internal discontinuities, transitory states that are not immediately apparent. It developed along fragmented, "dashed," lines into quite short periods entailing sudden changes of scenarios, inventive exploits, and unexpected dead ends.

The revolutionary decade consisted of two main periods: the core from late spring 1966 to summer 1968, when the most decisive events took place, and a long coda or "tail" that lasted until autumn 1976. Both periods consisted of stages internal to them. Here we shall concentrate mostly on the central period, the phase of pluralization. Only until the summer of 1968 did independent political organizations external to the party-state exist in China. In the eight years thereafter, the question of how to assess the significance and effects of those events remained open and was the subject of bitter controversies, as were a number of original experiments, especially in the factories and schools, which ceased only upon the arrest of the group of Maoist leaders in October 1976.

The original novelty during the first two years of the Cultural Revolution was the creation of an unrestricted plurality of political organizations: virtually anyone could establish his/her own political organization, whether the Communist Party approved or not.[6] Those independent organizations, known as the Red Guards (actually, this name applied mostly to student organizations), originally arose in the universities and secondary schools but then spread rapidly in the following months among factory workers and employees in all sorts of other institutions. Several of these organizations had their own independent press; they published newspapers, reviews and collections of articles, speeches, and dazibaos, even documents of the party-state that were normally for internal use only. It was the moment when freedom of the press was most widespread in China.[7]

In the central period, 1966–68, two main stages of pluralization are discernible: a *waxing phase* and a *waning phase*, the main political issues at stake being different in each. The subjective motive force changed radically within a few months. The decisive divergences in the first phase, from June 1966 to January 1967, concerned the *scope of pluralization*, that is, the extent of expansion that the organizational experiment could attain, while in the second phase the sole cause of disagreement involved not pluralization but the *annihilation* of a rival organization. The most enigmatic aspect of those events was this unexpected, dramatic change of scene.

Up until roughly the second half of 1966, the main question causing the subjective splits, the motive power of those political events, was how extensive the proliferation of political organizations might be. All disputes in this waxing phase were at every level essentially between those supporting the existence of self-authorizing independent organizations and those that in various ways impeded, or imposed basic limitations on, their existence. All the nuances and the intermediate positions divided across the fault line of this subjective split.

A contrasting process set in during the early months of 1967. The disputes no longer involved divergent statements pro or con self-organization. From spring 1967 to early summer 1968, a series of increasingly uncompromising clashes took place between symmetrically specular declarations and responses: each organization stated that it strove above all to destroy a rival organization. Underpinning the sudden change was the "seizure of power" issue. The various organizations clashed with each other to determine which group of leaders should hold power and which should be overthrown. Each organization considered itself the ultimate guarantee that power would pass into the hands of true revolutionaries and posited the annihilation of any rival faction as the basic prerequisite.

It is my contention that a major factor in the rise and ruin of the Red Guards was the degree of separation, or nonseparation, between the subjective energy for self-authorizing their political existence (the pluralization process) on the one hand, and the dynamics of intragovernmental bureaucratic competitiveness (the dismissal process), on the other. It is with this perspective that I propose distinguishing a waxing phase, even of impetuous growth, from that of a waning, declining phase in the existence of these independent organizations.

In terms of the descriptors discussed above, a peculiar subjective distance between pluralization and dismissal drove the waxing of these independent organizations and the expansion of that mass-scale political laboratory. Yet when the dismissal process later came to superimpose its weight on the pluralization, it caused the waning and final setting of those organizations, bringing the experiment and the extended laboratory to a close. The most evident manifestation of this decline was "factionalism" (派性 *paixing*). It was marked by brawls that were at times violent but, more importantly, increasingly lacking in real political content. In the span of about a year, from spring 1967 to summer 1968, the independent organizations ran out of any subjective novelty and finally ceased to exist.

Expansion of Independent Organizations

In the expansion phase, during which the number of Red Guards organizations reached several thousands, we can pinpoint at least three key moments. Each of them marked a decisive step in that political mass laboratory, overcame a set of specific hurdles, and tackled a peculiar experimental issue. Here is a preliminary list.

The onset ran from the publication of the Beida dazibao in early June 1966 to the end of July, when the failure of the "work teams" dispatched by central party authorities to "politically lead" the students, but in actual fact to keep them under control, became evident. The role of the party leadership in the course of these mass movements was the subject of heated disputes. The second period, over August and September of that year, saw the rapid growth of independent organizations. The "good class origin" criterion as a prerequisite for political activism played a very ambiguous role, which vigorous discussions among the students themselves counteracted and ended up supporting the principle of unconditional pluralization. The third period extended from the constitution in October of the first organizations of "Revolutionary Rebels" among workers in Shanghai to the "January Storm," when the city's governing Municipal Committee collapsed. The main experimental topic was the political value—the role—of the "working class" and its relationship to the party.

It is remarkable that during the expansion phase the main activity of these new organizations consisted essentially of declaring and defending their own existence as independent political bodies capable of issuing statements on fundamental questions of politics and the state itself without any prior authorization of the party-state. This was the case from the first dazibao at Beida. It was signed by Nie Yuanzi[8] and other young teachers and immediately supported by students, who initiated the true mass phase of the Cultural Revolution.[9] The key point in that dazibao is the declaration of a group of "imps" who claimed the right to make their own autonomous political statements and, hence, to organize their own independent political existence. They criticized the "black line" of the rector and the Beida party secretary for having obstructed this self-organizing capability, or, in the language of the time, for having imposed restrictions that did not permit the masses to "make revolution."[10]

The essential content of these political pronouncements was their capability for autonomously organizing themselves and formulating their critiques, but we should try to analyze them beyond the apparent tautology. The cause of disagreement was in fact an issue of the first magnitude. Apart from a certain number of formulas typical of that political culture (including "class," "revolution," "proletariat," "Mao Zedong-thought," etc.) that all the participants used and made the differences among the respective positions hardly distinguishable, the true demarcation line consisted of whether the existence of unrestricted forms of political organizations outside the class party was admissible or not.

The crux of the disputes raging from summer to autumn 1966 was thus a political proving ground targeting the fundamental issue of the organizational condition of politics. This problem did not concern China alone: there were countless grassroots political movements and debates about the "working-class party" and its actual validity throughout the world in the 1960s and 1970s. In fact, the creation of independent organizations in the first months of the Cultural Revolution soon became a mass political experiment to test the Chinese Communist Party and not merely a reaffirmation of the basic freedom of political association. The very concept of the Communist Party as the ruling apparatus of the socialist state claimed to have unquestionably surpassed any previous freedom of association, since it guaranteed the political existence even of those whom capitalism relegates to social inexistence, that is, the immense mass of wage-earning laborers. What the Cultural Revolution proved through a long and tortuous process is that without a surplus of mass political inventions, that "historical guarantee" was fictitious.

In the mid-sixties, this issue was not self-evident. Quite the contrary: it was extremely obscure. The Communist Party was at the core of a well-defined network of historical-political concepts. It was determined—let us mention something of the canonic doctrine—by the history of class struggle, the "dialectics between the development of productive forces and relations of production," the "national conditions," and so on, and even "overdetermined" by the peculiar circumstances of the Cold War era, not to mention the extremely tangled issue of the Vietnam War. Given these conditions, the very idea of a political experiment that would test the validity of China's Communist Party was for the dominant political discourse in the party-state not only unnecessary but also extremely dangerous: class enemies, imperialism, and so forth could easily take advantage.

The Difference between the Internal and the External

In fact, the reaction of the majority of central party leaders at the beginning of summer 1966 was either to obstruct the formation of independent student organizations or to keep them on a short leash in the hands of the party-state. The stakes appeared immediately so high that such top-echelon government leaders as Liu Shaoqi and Deng Xiaoping used their authority to contain the ongoing pluralization. Under their direct command, thousands of senior government officials were organized in groups called "work teams" (工作队 *gongzuo dui*) and sent to the biggest universities, first in the capital, to reestablish order. Their key argument was that "there is a difference between the internal and the external" (内外有别 *nei wai you bie*), that is, internal or external to the party-state. The exercise of political authority was obviously an internal prerogative, to which everything external was subordinate.[11] The Communist Party claimed to be the most advanced form of political organization, had historically transcended freedom of political association, and, a fortiori, admitted of no external interference.

In practice, the work teams were deployed to prevent the instantiation of independent student organizations. At first, they tried to direct the students' activism toward the more traditional organization of the Youth League, a ploy that proved unsuccessful since the students were aware that the members of the league were not politically independent operators. Many of these work teams then relied on the early Red Guard organizations, whose leaders were mostly the sons and daughters of senior party officials (高干子女 *gao gan zi nü*). As we shall soon see, while the early Red Guards, later labeled as "conservative" (保守派 *baoshoupai*), let students engage in political activity, their participation was subject to contrived criteria of class origin, which were simply pretexts to keep the situation under control. At the same time, other new political groups sprang up among the students. These were the embryos of new Red Guard formations, later known as "rebels" (造反派 *zaofanpai*), which would come into open conflict with both the conservatives and, more importantly, the work teams, challenging their authority and manifesting remarkable determination.

Incapable of handling the situation, the work teams ended up labeling as politically suspect the most radically activist students en masse. Although formed by thousands of officials invested with undisputed power and considerable prestige, the work teams never managed to curb the students' activism. The resistance of the latter, which was courageous indeed when you realize that young university students openly confronted senior party officials in heated discussions for several weeks, led to a further loss of the party-state's authority. The work teams, which the students had initially welcomed, thinking the teams had been sent by the party's central leadership to support their critiques of and confrontations with the leading officials on the campuses, found themselves openly and repeatedly criticized within a few days. A growing number of students accused them of imposing forms of discipline that reduced their intentions and political fervor to mindless routines of ritual propaganda.

The officials sent from party headquarters to the universities reacted with heavy-handed discipline. In order to silence their young, impatient critics, they immediately took action and labeled thousands of Beijing students as "rightists."[12] One must remember that in China at the time, as had already been the case in 1957, to label someone as rightist (右派分子 *youpai fenzi*) entailed political and professional disaster, which even extended to his or her family and social circle.[13]

The work teams thus counted on such steps in their efforts to create an effective deterrent. However, they found themselves at a dead end since criticism of them mounted, becoming even more strident and intractable. In order for such extensive coercive measures to be effective, repression on a massive scale would have been necessary. To brand thousands of students of the most prestigious Chinese universities a band of rightists turned out to be a reckless, adventurist decision—Mao said it was "leftist in appearance and rightist in reality."[14] It was the result of the panic that was engulfing almost the entire top leadership of the CCP (Liu Shaoqi and Deng Xiaoping were not alone) when faced with the possibility that the difference between internal and external was blurring. Obviously, the leaders who had organized the work teams justified their action in the name of a superior principle of organization that was strictly consistent—this was the key point—with a class-based vision of politics.

While Liu Shaoqi and Deng Xiaoping had stated that the brief of the work teams was to lead the revolutionary movement, it soon became clear that their real mission was to reestablish order in the universities. Their slogan, "to trace a firm difference between the internal and the external," meant that outside of the party there could only be disciplined, apolitical imps or a counterrevolution to be quashed as soon as possible. The steps undertaken by the work teams were highly censorious, albeit couched in ultrarevolutionary political statements. However, the incongruity between what the work teams were saying and what they were actually doing would soon become patently evident in their confrontation with mass political activism. Thus, not only did the work teams fail to reinstate party supremacy over the students; they were also rapidly discredited. Indeed, their efforts to quell and to disband the independent student organizations only served to reinforce the determination of the latter to endure.

That the president of the republic, Liu Shaoqi, with the full support of Deng Xiaoping, personally directed operations, and that the work teams were composed of middle- to high-ranking functionaries—at Qinghua University they were led incognito by no less a personage than Liu Shaoqi's wife, Wang Guangmei—created a stalemate at the top of the Chinese government.[15] If authority, according to Max Weber's well-known (and rather self-evident) definition, is the capacity to command obedience to an order, the failure of the work teams to obtain obedience in the Beijing universities by July 1966, despite having adopted such drastic punitive measures, led to a major collapse of the authority of the leading party-state elite. Subsequent to that failure, Liu Shaoqi and Deng Xiaoping actually did lose their top positions in late August 1966.

Pluralization and Class Origin

During the period of the largest expansion of mass initiatives, one major issue was how to understand and use politically the reference to "class." We have seen that during the controversy over *Hai Rui* the various participants used the reference to class with totally opposite intentions. During the early months of the mass phase of the Cultural Revolution, class was often an ambiguous argument for hindering mass participation in politics.

The disputes for and against pluralization added fuel to the fire of the political controversies raging inside and outside of the party throughout the following months until late 1966. August of that year saw the release of the Decision in 16 Points, the programmatic document in the ascendant phase of pluralization. Its fundamental thesis was, in synthesis: "In the Great Proletarian Cultural Revolution, it can only be that the masses educate themselves by themselves, free themselves by themselves [自己解放自己 *ziji jiefang ziji*], and nobody can use methods for acting on their behalf [不能采用任何包办代替的办法 *bu neng caiyong renhe baoban daitide banfa*]."[16] This meant that the existence of political organizations external to the party-state was not just fully acceptable but should even be welcomed as a very positive novelty.

However, the fact that forms of mass self-organization were held to be legitimate in principle did not attenuate, but rather worsened and complicated, fundamental contrasts. Everyone saw clearly that the very role of the Communist Party was at stake. The point was, how far could organizations created autonomously outside of the party spread? Should some criteria be applied to determine who might and who might not establish and participate in independent political organizations? Should, for example, the criterion of class, in the sense of belonging to certain social groups that were positively recognized by the state, be considered valid?

The answer to that question seemed to be a foregone conclusion because the class criterion was one of the founding factors in the organization of the state. Socialism operated a strict classification of the people and proclaimed that its own historical rationale consisted in a sort of radical affirmative action in favor of workers and peasants (we can assume that the US version of affirmative action imitated in its own way the socialist class model).

However, even if it meant a temporary reduction in social inequalities, class-based politics remained a device of state order. Though materialist, historical, and scientific, it actually functioned in the socialist state as cognate to the structure of every governmental power, which by means of the recognition of the various parts of a hierarchically structured society operates according to criteria that ritually discipline society's collective life. That this hierarchical structuring was in principle the inverse of the normal one, and that the final rationale of socialist classism went so far as to claim that it would, at some future moment in time, abolish all classes and even the state itself, in no way attenuated its intrinsically disciplinary function—if anything, it simply increased its fictional characteristic.

What emerged from the political clashes in those early months of the Cultural Revolution was that class-based politics might easily turn into an antipolitical criterion. In fact, from the beginning of the mass phase of the events, not only did the most controversial political issues inevitably involve classist references, but, even more remarkably, major hindrances to the pluralization process, which was the real issue at stake, were laid down in the name of class criteria, although in a rather tortuous way. For example, as mentioned above, most of the early Red Guard organizations in the universities and secondary schools of the capital set the issue of a good class background as the fundamental condition for participation.[17] These organizations, dominated by the offspring of the ruling elite, admitted only students from families of workers and peasants, besides, of course, those of revolutionary cadres.

Most of the early "conservative" Red Guard organizations even considered the political attitude of parents as a criterion for deciding participation in the new organizations. For example, students whose parents were labeled as right-wing elements in 1957, or who had less than a good "political reputation," were not to be admitted. However, many of the students at Chinese universities had a "bad" or imperfectly "good" class background, a grouping that included children of the urban middle-, petty-bourgeoisie class or whose parents had more or less explicitly been labeled as politically "backward." As student political activism became more widespread, many of the activists felt passionately involved in that mobilization but found themselves at first excluded from participating in the new organizations. The classist criterion was actually employed as much to ensure the hegemony of the offspring of party officials in the new organizations as to deflect any criticism aimed at party leaders.

The quarrels over the sociopolitical criteria required to take part in the independent organizations became increasingly bitter, and, given the growing political mobilization among students, the growing criticism of the class restrictions imposed by the conservative Red Guards became more and more difficult to quash. Some of the latter thereupon even started openly upholding a particularly obtuse version of classism, the so-called bloodline theory (血统论 *xuetong lun*). It was summed up in the slogan "from a revolutionary father a hero, from a reactionary father a bastard" (老子革命儿好汉, 老子反动儿混蛋 *laozi geming er haohan, laozi fandong er hundan*). No doubt it was a degeneration (a very puerile one, but children can be ferocious) that had nothing to do with Marxist theories. However, it proved highly influential for a while and was a sinister symptom of the effect that classist criteria can have on public opinion in a socialist state.

This aberrant "biological classism" was defeated after various clashes among student groups, the major reason being that such ideological tricks could not constrain the explosion of political activism. The Maoist group was particularly tenacious in criticizing those absurdities, with the added complication that initially they were widespread among student activists. In those months, the position of Jiang Qing became famous: she inverted the slogan and proclaimed that if parents were revolutionaries, then their children should follow their example, but if parents were reactionary, then it was better for the children to become "rebels."[18] Yet, despite being discredited on the political plane, the effects of the bloodline theory continued to poison China's ideological atmosphere in the following years.[19]

The conservative Red Guard organizations were responsible in the summer of 1966 for perpetrating some of the most gratuitous acts of violence against "bourgeois elements." Most of the latter came from families that had been well off before 1949 but that often carried no political weight at the time; some were artists and writers who became easy targets for the demagogy of petty politicians. Frequently, police commissariats even provided the students with the addresses of bourgeois elements. Most of the current images of blind destructiveness wreaked by the Red Guards hark back to these episodes.[20]

Amid all the equivocations concerning class targets, a series of *performances* by those whom one might call anything from "futurists" to "thugs" took place. The episodes were part of a so-called movement against the "four old things"—culture, ideology, customs, habits—and ranged from changing street and shop names to "revolutionary" ones, to plundering the houses of "old bourgeois elements" or damaging historical monuments. Perhaps the most "creative" episode was changing the name of the place where the Soviet embassy was located to 反修路 *Fanxiulu*, "Antirevisionism Road."

On the whole, destroying the four old things was an ambiguous campaign, seemingly supported at the highest levels of the party, whose aim was to direct the attention of student movements toward irrelevant objectives and deflect it from the real issues. By orienting student activism toward a series of obvious class enemies, it would be easier for those who were assigned to counteract pluralization to keep the situation under control.[21]

Finally, if we see pluralization as the basic issue at stake, let us look at one of the best known and most spectacular aspects of the Cultural Revolution in those months—the demonstrations of the Red Guards in Tian'anmen Square in the summer of 1966. Since Mao was also present along with millions of young Chinese from all over the country, they could easily be viewed through the lens of "charisma," "personality cult," and so on. However, if we look beyond the obvious charismatic aspect, the deeper significance of those demonstrations was unrestricted pluralization, given the fact that it would not have been possible to impose class limitations on the participation of millions of students in those demonstrations. As the demonstrations in Tian'anmen Square took place several times, it became clear that anyone could take part in them without any prior restriction pertaining to the social or political status of one's family.

Mao never gave a speech there, simply responding with a laconic 同志们万岁 *Tongzhimen wansui* [Long live the comrades] to the chorus of countless voices shouting 毛主席万岁 *Mao zhuxi wansui* [Long live Chairman Mao]. While he once added, "You must concern yourselves with the great problems of the state and carry the Cultural Revolution through to the end," there was really nothing else to say since the political significance of the demonstrations was precisely the being there of an unlimited pluralization, participation itself being unrestrictedly open to anyone.[22] However charismatic they may have been, the Tian'anmen demonstrations drew Mao's unalloyed support for pluralization and were among the decisive factors that destroyed the limitations arbitrarily imposed in the name of presumed class criteria. By August 1966, Mao's position was clear: "To make revolution you have to rely on yourselves" (搞革命要靠自己 *gao geming yao kao ziji*).[23]

While one should take all historical analogies with a pinch of salt, something about this stage in the Cultural Revolution recalls a similar turning point in the French Revolution. This was Robespierre's speech about the "silver mark." The question then posed to the revolutionaries was whether participation in the revolution should be restricted to those who could afford to pay a tax equivalent to a silver mark. At that time, the role of money as the general equivalent of commodity exchange was a modern "social" novelty of the bourgeois era, as Marx would say, that broke with many traditional bonds. Therefore, one could not take for granted that it might not also be a revolutionary political criterion.

Robespierre, however, was categorical: revolutionaries should reject the restriction of the silver mark because the chance to participate in the revolution depended solely on the "deepest, most heartfelt" convictions.[24] Note that Robespierre did not merely speak against economic inequalities (he was even somewhat fatalistic on the matter); more importantly, he referred to equality in terms of political subjectivities. We can better read Robespierre's standpoint as declaring that egalitarian subjectivities depend on decisions any individual can take and not on belonging to a particular social station—those capable of paying a tax in money—as recognized by established governmental circumstances.

Although the situation was radically different in 1966 China, and essentially incomparable, the pluralization process encountered a similar subjective dilemma. How was it possible to effect a principle of political equality for any single individual in those peculiar conditions when earlier criteria, such as those based on class, which also meant belonging to a certain social station recognized by established governmental circumstances, were turning out to be serious obstacles to mass political activism?

The Decline of Independent Organizations

After having overcome powerful obstacles to pluralization, how the events turned from a movement fueled by enormous, inventive mass energy into a self-destructive drive is an especially notable enigma. The independent political organizations that had sprung up in seemingly endless proliferation—literally tens of thousands set in motion initially by students in late spring 1966 and by workers and urban populations in the months that followed—had reached a dramatic impasse by spring and summer 1967. In events spanning little more than a year thereafter, they would expend their driving energies in a series of clashes among factions intent not to face any real opposing force but to compete for and claim an altogether imaginary political prize they saw as the "seizure of power." By summer 1968, at the height of a frenzy that had drained away any political novelty they had embodied, those organizations lost any capacity for the independence that had sparked them in the previous two years, and they dissolved. (In chapter 8 I will examine in detail the "conclusive scene" of this process.)

These groups had proliferated up to a certain date by a process whose particular political rationale I have attempted to reconstruct. The essence of that mass mobilization was the testing of the political core value of the CCP. The 1967 January Storm exposed the most burning problems of that experimentation. While the analysis of this turning point (see chapter 7) will be decisive for outlining new perspectives on the study of the phenomenon, I can submit here some preliminary hypotheses.

After the January Storm, in fact, the national political scene suddenly changed. In the following months, most of the independent organizations were weakened and finally exhausted by interminable internal conflict. While several details still require careful investigation, the general outcome was undoubtedly a political impoverishment of the new organizations that led to an insurmountable deadlock. From spring 1967 to the summer of 1968, center stage of Chinese politics was held no longer by heated controversies over the extension of pluralization but by the enigmatic phenomenon of "factionalism."

Almost everywhere in China, the thousands of organizations that had arisen in the previous months were involved in countless confrontations between two factions, that is, two opposed mass organizations. It was a radical change: from an unlimited multiplicity to the fixed number of two. Yet it was a "two" that should have turned into a "one," given that the declared intention of each contender was to annihilate the other—as in fact they ended up doing.

In virtually every city and every *danwei*, whether factories, schools, university campuses, government offices, or hospitals, severe divergences separated two factions or groups of factions. In most instances, the two factions resulted from a schism within a previous independent organization to which all the activists belonged. In some cases, various organizations made up two large rival groups in one city, as happened among Beijing students grouped into the "Sky" faction and opposed to the "Earth" faction. These aggregations created a web of alliances that aggravated the clashes between factions, especially among students. Nearly all the countless newly sprung subjective bodies underwent this type of structural schism.

Factionalism had an obscure essence but an apparent phenomenology. It reduced the unlimited plurality of independent organizations to a head-on clash between only two options, which, however many divergences they might initially have had, became formalist and lacking in political content as the months went by. One could easily assume that the most violent clashes of the Cultural Revolution, particularly the factionalist conflicts, were the outcome of an excess of political activism, a sort of hyperpoliticization that led to catastrophe. On closer inspection, however, what brought factionalism to the fore was a peculiar process of political depletion of the Red Guards. Those embryonic hotbeds of political inventiveness lost all their novelty when all the possible disagreements between the two factions were reduced to symmetrical stances, each pursuing an imaginary supremacy of power.

No longer were they the independent political bodies that had achieved their organization by self-authorization and that quarreled with anyone who sought to hinder this determination, as happened from summer 1966 to the early months of 1967. From spring 1967 to summer 1968, conversely, each organization predicated its own existence mainly upon annihilating a rival organization. At the height of this factionalism, each group claimed to embody the nucleus for the regeneration of the party and targeted its rival as the main obstacle to achieving that goal.

The political decline of the Red Guards was quite fast, but driven to a great extent by internal causes and far less by external constraints. In fact, the growing mutual hostility manifested a real political deadlock. The major terrain of disagreement between opposing factions was also two-sided: how the "revolutionary masses," that is, the various independent organizations, should participate in the new lead groups and how to reinstate the previous leaders, including how their roles and attitudes should change. To be sure, the attitudes of individual officials varied during the "storms" too. Higher cadres were often more hostile and lower ones more sympathetic, but virtually the whole system of the party-state's authority vacillated.

In fact, the problem of how to reorganize governmental order even at local levels was clearly not a simple administrative matter but, rather, a crucial political one. The crux of the issue was, given the principle "the masses can free themselves only by themselves," how to reconcile the continuing rise of forms of self-organization and the processes of readjusting the positions of authority in the various ranks of governmental order.

In the terms proposed above, the issue was how to articulate pluralization and dismissal. Mao was initially optimistic about the compatibility of the two processes. As he said in 1967, he hoped that by means of that great mass movement "a form, a mode" (一种形式一种方式 *yi zhong xingshi, yi zhong fangshi*) had finally been found to "reveal our dark side" (揭发我们的黑暗面 *jiefa women de hei'an mian*).[25] By "our" he meant the dark side of the Communist Party itself, namely the dark side of the desire to rule others. While the political experiment as a whole did, indeed, reveal many dark sides of the party-state, it finally proved that the simple combination of dismissal and pluralization under the aegis of the concept of seizure of power brought about a subjective impasse, without leading to the radical renewal in the party Mao had hoped for.

The experimental drive of the latter half of 1966 broke down over the following months into clashes that mimicked, often in the most brutal and grotesque form, bureaucratic infighting within the echelons of the government apparatus itself. Factionalism in our exploratory approach is to be seen as rooted in overlapping the process of pluralization and that of dismissal, the former being the specific phenomenology of egalitarian experimentation and the latter the automatism regulating the relations among governing subjectivities.

Sociological Perspectives on Factional Strife

One of the main obscurities of the factionalist phenomenon lies in its regularity: the schism into two factions was a sort of "social fact," in Durkheim's sense of a phenomenon endowed with an irresistible coercive force.[26] Nonetheless, sociological conceptualizations have hitherto been unable to throw enough light on the essence of the phenomenon. One such approach sought to explain factionalism as a response to given social conditions by interpreting the schisms as stemming from unequal access to economic and political resources.[27] Yet this "social" approach, even if it describes some aspects of the phenomenon, does not touch on the essential political impasse. The main limitation of this approach is that, as widely documented by other studies, activists of opposing factions often had very similar social and cultural profiles.[28]

Another interpretation of factionalism was attempted some years ago by Lynn White. He parsed the schisms as "unintended consequences of socialist state policies," designating the latter as "labeling, monitoring and campaigning."[29] White argues that the violence that erupted between opposing groups during the Cultural Revolution had its roots in the structure of state policies, which had become merely forms of social discipline, such as the use of categories like "class" or "good political behavior."

While the analytical perspective I suggest exploring is different from White's, he grasps an important point when he suggests that the organizational and ideological structure of the Chinese state in those years lay at the root of factionalism. Those students and their new independent political organizations completely failed to break down that scheme after a few months of political vitality. In a couple of years, their political novelty had evaporated. The factionalism of 1967–68, far from being a result of excessive politicization, was actually an effect of the "depoliticization" exercised by the bureaucratic model of the party-state.

One major issue is an adequate periodization, namely whether factionalism was a phenomenon that from the outset accompanied the independent organizations throughout their existence, as the few studies on the matter tend to argue. This is the thesis of Andrew Walder's *Fractured Rebellion*, undoubtedly the most extensive study of the Beijing Red Guards,[30] which considers factional splits as a unitary phenomenon ubiquitous throughout the events.

Although Walder maintains that the splits after 1967 were "unrelated to the factional divide of 1966 and had different causes,"[31] he nonetheless makes factionalism the main interpretive category for the whole period. He admits more than once that "the factional divisions [of 1967–68] were unrelated to the ... split of 1966,"[32] but he also maintains that in any event the Red Guard organizations were "divided at birth"[33] and "factions [were] reborn" after 1967.[34] In other words, Walder, on the one hand, states that the clashes between independent organizations in 1967–68 were not the consequence of the 1966 differences, but on the other hand, he concludes that factionalism was essentially a unitary phenomenon for the whole period 1966–68. I suggest instead that they were two different political phenomena, determined by different motive forces and issues at stake.

In fact, Walder's analysis yields mixed results. In the concluding chapters examining the situation from early 1967 to mid-1968 as the decline of the independent organizations set in, the author captures one key aspect of the situation. He notes that "The opening wedge for this new split was competition to seize power in state agencies."[35] However, the splits that occurred in the latter half of 1966 were not playing for the same stakes. The clashes among contending groups of Red Guards in those months essentially concerned the pursuit of their own independent existence and not the seizure of power.

In the summer and autumn of 1966, there were bitter disagreements over the very existence of independent organizations. The process was tortuous, indeed. The crucial divergences at the time involved profoundly different political choices and touched the essence of political experimentation. Conversely, the clashes between the factions from spring 1967 on essentially concerned symmetrical positions, the striving for power. Therefore, analyzing both the divergences in the second half of 1966 and those of 1967–68 as the same sort of factional clash ends up eclipsing any original political value the independent organizations possessed and leads one to conclude that all those events can merely be lumped together as mass participation in a series of bureaucratic conflicts.[36]

Joel Andreas comes to this conclusion in his sociological analysis of the factions at Qinghua University. Andreas proposes a more refined "social" interpretation, arguing that the split was rooted in the conflict between the "cultural capital" (the traditional, cultured elite) and the "political capital" (the new elite that assumed power after 1949). The typology picked out by Pierre Bourdieu's sociology seeks to provide theoretical consistency to the analysis. However, Andreas admits that in fact the two factions at Qinghua University, the "Jinggangshan" and "14th April"—we will see in chapter 8 the violence of their clashes—did not differ exactly according to the two forms of "capital," because one was highly critical and the other a firm supporter of both the cultural capital and the political capital.[37] Moreover, the distinction according to the typology of "capital," he writes, is applicable only for a few months to the junior high school attached to Qinghua University, which actually gave impulse to the Red Guard movements but was less important in the following developments.

In any case, for Andreas, the Red Guard movement was the result of a series of temporary contradictions within the Chinese elite, who in the end reached agreement and established the present-day constituent alliance of the "new class" in power. Those factional splits during the Cultural Revolution, he concludes, were "part of a longer process of inter-elite convergence."[38]

I suggest that only by starting from the original stakes of the independent organizations—experimenting with new forms of political organization—can their novelty, their point of impasse, and their decline be grasped. A precise periodization is indispensable in this regard. The controversies over the work teams, the disputes about class origin, or the conflict between the Revolutionary Rebels and the Scarlet Guards in Shanghai, which I will examine in chapter 7, although all moments of marked political division in the second half of 1966, are not comparable in content, violence, or duration to the formation and hardening of the factionalist splits in 1967–68. The key difference here is that the confrontations in the latter half of 1966 were political in nature. Their focus was a series of ongoing egalitarian inventions. By contrast, the clashes in 1967–68 were increasingly "absorbed" by the automatisms of intragovernment competition.

Some final remarks on the recent volume by Andrew Walder.[39] *Agents of Disorder* allows us to rethink the issue of factionalism in the light of the largest sociological study conducted so far. While the author confirms the perspective of the other volume (*Fractured Rebellion*), he greatly extends the scope of the analysis, aiming to capture an overview of factional struggles throughout China. Based on the annals that local authorities have published since the late 1970s, which he judges fundamentally reliable, Walder provides a remarkable quantitative description of a series of episodes that marked the factional period, also providing detailed localization and coherent periodization. The data, arranged by months and location, mainly list and correlate the number of violent clashes between factions or with military authorities, the "seizures of power" and the establishment of revolutionary committees, the interventions of the army, statistics of the dead and wounded, as well as individuals branded as "enemies" on one side or the other.

At this level, the analysis is primarily statistical and does not examine specific positions of the individual factions. The examination of those quantitative elements, however, illuminates essential aspects of the phenomenon. One reason not to examine the ideological and political differences between the factions might well have been that these were mutually specular, indeed more and more dictated by opportunistic choices. However, it would be interesting to dig on the political statements with which the actors articulated opposing positions.

Walder also elaborates on a series of theoretical hypotheses that highlight the contingent nature of the constitution of factions and their contrasts. The divisions, he argues, were the result of the interactions between the rebels, the civilian and military cadres—they were the primary "agents of disorder" in the specific circumstances of the collapse of state authority since early 1967. Those divisions did not ground on particular social affiliations, did not reflect vested interests, nor did they derive from the contrasts manifested in the political mobilization of the second half of 1966. Walder maintains as he did in the other volume that the "social interpretation" brought from the first studies on factionalism does not allow us to examine the phenomenon.

His analysis, which essentially covers the period from January 1967 to autumn 1968, shows two key elements. One, not enough examined by previous studies, is the role of the army in establishing and deepening factional divisions. The other key point is that the "seizure of power" was unconditionally the primary issue at stake of every mass episode of the two-year factional period, in particular of its most violent and destructive moments.

Among the elaborate statistics of the volume, there is no shortage of analysis of the number of "abnormal" deaths during that period, which the author estimates 1.6 million. The excruciating issue will probably push reviews and new estimates in defect or excess (I think, for example, of the very divergent estimates of the famine of the early sixties), but as far as it is possible to describe it precisely in quantitative terms, it will not solve the fundamental riddle. What was the essential source of what we can only call a violent death drive? Once ascertained that it did not reflect certain social circumstances, but depended on fresh contrasts risen in that peculiar conjuncture, what inexorable force dragged all its actors in a desperately destructive drift?

The problems that I suggest to explore are mostly two. If factionalism was a singular phenomenon, whose characteristics have been established only since January 1967, that is, in the high tide of the January storm, what role did the Shanghai events play? Moreover, while the divisions between the factions since 1967 appeared on new ground and with new stakes compared to the previous great mobilizations, they were nonetheless mostly composed by the same actors, ultimately the same empirical individuals, who had crowded the political scene in the previous six months.

In this volume, as in the previous one, Walder seems to oscillate between ascertaining the discontinuity and arguing that it was the evolution of the same phenomenon. The seeds of the divisions between the factions, he maintains, were already present in the constitution of the first independent organizations. In conclusion, he argues that the very "cellular" structure of those early organizations, their intrinsic fragmentation, was the preparatory ground for subsequent divisions. For Walder, what I have called pluralization, or rather hyperpluralization, has inexorably evolved into factionalism due to its intrinsic constitution.

However, if the thesis is correct that the factions since January 1967 were results of contingent interactions between the actors, reintroducing a criterion of structural continuity with the previous period does not help to clarify the issue. Walder examines the situation before January 1967 less in detail, also because local annals only record episodes since that time (this periodization of the archive deserves a better discussion). However, probably a comparative examination between the two periods (which the author certainly knows thoroughly) would show, on the level of those quantitative data, only marginal analogies. In fact, not only did the factions not derive from the previous disagreements, but they had entirely different stakes.

Indeed, the independent organizations that arose in the second half of 1966 were extremely fragmented, but the thrust to their existence was not the seizure of power. On the other hand, the fragmentation of the first independent organizations did not constitute a structural model of the subsequent factional division, because in the first case, the pluralization was unlimited. In contrast, in the second case, everything was inexorably linked to a unitary pattern. The first independent organizations multiplied indefinitely. Instead, factions or faction alliances since 1967 were only "two" everywhere, and above all, their essential thrust was to become the only "one" through the annihilation of the enemy.

The impetuosity of pluralization had, as its carrier, the affirmation of new possible forms of political organization. The knot of all the contrasts had been the attitude, favorable, contrary, or skeptical, toward these possibilities. Such mass political vitality could not have turned into violent, mutual, and symmetrical hostility without certain conditions. The hypothesis that I will discuss in the next chapter is that the transformation of those subjective energies into deadly thrusts must have entailed a key passage, an impasse that triggered the dialectical transformation of the former into their opposite.

In order to disentangle this impasse, the analysis will focus on the Shanghai events known as the January Storm. If the "seizure of power" constituted the stake, identical and contrary, and therefore mutually destructive, of the contenders, it will be necessary to examine the category carefully. It has never happened that "seizure of power" was the primary name of a period of mass riots so ruinous, prolonged, and widespread. What the "seizure of power" actually meant cannot be taken for granted.

The path followed in the next chapter will be the exam of the singular vicissitudes of the seizure of power in early 1967 in Shanghai. The existence of such a vigorous mass movement for six months and the progressive paralysis of the authority of the party-state had already destabilized ideologically and organizationally the horizon of revolutionary culture, within which that category occupied a central place. In January, in the space of a few weeks, the Shanghai events produced a point of no return. The main actors of political mobilization, the rebels and the Central Group of the Cultural Revolution, actually groped to seek the way out of an impasse. The decisions that Mao made at that time, including his hesitations and second thoughts, undoubtedly played a crucial role. In order to evaluate properly this passage, it is necessary to examine some detail, as will be done in the next chapter.

7

A Subjective Split in the Working Class

Students Waiting for the Workers

The mass phase of the Cultural Revolution, started in the universities, soon involved, by autumn 1966, widespread activism among workers. This development had a logical necessity. Since student activism had focused immediately on experimenting with new forms of political organization and called into question the monopoly of the Communist Party, the issue of workers' politics inevitably emerged, since the relationship of party to workers was the core of its organizational primacy. After all, the CCP was the avant-garde and supreme historical and political representative of the working class. Such an ambitious mass experiment dealing with its political value entailed the attitude of the workers as the decisive testing ground. The student mobilization, in this regard, heralded the arrival on the scene of the workers.

On this plane, the Cultural Revolution anticipated a phenomenon that occurred in national situations completely different from China. In Italy and France, as is well known, student movements similarly stimulated worker activism. The knot of universities (and students), factories (and workers), and party systems (particularly communists) in the sixties is very intricate and still in need of detailed exploration. Here we can only recall that the modern university, workers' politics, and the parties of the twentieth century have far more in common than meets the eye. The fact that at the worldwide level the university crisis and the crisis of the parties are rooted in the sixties is no accident. After all, the mass parties and the modern university (and state school systems) are the same age. They were formed through deeply connected processes at the end of the nineteenth century, and in the 1960s they were engulfed by interconnected crises.[1]

By summer 1966, when college students in China initiated experimenting with new forms of organization, the issue of the relationship between workers and party was necessarily going to emerge as central. In a sense, the rebel students were "waiting for" the rebel workers. With the entry of the latter on the political scene in the last months of 1966, the face-off between the new political subjectivities of the Cultural Revolution and the key revolutionary concepts reached maximum intensity. As we shall see in this chapter, the political experimentation in the following months inevitably involved at a deeper level the concept of class, which was the most basic historical-political concept (what made the political unity of the "working class"?), and more essentially that of the seizure of power, which in revolutionary culture was ultimately the compass of any political initiative.

An immediately apparent facet of this chapter on labor activism in Shanghai from late 1966 to early 1967 is the workers' notable level of political culture. The mass campaigns of political education in China had in less than two decades brought to the fore a generation of politically sophisticated workers capable of resolute and subtle argumentation. Yet, despite this circumstance, the relationship of their activist mobilization to their political culture was the crux and real epicenter of a problematic situation and the crucial events it triggered over that politically charged decade.

Independent Workers' Organizations?

The autumn of 1966 proved to be the decisive turning point for the entire central period of the Cultural Revolution, as well as for the decade as a whole. The question that then came to the fore was whether workers too, not just the students, could create independent political organizations. The issue became the decisive test of the political experiment. Since the matter concerned the workers, the class reference was obviously ubiquitous, though again playing an ambivalent role. The concept of the "working class" was even deployed as an argument to counter independent worker organizations.

The issue involved a web of theoretical and organizational references that were far more realistic than the sinister fantasizing of the "conservative" Red Guards on the bloodline theory in the previous months. Although bitter, the disputes all pivoted on one major political issue: the political role of workers under socialism and their relationship to the CCP. The first of the independent political organizations among workers appeared that autumn in Shanghai. While the Decision in 16 Points of the preceding August did not exclude them, it did not deal explicitly with the issue. Over the next two months, the party center issued contradictory directives that ranged between excluding or admitting this possibility. The dilemma was situated at the main crossroads between ideology and organization. Since in principle the CCP's historical task was to represent all the possible interests of the working class, independent workers' organizations outside of the party were unthinkable. If the grassroots emergence of independent student organizations had raised such controversy, the sprouting of workers' organizations could not but raise the temperature even higher.

The Shanghai Workers Revolutionary Rebel General Headquarters

When the first groups of workers announced the formation of the Shanghai Workers Revolutionary Rebel General Headquarters (上海工人革命造反派总司令部 *Shanghai gongren geming zaofanpai zong silingbu*; hereinafter WGH) that November, the entire leadership of the CCP was perplexed. Even the Maoists belonging to the Central Group of the Cultural Revolution (中央文革小组 *zhongyang wenge xiaozu*; CGCR) were initially unable to express a clear position. For their part, the head of the Shanghai Party Committee (SPC), Chen Pixian, and Shanghai's mayor, Cao Diqiu, were firmly opposed to the WGH and repeatedly and in unison declared it illegal.

The WGH therefore arranged for mass delegations to go by train to Beijing, where the great demonstrations had taken place in Tian'anmen, the symbol of unrestricted pluralization. They intended to meet the Central Group of the Cultural Revolution in order to argue that the WGH was a revolutionary political organization and not the counterrevolutionary movement the Shanghai party authorities had been stubbornly insisting it was.

The first group of demonstrators did not get very far. At Anting, a small railway station at the gates of Shanghai, the authorities blocked the train with two thousand demonstrators and kept it waiting for two days. The workers refused to leave the train and the authorities refused to grant them any concessions. The Central Group of the Cultural Revolution, surely at the request of the Shanghai party leaders, then sent an urgent telegram to the workers on the train. Drawn up and signed by Chen Boda, it did not address any of the workers' requests.

In wording that repeated canonic formulas, the telegram only invited everyone to calm down and go back to work in order to "take firm hold of the revolution and promote production," and it studiously avoided mentioning the issue of the revolutionary character of the WGH, which was the subjective core of the situation.² The demonstrators' reply, voiced by Wang Hongwen, one of the initiators of the WGH, left no doubt: the telegram could not but be "false"!³ The demonstrators insisted they wanted to go to Beijing to discuss the matter and to present their case directly to the party's central leaders.

The situation was unprecedented. In a socialist state founded on the dictatorship of the proletariat, here were workers declaring themselves revolutionary communists while affirming their intransigence on a fully political matter, namely their capacity to organize themselves autonomously. Their position was an open challenge to all forms of established political organization, including that of the Maoist group. As with the independent student organizations, the nub of the political declarations of the Revolutionary Rebel Workers concerned the fact that they alone authorized the establishment of an independent political body capable of autonomously formulating declarations about crucial political issues.

As noted above regarding the student organizations, the apparent tautology concerned the crucial issue of the situation. Declaring and defending the existence of their own independent organization was the requisite condition for participating in the ongoing mass political laboratory. The key point of the experiment was, once again, unrestricted pluralization. Conversely, to condemn the existence of "rebel" organizations was to reject any experimentation and to affirm the exclusive governmental nature of the CCP.

Nobody knew how to solve the problem, certainly not the SPC, whose refusal remained adamant. Even the ideas of the CGCR were quite hazy. While Chen Boda's telegram was not false in a factual sense, it certainly did not convey any "truth" able to come to terms with the singularity of the situation. Yet no one in the Beijing Maoist group had raised any objections or proposed alternative options. Not even Mao himself had expressed an opinion. In fact, it was impossible for those in Beijing to know exactly what was happening in Anting.

On November 11, the CGCR sent Zhang Chunqiao to Shanghai to deal with the problem, although without giving him any precise mandate. Zhang proved to possess outstanding political qualities: he managed to understand the novelty of the situation and reached a successful agreement with the workers in Anting. He carried out a thorough investigation, spoke to participants and observers, listened to the demonstrators' requests, and, within a very short time, personally assumed responsibility for and the risk of accepting the workers' demands.

However, Chen Boda's telegram was a de facto endorsement by the CGCR of the position taken by the Shanghai party authorities and circumvented the basic request of the Revolutionary Rebel Workers. Zhang thus ran the risk that both the CGCR and the local party authorities might turn on him. He also had to overcome considerable mistrust from the workers. Since Zhang was not only an envoy from Beijing but also a Shanghai official, many demonstrators in Anting initially saw him as a bureaucrat sent merely to placate them. The performance of the work teams in the universities some months earlier and the attitude of the Shanghai authorities in those weeks justified such misgivings. Only after intense negotiations did Zhang reach an agreement with the rebels, acknowledging that their declaration of an independent revolutionary organization was right. The Revolutionary Rebel Workers agreed in turn to discuss the problems in Shanghai, not in Beijing, in a series of meetings to be held over the following days.

The CGCR realized at once that Zhang had made the right decisions, and Mao complimented him on having been able to do so without any formal backing. The agreement, however, contradicted the standpoint of the party leaders in Shanghai and, since only Zhang had signed it, they did not recognize it as legally binding. The mayor and the head of the SPC repeatedly stated that Zhang had "capitulated" before people they considered thugs and he had, hence, renounced the very organizational principles of the CCP itself.

The Scarlet Guards

The Shanghai party authorities were initially confident they could outmaneuver the Revolutionary Rebels, who were, after all, only a small minority among Shanghai's workforce. Their first move was to sponsor the formation of a "loyalist" workers' group, backed by the official trade unions and the party organization in the factories. The loyalist organization, which was unsurprisingly set up immediately after the "Anting incident," assumed the name of Scarlet Guards (赤卫队 *chi weidui*), obviously flaunting an even brighter shade of red.

The name, as Walder notes, came from the groups of Russian workers who rose up together with the Bolsheviks.[4] The adjective "scarlet" therefore contained a reference to orthodoxy, which the rebels instead carefully avoided. Moreover, the adjective "scarlet" to designate loyalist organizations only appeared in the autumn, when "red" organizations had existed for months. Scarlet was a response to red, and even that nuance revealed that the whole tradition of relations between workers and communist parties was in question. At any event, the political program of the Scarlet Guards consisted of a single aim: to declare the existence of the Revolutionary Rebels unacceptable. The rebels, they argued, were counterrevolutionaries and enemies of the working class, which could only be represented by the SPC.[5]

The sponsoring of the Scarlet Guards by the local party authorities was as decisive in their rise as in their following collapse. Yet the initial popularity of the Scarlet Guards among the workers did not merely result from the support and the control of the SPC. The Scarlet Guards organized and exacerbated the bewilderment of a significant portion of the workers themselves, initially the majority, when faced with the appearance on the scene of the unknown political figure of "worker" that did not exist in the purview of the socialist state.

Most Shanghai workers initially supported the Scarlet Guards because of the solid prestige the party enjoyed among them. The argument of the loyalists can be summarized as "defending the acquisitions of Socialism."[6] In order to safeguard such acquisitions, the working class should exist politically only within the party's organizational framework and should firmly oppose all independent organizations of the workers as antisocialist and antirevolutionary. Yet the new body of worker political activism specifically took issue with this view. For them, the ability to create independent organizations was the sign of an even stronger revolutionary determination. The opposing fronts grew rapidly until there were hundreds of thousands of members on both sides. Within a few weeks, virtually all of Shanghai's working class was involved in the dispute.

The attitude of the Scarlet Guards ended up reflecting the predicament of the Shanghai party authorities, who had no strategy whatsoever for dealing with the new situation except remaining ensconced in their positions of power. The SPC could neither readily resort to ordinary repressive measures against the rebel organizations nor propose anything to their Scarlet supporters except the defense of the status quo at a time when unprecedented political activism flourished among the Shanghai workers. Thus, the activism of the Scarlet Guards was restricted to a series of confused provocations. In fact, collisions between the groups were never extremely violent, although there were of course very tense moments of physical clashes. However, given the immense political issues at stake and compared with the harshness of conflicts in other parts of China in the following months, these episodes were limited and finally secondary with respect to the ongoing subjective process. The Cultural Revolution in Shanghai was almost trouble-free.

The Scarlet Guards' real raison d'être, and the reason why they were sponsored by the SPC, was to oppose the very existence of the WGH. The rebel workers, who by December were attracting as many new activists as the Scarlet Guards, pressed the SPC leaders to reduce their pressure in opposition to the political existence of the WGH. Conversely, the Scarlet Guards insisted the ban on the WGH be kept and on several occasions clashed with them. Besides instigating episodes of senseless provocation (they even threatened to ransack the home of Zhang), the loyalists met with firm resistance by the rebels.

Incapable of dealing with the confusion it had stirred up, the SPC vacillated day after day between confirming support for the Scarlet Guards and accommodating willy-nilly some demands of the WGH. When in late December the Scarlet Guards rioted in front of the seat of the SPC, blaming their sponsor for having been too lenient toward the WGH, the SPC suddenly pulled its support from under their feet. It was a decision as unexpected as it was self-contradictory, since it disavowed the Scarlet Guards as being incapable of undoing the WGH while blaming them for behavior the SPC had intentionally instigated but that ended up increasing an instability that was severely undermining the position of the SPC itself.

The upshot on the one hand was that the WGH was now free to exist, even without the support of the SPC—its subjective determination was, if anything, considerably reinforced by its refusal to submit—and on the other hand, the Scarlet Guards suddenly collapsed without the support of the SPC. One can easily imagine the disorientation of hundreds of thousands of workers who for weeks had believed they were the collective personification of the loyal socialist worker.

Working Class, Industrial Danwei, and the Communist Party

Far from being a local case of riots involving opposing groups of the population, the divide in Shanghai's working class called into question the value and the universality that key concepts in the socialist political culture supposedly held, including that of the working class whose ideological and organizational role was foundational. To explore this fault line and its long-term consequences, we shall need to reconsider some theoretical issues. The Shanghai January Storm was a dramatic face-to-face encounter between a vision of communism as a set of experimental inventions, which the self-organization of the rebels brought into the political arena, and the vision of communism as a form of government, which was then hegemonic in the socialist states. The main divide between the Cultural Revolution and the revolutionary culture passed through these visions.

Of course, this was not the first time that revolutionaries had advocated an experimental vision of communism. Indeed, it played a decisive role in each key moment of modern egalitarian politics inspired by Marxism. Both Marx and Lenin engaged in bitter polemics against the idea of communism being primarily a peculiar form of the state, albeit in principle a transitional stage on the way to the extinction of the state itself. However, after having long been seen as a fully settled issue after the establishment of the socialist states, only with the Cultural Revolution did the reinvention of an experimental communist politics reappear as decisive.

Significantly, the divide separating the two ideas of communism reemerged as the most controversial factor at a time of intense political activism among workers. The January Storm was another major political test, this time conducted by the workers themselves, who brought their efforts to bear on their peculiar role in the very conception of the socialist state.

Socialism promised to bring political recognition to the worker and, hence, to radically change his or her social status. Capitalism recognizes the worker only insofar as he or she is a seller of labor force, an accessory attached to machine systems like the contemporary variant of the "animated tool" of ancient slavery, yet subject to the unconditional authority of factory command. Workers can sometimes bargain a bit over the price of their "commodity" (labor power), but it will be the free market that is the final arbiter. Even when workers engage in resistance vis-à-vis the technical despotism of factory organization, they must still face the absolute authority of factory hierarchies. The commodification of the labor force, the technical division of labor, and factory despotism are, to use a Maoist image, the "three heavy mountains" that oppress the workers in capitalist society.

Under capitalist conditions, the worker is an "inexistent," as Badiou would put it, or as Marx wrote, he has nothing to lose but his chains. The relations between worker and capitalist factory localize a void of sociality, a point of decoupling, or a loose thread in the social fabric. The main task of factory despotism is ultimately to prevent the consequences of this social decoupling. Today more than ever, no encomium of free enterprise as the prerequisite for democracy can conceal the fact that the capitalist government of labor is a model of integral dictatorship over wage laborers.

The socialist state in principle sought to turn this social inexistence into a complete social and political recognition of the workers and of their relations with the workplace. In the socialist political discourse, what Schurmann called "ideology,"[7] the major guarantee of this recognition was the very role of the communist party as the representative of the working class. Moreover, in the terms of what Schurmann called "organization," its peculiar institutions embodied the promised universal recognition of the worker.

To this purpose, one structural prerequisite of government in the socialist state was to include workers and factories within the organization of the state itself.[8] The socialist factory, like the *kombinat* in the Soviet Union or the industrial danwei in China, was not only a state institution; even its administrative structure provided a model of institutional organization for the entire Chinese urban society. In China even a university, a hospital, or a post office was a danwei.[9]

However, the danwei system was not merely some sort of supreme realization of the Hegelian ideal of the universal homogeneous state, capable of extending recognition (*Anerkennen*) even to the inexistent. It aimed primarily to break with the dogma of wage labor and proclaimed that it was possible to organize workers and factories in a way that was utterly different from that found in the capitalist system. The danwei was thus an inventive form of political organization, which even influenced the general forms of socialist government.

Factory and state were thus actually interdependent. In China, the socialist factory was a key articulation of a vast organizational apparatus that even played an essential unifying institutional role. On the other hand, only because it was included in the institutional framework of socialism could the industrial danwei exist as an exception to the capitalist factory. The danwei system thus had two faces. It was an organizational invention of a factory beyond capitalism and an apparatus for ruling the industrial labor power. As a form of government, however, the industrial danwei sought to prevent, albeit with methods different from those of capitalist command, the same risk of social decoupling intrinsic to the relations between worker and factory in the modern social world—that is to say, the void of sociality they compose. The danwei therefore included both of them in a sort of "small society" that was essentially a state institution whose constituent elements were purposed for managing risks that could lead to such a void. Especially in China, the latent contrast between its constituent elements—the audacity of the political experiment and the mere governmental function of a peculiar form of handling the industrial labor power—was a constant in the socialist factory.

A similar ambivalence was constitutive in the figure of the model socialist worker. With the abolition of private ownership of the means of production and, hence, the abolition of the labor market, workers no longer were sellers of labor power but part and parcel of a system of government that professed to be an alternative to capitalism. However, they remained subjectively suspended between the political activists, who had joined a universal political project, and the regimented figures in a government ceremonial who would end up being celebrated for their "heroic" productive capacities.

Such intrinsic discord in the major conceptual nexus of factory and worker was not self-evident. It came to be a critical issue only through the prolonged subjective controversies that involved several hundreds of thousands of workers and finally the entire city of Shanghai. On the one hand was the urgency, which the WGH acutely made manifest, of thoroughly rethinking the political role of workers in the government of the socialist state, and on the other was the anxious denial of that urgency, which determined the response of the SPC and initially of the majority of workers in the city.

It would be misleading, however, to consider the fault line as the divide between acceptance and refusal of the political role of workers in the governmental circumstances of Chinese socialism. Whereas the ritual version of the socialist worker was unproblematic for the loyalists, it represented a source of agitation for the WGH rebels, who would never relinquish their political role with respect to the government. They were, if anything, eager to engage in real political activism regarding issues of state. They immediately formulated their concerns in an effective prescription to the Shanghai government in the name of the general interest of the population. Early in January, as we shall see, they declared that the decisions taken by the SPC were inadmissible and "null," a statement that eventually led to the collapse of the SPC's authority.

During the January Storm, the rebels were proud of demonstrating a higher sense of collective responsibility. They were even able to replace the management of economic activities when the SPC pulled the plug on the Scarlet Guards. In effect, what is most impressive about the statements issued by the WGH is the evident strength of conviction they bore, since they were formulated from the singular space of their self-organized political invention and, hence, at a peculiar distance from the party-state.

It bears remarking here that the ability of the rebel workers to address the party-state without fully identifying with it necessarily involved a questioning of their supposed political existence. The identity the socialist worker received by inclusion as "working class" in the institutional framework of socialism had become dubious and required new exploration and political experiment.

The shattering of the privileged relationship between class and party inevitably destabilized the conceptual and organizational chain that bound the worker, or rather the working class, to the socialist factory through a Communist Party that represented it in the state. On the other hand, the destabilization of that conceptual chain—so crucial to revolutionary culture—disclosed that the working class, without thoroughgoing political reinvention, was merely part of a governmental device that by itself carried no guarantee whatsoever that workers could exist politically. The subjective divide in Shanghai ran not only between rebels and loyalists but, more essentially, into the very concept of the working class and its relationship to the governmental circumstances of socialism itself. Since the Cultural Revolution, it has been impossible to refer to the category of the working class without taking into account the deep-seated and long-term consequences of that subjective division.

Two Crucial Political Statements of the Rebels

The controversy between the WGH and the SPC reached its peak early in January. After having withdrawn its support of the Scarlet Guards as an organization, which led to the latter's disbanding in late December, the party authorities did not cease using their influence over the loyalist workers to obstruct the independent organizations and reestablish control over the situation. The SPC took two rather sensational steps that, in response, the WGH soon turned into the SPC's complete loss of authority.

The first step was to incite the loyalists to abandon their jobs and go to Beijing to "present their grievances" to the Cultural Revolution Central Group, as tens of thousands of workers actually did. The result was obviously to paralyze key economic activities in Shanghai, even threatening to cut off the municipal supply of water and electricity. This "strike from above" had the effect of creating chaos and anxiety among the population and was certainly seen as the prelude to an attempt by the SPC to return to center stage as the guarantor of public order that would sweep away the chaos it had deliberately created. The ultimate aim was undoubtedly to suppress the rebels.

At the same time, the Shanghai party authorities undertook a mass distribution of money to the workers under such guises as wage increases, bonuses, travel subsidies for "exchanges of revolutionary experiences," and so on. They expected to meet immediate and indisputable favor among the workers for the monetary benevolence showered upon them.

The prompt response of the independent workers' organizations gave a dramatic turn to these events. The following days saw the WGH and other rebel organizations publish two crucial political pronouncements—the "Appeal to All Shanghai People" and the "Urgent Notice"—each proof of remarkable acumen in grasping the singular stakes of the situation and the difficulties to be overcome regarding both the loyalists and the SPC.[10] The two statements, whose very titles stressed the gravity of the situation and the urgent need for a clear stance, dealt with the two main political issues of the situation: the split among the Shanghai workers and the attitude of the SPC.

The rebels addressed their messages to the newly disbanded loyalists and to the still powerful SPC in strikingly different tones. They called the Scarlet Guards "the broad sections of our class brothers who want to make revolution" and invited them to join their resolute political struggle and not be hoodwinked by the SPC. As to the latter, conversely, the rebels demanded the SPC immediately stop inciting workers to walk off the job and to withdraw the decisions concerning the bonuses and wage increases. The documents were thus a deliberate warning to the local party authorities, declaring them liable for all the waste of money and destruction of public resources resulting from their actions, which the rebels inevitably labeled a "bourgeois reactionary line."

The distinction made by rebels was indeed remarkable since it was not easy to disentangle the behavior of the disbanded loyalists from the moves of the SPC. In fact, the Scarlet Guards were becoming even more easily manipulable by the SPC after self-dissolving as an organization. In the bewildering situation that followed, when the loyalists were invited to walk off the job and even encouraged to do so by the substantial financial incentives the party authorities were offering, they could seemingly have their cake and eat it too by way of compensation and personal revenge.

The SPC, meanwhile, was employing tactics typical of the way government authorities react in situations where the rise of mass independent political organizations haunts them but they cannot directly resort to repressive methods. The powers that be invariably try to create confusion in such cases, to fish in troubled waters, in order to pit one side against the other and to divert the original subjective intentions of the newly formed mass organizations toward irrelevant goals. Had there been a follow-up move, it surely would have called upon the repressive apparatus to complete the task of restoring law and order. But in those early days of January the SPC decided to sponsor a sort of huge protest strike by the disbanded loyalists while spreading a lot of seed money around as encouragement.

The deliberate purpose of the Appeal and the Urgent Message was to clarify waters that the gambit of the SPC had made extremely muddy. They reaffirmed their political novelty as independent organizations, criticized the attitude of the SPC, and confuted the version of the situation that the latter was trying to pitch among the workers. The issue at stake was the relationship between the existential determination of independent worker organizations and the attitude of categorical refusal by the Shanghai party authorities. In the language of the rebels, the question they posed to the SPC boiled down to whether it wanted to promote the revolutionary activism of workers or implement a bourgeois reactionary line.

In acting as it did, the SPC left the rebels in no doubt about its intentions. Their response was immediate and quite clear-cut: they declared the steps taken by the Shanghai party authorities—the cash windfall and permission for temporary leave—"null and void." By contrast, the register of the two statements for the Scarlet Guards and for all the workers involved had a more persuasive tone, arguing that the aim of mobilization was to affirm their political existence, not to negotiate wage increases nor as a form of struggle intended to halt production by means of a strike.

It was strange indeed, the rebels said, that the government magnanimously granted wage increases and bonuses without an obvious motive, which in the view of the rebels could only be to curb the political intentions of the workers through corruption. Moreover, the SPC now displayed a rather lenient attitude toward the workers taking a leave of absence, whereas it had roundly decried the formation of the WGH in November as damaging to the official line of "make revolution and stimulate production."

A remark on this point: It was seemingly contradictory that in the end the rebels adopted this slogan to defend their own position against the SPC and to appeal to the Scarlet Guards to refrain from quitting the workplace. Clearly, "make revolution and stimulate production" was entangled in the intrastate web holding workers under socialism—that is, the inclusion of workers and factories in the state sphere—and certainly lent itself to being used as a Stakhanovist slogan, as in fact occurred.

For the rebels, however, the slogan's tail, "stimulate production," was intended to be part of their appeal aimed at redressing the near economic paralysis caused by the loyalists walking off the job, an action that also put at risk the existence of independent organizations. Note that throughout these events, the rebels never repudiated the peculiar position assigned to them in the socialist state. In fact, while they were even rather proud of it, they managed at the same time to keep their distance from the ritual, and finally apolitical, role it entailed. Apart from and beyond the obvious rhetorical note, "make revolution" was the touchstone for reinventing their political role within socialism.

Another remark is necessary concerning the "criticism of economism." Here, too, the rebels pursued an immediate goal. The SPC's distribution of funds was clearly intended to corrupt workers as well as to create confusion over the existence of independent organizations. On the other hand, some studies point out that the various organizations that arose in Shanghai that January included groups of workers whose appeal was based on economic demands.[11] There were, in fact, several inequalities in the status of the Shanghai workers, such as between those on contract, a category that had swelled quite a bit by the early sixties, and those permanently incorporated in the industrial danwei.

While these elements were certainly part of the overall social situation of Shanghai's workers at the time, the problem is whether economic demands were part of the core political issue at stake—rethinking the role of workers under socialism. In fact, the discontinuity between the social status of workers and their possible political existence has been one of the thorniest problems of the revolutionary tradition of the twentieth century. By using the term *economism*, rebel workers explicitly raised the issue of the singularity of the political figure of the worker with respect to its social position.

For Lenin, the founder of the concept of "criticism of economism," it is not possible to infer the political figure of the worker from his social position. As noted above, the worker under capitalism has in principle no existence, except that of being one commodity among many others; labor power is simply sold in exchange for wages. However, the mere negotiation of this purchase, although indispensable for surviving under capitalist conditions, not only does not guarantee such a political existence; it even obscures the political stakes at play. Lenin wrote that the political existence of organized workers is a "deviation" with respect to their social status. The SPC attempted to quash this deviation, whereas the rebel workers refused to allow their political activism to be reduced to bargaining for wage increases.[12]

Obviously, the rebels were aware that economic inequalities among workers did exist, and they were surely not for perpetuating them. What was essential for the rebels in counteracting the maneuvers of the SPC was to make it crystal clear that their struggle had nothing to do with a workplace strike. Put another way, they eschewed both the role of labor-selling workers of capitalism and the ambiguous ritualism of the workers' status in the socialist state. This dual deviation from both twentieth-century models of the worker created an absolute novelty in the January Storm. It was the manifest strength of this political novelty in the Appeal and the Message that eventuated in the collapse of party authority.

What political consequences the revolutionaries drew from this collapse was a primary issue in the following days. The formula adopted quite soon, on Mao's initiative, was to call the January Storm a "seizure of power." In fact, the first indubitable result of the two statements was to deprive the SPC of authority. When the rebels declared its actions to be inadmissible and its decisions null and void, the SPC no longer commanded obedience and collapsed.

Seizure of Power

Since the January Storm was ultimately the test bed of the relations between the CCP and the working class, its consequences for later developments in the Cultural Revolution were far-reaching and inevitably entangled both in Shanghai and in the rest of China.

Those events marked the pinnacle of pluralization and the furthest extent of the experiment's reach. Moreover, I suggest that the watershed between the expansion and decline of independent organizations must be searched for in the aftermath of the January Storm. Yet how was it possible that the zenith of pluralization was also the immediate antecedent of its waning? The discontinuity between the two periods is far from self-evident.

The path I propose for examining the dramatic change of scenario focuses on the seizure of power as a key issue for the entire framework of Marxist-Leninist political knowledge, and examines the effects of this conceptual knot on the political situation of the early months of 1967 in China.

Historical materialism intended to provide a rational anchor for the concept. In principle, seizure of power in revolutionary culture was the result of the class struggle, which involved radical oppositions between different visions of politics and the state. It was not merely the "fight for the acquisition and distribution of power," which Weber considered the essence of "politics as a profession." In fact, the Weberian concept merely describes a sort of "instinct" that is omnipresent in any governmental subjectivity, which in itself is simply power for the sake of power, without any difference in principle among competitors.

It is true that in the revolutionary history of the twentieth century, the concept of seizure of power had also been a source of opportunism, arbitrariness, despotism, and even of a terrorist vision of the socialist state. The nodes of all these ambiguities came to a head during the Cultural Revolution. Yet the "seizure of power" in the ideology of the communist parties of the twentieth century, despite all, claimed to be a rational principle, the crux of a historical vision of politics. The revolution was the "locomotive of history," and seizure of power was its strategic task.

Mao on the Seizure of Power in Shanghai

Since the declaration that the January Storm was a seizure of power came first from Mao, we should start discussing his positions during those weeks. Once again, focus on declarations will make the narrative somewhat heavier, but the political issues at stake, I hope, will be clearer.

Mao played a crucial role in the January Storm. He kept constantly abreast of the unfolding events, and all his interventions demonstrated a detailed knowledge the situation. The most problematic is his suggestion in mid-February to change the name of the Shanghai Commune to the Revolutionary Committee. Was it a retreat? A compromise? A step forward? In order to find a path for discussing the issues, a close reading of Mao's statements in January and February is indispensable. We can put them into three groups.

Those making up the first group came in response to the Appeal to the Shanghai People and the Urgent Message the WGH rebels issued early in January, which we have already mentioned above. Mao warmly praised them as definitely well written, "much better than our articles," he remarked. At his urging, the Central Committee sent the rebels a congratulatory telegram and the *Renmin ribao* reprinted both texts accompanied by editorial notes that emphasized the novelty and accuracy of the declarations of the rebel organizations.

The second group, which we shall explore in detail, includes three articles published in the following weeks in 红旗 *Hongqi* [Red Flag], the party journal, and in *Renmin ribao*, the central newspaper. Personally inspired and revised by Mao, the articles introduced the concept of seizure of power as the criterion for evaluating the situation and for organizing the struggle.

The third group of statements, which we will examine later, consists of conversations that Mao had in mid-February with Zhang Chunqiao and Yao Wenyuan about the issue of "Shanghai Commune" as the name of the new organ of power. A summary of Mao's remarks on this issue immediately circulated among the Shanghai rebels and independent organizations all over China.

Let us consider first the second group of Mao's statements. Very dense and fraught with consequences, the three articles inspired by him on the issue of the seizure of power were published respectively on January 16, 22, and 31.

The earliest of them was a "Commentary" published on January 16 in *Hongqi*, praising the Shanghai rebels for having "provided the correct orientation, policies, and forms of organization and methods of struggle" (提供了正确的方针、政策、组织形式和斗争方法 *tigongle zhengquede fangzhen, zhengce, zhuzhi xingshi he douzheng fangfa*). The January Storm, the "Commentary" noted, was a "new stage in the Cultural Revolution." Its main tasks were the seizure of power (夺权 *duoquan*) from a handful of "persons in positions of authority in the Party that follow the capitalist road" (a definition already present in the May 16 Circular, often shortened to "capitalist roaders" [走资派 *zouzipai*]), and "the establishment of the new order of the Great Proletarian Cultural Revolution."[13] This was the first statement that termed the Shanghai events as a seizure of power.

Such a seizure of power, the "Commentary" went on, quoting a recent statement of Mao, was "a revolution of a class that overthrows another class, under the conditions of the dictatorship of the proletariat, namely the revolution of the proletariat for destroying the bourgeoisie" (在无产阶级专政条件下，一个阶级推翻一个阶级的革命，即无产阶级消灭资产阶级的革命 *zai wuchanjieji zhuanzhen tiaojian xia, yige jieji tuifan yige jieji, ji wuchanjieji xiaomie zichanjieji de geming*). In the struggle against the capitalist roaders, the article clarified, it was indispensable to "seize power from them" and "exert the dictatorship over them" (对他们实行专政 *dui tamen shixing zhuangzheng*). To evaluate the weight of this statement, one must have in mind that the political essence of such a dictatorship will become the ultimate question of the revolutionary decade. As we will discuss in the fourth part of this volume, one of the major issues raised by Mao in 1975 was "Why the dictatorship over the bourgeoisie?"

A more incisively argued case for the seizure of power appeared in an editorial of *Renmin ribao*, also inspired by Mao, published a week later on January 22, entitled "Proletarian Revolutionaries Form a Great Alliance to Seize Power from Those in Authority Who Are Taking the Capitalist Road!"[14] It was a fervent political appeal whose thesis was stated in a resolute introduction: "The basic question of revolution is political power." The Cultural Revolution was therefore "a struggle for the seizure of power, . . . the arousing of hundreds of millions of people to liberate themselves and to seize power from the handful of people within the Party who are in authority and are taking the capitalist road."

If, in the months before, the road was twisting and the rebels had suffered defeats, the editorial said, it was "due precisely to the fact that they did not seize the seals of power with their own hands." As repeated exclamation points hinted, the entire editorial vigorously enunciated the necessity of the seizure of power.

> Of all the ways for the revolutionary masses to take their destiny into their own hands, in the final analysis, the only way is to take power! Having power is to have everything; not having power is to have nothing [有了权，就有了一切，没有权，就没有一切 *youle quan, jiu youle yiqie; mei you quan, jiu mei you yiqie*]. . . . Of all the important things, the possession of power is the most important! Such being the case, the revolutionary masses, with a deep hatred for the class enemy, clench their teeth and, with steel-like determination, make up their mind to unite, form a great alliance, seize power! Seize power!! Seize power!!! . . . The proletarian revolutionaries, the real revolutionary Left, have their eye on seizing power, think of seizing power, and act to seize power!

Comparing the variations in Mao's statements on the issue at a few days' distance gives the sense of how momentous was the passage. About a week later, on January 31, a third text on the seizure of power appeared as an editorial signed jointly by *Hongqi* and *Renmin ribao*, though with fewer exclamatory flourishes. Adding significant issues and nuanced arguments, the article, also in this case inspired and revised by Mao, was entitled "On the Proletarian

Revolutionaries' Struggle to Seize Power."[15] While endorsing the seizure of power from the "handful of capitalist roaders within the Party" as the "strategic task," it discussed a series of new, urgent, theoretical and political "questions [to which] great attention is to be paid."

First, the capitalist roaders would not readily acquiesce in any stripping of power and would do their utmost to regain their lost authority by any means. However, the revolutionaries must be able to make "a strict distinction between contradictions between ourselves and the enemy and those among the people." The key point in this editorial was the necessity of building a "great alliance" among the broad masses as the prerequisite in the struggle to seize power.

In fact, the editorial of January 22 too had clearly raised the alliance issue, warning that lacking a great alliance, the seizure of power would "remain empty talk." Even Mao's famous 1919 "The Great Union of the Popular Masses," a pre-Marxist essay written in the high tide of the May Fourth Movement, was cited there as a major reference. However, while the editorial of January 22 put more stress on the importance of being vigilant toward "a tiny number of bourgeois diehards" who "hypocritically fly a flag of revolutionary rebellion" in an attempt to seize power from the proletariat, the editorial of January 31 posited a series of self-critical issues for the rebels as more decisive.

"Mass organizations that have seized power and the leaders of these organizations," the editorial wrote, "should adopt the principle of unity toward the masses and mass organizations holding different views." "Erroneous tendencies" such as "small group mentality," the editorial noted, "hamper the great alliance of the proletarian revolutionaries," and since they are "questions that fall within the category of contradictions among the people," they must be carefully resolved with the method of "doing more self-criticism, and not attacking one another," otherwise "the nonantagonistic contradictions can turn into antagonistic ones."

In line with this concern, the editorial raised a theoretical issue that was to become crucial in the disputes of the following weeks and months. The seizure of power, it argued, involved a "change of position" that the rebels must carefully consider. Remarkable here is the attention to the effects of this change on subjective choices. Since the strategic issue was the reinvention of a possible new political role of workers in socialism, the rebels should strictly survey the counter-effects of the seizure of power.

> Once the revolutionary mass organizations have seized power in a particular department, their own position alters. At this time, the bourgeois ideas

and petty bourgeois ideas in the minds of certain comrades easily come to the fore. We must be highly vigilant. We must rid ourselves of all selfish ideas and personal considerations and make a revolution to the depth of our souls. Everything must proceed from the fundamental interests of the proletariat. We must attach the utmost importance to the interests of the whole instead of concerning ourselves with personal prestige and position.

The editorial discussed at length another extremely sensitive issue in that peculiar situation: how to resolve the contradictions between cadres and rebels. The rebels must pay "adequate attention to the role of revolutionary cadres in the struggle to seize power," and on their part, the cadres must not underestimate the ability of young rebels, despite "minor errors."

"The overwhelming majority of the ordinary cadres," the editorial wrote, "are good and want to make revolution." To regard all persons in authority as untrustworthy is wrong. As for the cadres that had already distanced themselves from the wrong decisions of the local party authorities and supported the rebels, the latter must welcome their participation in the struggle and consider that "the seizure and retention of power will be helped immeasurably by their inclusion in the core of leadership." Moreover, the cadres who had made errors should be treated correctly and "should not be overthrown indiscriminately but be allowed to correct their errors and be encouraged to make amends for their crimes by good deeds."

The cadres at all levels, it continued, "should not rest on their past achievements, think that they are so wonderful, and lightly regard the young revolutionary fighters who have now come to the fore." They must correct the wrong attitude of "seeing only one's own past merits but not the general orientation of the revolution today" and "seeing only the shortcomings and mistakes of the newly emerged young revolutionary fighters, but not to recognize the fact that their general orientation in the revolution is correct."

The editorial then stressed that the "current seizure of power is not effected by dismissal and reorganization from above, but from below by the mass movement," and pointed out that it was "essential and extremely important" to set up provisional organs of power. "Through a period of transition, the wisdom of the broad masses will be brought into full play and a completely new organizational form of political power better suited to the socialist economic base will be created." The editorial cited the Paris Commune as the major reference point of such new organizational forms, recalling that in June Mao had praised the first Beida dazibao as "the Manifesto of the Beijing People's Commune of the sixties in the 20th century." That statement, the editorial argued, was the prediction that with the Cultural Revolution "our state organs would take on completely new forms."

By mid-January, the problem of the rebels was primarily how to nourish their political existence after having caused the collapse of the SPC. On the other hand, since the central government had not officially declared the dismissal of the SPC officials, the SPC cadres were still formally in office, yet discredited in the eyes of both the independent organizations and the loyalists.[16]

Mao's on-the-spot decision to adopt "seizure of power" for labeling the events appeared to manifest a dual concern: how to deal with the collapse of the SPC, which he considered irreversible, and how to consolidate the political potential of the rebel workers. Mao saw them as capable of fully mastering the new situation. In the last few months, the rebels had grown politically by overcoming powerful obstacles, and in those very days they were proving their ability to deal with a chaotic situation. Mao praised, for example, the fact that the workers had even organized and mobilized the Red Guards among students to temporarily replace the Scarlet Guards who had walked off the shop floor and blocked the port of Shanghai. The SPC, meanwhile, was certainly on the defensive, but surely ready to resume the offensive at the first ebbing of the rebel tide.

Declaring that the rebel organizations were in the process of seizing power was primarily meant to support their capacity for independent political action and the steps they took to deal with the overall situation, including the form of government, while at the same time acknowledging the collapse of the SPC's authority and checking its capacity to react. Briefly put, the statement asserted the need for a radical change, a discontinuity, in the local government to be effected via the capacities of the rebels.

The three articles discussed above, the "Commentary" and the two editorials, were decisive in the political situation in Shanghai and exerted a profound and prolonged influence on the overall development of events. In effect, not only did they pinpoint a series of urgent political tasks that the rebel organizations were facing at that time in Shanghai; they even anticipated issues that would come to mark the situation in China for over a year and a half thereafter.

We encounter again the intricacies of our periodization. This time span, running from the early months of 1967 to mid-1968, corresponds to the decline of the independent organizations, marked by factionalist squabbling within and among the independent organizations as their focus shifted to the issue of power. So why, then, did the strategic and tactical arguments that were clearly set forth in the two cited *Hongqi* editorials, especially in the second, fail in the end to avert factionalism, despite all precautions adopted in circumscribing the concept of seizure of power, both theoretically and politically?

This question also provides an obvious link to the other two questions noted above—why the zenith of pluralization in Shanghai was the immediate antecedent of the decline into factionalism, and why an exceptionally experimental and violence-free political atmosphere prevailed in Shanghai over the following years. Since, as suggested above, the descent on the slippery slope of factionalism resulted from the political waning of independent organizations, let us now focus attention on the effects of seizure of power as a political concept in that singular situation.

The Seizure of Power and the January Storm

In the framework of concepts available in the revolutionary culture—it is necessary to stress this delimitation—Mao's statement was the most vigorous possible. Its first result was in fact to strengthen the rebels and to prevent the Shanghai Party Committee from organizing a counteroffensive. In this sense, Mao's choice of terms was timely and well-grounded and, as we have seen, he even acknowledged the danger of some serious fallout from the "change of position" effected by the rebels.

However, as noted above, seizure of power, far from being just one concept among many in the revolutionary culture, was the focal point of that vast conceptual system, which moreover had reached a stalemate in the Shanghai events. Let us summarize once again the main points. In class-based politics, seizure of power had boasted a strong historical, economic, and even philosophical genealogy. In the revolutionary culture, the official doctrine of the communist parties of the sixties, it marked the crucial stage in the history of class struggle, in which the proletariat, the promoter of the new productive forces, overthrew the bourgeoisie, the representatives of the old relations of production. The connection between workers and party was its central pillar. The political subjectivity of the working class was fully inscribed in the Communist Party, the class vanguard that would lead, through the seizure of power, the transition from a socialist to a communist society.

So, in the January Storm, what could seizing power mean, not in any Weberian sense but in the framework of revolutionary culture, at a moment when the rebel workers had called into question the historical-political connection between the working class and the Communist Party? Indeed, despite the cataclysm that struck the class-based revolutionary culture in the January Storm, or rather just because of it, the concept of seizure of power not only did not lose its previous prestige, but also, paradoxically, gained disproportionate extra traction.

The concept of seizing power, it is true, gave political impetus to the Shanghai rebels. A further rapid expansion of pluralization was clearly signposted when we consider that thirty-two independent organizations had cosigned the Message and the Urgent Notice by early January, and over a hundred organized groups existed later that same month. On the other hand, seizure of power was also invested with an extraordinary role, which we might call "substitutive," for it acted as the main guarantor of revolutionary culture's solidity *after* the January Storm. How could the category of proletariat be understood after the subjective split between Worker General Headquarters and Scarlet Guards? Where, exactly, was the bourgeoisie? Who represented the new productive forces? Who defended the old relations of production? Above all, what was to be done with the Communist Party, its leaders, and its cadres, when the Shanghai party's authority had collapsed after having stubbornly opposed the new workers' organizations for over two months?

It was at this point that seizure of power became a "conceptual vicar." In other words, it became a stabilizing principle for the same conceptual framework that the very existence of independent organizations had made precarious. As unifying vicar, the concept thus dramatically enhanced its prestige. The first of the two *Hongqi* editorials examined above, despite all the precautions and the details explaining the singularity of the situation, unreservedly made seizure of power the compass and the touchstone of revolutionary determination.

Yet the path was soon revealed to be quite tortuous. The difference in register that we have observed between the first and second of the *Hongqi* editorials inspired by Mao, of January 22 and 31, respectively, with the latter stressing the need to be more self-critical and to form a grand alliance among the rebels, was pitched to respond to the rapid development of the situation in Shanghai. In fact, during the pluralization of mid-January, an embryo of factional competition did appear as several organizations claimed to possess greater revolutionary mettle than the others did. Even within the WGH, a sizable group sought to pursue an autonomous role based on alleged revolutionary merits acquired in mass demonstrations some days earlier.

The very idea of seizure of power soon became a source of division among revolutionaries. Those days saw five seizures of power by different rebel organizations, which in actual fact temporarily occupied government offices that in all likelihood had already been abandoned by their official occupants. Some rebels even took too literally the seals-of-power metaphor by taking possession of the official stamps affixed to official government documents.

These tactics, however, were short-lived, for they resolved neither the problem of relations among the growing number of independent organizations nor what to do about the governmental institutions of the city. The Shanghai rebels realized almost immediately that they were about to enter a cul de sac, and it was necessary to correct course if they were to come to grips with the real situation. The turnaround came in late January when various organizations led by the majority of the WGH decided to form the grand alliance the CGCR had repeatedly urged. The second *Hongqi* editorial was certainly an inspiration, especially with its reference to the Paris Commune as the emblematic name of a new form of government organization. In early February the WGH and several other organizations decided to establish the Shanghai People's Commune to replace the SPC.

The Commune

The foundation of the Shanghai Commune, which, as is well known, was quickly replaced by the Revolutionary Committee, was one of the most eventful and intricate steps of the Cultural Revolution. Obviously, the official narrative of "thorough negation" has nothing to say about it except to hurl a series of insults at it and portray the rebels as ambitious thugs easily maneuvered by powerful sponsors. This prevails as a profoundly distorted version of events that attributes all developments to "conspiracies" by Zhang Chunqiao.

Yet the extensive documentation available makes it possible, I submit, to explore another path. As I will argue below, the political ability of the Shanghai rebels to "downsize" the concept of seizure of power—that is, to limit much of its imaginary resonances through a broad-based collective debate over the destiny of their political invention—is the sign that marks the way. I will try to reconsider under this perspective the passage from the Commune to the Revolutionary Committee.

Early in February, the decision to set up the Shanghai People's Commune taken by the thirty-two organizations that had signed the Urgent Appeal on January 9 was therefore a step intended to overcome a deadlock, the sign of an incipient factionalism in fact, though the process was quite complex. According to an account Zhang Chunqiao gave shortly thereafter, when the rebel organizations informed him about their intention to set up the Commune, he and Yao Wenyuan immediately agreed. The Maoist CGCR objected, though, that the Central Committee in Beijing would recognize the new organ only on condition that some leading cadres of the former city government also joined. In other words, the Central Committee would not approve a new ruling organ that excluded Shanghai cadres, that is, that excluded the Communist Party.[17]

The main problem, however, was that in the preceding weeks most of the top Shanghai cadres had followed, or at least had not objected to, the hard line of the SPC. There were then about six thousand mid-level and six hundred top-level cadres in the city, but only a minority, mostly mid-level, openly supported the rebels, the municipal "writing group" being an example. When Zhang Chunqiao informed the CGCR that none of the local top-level cadres had expressed any willingness to join the Commune, the CGCR suggested that at least he and Yao Wenyuan do so in their capacity as local Shanghai officials.

The rebels accepted at once, thereby at one stroke overcoming another major but implicit obstacle, since the inclusion of Zhang and Yao also signaled that in principle the Commune was open to the participation of cadres. Yet another problem now came to the fore. While the thirty-two organizations that were acting as collective midwife to the birth of the Commune also claimed full parental rights by virtue of their having signed the document ousting the SPC, no fewer than seventy new independent organizations had formed in the weeks between conception and inception. While the latter were smaller organizations that were riven to varying degrees by conflict, several felt excluded from the new ruling alliance and voiced their readiness to form a "Second Shanghai People's Commune," a step that would obviously have vitiated the purpose of the first Commune.

Zhang Chunqiao once again stepped into the breach. He told the new rebel organizations that the CGCR required some cadres to be part of the new governing body, but that the only two available, Yao and himself, were already part of the first Commune. He then proposed that the thirty-two organizations sign the founding act not as "components" (组成 zucheng) but as "initiators" (发起 faqi) of the Commune, thereby ensuring that all the others could join subsequently. Once his proposal was accepted, the Commune formally came into being on February 5, accompanied by a "Manifesto" and enthusiastically acclaimed by a demonstration of a million people in the city's central square.

It soon became clear, however, that the CGCR still harbored reservations. Unlike the endorsement given to the two documents of the rebel organizations early in January, this time it sent no message of congratulations, and the Manifesto was published by the Shanghai *Liberation Daily* but ignored by the national press. One week later, Zhang and Yao went to Beijing, where they met several times with Mao, who proposed that they renegotiate the name and statutes of the Shanghai Commune with the rebel organizations. This was a rather unexpected turn of events given that Mao's carefully revised January 31 editorial citing the Paris Commune as an essential reference point had appeared almost on the eve of the foundation of the Shanghai Commune. What had changed in such a short time?

The Manifesto

While the political statements of the protagonists in those weeks deserve to be discussed more systematically than space allows here, we can at least proceed with a close reading of the Commune's Manifesto. Though seldom dealt with in detail even by the few studies that mention it to any extent, the Manifesto sets forth a thesis, all of whose arguments revolve around seizure of power. "The central task of all of our tasks," it notes, "is to take power. We must seize power, seize it completely, seize it one hundred percent."

It even lifted a sentence from a 1933 speech by Mao to buttress its claims and further amplify its political intent: "All revolutionary struggles in the world are made to take political power and strengthen it." That specific sentence, however, was intrinsic to revolutionary culture, and any Marxist revolutionary of the thirties could have uttered it—no copyright did or could cover it. After the January Storm, so insistent a mention of seizure of power was bound to signal a predicament.

After invoking two lines of Mao's 1963 poem "Response to Guo Moruo"— "The Four Seas are rising, clouds and water raging / The Five Continents are rocking, wind and thunder roaring"—the incipit of the Manifesto struck a solemn note: "We proletarian revolutionaries of Shanghai proclaim to the whole country and the whole world that in the great January Revolutionary Storm the old Municipal Committee of Shanghai has collapsed, and the Shanghai People's Commune was born." It declared its resolute political enthusiasm and a strong universalistic determination ("we proclaim to . . . the whole world"), and the reference to the Paris Commune bore yet more witness to its decidedly internationalist intent.

The Manifesto then declared that the Commune was only "a first step" concerning the main political tasks ahead. However, it said nothing of the next steps other than a few cliché-ridden formulas—workers were to "make the revolution and stimulate production," students and intellectuals were to "self-reform" and to "reform education," the army was to "support the revolutionaries," and the cadres were to "criticize revisionist authorities." In the event, all of these next steps related mainly to the seizure of power in "all fields" and highlighted the need to prevent revisionist authorities seizing back power.

While the Manifesto's tone is more stridently radical than that found in the Message and the Urgent Notice, the latter showed that the rebels had grasped the crucial points by clearly indicating the tasks and attitudes for dealing with the Scarlet Guards and the SPC. The Manifesto, on its part, makes no mention of the most pressing issues then at stake—how to resolve the discord among the rebel organizations and how to treat party cadres at various levels of the Shanghai government. These omissions are further underscored by the relentless repetition of "seizing power"—sixty-three times in a few pages, accompanied by several exclamation marks.

Riding the tide of mass enthusiasm for the declaration of the Commune, no less than the patient work of Zhang Chunqiao, the rivalries among and within organizations were temporarily smoothed over but were still far from being resolved. Indeed, they were ready to burst into the open as early as the next day over whether the role assigned to each participating organization in the new body was proportional to the revolutionary merits achieved in the January Storm. Even within the WGH a minority group was contesting the leadership of Wang Hongwen and insisted on due recognition until the day before the Commune's declaration, agreeing only at the last minute to participate in the ceremony. While the Manifesto called for maximum unity, an alliance among the various organizations cemented amid those tensions merely by seizure of power only created a precarious truce under conditions where discord could readily flare up.

When it came to party cadres, the Manifesto announced that having overthrown the municipal committee was not the same as having overthrown the party. The complication was that the role of the Communist Party was indistinguishable from that of the government apparatus. Despite the recurrent formula that the target of the struggle was the "small group of people in positions of authority that follow the capitalist road," the destiny of the local apparatus of the party-state as a whole remained undecided. The announcement of having created "a new form of state institution of the dictatorship of the proletariat at the local level" clearly indicated neither the role of the rebel organizations nor how to deal with the existing state agencies, and postponed all related issues to further seizures of power.

Two Questions for the Rebels and Second Thoughts for Mao

The name Commune was changed, about two weeks after being established, to Revolutionary Committee following a series of meetings Mao had with Zhang and Yao, the two Maoist leaders in Shanghai. This was a crucial episode, a focal point for any meticulous investigation of the events then unfolding and the problems they entrained. An issue under discussion is whether the abandonment of the name Commune was the abandonment of the previous political thrust or its continuation under new conditions.[18]

I suggest that focusing on the Commune as the apogee of political invention risks losing sight of the uniqueness and intricacy of the entire course of a political process that began in November, its stakes, the obstacles it met, and the efforts deployed to overcome them. The main criterion for examining those events and their scope should not be limited to one form of government, however extraordinary, that the revolutionaries of Shanghai tried but failed to achieve.

The essential issue at stake in the events in Shanghai was the experimenting with a new political existence for workers who were no longer under the sway of the Stakhanovite model and, hence, were able to organize their own collective existence regardless of whether the party-state would endorse such an action. The political distance that the independent organizations were able to keep from the party-state was a prerequisite for experimentally testing its political mettle. The question, therefore, is whether the Commune was the moment of that peculiar political invention's greatest expansion as embodied in those weeks by rebel worker organizations.

The turn from Commune to Revolutionary Committee involved both workers and local Maoist leaders. Arriving at the change was clearly not a spontaneous leap. Indeed, the decision was the result of a complicated series of collective negotiations, hashing and rehashing amid diverging lines of thought. Mao certainly played a leading role in the events, including the theoretical pondering and inevitable hesitation that accompanied the concrete decisions he took as the events reached such a crucial juncture. However, to maintain that Mao, when faced with a political situation that for months had generated the active involvement of millions, had first taken a decision only to reverse it in a cold calculus of power underestimates the intricacy of this passage. As we have noted, the Shanghai rebels were not easily deterred from the course they had set upon. Indeed, they proved their mettle by facing down views even from the Maoist group within their ranks.

A series of meetings in Beijing between Mao and Shanghai officials Zhang Chunqiao and Yao Wenyuan in mid-February surely covered more topics than those in the account Zhang rendered publicly upon returning to Shanghai. Yet the few pages of his account likely focus on the core of Mao's thinking vis-à-vis the Shanghai events.[19] Worth noting is how measured Mao's words and tone were in these talks, and how far removed his comments were from the image of mercurial despot current historiography attributes to him. Mao makes a point of persuading the Shanghai officials to ponder carefully the options before making any decisions. The focal points of the reported discussion essentially regard his critical second thoughts about the name of the Commune and two questions he posed to the rebels. Let us first take up the latter as they are the fillip for his second-thought remarks about the name. Mao addressed his queries to Zhang and Yao, the message bearers who were to deliver them to the rebels in Shanghai. Briefly put, they are: What exactly is your new organization? What are you going to do about the Communist Party?

Mao noted in regard to the former that a political organization, an "organizing nucleus," is indispensable. It can be called, he said with a hint of sarcasm, even Guomindang or Yiguandao, the latter being the name of a Taoist sect that was outlawed in China after 1949. In the event, there is no revolutionary politics without an organization. So the first question for the Shanghai rebels boils down to this: Is the Commune your organizing nucleus? Indicatively, Mao here did not presume to take for granted what the organization must be. Indeed, he even remarked that what was really at stake was the reinvention of political organization itself.

Put this way, the first is a crucial question pertaining to the entire course of the Cultural Revolution after June 1966, when Mao approved the first Beida dazibao: how to reinvent the egalitarian political organization. All the developments the events of the preceding eight months eventuated turned on this issue. The second, equally crucial question was: What is the role of the Communist Party in this reinvention? There is no reason to think that the Shanghai revolutionaries wanted to do away with the party. They certainly leveled much harsh criticism at the bureaucratic apparatus and its big and small despotic ways. Yet at the core of the storm was the issue that the Communist Party was not the only form of political organization and, hence, it was necessary to invent new ones by experimenting with an unrestricted pluralization of forms and modalities of organization.

The situation in China in 1967 was in no measure comparable to the dissolution of the Soviet Union's Communist Party or those of its satellites in the late 1980s. Nor was it comparable to the disrepute heaped on the CCP following the bloody repression of the mass movement in spring 1989. The issue for the revolutionary rebel workers was not to eliminate the CCP but to rethink root and branch what its place and role within the political experiment then underway were to be.

Mao's two questions were thus notably precise as well as pointedly circumstantial. They emphatically threw into relief the key issues facing the Cultural Revolution in general and the Shanghai revolutionaries in particular. The thorniest problem the latter faced at that moment was how to put together a stable alliance among the numerous rebel groups whose contrasting views had been only temporarily resolved. When it had to deal with the problem of the Communist Party, the Commune resorted to a symbolic gesture by drafting Zhang and Yao into it. While this move indicated that party cadres at all levels would be welcome, it was only a tentative step to solve the many big problems looming on the horizon.

Let us now backtrack to the second, critical, thoughts over the name of the Commune that Mao ventured in his conversations with Zhang and Yao. Mao repeatedly spoke of the "name" (名称 *mingcheng*) problem, insisting that it not be confused with the "real" (实际 *shiji*). The Commune was just a name whose importance was not to be exaggerated because "names come and go" (名称变来变去 *mingcheng bianlai bianqu*). But where does the "real" of the name Commune lie and, more specifically, what is the point, the meaning, of "real" in the remarks Mao was then making?

It certainly did not escape his Shanghai conversation partners that Mao was correcting himself, taking a step back with regard to the positions he had espoused up to then. But exactly what was he stepping back from? Everyone was well aware that Mao had championed the Commune as a decisive milestone of the Cultural Revolution since the previous June, when he supported the first Beida dazibao. Moreover, as we've seen, the Mao-inspired editorials in January had systematically underscored the reference to the Paris Commune and in turn served as a source of inspiration for the Shanghai Commune.

Mao was thus speaking to guests who, like himself, had enthusiastically embraced the reference to the Paris Commune he had fostered and whom he was then inviting to share in his second-thought musings. He began with a rhetorical question: "Didn't we all say that the Commune, the Paris Commune, had been a new political power [新政权 *xin zhengquan*]?" The meaning seems obvious: Yes, we all said so, you and I, all of us found it convincing; the Paris Commune was synonymous with "new political power" for all of us.

Mao's interrogative phrasing hints at a first response to the question. He was saying that surely one cannot believe that Commune is some kind of magic name that conjures up invincibility. The reality of the question being posed concerns the issue of political power in general. A name that until a few weeks before had been synonymous with the ideal form of a new political power for everyone, Mao was now signaling, was not quite what it seemed, and he intended to downsize the "omnipotence" that the name Paris Commune can evoke. He even said that in his view the Paris Commune, meant as a form of government, was almost certainly destined to failure, for the French bourgeoisie would never have allowed the working class to retain a hold on power of that magnitude.

A SUBJECTIVE SPLIT IN THE WORKING CLASS

Taken at face value, it's a rather strange comment coming from a Marxist revolutionary leader like Mao. Yet it is of a piece with his entire rethinking of the idea of victory and defeat in the arena of politics. We have already noted that for Mao "victory" was not the sole criterion of revolutionary politics, since it also encompasses a number of counteracting effects that have to be taken into account. This, as we have seen, was one of the concerns connected with the term *seizure of power* in the January editorials. On the other hand, even if defeat were to be "the most likely probability," that should not impede the will to political action but, rather, make it all the more urgent.

In the event, Mao was not indulging in capitulationist pessimism but pondering all the "victory-hailing" rallying cries in revolutionary culture. The Commune was as much an object of his rethinking as was the name "Soviet." The latter too had been a new form of political power. Lenin was "quite pleased" with the name, holding that it was a "grand creation of workers, peasants, and soldiers," a "new form of the dictatorship of the proletariat." However, said Mao, Lenin "did not expect [没有料到 *mei you liaodao*] this form" (这种形式 *zhe zhong xingshi*) could be used not only by workers, peasants, and soldiers, but also "even by the bourgeoisie." In effect, he concluded, "today Lenin's soviets have become Khrushchev's soviets."

Mao was arguing in essence that nothing, even less their names, ensured the invincibility of these two notable forms of power because "the problem lies not in the name but in the real, not in the form but in the content" (问题不在名称而在实际, 不在形式而在内容 *wenti bu zai mingcheng er zai shiji, bu zai xingshi er zai neirong*). It was for Mao a very pressing issue at the time. Given that "the founding experiences"—the Paris Commune and the soviets—ended up as they did, we are entitled to think, said Mao, that the same holds as well for the People's Republic of China. If we were to be overturned and the bourgeoisie to take power, "they might not even change the name" (他们也可以不改名字 *tamen ye keyi bu gai mingzi*).

The latter was another forward-looking prediction, once again in the register of the "probable defeat." Here, however, Mao's statements made the symptom much more explicit, that is, his intention to rethink the theme of proletarian political power. In the remarks that Mao addressed to Zhang and Yao, his proposal to give up the name of Commune expressed the need, more than for a step backward, for one more step. Mao said clearly, and in an obviously self-critical sense, that "Commune" as a synonym of "seizure of power" and "certainty of victory" was not only not enough, but led us astray, and that the problem of the form of political power was inessential if a new way of thinking about the nucleus of revolutionary political organization was not found.

Ultimately, Mao posed two orders of problems, a tactical one and a strategic one. On the level of immediate tasks, he said that it was unclear how the newly established Commune intended to solve the problem of the organizational nucleus—in other words, how to deal with the problem of place in the new organs of the Communist Party, or more precisely of the "leading nucleus" at that moment, and at the same time, how to create a "great alliance," that is, how to overcome the divisions between the different mass organizations.

Moreover, Mao raised a long-term problem that had actually been at the center of his political thought since the second half of the 1950s, namely that of assessing the historical experience of the dictatorship of the proletariat, from the Paris Commune up to the People's Republic of China. As we will see in the fourth part of this book, Mao would bring up the issue in an even broader way in his last two years. In this 1967 conversation he states that the sole reference to the Commune as "a new form of proletarian political power" is insufficient. In fact, the reference to the Paris Commune as a "first seizure of power" had no value without posing the problem of how to "break the bureaucratic-military machinery of the state." These were the theses of both Marx and Lenin, which the Maoists would repropose in the vast study movement on the theory of the dictatorship of the proletariat in 1975.

In 1967, the abandonment of the name "Commune" explicitly concerned the need to clarify what the reality of that reference could be beyond a name. Taken only as a synonym for seizure of power, Mao said, "Commune" does not solve the more urgent problems, and at the same time obscures a strategic task of the Cultural Revolution, namely the reexamination of the historical and conceptual references of revolutionary culture.

Shanghai as a Place for Political Experimentation

The long-term consequences of abandoning the name Commune and establishing a Revolutionary Committee are largely still to be explored. What was the personal and collective destiny of the rebels? How were the independent workers' organizations transformed after the creation of new governing bodies? What were the role and attitudes of the leading party cadres that had been overthrown in January 1967? These are essential questions that need to be answered in a new way.

It is essential to focus on the political experiments that took place in Shanghai in the revolutionary decade and to see past the strict censorship that the Chinese government continues to impose on the study of those events. All Chinese books on the subject thoroughly deny any political value to those experiments, assuming that they were pure rhetoric or the result of palace plots and intrigues.

In point of fact, however, Shanghai was one of the most politically active places of the decade in China, with avant-garde initiatives, especially in the factories. We will discuss in chapter 9 the value of inventions such as "workers' universities" and "theoretical workers' contingents" that took their impulse from experiments in Shanghai. The main ground of experimentation was how to reduce the division of labor, how to get the workers involved in technical and administrative decisions, and vice versa—how to get the cadres and technicians to take part in manual labor. At the same time, those experiments emphasized the need for the workers to increase their theoretical abilities. From the late 1960s to the mid-1970s in Shanghai there was an immense openness to the intellectual activity of the workers.

Certainly, the impulse to experiment came from the January Storm, but it also came from the fact that that drive was not dispersed into factionalism. A condition that made Shanghai a privileged place for those experiments was that the city, in fact, unlike almost the rest of China, had a very limited presence of factional quarrels, which marked the political decline of independent organizations.

Official Chinese historiography, even if at times forced to admit that the climate of the decade in Shanghai was relatively peaceful, tries to find explanations compatible with the obligations of "complete negation." Some even claim that the almost complete absence of violent confrontations after January is to be attributed to the control over the situation exerted by Maoist leaders Zhang Chunqiao and Yao Wenyuan, who wanted to impress their mentor.[20] Yet, if this were so, one might try explaining why Mao himself was unable to control the eruptions of violent demonstrations by rival student groups that convulsed Beijing. Indeed, as we shall see in the next chapter, Mao himself was at a loss for words to explain these clashes.

The role played by Zhang and Yao, especially by the former, was indeed essential. Yet it makes no sense to say they held "integral control" over a situation whose pulse ran through the subjective arteries of millions of people in public demonstrations during one of the most politically charged periods of the twentieth century. The leitmotif running through Zhang's speeches and statements at the nearly countless meetings and assemblies with the rebels in 1967 is phrased in altogether different tones, none of them bearing any resemblance to those about imposing his "control" in order to curry favor with Mao.

In Zhang's and Yao's interventions in the meetings with the various independent organizations in 1967, for which there is ample documentation, the two Maoist leaders were committed to arguing with the rebels as comrades with whom they were sharing the same concerns. For months on end, the main problem Zhang almost always had to address was how to dissipate the imaginary aura that the term *seizure of power* had taken on. For example, he said more than once that some seizures of power in January whose revolutionary merits were claimed by some organizations amounted to nothing more than "the seizure of a few rubber stamps and occupation of a few empty rooms."[21]

Zhang even spoke to them about Cao Diqiu, the mayor of Shanghai whom the rebels had stridently criticized for his "reactionary bourgeois stance." Zhang reminded them that Cao had fought in the War of Liberation, took part in the Long March, and had even been a military hero who had overcome great odds, but that his position of power had changed his subjective attitude. He then said they all, the rebels and himself, had to be careful so as not to end up in the same changed state. Rather than boasting about their revolutionary merits in order to gain primacy in the seizure of power rankings, the organizations should busy themselves with establishing a grand alliance.

The range of political developments following the founding of the Revolutionary Committee certainly requires detailed research. Yet it is possible to advance the hypothesis that the essentially nonviolent political atmosphere that pervaded Shanghai, unlike what occurred elsewhere in the country, was due to both the political acumen acquired by the rebels during the January Storm and the intelligent guidance throughout the unfolding developments provided by the steady hand of Zhang Chunqiao.[22]

Moreover, the turning point from Commune to the change in name can even be seen as a kind of "vaccination" against the destructive virus carried by the mystical aura of the substitute concept "seizure of power." Since the name *Commune* had been adopted as synonymous with the concept of seizure of power, that is, of a specific state form, having abandoned that name diminished the value and the extent of that concept. I suggest that such a downsizing enabled the subjective energies that appeared with the January Storm in Shanghai not to break down into factional struggles.

A Recap

I will try to recap the main points of the complex process that led to the Commune and its symptomatic abandonment. The perspective I propose is that, with the January Storm, a conceptual congestion was created in the face-to-face encounter between Cultural Revolution and revolutionary culture. At its source was the subjective division of the working-class concept under the pressure of rebel revolutionaries who sought a new path for the political existence of workers under socialism. Such an internal division of the working-class concept destabilized and finally paralyzed party authority, since this was founded on the premise of its being the vanguard of the working class, that is, its only legitimate organizational principle.

Obviously, this authority had begun to falter already with the first Beida dazibao, when an embryo of independent organization had appeared. When the phenomenon extended to the workers, the Shanghai Party Committee was soon deprived of authority. However, in that situation, calling the loss of authority of the municipal committee a seizure of power created a sort of conceptual short-circuit. Seizing power was the key concept of revolutionary culture, that is, the ideological and organizational framework of twentieth-century communism, but the events of Shanghai had gone beyond the horizon of revolutionary culture, requiring new ways to be found in order to reinvent the political existence of workers under socialism.

The declaration of the seizure of power, on the one hand, galvanized the rebels and prevented repressive backlashes from the Shanghai Party Committee (which was formally still in office), but on the other hand it immediately set in motion a transformation from pluralization to factionalism. There was soon a hyperpluralization, involving more than one hundred rebel groups, and therefore a positive phenomenon of extension of independent organizations. At the same time, however, there were lines of contrast between the main independent organizations concerning the primacy of each group with respect to the seizure of power.

In this sense, pluralization started to be associated with the dismissal process and immediately tended to be reabsorbed into the latter. The hypothesis I propose, in order to deal with this tangle, is that in mid-January 1967 in Shanghai the first overlap of the two processes was manifested, and that the first embryo of factional quarrels was created around the theme of the primacy of the seizure of power.

At this point, thanks to the awareness of the main rebel organizations (especially the WGH) that the situation was coming up against a dead end, and under the pressure of the Central Group of the Cultural Revolution, which urged the rebels to create a great alliance, the Commune was founded. While this passage immediately attenuated the factional divergences around the seizure of power, at the same time the reference to the Commune was itself taken as a synonym for seizure of power.

Mao grasped the impasse, at the source of which there was, however, his own declaration on the seizure of power in Shanghai and ultimately also the equivalence "Commune = seizure of power." He therefore proposed giving up the name Commune, and did not hesitate to do so in a self-critical way, explicitly inviting the revolutionaries to make a historical and conceptual assessment of proletarian political power.

My assumption is that if in Shanghai they had kept the name Commune, this would have increased the tendency to clashes between factions. In Shanghai, giving up the name Commune mitigated the effect of the "substitute concept" of taking power. We have seen that in declaring the foundation of the Commune the rebels had merely foregrounded the repetition of that concept. Giving up that name allowed that repetition to be interrupted.

However, the concept of seizing power, while in Shanghai it was resized as to its imaginary resonances, was by no means abandoned at the national level. In the following months, the formation of Revolutionary Committees throughout China took place under the banner of that concept, which the group of central Maoist leaders declared as the prerequisite for the establishment of the new organs of power.[23] Despite the CGCR often insisting that it was a "takeover of power from below," based on the great alliance and the ability of rebels and cadres to treat each other in a nonantagonistic way, the issue of seizing power became in the following months one of the main obstacles to the political growth of the revolutionaries. While in Shanghai it was diminished, elsewhere it became more and more the compass of rebel political subjectivity.

Nearly everywhere else in China, the concept ended up sweeping away rebel organizations in a tide of self-destruction. By the spring of 1967, the independent organizations established in the preceding months began showing divisive cracks among and between them. These developments, however, did not result in the spread of pluralization but in the onset of its decline and eclipse in a radical impasse. We shall examine this crucial course of events in the next chapter through the lens of an episode that personally involved Mao in July 1968.

At that juncture, Mao was caught in a cross fire. Despite openly criticizing the senseless clashes among factions, and while still making decisions affecting the course of those events, he nonetheless showed notable uncertainty in assessing the origin and nature of a phenomenon he had not foreseen and that led to an impasse in the set of political experiments that had begun two years before. It may even be that Mao initially viewed the division into factions as a further spread of pluralization. Whatever the case, he finally said that he could not fully understand the phenomenon.[24]

A Symptomatic Reading of Seizure of Power

To better reconsider Mao's oscillations and indecisions between January 1967—the highest moment of the mass phase—and July 1968, the moment of the independent organizations' definitive implosion (which I will examine in the next chapter), it is worth returning once more to his "seizure of power" declaration by way of a symptomatic reading.

As is known, Althusser proposed this kind of interpretation in regard to certain concepts of Marx's *Das Kapital*, which he called "voids in discourse," corresponding to new though not yet formulated concepts, but also essential for devising a theoretical innovation. These new concepts, necessary for the new theoretical formulation but still beyond the available discursive resources, constitute "voids," argued Althusser, which are in turn filled with old concepts that take their place. They are "vicarious concepts" that take their name from a previous theoretical horizon and play a substitute role in a completely new framework of thought.

I suggest this as the function that, from mid-January 1967, the concept of seizing power filled.[25] The problem was, especially in this case, what retrospective action exercised the "vicarious concept" on a thought at the height of the political innovation then in progress, and therefore on the political invention itself? In any case, it was not a neutral role, a temporary, inconsequential substitute. That substitutive concept is not limited to filling a void, but functions retroactively to bring the political innovations in progress back within the conceptual framework with respect to which those innovations had appeared in excess. In fact, seizing power, as I have argued, was the keystone of the entire revolutionary culture, the unifying principle of the ideological and organizational framework of twentieth-century communism.

It is significant that, just at the moment when that space of political knowledge was crossed by an invention that irreversibly marked a radical discontinuity, the name assigned to this discontinuity was the unifying principle of the previous conceptual space. It was as if an automatism were immediately put in place to rearrange the encyclopedic unity of revolutionary culture. The definition Mao gave of the January Storm certainly corresponded to his intention to go all the way in support of the rebel workers of Shanghai. Thus, Mao stated that their political value consisted in having seized power. That was the strongest term available in the "language of the situation," as Badiou would put it, but as such it had two converging results that transformed it into a factor of radical weakening. It is really true that, under certain conditions, everything can turn into its opposite.

On the one hand, the name produced a recomposition of the space of the political knowledge in which the party-state operated both ideologically and organizationally, with the complication that, given the radical rift in the party–working class relationship, which embodied the unifying consistency of that framework of political culture, seizure of power immediately took on the exorbitant value of a completely imaginary name endowed with the virtue of recomposing the lost unity of that space of knowledge.

On the other hand, seizure of power brought the current political invention back to the preceding condition of its existence. Within a few days, the first consequences of that definition involved a weakening of those political inventions that had arisen in the preceding weeks. Seizure of power immediately became a sort of categorical imperative that was supposed to inspire political activism. It actually nourished a destructive and self-destructive narcissism, devoid in reality of any political idea, which led some organizations to affirm their own bureaucratic supremacy over other organizations. This was to be the general model of factional decline over the next year and a half.

8

Facing a Self-Defeat

The discussion of factionalism in the preceding chapters could only sketch a few working hypotheses. Let me suggest a case study here that may delineate more clearly the direction a fruitful study of factionalism can take.

I have already had occasion to review transcripts of meetings in preceding chapters. I propose here a detailed look at the transcript of a meeting that played a decisive role in the events it was convened to deal with. The meeting took place on July 28, 1968, and its participants were Mao, members of the Maoist Central Group of the Cultural Revolution, and the leaders of the main Red Guard organizations on the campuses of Beijing's universities. What makes this document so extraordinary is that it renders in a strikingly realistic way, down even to the finer points of stylistic nuances, one of the most dramatic moments associated with those events—the "closing scene" of the mass-movement phase of the Cultural Revolution.[1]

Well known even outside of China since the mid-seventies, this document has not been widely cited, a circumstance that may largely be due to the fact that it contradicts many clichés surrounding the Cultural Revolution, not least of which were the relations between the leaders of the Maoist group and the Red Guards, as well as the political and personal style of Mao himself. For example, it is impossible to use this transcript as evidence supporting the image of Mao as a utopian, even bloodthirsty despot now current in the historiography of the "thorough negation." We shall see that style as it really was—how Mao addressed the other leaders of his own group and the young student leaders at such a critical juncture in time. In a more overtly subtle way, too, the transcript brings into sharp, realistic relief the subjective tone of the participants, how they hesitated, and how they realized that the situation had come to an impasse of their own making. As a detailed document of the conclusive moment of the political experience of those independent organizations, the transcript of that meeting also points in several directions that can be explored to elucidate the nature of factionalism as a political phenomenon.

It is worth noting that from the outset the transcript takes the form, spontaneously it should be said, of a *pièce de théâtre*, a play.[2] It is perhaps no accident that the opening scene of the Cultural Revolution had a prologue in the theater, and the closing scene of that mass movement has come down to us in a document of such a markedly theatrical nature. We have noted too that the theater is on intimate terms with politics because it places the value of declarations at center stage. So let us now take a close look at the transcript, focusing on the decisive political turning point it elucidates through the crucial statements, even the tone of voice, of the actors and the meeting in which they were uttered.

Mao's Last Meeting with the "Little Generals"

In the very early hours of July 28, 1968, some of the most famous figures of the subjective turbulence that in the two previous years had affected the fundamental conditions of politics in China—the Red Guards and the Maoist leaders—met in a long and dramatic face-to-face meeting, a transcript of which was kept in such a deliberately meticulous way that even the emotional tones of the dialogue were recorded. The result, thanks to compilers endowed with a remarkable literary culture (probably one or more of Mao's secretaries), is much more than the bare proceedings of the meeting. One would be inclined to call it rather a play whose "authors" are the characters themselves. These characters were subjective figures who met in the final moment of the political situation in which their existence was grounded. By the next day, the situation would be totally different—the Red Guards would no longer exist as independent organizations, and in the following months they would be dissolved, with consequences that would unavoidably rebound on Mao and on his allies.

The meeting was held in a hall at Zhongnanhai, the small lake in the center of Beijing, around which the headquarters of the party-state are situated. On one side were Mao and the Central Group for the Cultural Revolution, the restricted group of central leaders who had remained politically active over the last two years (most of the high ranks of the party-state had been paralyzed since the summer of 1966). On the other side were the five most important leaders of the Red Guards on the Beijing campuses. The meeting's main topic was the consequences of the political exhaustion of the Red Guards. In August 1966 they had been greeted as "new forms of organization created by the masses" that were to have a "permanent character" of political and institutional innovation (as declared in the Decision in 16 Points, the main programmatic document of the Cultural Revolution). However, especially during the preceding year, they had decomposed into small paramilitary groups lacking any political distinction, engaged in increasingly grotesque brawls to establish the absolute supremacy of their own faction.

In the last few months most of the militants, bewildered by the political crisis of their organizations, had quit all forms of activism and swelled the ranks of the so-called faction of the disengaged (逍遥派 *xiaoyaopai*), which in fact was not a real "faction." On the other hand, the more the number of militants decreased, the more violent the clashes became on some Beijing campuses, particularly at Qinghua University, where with crude but deadly weapons the "hardliners" of the two factions (a few thousand people altogether) continued to fight.

The day before, July 27, on Mao's initiative, and following crowded meetings in several factories, tens of thousands of unarmed workers entered the Qinghua campus peacefully, shouting slogans against the armed struggle, with lines of demonstrators standing between the two factions to prevent them from fighting.[3] The workers had been violently attacked by the students (five workers were killed and hundreds wounded), but, with an extraordinary sense of self-discipline, the workers' only reaction was to continue to shout slogans against the armed struggle. The workers finally were able to disarm the two factions and occupy the key spots of the campus. At the moment of the meeting in Zhongnanhai, which began at 3 A.M. and lasted until 8 A.M. (the preferred working hours for Mao and other Chinese leaders), the fighting at Qinghua had just ended.

The exceptional archival condition of the meeting's transcript, which allows a close reading of that event, crystallizes the singular political character of its lead actor. Mao himself had required the recording and had also decided that its contents should be widely distributed for a reason that he clearly explained to the Red Guard leaders: "Otherwise, on your return, you will interpret what I have said today as you like. If you do so, I'll have this tape aired."[4] The issue at stake was how to deal politically with the end of the political experiment of the independent organizations that had begun two years before. The publication of the exact minutes of the meeting, held at the apex of a month of crucial initiatives from the Central Group for the Cultural Revolution (July 1968 is a decisive month for the years 1966–76), was therefore considered essential for the success of Mao's initiatives.

The Black Hand and the Red Guards

Accuracy was hence a prerequisite, but not the only quality of the document. Sensitive to subjective details, the transcript from the first sentences is an accurate record of the register of the various figures' statements and reciprocal interactions.[5] At least some passages of this long and highly nuanced piece of "documental theater" should be quoted extensively. Following the interlacing dialogue is a good introduction to the tangle of the matter. Here is the starting point of the document, testimony, and at the same time integrating part of the conclusive scene.

> *Nie Yuanzi, Tan Houlan, Han Aijing, and Wang Dabing [four leaders of the Red Guards] walk into the conference room. The Chairman stands up and shakes hands with each in turn.*
>
> CHAIRMAN: You're all so young! (*Shaking hands with Huang Zuozhen, a military commander*) Are you Huang Zuozhen? I've never met you before. I'd heard you'd been killed.
> JIANG QING (*addressing the four leaders of the Red Guards*): Haven't seen you for a long time. You're certainly not putting up dazibao anymore.
> CHAIRMAN (*addressing the four Red Guards*): We only met at Tian'anmen [in the summer of 1966], but we didn't talk. This isn't good. You only come up to the Triratna Palace when there's important business [a proverbial formula, "you never come to see me"]; but I have read all your newspapers and I know your situation. Kuai Dafu [another student leader] hasn't come. Is he unable to come [from Qinghua campus] or unwilling?
> XIE FUZHI [vice-premier]: I am afraid he's unwilling.
> HAN AIJING: Impossible. In this moment, if Kuai knew there's a meeting with the Cultural Revolution Group of the Central Committee and could not meet the president, he'd cry. For sure, he's unable to come.[6]

The dialogue introduces from its first lines the most burning topics of the meeting and the relationships between the characters. With the exception of Nie Yuanzi, an instructor and cadre of the Philosophy Department at Beida and the author of the famous first dazibao of the Cultural Revolution, who was a woman in her forties, all the other Red Guard leaders who attended the meeting were in their early twenties. The seventy-five-year-old Mao, who stands up and shakes hands, begins with "All so young!" almost amazed at something that he is surely aware of but that, nonetheless, he gives all due consideration to in addressing them. The "Triratna palace"[7] is one of those learned references pronounced with a popular tone with which Mao liked to color his speech, especially when he meant to be polemical. The expression is in fact idiomatic. Here he seems to use a joke to attenuate hierarchical relationships. The words spoken to Huang Zuozhen ("I heard you'd been killed"), a military leader who accomplished the difficult task of keeping in touch with the leaders of the Red Guards as well as organizing their coming to Zhongnanhai, may exemplify the climate—fights at Qinghua had been bloody and even an "ambassador" like Huang had taken serious risks. Mao's remark is probably intended to downplay the moment, defusing the situation by exaggeration.

Jiang Qing opens sarcastically. "You're certainly not putting up dazibao anymore" implies: "Now all you do is fight." She will keep this tone even in her following remarks, showing much anguish and disappointment, too. She says to them: "We are all in great anguish," "I am deeply grieved for you," and even "I have spoiled you," "spendthrifts" (败家子 *baijiazi*). Mao will interrupt her several times, admonishing her not to translate her anxiety into hierarchical superiority ("don't get so puffed up," he tells her at one point, almost revealing a small scène de ménage). He will do the same with the other Central Committee leaders, often insisting that they should not underestimate their interlocutors because of their youth and telling them not to suffocate them with criticism: "Don't put on the airs of veterans."

Together with Nie Yuanzi, the leader of the majority faction at Beijing University, called "New Beida (Commune)," three other "little generals," as the student leaders are affably called during the meeting, enter the hall. They belong to the two opposing factions ferociously struggling for "power" on Beijing's university campuses: the "Earth" faction (地派 *Dipai*) and the "Sky" faction (天派 *Tianpai*). These names, which sound so imaginative, were in fact rather bureaucratic: two university institutes (Sky was based at the Institute of Aeronautics, Earth at the Institute of Geology) whose majority factions wove a complex tangle of opposing alliances on other campuses, but by then lacked any difference in principle. At a certain point Mao will admit, "All this Sky and Earth stuff is not clear to me." Moreover, the names of the organizations symptomatically overlapped each other, creating bizarre homonymies.[8]

Wang Dabing, a student at the Institute of Geology, heads the Earth faction; he is fully absorbed in his "little general" role, like the others. Mao will address him with good-natured irony, though his tone remains completely unperceived.

Tan Houlan, a woman, leads the majority faction at the Normal University, which belongs to the Earth faction, too. She is quite young, but rather feared by her adversaries: "Comrade Tan Houlan has two small braids," says Lin Biao. But "she has cannons pointed against Nie Yuanzi [of the opposing Sky faction]," Mao says, commenting: "Two of you are women [Tan and Nie]—extraordinary indeed!"

During most of the meeting, one of the invited student leaders, whom Mao is impatient to meet, is absent: Kuai Dafu, the most famous Red Guard in the country, leader of the "Jinggangshan (Headquarters)" faction of Qinghua University that led the deadly attack on the workers (the opposing faction, by contrast, welcomed them). Kuai Dafu will arrive at the meeting after a long delay, and this increases the already considerable tension: "Is Kuai Dafu unable or unwilling to come?" Mao and the others of the Central Group ask repeatedly.

It is often Han Aijing who speaks in Kuai Dafu's place, defending him in heroic-dramatic accents. Han, a student at the Institute of Aeronautics and leader of the Sky faction, is the only one among the four little generals who intervenes at turns with resolve, overflowing pathos more often, and weak argumentation. He says: "I love Kuai Dafu. Since we have done many things together, I know that I will be compromised. I feel that I must do everything to protect him and not allow him to be undone. His destiny is linked to that of the country's Red Guards."

With the exception of Mao, who addresses Han both sternly and sympathetically, the others of the Central Group show their impatience: "You always think you're right," "Kuai is the commander and Han the political commissar" are their ironic comments.

Kuai Dafu will enter the scene in a theatrical way, toward the end of the meeting, crying out as predicted to his friend and ally. But even though Kuai was absent at the start of the meeting, he is the one whom Mao addresses first. The day before, Kuai had sent an urgent telegram to Mao and to the Central Group to denounce the workers, who, "unconsciously maneuvered by a Black Hand" (that is, by a hidden power that planned to quash the Cultural Revolution), "had surrounded and invaded Qinghua University."[9] This was Mao's response to the letter, which he will confirm when Kuai eventually joins the meeting.

CHAIRMAN: Kuai Dafu wants to capture the Black Hand. All these workers sent to "repress" and "oppress" the Red Guards. Who is the Black Hand? He hasn't been captured yet. The Black Hand is nobody else but me! And Kuai has not come yet. He should've come to take me! I was the one who sent the security guards of the Central Committee and the workers of the Xinhua Printing Plant and the General Knitwear Mill there. I asked them how to solve the armed fighting in the universities, and told them to go there to have a look. As a result, thirty thousand went.[10]

The meeting of July 1968, in fact the only one in which Mao spoke with the student leaders directly, shows that the relationships between the Central Group for the Cultural Revolution and the Red Guards had been rather sporadic and contradictory. During the meeting, Mao regrets not having talked with the students before, but he also says that he has tried to avoid any interference in the situation. The mobilization of the workers was decided only after taking into account other possibilities, among which was the opportunity to let the students solve their own problems. Mao continued:

What do you think? What should be done about the armed clashes in the universities? One approach is to withdraw completely and have nothing to do with the students. If they want to fight, let them. So far, the revolutionary committees and garrison commands have not been afraid of the disorder caused by armed conflict in universities. They have not exerted any control or any pressure, and everyone has considered this as proper. Another way is to give them [the students] a bit of help. The workers, the peasants, and the majority of the students have praised this method. There are more than fifty institutions of higher learning in Beijing, but only in five or six were there fierce clashes and your ability was put to the test. As far as solving the problem is concerned, some of you should go live in the South, and some of you in the North. All of you are called "New Beida," adding "Jinggangshan" or "Commune" between parentheses, just like the Soviet Communist Party adds [between parentheses] the name *Bolshevik*.

As noted above, both Beida factions had the same name, "New Beida," but were distinguished by the label "New Beida (Commune)" and "New Beida (Jinggangshan)." Mao, in this case quite skeptical of the names, here remarked that they were imitating the specification "Bolshevik" in the title of the Russian Communist Party, to distinguish it from the "Menshevik" Communist Party. Mao was quite ironic about the formalistic language with which the opposing student factions obstinately quarreled over the ownership of the great revolutionary names, mutually treating each other as counterrevolutionaries. Yet on the crucial issue he was very direct: "If you cannot solve the problem, we may have to resort to military control and ask Lin Biao to take command. We also have Huang Yongshen [chief of the general staff]. The problem has to be solved, one way or the other!"[11]

Of the first solution (some go South, others North), Mao will presently explain the meaning: the factions had to be dispersed. Personal animosities had become so exacerbated that the two factions could not remain in the same college or the same city without igniting new fighting. (This was one of the main reasons why "educated youths" and cadres were sent to the countryside the following year.) Far worse, the violence was inversely proportional to any serious distinction of principle between the factions.

Of the second possible solution, it was obvious that it was quite easy to resort to military control in Beijing, considering the reduced number of students effectively involved in the clashes. However, the difficulty was how to deal with the problem as a political situation, that is, not just in terms of law and order—it was, in fact, a rare example of a nonmilitary intervention for a crisis of that kind—but as an outcome of a subjective process that Mao described as follows:

> You have been involved in the Cultural Revolution for two years: struggle–criticism–transformation [斗批改 *dou-pi-gai*]. Now, first, you're not struggling; second, you're not criticizing; and, third, you're not transforming. Or rather, you are struggling, but it's an armed struggle. The people are not happy, the workers are not happy, the peasants are not happy, city residents are not happy, students in most schools are not happy, most of the students even in your schools are not happy. Even within the faction that supports you, there are unhappy people. Is this the way to unify the world [统一天下 *tongyi tianxia*, "unify everything under the sky"]?
>
> (*Addressing Nie Yuanzi*): In the "New Beida," you have the majority, you "Old Buddha" [老佛爷 *Laofoye*]. You're a philosopher. Don't tell me that in the "New Beida (Commune)" [the majority faction] and in the Revolutionary Committee of the University [under Nie's control] there is nobody against you. I'd never believe such a thing! They won't say anything to your face, but they make snide remarks behind your back.[12]

The student leaders purposely addressed by Mao with sarcasm had been central figures in the last two years. The one whom he called "Old Buddha," in the sense of "a person who gives himself/herself an air of higher authority," was Nie Yuanzi, whose dazibao had sparked the student movement at Beida and had been exalted by Mao in 1966 as a crucial political declaration, praising it as "the first Marxist-Leninist dazibao of China," or even "the declaration of the Chinese Commune of Paris of the sixties of the twentieth century."[13] Two years later, Nie was, among the five little generals present at the meeting, the one who irritated Mao the most, possibly because she lacked any extenuating circumstance because of young age.

The one to whom Mao mockingly revealed himself as the Black Hand was Kuai Dafu, the Qinghua student who led the resistance to the work teams sent by Liu Shaoqi and Deng Xiaoping to liquidate the newborn student movement on the Beijing campuses in 1966. Kuai had shown a personal courage that Mao continued to esteem ("Kuai [said Mao] is one who takes personal risk"). However, the situation was radically different as compared with two years before: the Red Guard organizations were at an impasse from which no one among their leaders was able to find a way out.

Despite the irritation expressed by Mao and the other members of the Central Group, the discussion was carried out in an atmosphere much more egalitarian than could be expected given the differences in the hierarchical positions of the participants. Mao deals with the issues with strictness, yet often he shows himself to be even lenient, given the circumstances. He addresses his young interlocutors with pointed criticisms, but he treats them all as comrades with whom he has shared many positions in the last two years and with whom he continues to sympathize. Mao accuses them of having become petty militarist politicians incapable of any original thought about the singularity of the situation. However, during the meeting Mao refuses any role of "master" or "higher authority" possessing the solution of subjective dilemmas ("Do not say that I am giving 'instructions,'" he says, addressing his colleagues).

The current images of this turning point in the relationship between Mao and the Red Guards, found in historiography as well as in some memoirs of former Red Guards, speak of a charismatic chief who used the mystical infatuation of ingenuous adolescents to overthrow his adversaries at court.[14] At a certain point, so the story goes, he decides to get rid of those uncomfortable supporters, liquidating their radicalism for raisons d'état. However, the record of this meeting, thanks to the realism of its unknown stenographer, shows that their relationships involved authentic dilemmas.

The student leaders, all well versed in public speaking and redoubtable polemicists, could offer only inconclusive excuses in response to Mao's criticisms—not because of hierarchical inferiority but because, in the pursuit of an imaginary armed struggle for power, they had politically exhausted the organizations that they had managed to constitute two years before. They prove themselves unable to understand the meeting's ultimate meaning, considering that some of them continue, more or less directly, to ask for army intervention on their behalf in order to overwhelm the opposing faction. The little generals, stiff and dazed, are not even able to perceive the friendly skepticism with which Mao deals with the so-called contrasts between left and right, and the way he replies to them when they pretend not to be involved in fighting at all. Here they are in a scene where the dialogue is particularly closely woven.

> CHAIRMAN: Wang Dabing, is your situation easier [compared with that of Nie Yuanzi]?
> WANG DABING: There were some who opposed Xie Fuzhi, but they've fled. [He claims the fighting is over at his university and probably wants to show his allegiance to Xie Fuzhi, of the Central Group, although the latter reacts sarcastically].
> XIE FUZHI: His second-in-command wants to seize power and calls him a rightist.
> CHAIRMAN: Is he [Wang's second in command] then so much of the Left? So Marxist?
> WANG DABING: They're trying to sow discord between us. He's a good comrade, with good social origins. He's suffered bitterly and nurses deep hatred. This man is very straightforward and full of revolutionary energy. He's got a strong revolutionary character. He's just a bit impatient. He's not really capable of uniting people, and his methods are a bit rigid.
> CHAIRMAN: Could you unite with him? One is Left, the other Right, it should be easy for you to unite. Come here; sit by my side.
> LIN BIAO: Come over!
> XIE FUZHI: Go! Go! (*Wang goes to sit down beside the Chairman.*)
> CHAIRMAN: Sit down; sit down.
>   In these matters, we should have some leeway. After all, they're students, not criminal gangs. . . . The key point is that the two factions that are so thoroughly locked in armed struggle have put all their heart in armed struggle. Such a struggle–criticism–transformation doesn't work, better perhaps is struggle–criticize–quit [斗批走 *dou-pi-zou*]. Aren't the students themselves talking about struggle–criticize–quit and struggle–criticize–disperse [斗批散 *dou-pi-san*]? There are so many students in the faction of the disengaged. Increasingly

unpleasant words are said publicly about Nie Yuanzi and Kuai Dafu. Nie Yuanzi doesn't have all that much cannon fodder, nor does Kuai Dafu. Sometimes 300, other times 150 men. How can this be compared with the troops of Lin Biao or Huang Yongshen? This time, at one shot, I sent in 30,000.[15]

The formula "struggle-criticism-dispersion" parodied the slogan of the two previous years, "struggle-criticism-transformation" (dou-pi-gai), which identified the targets of the Red Guards in the universities. It was never officially quoted, but it was the one actually adopted after the meeting: the factions were "dispersed" and the Red Guard organizations, which most of the students had already abandoned, were dissolved. As for the transformation of universities, a different path was tried.

Very remarkable in this meeting, where a political and not a simply military solution is attempted (the power of the repressive machine is obviously overwhelming), is that Mao often emphasizes the subjective relations then at stake, including those expressed within the meeting itself. Several times he puts a stop to the most irritated comments of the other members of the Central Group, reminding them that they are facing students who have shown themselves unable to go beyond a heroic and militaristic imagery of politics but who should not be disregarded just because of their youth. The severity they deserve should be limited to the solution to their political impasse. However, for all the meeting's participants, finding an adequate solution was still equally hazardous. Neither the hierarchies founded on age nor those founded on state functions would have been enough to warrant a set of decisions flexible enough to deal with the situation's singularity.

Here is another passage during which this kind of tension is manifest. Mao asks himself, altogether perplexed, what really led to the impasse, how to explain ("historically," he says) the degeneration into factions.

> CHAIRMAN: What has happened must have historical reasons. It must have a history. These things don't happen by accident. They don't just crop up suddenly.
>
> CHEN BODA: Follow the Chairman's instructions closely; act resolutely in accordance with them.
>
> CHAIRMAN: Don't say I have issued instructions.
>
> YAO WENYUAN: The Chairman's words today are sincere and earnest.
>
> CHEN BODA: The first half of 1966 was relatively good. The colleges and the universities of the capital did fan the flames throughout the country. Touching off the revolutionary storm was right. Now,

they've got swelled heads, they think they're extraordinary. They want to unify the world [tongyi tianxia, as above, but likely in a sarcastic sense: they want to keep everything under their control]. Kuai Dafu and Han Aijing reach everywhere with their hands, but they're ignorant.

Mao intervened at this point, as in other phases of the meeting, to mitigate the intolerance of the other central leaders toward the students.

> CHAIRMAN: They're only twenty years old. Don't despise young people. Zhou Yu [AD 175–210, famous general of the Kingdom of Wu] started as a cavalryman, he was only sixteen. Don't give yourselves airs because you're veterans.
> JIANG QING: We took part in the revolution when we were teenagers.
> CHAIRMAN: Don't swell up; when the body swells, one has dropsy.
> CHEN BODA: Han Aijing, you've not reflected duly on the thought of Chairman Mao and on the opinions of the Central Committee. You've not pondered them. You've called secret meetings relying on hearsay. By putting yourself first, you're on a slippery slope.
> CHAIRMAN: The first point is of my own bureaucratic making. I've never met you before. If they had not wanted to capture the Black Hand, I would not have asked you to come. Let Kuai Dafu wake up.

Despite Mao's interventions, however, the irritation of the other members of the CGCR toward the little generals remained high.

> LIN BIAO: Kuai Dafu, wake up, stop your horse at the edge of the cliff. Admit your mistakes!
> CHAIRMAN: Don't say, "Admit mistakes."
> CHEN BODA: Kuai Dafu has no respect for the worker masses. If he still refuses to listen to us, it means he's contemptuous of the Central Committee, that he disrespects Chairman Mao. That's a dangerous path.
> CHAIRMAN: Quite dangerous. Now is the time for the little generals to make their mistakes.
> ZHOU ENLAI: The Chairman has been saying "now is the time for the little generals to make their mistakes" for a long time.

Here the premier seems quite fatalistic, but implicitly means that "now it is time" to help them correct those mistakes. Later in the meeting Zhou will be much more determinate. Mao goes on:

CHAIRMAN: Tan Houlan's opponents only number two hundred people, but one year later she has yet to subdue them. In other schools, there are even more opponents, how can they be subjugated? Cao Cao tried to use force to conquer Sun Quan but was defeated. Liu Bei used force to conquer Sun Quan; he lost Jieting and was defeated. Sima Yi failed to conquer Zhuge Liang by force. The first battle lasted a long while, but Zhang had only one horse left at the end.

YE QUN: That was the loss of Jieting.[16]

In the punctuated flow of the dialogue, several passages echo remote references. The last sentences contain a closely woven fabric of historical references (about the collapse of the Han Dynasty and the rivalries among the Three Kingdoms at the beginning of the third century), surely known to the participants, quoted as examples of military tactics that failed because they were centered on attack. In his military writings of the 1930s, Mao had subtly argued the strategic superiority of defense over attack—a line of thought shared by other great dialecticians of war including Sun Zi and Clausewitz—and such a theory had been effectively pursued in the People's War.

However, political situations are unique and unrepeatable. Further evidence of this rule is given by the fact that, although the names chosen by the Red Guards bannered the glories of the People's War that had characterized its founding moment (like the Jinggangshan red bases), their "military" style reproduced an insurrectionary imagery based on attack. Instead, the Jinggangshan bases were made possible only when, at the end of the 1920s, Mao abandoned the insurrectionary vision, by then dominant in the Chinese Communist Party, and elaborated a military strategy based on the strategic primacy of defense.

Here it seems that Mao was musing on the situation and did not mean to give a lesson in military history to the Red Guards. He considered the fighting on the Beijing campuses totally absurd even on the military plane: "What kind of war are you fighting? It amounts to nothing! You only have homemade weapons." Mao tells the students: "If you are capable of it, you should lead the war on a large scale." But here it was clear that they were only mimicking a revolutionary military heroism that was completely imaginary and that they were being allowed to do so just because the state's military apparatus had thus far decided not to intervene. "This little civil war is not a serious thing," concludes Mao, and it must be stopped soon. On this issue, Lin Biao argued in a classical Chinese-style dialectics to confirm the nonnegotiable demand to stop the armed struggle: "In all the great events in the world, it should be unity after long disunity and disunity after long unity. All your defenses aimed at armed struggle must be dismantled. All hot weapons, cold weapons, knives, and rifles should be shelved."[17]

The discussion involved several details about the situation that would require elaborate annotations. I therefore limit myself to the two main concerns that animated the meeting: the urgency of stopping the fighting between the factions and, parallel to that, the even more uncertain problem of the destinies, both political and intellectual, of the university.

"We Do Not Want Civil War"

"These are our reasons: first, we want cultural struggle, we do not want armed struggle"; "The masses do not want civil war." These are the two main arguments that Mao and the other members of the Central Group address to the students. Mao admits there are different points of view between the factions and that, in the final analysis, he agrees more with one faction than with another. However, he notes that none of this justifies the absurd war being fought by the students on the campuses.

He quotes, for example, the "theory of the certain victory" formulated by the "April 14th" faction hostile to Kuai Dafu, according to which the faction was sure to achieve victory in the struggle for power on the basis of the principle that "those who conquer power are not capable of governing." In other words, Kuai, who had overthrown the former authorities and "conquered power" at Qinghua, could do nothing but hand over power to April 14th because the latter had been formed later. As for the value of the arguments supporting the "historical law" expressed by April 14th, it was apparently a rather instrumental theory, aiming only at justifying April 14th's opposition to Kuai Dafu. Mao declares, in fact, that he does not feel any special sympathy for the doctrine of "certain victory," while stressing nonetheless that it should be free to exist exactly because it strives to be a political theory: "April 14th has a theorist called Zhou Quanying. Why should we arrest a theorist? He's a theorist of a school of thought. He writes articles. Why should you arrest him? Release him. He has his opinions. Let him write again! Otherwise, they'll say there's no freedom."[18]

It should be recalled that freedom of political thought, here openly defended by Mao even in the case of a rather poor "theory," was the key issue in constituting the Red Guards since the second half of 1966. In the declining phase, factionalism was increasingly marked by mutual harassment by organizations involved in the struggle to cut each other off. These eventually considered the annihilation of their opponents as the prime condition for their own existence, each of them regarding itself as the nucleus of the regeneration of the party-state. This was the main motive that led to the present sticking point. Mao continued in his colorful polemic register, addressing Nie Yuanzi:

> I say that you, Old Buddha, should be a little more generous. There are several thousand people in Beida's Jinggangshan [the faction adverse to her]. If they are released like a torrential flood, they will wash out the Dragon King's Temple [Nie's headquarters]. How can you stand for that? Otherwise, Old Buddha, we shall impose military control. The third method is to act according to dialectics: you cannot live in the same city, one divides into two, either you or Jinggangshan moves to the South. If one is in the South and the other in the North, you will not see each other and you will not be able to fight. Each puts its own affairs in order and then the entire world will be united [*yi tong tianxia*]. Otherwise, you also will be afraid. If they launch an attack on the nest of the Old Buddha [another sarcastic name for Nie's headquarters], you won't be able to sleep. You're afraid and they're afraid too. It's necessary to hold back a little. Why should you be so tense?[19]

Mao and the other members of the Central Group repeatedly expressed their great indignation about the gratuitous cruelties the factions inflicted on each other and the complacent slogans that threatened to "slaughter" and "cook" their adversaries. Furthermore, the arguments that each faction used to accuse their opponents of being counterrevolutionary and to treat them as war enemies were ludicrous. When Mao asked Nie Yuanzi why she regarded the adverse faction as counterrevolutionary, she answered: "They organized a reactionary block that viciously attacked Chairman Mao and Vice-Chairman Lin." Mao sharply replied: "What is the matter if they slander us a bit?" The evidence Nie produced about the "political crimes" of her adversaries were null: "Let them criticize us," Mao said several times. "How would it be possible not to have opponents?"

On the tortures inflicted on their opponents by the little generals who claimed to emulate the glories of the People's War, Mao reminded them how far more civilized was the style of the People's Liberation Army despite the fact that it was composed of soldiers and even generals with very poor formal education. "Two rough fellows" (土包子 *tubaozi*), Mao said, jokingly referring to the chairman and the vice-chairman of the general staff present at the meeting, who had attended only a couple of years of primary school, compared with the long curricula of the Red Guard leaders, who could definitely be considered "intellectuals" (知识分子 *zhishifenzi*). Whereas in the army, Mao said, deserters were not put under arrest anymore and isolation was no longer used as a punishment, in the student factions arrest was frequently used and the opponents were treated as "prisoners of war to be subjected to coercion and forced to confess"; those who refused to confess were beaten to death. "I think the intellectuals are the most uncivilized [commented Mao sourly]; you say they're the most civilized. I don't think so. The less educated are the most civilized."

Among the members of the Central Group, Jiang Qing was the one who was the most distressed about the treatment of opponents. At the Normal University, where Tan Houlan was in command, many students of the opposing faction had been put under arrest and imprisoned for several days in the dark without food or drink. Jiang Qing addressed this fearsome "girl with braids" with heartfelt indignation.

> JIANG QING (*addressing Tan Houlan*): ... How could you have done this? As soon as they told me, I could not help crying. These hundreds, or dozens of persons, after all they are the masses. ...
>
> I have no friendly feelings toward your opponents. It is said that [they] are against us. We are not speaking in their name, but release them! Proletarians should stress proletarian humanitarianism. These dozens of counterrevolutionaries are, after all, youths.
>
> They want to strangle me to death. I am not afraid of being fried in oil. I've heard that Beida Jinggangshan wants to fry Jiang Qing.
>
> YAO WENYUAN: Frying is just a figure of speech.
> CHAIRMAN: They even say strangle Kuai Dafu to death.

The violence of the language used by the Red Guards, and even the brutality of their behavior, is inversely proportional to their political capabilities. Jiang Qing then addressed the same rebuke to Nie Yuanzi for her senseless violence on the Beida campus.

> JIANG QING: Nie Yuanzi, have I still a right to speak? I'm deeply grieved by all of you. Now you are all masses struggling against other masses, and the bad people are hiding. ... April 14th says they are definitely going to win. April 14th is especially against the Central Group of the Cultural Revolution [that is, against the leaders present at the meeting]. They are also against the Premier [Zhou Enlai] and Kang Sheng [of the Central Group]. Nevertheless, they are a mass organization.
>
> You know where I live. If you want to strangle me, go ahead. If you want to fry me, go ahead. We were in trouble and adversity together. If you cannot tolerate others, how can you rule the country

and bring peace to the world [治国平天下 *zhi guo ping tianxia*; the same *tianxia* as above, but not sarcastic]? I think you are not studying the Chairman's works, and you are not learning his working style. The Chairman always seeks unity with those who oppose him.

CHAIRMAN ... (*addressing Nie Yuanzi*): What you cited [as the crimes of your opponents] are nothing but [their] attacks on Jiang Qing and Lin Biao. We can write them off at one stroke. They only talked among themselves privately, they didn't go out to post dazibaos.

JIANG QING: Even if they post dazibaos, I'm not scared. . . .

CHAIRMAN (*addressing Nie*): . . . You cannot get rid of thousands of members of the Beida Jinggangshan.

Nie tries to prove that all is well, that she has defeated her opponents, keeps them under control, and even forced them to participate in study classes, presumably to "correct their mistakes" and to switch them to her side. But Mao denies it decisively.

NIE YUANZI: More than a thousand have left the Jinggangshan. They're holding study classes.

CHAIRMAN: You cannot rely on those who leave Jinggangshan. Most of them are physically with Cao Cao, but, in their hearts, they are with the Han.[20] Physically they are with the Old Buddha, but their minds are with Jinggangshan. Do not do anything to Niu Huilin [leader of the opposing faction], let him go with Jinggangshan, let him be. We must not compel or insult others, especially not beat people and not extort confessions. In the past, we committed many mistakes. You're making this mistake for the first time; we cannot blame you.[21]

Since the hostilities among the Red Guard factions were deeply entangled with the relations the student leaders had established with individual members of the Central Group,[22] Mao and the other central leaders repeatedly emphasized that to be for or against some of them did not constitute any possible reason to continue the struggle.[23] The Central Group was united and resolute in its request for an immediate cessation of the fighting.

The intransigence of the Central Group on this point was augmented by the trend, worsening in the recent months, of an interlacing between student factionalism on one side and, on the other, a series of divergences among military commands that, if fully developed, could have turned the fighting among small student factions into conflicts among real warlords.[24] The student leaders, for their part, seemed not to be worried about that possibility. Some indirectly advanced the request for the army's support for their faction in order to overwhelm their adversaries. Nie Yuanzi went further in asking the support of a particular army unit that she considered close to her faction. "You want everything served to you on a platter just the way you want it," Mao replied with anger.

Interference in student factionalism by the military was one of the meeting's hottest issues, and it emerged very excitedly when a worried Zhou Enlai remarked about a meeting of the Scientific Committee of National Defense that some student organizations had called at the Beijing Institute of Aeronautics. It is clear that the Scientific Committee was an organ situated at the institutional juncture between military and academic-scientific apparatuses and that the Institute of Aeronautics was closely connected with the programs of national defense. "How did you dare call that meeting?" Zhou Enlai thundered to Han Aijing. "You know it deals with secrets of national defense." Han's long answer reveals the superficiality with which he and the main leaders of the Beijing Red Guards had treated such an intricate point of the situation.

> HAN AIJING: We didn't call that meeting. You can check. Wu Zhuanbin of Guangdong called the meeting. I was ill, and before going to the hospital, I lived at the School of Physical Education. A telephone call came from the school asking me to receive two standing members of the provincial revolutionary committee. People say: "Up there is Heaven; down there is Beijing Aeronautical Institute." I did not enthusiastically welcome the leaders of the May 4th Students' Congress and the various leaders of the rebel factions from other provinces. So we were criticized for being conceited and arrogant; they even said we were rich peasants and not revolutionary anymore. Thus I accepted to receive them. As they were leaving, they wanted to call a meeting to discuss the national situation. I told them that if they call such a meeting in Beijing, it would be a black [that is, a reactionary] meeting.

Han, the most talkative among the little generals during the meeting, continues with more and more inconclusive justifications, trying to minimize his involvement in the episode that infuriated Zhou Enlai.

> In Beijing, the situation is very complicated—there is a Sky faction and an Earth faction. I agreed to have a chat with some reliable leaders of rebel factions and the responsible persons of revolutionary committees, just to talk about the situation, without discussing any specific measures. Both Kuai [Dafu] and I went to those talks; then I entered the hospital. As soon as the

meeting started, everybody felt that things were going wrong. Those from the Geology Institute, after having attended the preparatory meeting, did not attend the other ones. Kuai Dafu, after listening for a few minutes, ran away scared from the meeting, and the representatives of Jinggangshan did the same. One after another, schoolmates informed me; I said we must hasten to write reports; who would have thought we were already being criticized.[25]

Faced with these explanations, as embarrassed as they are incongruous, Zhou does not even find it necessary to reply. A mix of complacency, adventurism, and tactical opportunism had led the little generals to an impasse disproportionate to their capacities.

Another essential reason to ask the Beijing student leaders to end the struggles between factions was due to the national echo that the events unavoidably gave rise to. The fighting in Beijing actually involved only a few thousand students at five or six campuses, but in the last months in some provinces, especially in Guangxi Province, there had been much more serious fighting. In the face of the situation in Guangxi, the Central Group of the Cultural Revolution had issued an appeal on July 1 asking for the immediate cessation of the armed struggle.[26] The continuation of fighting on some Beijing campuses (the organization of Kuai Dafu stated that the announcement was applicable only in Guangxi, not in Beijing) influenced the situation in the whole country, because of the prestige enjoyed by Beijing's Red Guard leaders. About the cessation of the armed struggle, Mao was adamant. Whoever kept on fighting would be dealt with as a criminal.

> CHAIRMAN: Somebody said that notices issued on Guangxi are applicable only in Guangxi and those on Shenxi are applicable only in Shenxi. Now, I issue another nationwide notice. If anyone goes on running counter to and fighting the People's Liberation Army, destroying means of transportation, killing people, or setting fires, he is committing crimes. Those few who turn a deaf ear to persuasion and persist in not changing their behavior are bandits, Guomindang elements subject to capture. If they stubbornly continue to resist, they will be annihilated.

On the situation in Guangxi, Lin Biao and Mao both show maximum determination. The clashes of paramilitary groups, fires, and destruction are intolerable.

> LIN BIAO: At present, some of them are true rebel groups; others are bandits and Guomindang elements that are using our flag for rebellion. In Guangxi, one thousand houses have been burned down.

CHAIRMAN: In the notice it should be written clearly and explained clearly to the students that if they persist and do not change, they will be arrested. That's for the minor cases; the serious ones will be surrounded and suppressed.

LIN BIAO: In Guangxi one thousand houses have been burned down and they were not allowed to put out the fire.

CHAIRMAN: Was not the Guomindang just like this? This is like the desperate agony of class enemies. Burning houses is a grave error.

LIN BIAO: During the Long March I entered Guangxi, where I defeated Bai Chongxi. He too used this method: he burned houses and tried to pretend the communists did it. It is the same old tactic used again.

At this point, Han Aijing tries again to justify Kuai Dafu, and therefore himself, claiming that he has been overwhelmed by events. Mao, however, cuts him short.

HAN AIJING: Kuai Dafu is riding a tiger from which he cannot dismount.

KANG SHENG: It's not that kind of situation.

CHAIRMAN: If he cannot get off the back of the tiger, then let us kill the tiger.[27]

"To kill the tiger" meant to declare the end of the Red Guards as politically independent organizations, which was in fact was the main result of the meeting. The arrival of Kuai Dafu confirmed the subjective breakdown that the meeting was trying to deal with. Kuai broke into the hall two-thirds of the way through the meeting, sobbing theatrically, just as his friend Han Aijing indirectly had anticipated at the beginning. The tragicomic effect, as the transcript scrupulously recorded, clearly showed on Jiang Qing's face: "Huang Zuozhen reports that Kuai Dafu has arrived. Kuai enters crying out bitterly. The Chairman stands up, goes toward him, and shakes his hand. Comrade Jiang Qing is laughing. Kuai, still crying, introduces his case (告状 *gaozhuang*, "'introduces his complaints to superiors'"); he says that Qinghua is in extreme danger, that the workers, manipulated by the Black Hand, entered Qinghua to suppress the students, and that there is a big plot behind it all."[28]

To understand how different the situation was, one should consider that in June 1966 Kuai emerged as a brave leader of the student rebellion at Qinghua, writing an "open letter" to the "hesitant," whose general tenor was captured in the following: "I sincerely hope that in this difficult and crucial moment you remain firm. The train of the revolution, which is running at very high speed, is entering a sharp bend. Keep a firm grip on yourself if you do not want to fall down and shatter."²⁹

Two years later, Mao met a whimpering Kuai Dafu, to whom he could not but repeat what he had already said to the others, adding serious criticism for the bloody attacks led by Kuai's faction against the workers at Qinghua the day before. The opposing faction, April 14th, had in fact welcomed the workers, while the Jinggangshan of Kuai Dafu, to which Mao said he was more sympathetic, had launched a deadly attack against them. After going to shake hands with Kuai, Mao calls to him harshly, but continues to show sympathy.

> CHAIRMAN: You want to arrest the Black Hand. I am the Black Hand. There was no other possible way to deal with you. We're more sympathetic to your faction. I cannot accept April 14th's idea of a "sure victory," but we must win over their masses, including some of their leaders. The main idea of Zhou Quanying is that those who conquer power cannot rule, thus Kuai Dafu cannot but transfer power to April 14th. We asked the workers to do some propaganda work, but you refused. You well knew how many people were coming for propaganda—Huang Zuozhen and Xie Fuzhi had talked to you, there was nothing else to do. The workers were barehanded, but you reviled them and attacked, killing and wounding them. In the case of Beida too, we are more sympathetic to Nie Yuanzi. We're more inclined toward you five great leaders, but did you not know what those tens of thousands of workers were coming to do at Qinghua University? If there had been no decision of the Central Committee, how could they have dared to go there? You have been very passive. On the contrary, April 14th has welcomed the workers; you of the Jinggangshan, instead, did not welcome them, and you were wrong.³⁰

According to Hinton, the attitude of April 14th was due to serious "military" difficulties at the time and to the fact that they were on the point of being overwhelmed by the Jinggangshan. In a sense, they welcomed the workers as their rescuers. Those of the Jinggangshan, who believed themselves to have almost reached complete control of the situation, were particularly fierce against the workers, whom they saw as stealing away their victory. This detail further confirms the total political groundlessness of the armed clashes at Qinghua.

Unable to reply, Kuai was so confused that Mao, after criticizing his "passive" (in the sense of politically incapable of taking the right decision) behavior, did not insist too much, and eventually he just suggested Kuai find a place to rest. Zhou Enlai, for his part, recommended that Han Aijing take care of his ally and help him find a way out. The attitude of the Central Group of the Cultural Revolution toward Kuai and the other student leaders was very patient, notwithstanding the gravity of the situation.

Mao had also expressed a precise evaluation of the paroxysm of student rebellion during the previous months: "There is quite a bit of anarchism. In this world, anarchism [无政府 *wu-zhengfu*, 'no government']) is correlative with government. As long as there is government in the world, anarchism cannot be eliminated. [Attitudes of] servility and 'docile tool' that in the past have been told [to youth] now turn contrary. This is the punishment of right opportunism, the punishment for the right opportunism of the Central Committee."[31]

It could be said that, after all, any "censorship" always has a corresponding "return of the repressed." However, against the backdrop typical of Mao of a general philosophical fatalism about the unavoidable side effects of the very existence of "government," what he was proposing was a properly political judgment on the situation. Did not the party-state disseminate and impose, especially among the youth, acquiescence and docility as qualities of a "good communist"?[32] The present "anarchism" was the opposite result, commented Mao. It was a sort of Dantean *contrappasso*, the "retaliation" that the "right opportunism of the Central Committee" had fully deserved.

The meticulous methods, in no way inferior to those of the Jesuit colleges in the European Renaissance, for disciplining schools and university students in the early sixties would deserve specific research.[33] Many episodes of brutality and even cruelty by the Red Guards—this was the sense of Mao's bitter remark—were the tragic result of a basic failure of the "pedagogy" of the party-state and of the program of moral "perfecting" of the youth in which the Chinese educational apparatus was engaged during the previous two decades.

"Should We Still Be Running Universities?"

Besides the fighting at Beijing universities, the other important topic discussed that day unavoidably regarded the institutional and intellectual destinies of the universities. The issue, about which the uncertainty was probably greater than that about how to stop the armed struggle, was crucial for several reasons: the central place occupied by the university system in the Chinese state apparatus in the 1950s and 1960s; the obvious failure of any attempt to reform university education through the Red Guards' activism (the "struggle–criticism–transformation" that degenerated into brutal brawls); and, not least, the 1968 worldwide university crisis that the Chinese university system largely anticipated and finally concentrated in itself through a prolonged institutional paralysis.

Note too the difference in register Mao adopts here regarding the radical educational program of the letter of May 7, 1966, about the "Great School." His tone is also cautious and probing in the approach needed to transform China's university system vis-à-vis the evident "barricade" the students themselves erected to forestall university reform. It was July 1968, the moment of maximum uncertainty for modern university education, when Mao asked:

> Should we still be running universities? Should universities enroll new students? Not to enroll students will not do. I left some leeway in my remarks. We should still run universities: I've mentioned science and engineering colleges, but I did not say that humanities colleges should not be run. If these latter are unable to make any achievement, then forget about it. As far as I can see, colleges offer more or less the same basic courses as those offered in junior and senior high schools and in the last years of primary school. One should go to school only for six years, ten at most. In senior high school, the courses repeat those in middle school, university courses repeat those in senior school. As for the basic courses, they are all repetitious. As for the specialized courses, even teachers do not understand them. Philosophers are unable to talk about philosophy. What is studying for?

Mao tries to involve Nie in the discussion on this point, but she declines the invitation, provoking the sarcasm of Jiang Qing.

> CHAIRMAN: Nie Yuanzi, aren't you a philosopher?
> NIE YUANZI: No, I'm not a philosopher.
> JIANG QING: She's an Old Buddha.
> CHAIRMAN: What's so worthwhile about the study of philosophy? Is philosophy something that one can learn in college? If one has never been a worker or a peasant and goes to study philosophy, what kind of philosophy is that?[34]

Questions like these would horrify philosophy teachers bound too much to school programs, but not necessarily all philosophers. Is it possible to learn how to philosophize only inside the university? Lin Biao, who during the meeting showed a flash of humor from time to time, answered with a sarcastic joke: it was not 哲学 *zhexue*, "philosophy," but 窄学 *zhaixue*, "shrinking study": "The more one studies the more [the mind] shrinks."

Mao posed the same question for literature: Is it possible to learn how to write literature in the university? This time it was Zhou Enlai who bitterly commented: "When they go to university their brain petrifies," citing the case of a self-taught writer of peasant origin, Gao Yubao, who had been rewarded and sent to university. Before the Cultural Revolution, his case was the subject of a large propaganda effort as the result of the democratization of the Chinese school, but as soon as Gao entered university, he stopped writing altogether.[35]

The skepticism about the results of previous educational policies was almost total. "Look at some of our boys who attended school for more than ten years [said a disheartened Mao]; they are so physically destroyed as to be unable to sleep. A boy studies history, but he does not understand the class struggle." In other words: Is to philosophize, to write novels, to make politics in a thoughtful way, intellectually consistent with the system of university knowledge and its transmission? In the summer of 1968, these were key intellectual questions worldwide. According to Mao: "When studying literature, one should not study the history of literature, but should rather learn to write novels. Write me a novel per week. If one is unable to do it, go to a factory to work as an apprentice. During his apprenticeship, he should write about his experience as an apprentice. Nowadays those who study literature are unable to write novels."[36]

Besides showing an overt aversion to "literary history," Mao here talked about going to factories and the countryside to become an apprentice or a peasant in order to be able to write novels, certainly a thorny problem and open to various misunderstandings. However, what writer has really learned more of his art from university education than from experiencing the reality of relationships among people? Factories and countryside here meant the existential horizon of 90 percent of people in China at that moment.

On the other hand, looking at the blossoming of Chinese literature in the 1980s and 1990s, it is significant that great poets like Bei Dao, Mang Ke, and Yang Lian, or novelists like Han Shaogong,[37] began to write at the end of the 1960s when they had been sent as "young educated people to the countryside" and that none of them ever attended university. Can anyone assert that the interruption of university teaching of literature during those years was decidedly harmful to contemporary Chinese literature?

What was at stake, after all, was the role of the modern university in the relationship between intellectuality—of art, politics, and philosophy—and its didactic transmissibility. The university apparatus of the socialist state, which in those years in China was modeled on the Soviet system, had pretended to embody the perfect balance between thought and knowledge. Yet this was exactly what the current crisis was radically refuting, impelling China to find new paths.

Thus, Mao, who was far from being persuaded of the superiority of the socialist university, emphasized that Marxism—the core of Chinese university knowledge at the time, and of the philosophy departments in particular—had not been formed in the university. No one among the great Marxists, Mao remarked, had graduated, except Marx, who to be sure did not follow an academic career. As for the school records of the others, as Mao recalled, Engels began to make inquiries on workers while he was a bookkeeper in his father's factory and tutored himself at the British Library. Lenin attended university for two years; Stalin only some years at a secondary school ("run by the church," Mao specified, perhaps not without irony). Gorky went only two years to a primary school, less than Jiang Qing, who attended some years more, and less than Lin Biao, who, having attended some years of middle school, could be called an "intellectual," as Mao jokingly commented.

Mao said he had not been a good student ("I only tried not to be thrown out of school"), but this should not be taken too literally. As a student and later as a teacher at the Normal School of Changsha, he was for several years a young militant educator who took part in important initiatives in the most advanced currents of educational reform of the May Fourth movement. Traces of those experiences emerged in this meeting, as for example the Hunan self-study university (自修大学 zixiu daxue) that Mao founded in 1921 and that produced a significant echo at the national level (Mao would in fact propose a self-study system in 1968).[38] Peculiar to those experiences, as well as to the school policies of Yan'an in the 1930s and 1940s, was the consideration of school and university policies as a crucial terrain of political and intellectual experimentation, and not only as structural elements of the modern state system to be taken for granted. They in fact created remarkably inventive forms of schooling.[39]

Other leaders present at the meeting had been protagonists of those experiences, like Zhou Enlai, who in his youth was active in the intellectual and educational vanguard of reform currents of May Fourth, and Lin Biao, who at Yan'an directed the University of the Anti-Japanese Resistance (抗大 Kangda). Although they avoided boasting of any special expertise in the educational field and proudly declared themselves to be self-taught, a number of the leaders present at the meeting were in fact well versed in the issue. Nevertheless, with the irreversible crisis that the school and university policies of the socialist state revealed in that moment, the issue of what new criteria might inspire an educational reform was then the most uncertain for all the participants. The evaluation of the last two decades was for them largely negative, and the experience of the last two years did not show any new path.

"No steps forward have been made in educational reform," a member of the CGCR said during the meeting. "If no steps forward are made in educational revolution [Mao replied to the students] we too will not take any step forward, let alone you. The old educational system damaged you." Moreover, if the situation was to be blocked by the fighting between student factions, it would be impossible to find something new:

> CHAIRMAN: . . . As I see it, if all boils down to these few matters [of the student factions], what revolution in education can we start? If we fail, let us disperse [*san*]. This is what the students are saying. It's not information that I get from the disengaged [*xiayoapai*]! . . .
>
> YAO WENYUAN: I'm inclined to accept that in some schools there should be struggle-criticize-dispersion [dou-pi-san], or struggle-criticize-quit [dou-pi-zou].

Mao quotes his idea, which he had developed since the early 1920s, that the way to scholastic reform should be based, in addition to the participation of students in all kinds of social activities, on "self-study."

> CHAIRMAN: With the two factions going on like this, I think that even if they do not want to quit they should quit [the campuses]. . . . When they have vacated the field, let in people to take their place for self-study [自修 *zixiu*] of how to write a novel. If you study literature, you should write poems and drama. Those who study philosophy should write family history, the history of the revolutionary processes. Those who study political economy should not learn from the professors of Beijing University. Are there any famous professors at Beijing University? These topics do not need professors. Professors who teach is a harmful method. Organize a small group and study by yourselves, [run] a self-study university [自修大学 *zixiu daxue*]. Come and go, half a year, one year, two years, three years.

Another strong point for Mao was his aversion to exams and grades. As is well known, this was a fundamental theme of all radical pedagogy in the 1960s.

> CHAIRMAN: No examinations: examinations are not a good method. Suppose ten questions are asked about a book which contains one hundred viewpoints: do they not cover only one-tenth? Even if you answer correctly, what about the other 90 percent? Who examined Marx? Who examined Engels? Who examined Lenin? Who examined Comrade Lin Biao? Who examined Comrade Huang Zuozhen? The needs of the masses and Jiang Jieshi have been our teachers.[40] This was the case for all of us. Teachers are needed in middle schools, but everything should be simplified and the superfluous eliminated.

YAO WENYUAN: Open a few good libraries.

CHAIRMAN: Give workers, peasants, and soldiers time to use them. To study in a library is a good method. I studied at a library in Hunan for half a year, and in the library of Beijing University for another half a year. I chose books by myself. Who taught me? . . . Universities are run in such a lifeless way. There should be more freedom.[41]

All these were crucial topics worldwide. Was not the intellectual value of the modern university, and in the long run even its institutional existence, at stake as much in China as in France and elsewhere? It is usually said that China had been isolated from the rest of the world for ten years. But any university student or teacher in July 1968 who was not asking himself somewhat radical questions—about the usefulness or the damage of academic curricula, or the intolerable bureaucratic exercise of exams, or the need for freedom of choice in study—lost a great chance to reflect on the essential circumstances of his own intellectual existence.

A Strategic Retreat

After the end of the meeting, the five little generals were kept a little while at Zhongnanhai. "What about today? Do you think we're going to arrest you and to put you in isolation?" Mao had said sarcastically, blaming them for the cruelties against their opponents and for the deadly attack against the workers at Qinghua. The student leaders were in fact treated much less severely than they could have expected. They were only asked to sign a brief summary of the discussion and then disseminate it on their campuses: two pages in all, containing the main arguments with which Mao and the others of the Central Group had harshly criticized the student leaders for their behavior and asked for the immediate end of the fighting.[42]

The meeting confirmed that the situation had reached self-destructive gridlock, because by that time the Red Guard organizations lacked any political content. Two years before, the Red Guards had been welcomed by the Decision in 16 Points of August 1966 as "an excellent bridge that allows our party a closer tie with the masses." They should be considered, continued the document, "not as temporary but as permanent organizations," destined "to operate for a long time" and not only in the schools and universities; their expansion to "factories, mines, neighborhoods, towns, and countryside" should also be welcomed. In July 1968, with the dispatching of the workers at Qinghua and with this meeting, Mao and the Central Group declared that the subjective existence of that kind of organization should be considered as concluded. As for the political experiment started in June 1966, those independent organizations in which the "masses liberate only by themselves, and no one must in any way act in their place," as expressed in another famous statement of the Maoists in August 1966, had come to an end.

With the demise of the "rebel organizations," the most difficult problem for Mao and the Central Group was no longer how to halt armed struggle on the campuses but how to handle the student factions—disarming them and envisaging their dissolution—without destroying the subjective energy that allowed their existence. It is remarkable that the main steps taken by the Central Group at the end of July 1968 linked the theme of the university with that of the factories and the workers. The decision to involve the workers and factories in educational issues can be considered, using a military principle Mao had often adopted, a "strategic retreat." That retreat would be made only after having identified a terrain on which to orient themselves, to keep the chances to experience new forms of egalitarian politics alive, on the basis of the political energy of the last two years.

Sending the workers to the Qinghua campus was above all a way to deal with that situation as a political matter, rather than simply as an unavoidable police operation. The workers entered Qinghua to disarm the students, shouting slogans such as "use reason not violence, lay down your arms, form a big alliance," and thanks to this rationalist discipline, altogether rare in this kind of event, they accomplished the task of stopping the fighting.[43] Mao mobilized the workers as possible protagonists of political invention and not as substitutes for the state's repressive apparatus. The demonstration of the workers at Qinghua, to be sure, also filled a highly symbolic role, thanks to the prestige of the category of "working class" in the ideology of the socialist state. However, Mao was not leaning on a fixed and stable point.

Although that decision seemed to arise from the canonical options of Marxist-Leninist culture, and to bring the issue back to the relationships between the socialist state and its "worker base," as we have seen, those relationships during the Cultural Revolution endured a political cataclysm in Shanghai's January Storm of 1967.

Yet, as we noted in previous chapters, Shanghai was also the city least affected by factional fighting and the most open to political and institutional innovation. Shanghai's revolutionaries managed to turn the consequences of that cataclysm into a stimulus for political experimentation, and until the mid-1970s the city was the site of important attempts at rethinking politics in the worker–factory relationship.

Mao tried to rely on those possibilities, although gropingly, when he urged the mobilization of workers as a way of solving the factional fighting. Just a week before the meeting with the Red Guards, Mao had published an article accompanying a report from a Shanghai machinery factory that announced the opening of a "worker university." Mao's remarks, emphasized by the national press, enthusiastically supported the initiative, praising it as "the path to follow" in the transformation of the polytechnic-scientific universities. Those strange "worker universities"—which in the following years were one of the strongest points of the Maoist group—audaciously linked the university's destiny to the experimentation with new political possibilities in worker–factory relations. We will discuss the political value of those experiments in the next chapter.

In conclusion, let me suggest that the three main steps taken by the Maoist group at the end of July 1968—the publication of Mao's remarks on the worker university of Shanghai, the dispatching of the workers to Qinghua, and the Zhongnanhai meeting—formed a coherent, although precarious and risky, set of political decisions. The wide distribution of the minutes of that meeting, both in the form of a summary and in full text, played a crucial role in attempts to find a political way out of the impasse created by factional exhaustion, in fact by the self-defeat, of the Red Guard organizations.[44]

Revolutionary Culture and Factional Heroism

As I have suggested, this self-defeat was the result of a retroactive response of revolutionary culture, that is, the ideological and organizational thrust of socialism, vis-à-vis the Cultural Revolution, that is, the experimenting political subjectivities of the time taken together. A recent study by Yang Guobin provides a detailed look at the role revolutionary culture played in factionalism periodizing the phenomenon as subsequent to January 1967 in reference to "seizure of power."[45] For the reasons set out in the chapter 7, I agree that factionalism, meant as a striving to seize power, occurred only after the January Storm.

Yang accurately portrays the features of the "imaginary heroic," facets that though clearly outlined already in the second half of 1966, by early 1967 overwhelmed whatever novelties had appeared up to that point. In a well-wrought pondering of factionalism's tragic outcomes, Yang cites a beautiful poem by Gu Cheng entitled "Adieu Tomb" that is dedicated to the grave of a Red Guard. It is a poem that I have always admired for its elegiac intensity and political acumen. A few months before his tragic death, in an interview accompanying publication of its translation in Italian, Gu Cheng observed that the Cultural Revolution was not only a unique event—"as if the Sky had fallen upon the Earth"—but, more importantly, a moment when "a hundred flowers of all seasons blossomed."

What caused the frost that killed the flowers? What returned the Sky to its place and quashed in a fury of self-destruction the hyperpluralization of independent organizations? The ruin of the Red Guards was essentially of their own making. Gu Cheng's poem subtly captures the "primacy of internal causes" in the destruction of those political novelties:

> Interweaving among yourselves
>
> you have fallen below ground
>
> weeping tears of joy
>
> clasping imaginary rifles.
>
> Your fingers
>
> are still clean
>
> they have leafed through only schoolbooks
>
> and stories of heroes.
>
> Perhaps spurred on
>
> by a common habit
>
> on the last page
>
> you have portrayed yourselves.[46]

The system of tropes embedded in the composition of these lines can, to a great extent, be immediately recognized. In their senseless brawls, the Red Guards' organizations destroyed one another, all falling together into a mortal weft. The Red Guards ended up expending all their energies in a quite imaginary and tragicomic petty civil war driven by a particularly schoolbook, rote-learned version of a "historical" vision of politics that was aggravated by a "heroic" attitude ("only schoolbooks / and stories of heroes"). On the "last page" of the book of revolutionary heroism, they claimed to "portray" themselves. They did so, the poet remarks, "spurred on / by a common habit," that is, the catastrophic effect of a social consensus. In the last analysis, they reflected themselves in the image of a revolutionary "ideal of the Ego" that was far removed from the political novelty they were creating and that eventually destroyed them.

The eye of the poet helps us shed light on our approach to the issue we're exploring. Aside from exterior attitudes, slogans, heroic posturing, and the like, revolutionary culture was, as noted more than once, a framework compacting in its spatial articulation the political, historical, economic, and even philosophical insights, the body of knowledge, that provided the institutional structure of the state's entire system. The proposition we are exploring is that revolutionary culture responded in the most rigid, stereotypical, and, in the end, most self-destructive reaction to the ongoing political experimentation. The propulsive, probing thrusts of the latter were shaking the vital joints of that framework's political beams and organizational nodes by calling into question the primacy of the Communist Party as the sole organizational principle at its core.

In the perspective I am exploring, two factors converge at the roots of factionalism. On the one hand, the ideological and organizational body of the governing system responded by closing ranks in the face of the threat, that is, the calling into question of the CCP's authority, its revolutionary cultural leadership, posed by the political subjectivities in the form of the independent organizations that had sprung up at the time. On the other hand, the revolutionaries proved unable to stake out a middle ground as a buffer between their mass egalitarian self-organization and the workings of that governing machinery.

The fulcrum of my proposition is the turning point that occurred in January 1967. In the latter half of 1966, when the mass student–worker activism converged with the "symptom" of the "probable defeat," the mobilizing anxiety of the latter was treading on unexplored territory. The path led to an uncharted field of political experimentation that swiftly overcame the hurdles embedded in socialism's ideological and organizational groundwork. The "difference between internal and external" vis-à-vis the party's organization, the class origin, and even the "natural" membership in the working class of the party-state's ritual guidelines were examples.

However, when in January 1967 Mao declared seizure of power as the main task (I have already noted the particular conditions prompting the utterance and his numerous second thoughts), the Cultural Revolution's political anxiety, that is, the experimenting subjectivities as a whole, began to recoalesce within the framework of revolutionary culture. But there was one complication. That framework had been struck and destabilized by an unprecedented political novelty. Given its central role in that "epistemic" fabric, the concept of seizure of power ended up acting as a recompacting factor but in an altogether formalistic way that was inversely proportional to the structural weakening it had induced. The result was that it drained the ongoing experimentation of its political vitality.

As a contribution to a work largely yet to be undertaken, I have proposed in this chapter a close reading of the transcript that faithfully records the statements of the protagonists at the height of factionalism, or rather at the time of the implosion of the factions on the Beijing campuses. The little generals were convinced that they were engaged in a heroic struggle to seize power, even as they and their groups had lost all political purpose and were on the verge of dissolving. Yet, no matter how self-destructive, their resolve was nurtured by the conviction of being called to save the weave of the entire framework's political and intellectual fabric. Rather than contesting the powers that be in this or that university, factory, or state agency, the Red Guards threw themselves headlong into an imaginary seizure of power to save nothing less than revolutionary culture itself.

Conclusions

In these three chapters on the first two-year period of the revolutionary decade, I have argued at various points for the need to distinguish two political processes, *pluralization* and *dismissal*, which were copresent, but which turned out to be intransitive. This distinction aims to dissolve the fog that enveloped those events and to call into question the image of a completely irrational turmoil in which the entire Cultural Revolution has been embalmed for decades. These two descriptors have served to find a path toward analyzing the peculiar political logic of the mass phase, its advances with respect to powerful obstacles, and its final impasse. In this perspective I have outlined the internal periodization of the two-year period, arguing that the separation and overlap of the two processes of pluralization and dismissal marked, respectively, the expansion and decline of organizational experimentation.

Countless independent organizations arose and expanded in an unexpected and singular way. They were certainly fully supported by Mao, but he himself neither conceived nor initiated them. The political objective of the revolutionaries was to search for a new principle of organization. The Communist Party, which effectively duplicated the entire state bureaucratic apparatus, was, in Mao's estimation, incapable of preventing on its own the undermining of socialism and the restoration of capitalism in China—what a farsighted prediction!—that is, the reestablishment of the rule of government over the modern world. This was the key point on which Mao's political anguish and that of the masses of "rebel" students and workers converged throughout the second half of 1966. The indeterminate pluralization of the organizational forms of revolutionary politics was the main ground of experimentation they undertook.

On the other hand, what I have called the "dismissal process" did not involve any real political experimentation. It was intrinsically in line with the seizure of power, whose synonym, ultimately, was "dismissal." One takes power when one dismisses another from power. Dismissal is what governmental subjects of all times and countries have always practiced. The fact that in the case of socialism it was argued in the name of communist and egalitarian revolutionary principles only served to make its function more ambiguous.

However, dismissal is not at all transitive to egalitarian experimentation, as the Cultural Revolution dramatically demonstrated. When the processes of egalitarian mass invention established their objectives around the seizure of power, meaning the dismissal of certain powers and their replacement by others, those inventions annihilated themselves; indeed, they served as a lever for a change of hands between powerful entities that did not know what to do with egalitarian political experimentation.

The unresolved problem that the Cultural Revolution left behind was, first of all, how to find and maintain the necessary political distance between the two processes. During the revolutionary decade, politics was riven by a radical discontinuity that penetrated the revolutionary subjectivities themselves, and that ultimately concerned the face-to-face confrontation that took place between the Cultural Revolution and revolutionary culture.

Reflection on such discontinuity, indispensable for a political assessment of factionalism and in general of the mass phase of the Cultural Revolution, remained an unfinished task. As I will discuss in the next chapters, the prerequisite for such an assessment should have been a rethinking of the entire horizon of revolutionary culture, starting from its most basic concept, the dictatorship of the proletariat.

PART IV

At the Edge of an Epochal Turning Point

9

Intellectual Conditions for a Political Assessment

While the Zhongnanhai meeting of July 28, 1968, did indeed manage to stem the self-destructive effects of the political exhaustion of the Red Guards, Mao himself was not able to formulate a precise thesis to explain factionalism. He suggested it could be the manifestation of an anarchism as a sort of negative correlative to the very existence of any government, or a side effect of the pedagogy of the "docile tool" that the CCP had propagated in previous years. However, these were provisional suppositions that did not fully explain the dissipation of the experimental drive of independent organizations. Yet to leave unresolved the question of the impasse of the great political innovations of the first two-year period was tantamount to leaving open the general assessment of the Cultural Revolution, which evidently constituted an element of serious weakness for the Maoists. The main obstacle, as discussed in previous chapters, was that the impasse remained inexplicable within the cultural horizon of the politics in which it had taken place. The hypothesis that I propose in this last part of the volume is that the political problem of the decade's final phase was how to overcome the difficulty of that assessment.

I will not examine all the tortuous developments of the post-1968 political situation. The most catastrophic episode was undoubtedly the attempted coup of Lin Biao in 1971, of which only partial and unconvincing reconstructions are available. On the basis of what little is known—an attempt to assassinate Mao and Lin's ruinous airplane flight to the USSR—it is extremely difficult to outline research prospects. My tentative reading is that the political clash at the summit of the revolutionary leadership group itself concerned the assessment of the events and in particular the problem of how to deal with the vacillation of the ideological and institutional stability of the party-state.

As we saw in chapter 5, Lin Biao had tried since 1966 to appeal to Mao's "absolute authority" as a factor of supreme stabilization. Mao initially replied sarcastically about "Wife Wang boasting pumpkins to sell at the market." Much more drastic was his response when in 1970 Chen Boda, another key figure in the Maoist group, who was close to Lin's positions, pledged to theoretically support the need to proclaim the "genius" of Mao's thinking. Mao refuted Chen with the utmost determination, criticizing his position as a serious political error. Incidentally, the site of that clash at the summit of the CCP was again, as in 1959 with Peng Dehuai, the enchanted landscape of cloud-shrouded Mount Lu.

Contrary to the image of him often painted by the right as much as by the left, Mao did not believe that his thought possessed any absolute authority. In fact, the path he proposed was completely at odds with the exaltation of his genius. The initiatives on which he worked the most in his last three years were, indeed, aimed at stimulating the growth of a mass political intellectuality capable of dealing with the tangle of new problems that the Cultural Revolution had opened up. His strategic goal, I will argue, was to open up a critical mass rethinking of the Cultural Revolution. A first step toward achieving this was to thoroughly review the fundamental categories of politics.

In this last part of the volume, I will examine two key passages from the last days of the decade. In this chapter, we will discuss the peculiar theoretical character of the mass political movements launched by Mao in those years; in the next chapter I will show how the ability of Deng Xiaoping to firmly oppose Mao's latest initiatives was the foundation of his strategic affirmation.

In those years, the politics of the Maoists explicitly revealed the urgency for a theoretical reexamination of the whole framework of political culture available to the revolutionaries, which had already appeared "symptomatically" throughout the decade since the prologue. In 1975, that urgency had a specific political objective: to broaden the theoretical horizon of "the whole country," as Mao said, in order to achieve a reexamination of the entire experience of the Cultural Revolution, starting with its limits and errors. The final years of the Cultural Revolution were Mao's "last battle," which remained unfinished with regard to that strategic objective. His failure to achieve that political assessment was the main factor in the defeat of the Maoists, and Deng

Xiaoping's obstinacy in preventing that assessment was the decisive factor in his victory.

The last political movements launched by Mao were essentially "study movements" that aimed not only at raising the mass cultural level, but at developing vast critical capacities on highly controversial theoretical issues. The two main movements were the "critique of Confucianism" in 1973–74 and the "movement for the study of the theory of the dictatorship of the proletariat" in 1975.

In this chapter I will examine in more detail the second of these study movements, limiting myself to some theoretical hypotheses for the first. Indeed, basic research work remains to be done on the critical movement on Confucianism in those years. The critiques of Confucianism in those years entail a reexamination of the theoretical perspectives on the political history of China as a whole.

Lin Biao

Even in a limited review of the key themes of the anti-Confucian campaign, one cannot avoid looking at a hypothesis about one of its most problematic points, namely the association of Confucianism with Lin Biao. The official name was indeed "Criticize Confucius, Criticize Lin Biao" (批林批 *pi Lin pi Kong*). That Lin Biao was well versed in the calligraphy of Confucian maxims, as was said in the first accusations addressed to him after his fall, explains absolutely nothing. Most of the Chinese government elite delighted in that pastime. His relationship with Confucianism concerned something deeper, and more obscure, which certainly did not involve just his individually understood positions.

Lin's "attempted coup d'état" is a shadowy episode still without reliable elucidation. That he had stood next to Mao, first as his "closest comrade-in-arms" and then as his designated successor during the CCP's Nineteenth Congress in 1969, has made the entire incident even more obscurely enigmatic. However tense and fraught with differences relations between them may have been, Mao had always acknowledged a warm, long-standing political comradeship with Lin. The May 7th letter of 1968 reviewed in chapter 5 bears eloquent witness thereto. Mao certainly counted on Lin to see that the People's Liberation Army cultivated egalitarian virtues, even in the event of world conflict (something that could not be ruled out at the time).

Briefly put, Lin was as inextricably linked to Mao in his position as both were associated with the Cultural Revolution's phase of mass movements. The fallout from the "Lin Biao affair" thus retrospectively discredited any experimental merits of the pluralization process of 1966–67.

For the Maoists, taking the political initiative following the Lin Biao affair was an altogether uphill climb. It would have meant marshaling the will and means for reappraising the core years in which the mass movements arose and unfolded, no easy feat to begin with, and one that would have to deal at the same time with a political disaster that overshadowed Mao personally as well as all the party leaders of the Cultural Revolution. The situation was further exacerbated by the fact that the Lin incident had exploded in ways and places entirely upon and within the sphere of the governing powers without involving any mass political movement, thereby making it even more difficult to reopen mass political experimentation.

In his famous 1966 letter to Jiang Qing noted above, Mao wrote that under the circumstances he was unable openly to refute the way Lin was extolling his persona or portraying the Cultural Revolution as a necessary preemptive strike against a reactionary coup d'état. He added that to say so publicly would put a damper on "the left, all of whom speak like that." What then, apart from the name of an individual, did Lin Biao stand for if not everyone "of the left," including Mao? If he felt unable to come out publicly against Lin's exhortations—even while noting that it was the first time he was compelled to compromise a principle against his will—it was because all the cultural revolutionaries, including himself, were to a greater or lesser extent "Lin Biao." Far more than the name of a person who had betrayed the cause, Lin Biao had become the name that up to a few years before had been the political "us" in revolutionary China. Indeed, I am tempted to translate pi Lin pi Kong as "Criticize Ourselves, Criticize Confucius," or "Criticize the Confucianism in Each of Us."

The Criticize Confucius campaign should thus be recast as arising from the need to radically reexamine the entire Cultural Revolution itself, or better yet, as an initial step in taking its political stock. How much vision-obstructing Confucianism, that is, politics meant as a set of bureaucratic rituals for governing others, did the Chinese revolutionaries have to wash away? How were they to reexamine a Confucian tradition that was so deeply rooted in the cultural soil of China's politics?

China and Historical Materialism

As for the pi Kong, that is, the critique of the Confucianism of the movement of 1973–74, I will focus on an issue that more directly concerns the general topic of this book, namely the twist that the Cultural Revolution produced on the fundamental concepts of revolutionary culture, specifically on the place of China in historical materialism. The rereading of the country's entire history as a "struggle between Confucians and Legalists" (儒法斗争 *rufa douzheng*), which was at the core of that movement, resulted in a conceptual dissonance of the first order in the theoretical framework that had made it possible to situate China in history for more than half a century.

As I have observed since examining the initial controversy over *Hai Rui*, history in the political and academic discourses of revolutionary culture that shaped the structure of socialism's governing order was perceived as a doctrine encompassing sequential epochs of relations of production. These epochs evinced given tiers of development for the productive forces on the one hand and the "superstructure" on the other. The general law of that history as a succession of production modes called for the superstructure—the various ideological forms and governing circumstances reflecting the differing modes of production—to be modeled on the economic and political interests of the dominant classes that varied within those relations. When, for example, given relations of production can no longer resist the thrust of new productive forces, a new dominant class arises to represent them and ends up overthrowing the political power and ideological dominion of the old dominant class. This was the historical core of the category entry headed "revolution" in revolutionary culture.

However, the fact that during the anti-Confucian campaign the Maoists argued that Chinese political and ideological history had been shaped for over two millennia by the struggle that opposed the visions of politics and the state, respectively, of the Confucians and the Legalists opened a front of unusual issues with regard of historical materialism. The study campaign was also called "Criticizing Confucianism, Discussing Legalism" (批儒评法 *pi ru ping fa*). Without going into scholarly details, let me attempt to summarize the essential outlines of a set of issues that would necessarily entail a much more meticulous treatment.

China was unified in 221 BC by Qin Shi Huangdi (260–10 BC), founder of the first imperial dynasty, which lasted only a few years but had decisive consequences for the whole history of China's forms of government. The unification of the written language, weights, measures, and so on, as well as the first Chinese legal codes, were among the most important results. The first emperor was influenced in his political philosophy by the intransigently anti-Confucian Legalists and, most notable among them, by Han Feizi (?–233 BC), whose political writings rank in the first magnitude with those of Montesquieu and Machiavelli. Han Feizi was the author of a wide-ranging theory of the state and sovereignty that developed and systematized the ideas of a Legalist school of thought that had flourished under renowned political theorists prominent in preceding centuries. As is well known, for two millennia the Confucians held Qin Shi Huangdi and his theoretical inspirers as the epitome of despotism and cruelty.

The unification of China was thus guided by a political and philosophical vision that was radically at odds with Confucianism and championed an altogether different form of government based on the "law" (法 fa), and not on the "rituals" (礼 li), which were at the core of Confucian political ideology. However, by the advent of the Eastern Han (AD 25–220), not more than two centuries on, Confucianism had once again become part and parcel of imperial state ideological scaffolding and would remain so for two millennia.

It was precisely on this point that the campaign criticizing Confucianism and reevaluating Legalism constituted a major dissonance with historical materialism. Confucianism in revolutionary culture's scheme of things was the ideology reflecting the relations of production dominated by the class of slave owners, and Legalism was that reflecting the interests of the landowners. The latter had represented the new productive forces, brought about a political revolution under the banner of Legalism, unified China, and created a new form of state supportive of new relations of production.

In this perspective, however, the very idea of a China shaped historically by a succession of production relations, in turn reflected by the ideological and state superstructure, encountered an essential aporia. Legalism, the ideology of the new feudal production relations, created the conditions for imperial unification, but was then replaced as the dominant ideology of the imperial governments by Confucianism, which represented the old slave production relations. How was it possible to define the class character of the ideology of the imperial state? Was China in the final analysis shaped by a revolution followed by two thousand years of restoration?

The Maoists expended energy to demonstrate that, although Confucianism was the dominant political philosophy, Legalist thought had been the default position for the promoters of radical political innovation at key turning points in Chinese history. The Maoists argued that Chinese ideology had developed a long series of internal divisions that Confucian supremacy had merely repressed but never resolved. The resolution they sought tried to be coherent with the view that attributed all progress within the ideological superstructure to the Legalists, representatives of the new production relations.

Yet this left unresolved the theoretical dissonance in the conceptualization of base/superstructure and productive forces/relations of production. While the Maoists never managed to openly discuss this aporia, they were always resolute in declaring themselves the political heirs of the Legalists. Even Mao considered his being compared to Qin Shi Huangdi not without merit. It was rather polemical posturing on his part, however, a stance having more to do with that of the French revolutionaries vis-à-vis the ancient Roman Republic than with textbook historical materialism.

Although the anti-Confucian campaign is the subject of a special censorship and self-censorship in contemporary China, it was in fact a very intense moment in twentieth-century Chinese intellectual history, with a peculiar combination of specialized scholarship and openness to mass study. There were, of course, reprints and new editions of classic Legalist writings, just as there were historical reconstructions of the disputes with the Confucians.[1] Yet the pi ru ping fa campaign also provided the thrust for archaeological excavations at sites connected to the era of the first emperor.[2] All of resounding scholarly and scientific interest, none of these discoveries would have been made if, as the official Chinese government websites continue to insist, pi ru ping fa had been a ploy of palace intrigue and deception.

The mass dissemination campaign accompanying the issues being debated and the historical finds unearthed during pi ru ping fa were no less spectacular. They made available to nonspecialist readers thousands of articles and documents, access to which was usually restricted to a small circle of academic scholars. Indeed, the pi ru ping fa campaign itself was the subject of widespread debate in Chinese factories, where workers formed study "groups for theory," one of that era's most original political novelties in China. A key objective of the campaign was obviously intended to raise theoretical appreciation to a mass level. Yet the task at hand was riddled with complexity, for it aimed to popularize not so much acquired historiographical developments, even less orthodox viewpoints, but issues that were as controversial in their subject matter as in their attendant details.

Indeed, the most evident paradox concerned the history of China as a succession of production modes. The crucial issues of contemporary Chinese politics were clearly being stirred up in the cauldron of the anti-Confucian campaign. The most relevant issue, I suggest, was its manifestly urgent drive to rethink the historicity of China as a prerequisite for assessing the Cultural Revolution per se and dealing with the challenges of the new political horizons it had brought into view. That historicity could be revisited neither through the lens of the historicist teleology of historical materialism in its Stalinist perspective, nor in terms of some presumed Chinese-ness.

In the perspective of the anti-Confucian campaign, whatever destiny awaited politics in China, it could not confidently be charted on any master map of the logic of history. If the development from slavery to feudalism—

however much such designations might be applicable to China—was unthinkable as a linear historical progression, even less could the coordinates marshaled to trace the steps from socialism to communism be taken for granted. These were in fact the key issues of a second mass campaign launched by Mao in late 1974 and purposed to a theoretical reappraisal of the entire matrix constituting the cultural horizon of communist politics itself, from the *Communist Manifesto* to the Cultural Revolution.

Why Did Lenin Speak of the Dictatorship over the Bourgeoisie?

In January 1975, when a new ministerial cabinet was established and a new constitution approved during the Fourth National People's Congress, a formally positive evaluation of the Cultural Revolution was also sanctioned. Mao himself contributed to this constitution, to which he added the key point of the freedom to strike.[3] This was an issue that would previously have been inconceivable in the classical doctrine of the socialist state. In a state that had declared itself fully representative of the workers, the latter had no major reason to express any disagreement or dissatisfaction.[4] In proposing to mention explicitly the right to strike, Mao pointed out how fanciful that earlier vision was, because contradictions between the workers and the system of power in the factories were the norm, not only under capitalism but in the socialist state as well, and should therefore be legally recognized.

In any case, Mao considered neither the new constitution nor the formally positive evaluation of the Cultural Revolution expressed in the People's Congress to be decisive. The crucial question, he felt, remained unresolved because the basic political concepts for weighing up the achievements and failures of those events had been radically destabilized by the events themselves. In other words, what was needed was a solution to how that theoretical-political destabilization might be dealt with and how new concepts for evaluating the Cultural Revolution might be devised. In fact, Mao's initiative started in December 1974, precisely at the conclusion of the preparatory work for the Fourth National Congress and the new constitution. When a new version of the supreme law of the state was on the point of being passed, Mao launched a battery of theoretical questions involving the concepts of "right" and "legal power."

Mao's opening move was apparently highly abstract. He proposed a series of topics for theoretical study concerning nothing less than the dictatorship of the proletariat—the basic concept of Marxist political culture. The problem was that not only did the events of the preceding decade belong to the political-cultural network that pivoted around the concept of the dictatorship of the proletariat, but they had also created a predicament within that very conceptual network. How might the concept of the dictatorship of the proletariat be conceived after the Cultural Revolution?

The latter was formally praised at the Fourth National Congress in January 1975 for having "strengthened the dictatorship of the proletariat." But what did that really mean? What sort of concrete achievements in the form and function of the state had it introduced? Without forgetting, however, that reinforcing the dictatorship of the proletariat meant for Marx and Lenin radically resizing the separate state functions and dispersing them among the common people, in what sense could those events be conceptualized within the theoretical framework of a socialist state led by a Communist Party representative of the proletariat and its long-term alliance with other working classes? What was the political content of that "special government" (which is, in Chinese, the name for "dictatorship": 专政 zhuanzheng) of one class, the proletariat, over another class, the bourgeoisie? The political value of all these concepts, even the very distinctiveness of the socialist form of the state, Mao maintained, were unsolved key questions, obscure points that "had to be clarified" (要搞清楚 yao gao qingchu).

It is remarkable that of all Mao's theoretical theses in late 1974, the initial one was merely a question, one to which he gave no answer: 列宁为什么说对资产阶级专政? *Liening wei shenme shuo dui zichanjieji zhuanzheng?* [Why did Lenin say dictatorship over the bourgeoisie?].[5] Mao's question was not rhetorical but an appeal, to virtually anyone, for a concerted theoretical reconsideration of a fundamental principle: 要使全国知道 *yao shi quanguo zhidao* [The whole country should be informed of this question]. 这个问题要搞清楚 *Zhege wenti yao gao qingchu* [This problem must be clarified], Mao warned, because 这个问题不搞清楚 *zhege wenti bu gao qingchu* [without such a clarification], 就会变修正主义 *jiu hui bian xiuzhengzhuyi* [a probable revisionist transformation would occur].

Given the conditions of the time of both the Chinese state and the economy, Mao stated that 在中国搞资本主义很容易 *zai Zhongguo gao zibenzhuyi hen rongyi* [in China it was easy to make capitalism]. The fundamental reason was that capitalism is the rule of the modern world, whereas socialism had been the exception for only some decades. Without a theoretical clarification on the nature of that exception and without a mass political push to reinvent it incessantly, it was therefore very easy to restore capitalist rule. As noted in chapter 4, it was a prediction Mao had first uttered in the early sixties. By the mid-seventies it was further complicated since the criteria for distinguishing capitalism and socialism had undergone a radical upheaval during the Cultural Revolution. For Mao, those criteria had started to become uncertain much earlier, at least at the time of the ideological dispute with the Soviet Union in the second half of the fifties. In 1956, the first official text by the Chinese communists that initiated the controversy with the Communist Party of the Soviet Union (CPSU) was an editorial in the *People's Daily* entitled "On the Historical Experience of the Dictatorship of the Proletariat," to which Mao made important revisions and additions.[6] Twenty years later, the political worth of that concept was for Mao an even more essential issue. It was something that had become obscure and thus needed to be fully reexamined from its very outset.

In raising the question of bourgeois right under socialism, Mao distanced himself from the Stalinist viewpoint, according to which socialist legality was a radical alternative to the capitalist's, and definitely superior to it. The socialist form of the state was in Stalinism the only true and rightful legality, while that of the enemy camp was just a smokescreen for concealing the capitalist relationships of exploitation. Mao, on the contrary, considered that the socialist forms of "right" (or "legal power," 法权 *faquan*, according to the lexicon used in this debate) were basically congruent with those of the capitalist forms. Far from suppressing "bourgeois right" (资产阶级法权 *zichanjieji faquan*), the socialist state had inevitably to introject them as a major criterion in its operative system. In socialism too, Mao argued, production remained essentially a production of commodities to be regulated by the law of "exchange at equal value." The legal framework securing the operation of the "law of value," or bourgeois right, was shared by both the capitalist and the socialist forms of the state. On this plane, "there are not many differences" (没有多少差别 *mei you duoshao chabie*) between capitalism and socialism. Yet Mao pointed out a difference, which I will discuss below: "the form of property has changed" (所不同的是所有制变更了 *suo butong de shi suoyouzhi biangeng le*).

We should recall in this connection that the generalization of exchange at equal value is for Marx the basic condition of the capitalist mode of production, which plays a special role in the bourgeois social order. Exchange at equal value is, according to Marx, a fiction that obliterates the different conditions under which commodities are produced. The equality of the exchange of commodities, Marx wrote, constitutes a fetish ("The Fetishism of Commodities and the Secret Thereof" is the title of a famous chapter in *Das Kapital*), since it reflects on the producers an "image" of social relations that are totally abstracted from the social differences that structure the real fabric of sociality. It therefore exacerbates social inequalities, masking them and thereby making them harder to restrain by the mere logic of the exchange of commodities.

The relations between workers and capitalists are for Marx the most elaborate instance of the ideological role of commodities: formally they are exchanges of equivalent commodities (labor force) for their general equivalent (money), but in fact they are dominated by radically unequal relations between the owners of the means of productions and the "owners" of their labor force. Only the fiction of the equality of each commodity with its general monetary equivalent, Marx argued, permits a social consensus in the real system of inequality in the market for the labor force. Thus, according to the modern *doxa*, the structure of opinion that supports the forms of government of the modern world, labor force is equal to any other commodity through the "arcane" transubstantiation fulfilled by the "general equivalent." Thus, everybody can be recognized as an "owner" who goes to the market taking commodities to buy and sell; all men are equal in the face of the market, or rather, in the face of money, as we are constantly told.

The socialist state, Mao argued, had inevitably inherited this condition, and, hence, a mere change in the form of ownership would not be really decisive. Not only did bourgeois right persist in the socialist state, he said; it was also necessary to protect them. The production of commodities and their exchange at equal value were a major factor in economic development and, hence, their growth should be welcomed. As Zhang Chunqiao, who in this case proved to be one of the most talented theoreticians in Mao's group, wrote during that period: "We have always asserted that our country, instead of having too many commodities, does not have them in abundance."[7] On the other hand, as Marx had pointed out, bourgeois rights played the specific ideological role of the sole criterion of equality, thereby masking the real conditions of inequality and hindering policies for reducing them.

What was to be done? Mao's solution in no way simplified matters. On the contrary, it made the theoretical framework more complicated. The persistence of bourgeois right, he said, could not be suppressed, but "could only be limited" (只能加以限制 *zhi neng jiayi xianzhi*) "under the dictatorship of the proletariat" (在无产阶级专政下 *zai wuchanjieji zhuanzheng xia*). It should be noted that this formulation of bourgeois right in the socialist state was apparently new. The Marxist-Leninist doctrine of the state spoke of "overthrowing the bourgeois state," "breaking the state machine," and even considering it as a "half-state." However, the concept of 限制 *xianzhi*, "limiting" an essential function of the state (in this case, the fact that the socialist state must protect bourgeois rights) was new to this conceptual framework, with the further complication that the instrument of this limitation was, for Mao, to be the very dictatorship of the proletariat. But was the dictatorship of the proletariat not precisely the most obscure point in 1975? It is clear that this conclusion led back to the original dilemma.

Mao's argument could not avoid a paradox, nor in fact did it try to do so. The limiting factor of bourgeois right should certainly be political, but the supreme ideal of politics in China at the time coincided with the most unstable concept of the entire web of theoretical references. How could the dictatorship of the proletariat restrict bourgeois right if it was unclear why Lenin said "dictatorship over the bourgeoisie"? Mao's arguments began with an interrogative, which equated to a radical questioning of the theoretical worth of a basic concept but ended up using the same concept again in the same key place within the theoretical device.

The Impact of the Cultural Revolution on the Danwei System

To urge virtually everyone in China to study this problem—"The entire country should be informed of it"—was indeed an arduous task that involved a tangle of economic, political, and philosophical concepts. The "movement for the study of the theory of the dictatorship of the proletariat" (according to its official name in the Chinese press in those days), shortened to "movement for the study of the theory" and initiated by the publication of Mao's above-quoted theses in February 1975, was an effort at reconsidering unraveled theoretical knots, not a campaign for popularizing an established doctrine.[8] But which forces, even potential ones, could be mobilized to engage in political research at such a level of theoretical abstraction?

Although Mao's urgent appeal was addressed to "everyone" without any further specification, some recipients were arguably closer to Mao's intent. Since 1968, Mao had mentioned factories as a crucial point of strategic retreat after the failure of the independent student organizations (see chapter 8). In fact, a number of political experiments had begun in Chinese factories in the late sixties and will be discussed later in this chapter. In 1975, several factories were deeply involved in the campaign to "study theory." Not only were study groups of workers formed dedicated to Mao's theoretical issues, but the question of what the socialist factory itself should be became a crucial political topic in the debates.

As we noted in chapter 7, the socialist factory had been a major epicenter in the mass phase of the Cultural Revolution. From the autumn of 1966, political activism among workers, culminating in the January Storm, resulted in a general crisis involving the whole system of power in Chinese factories. Eight years later, that crisis remained in most aspects unresolved, revealing itself in the end to be unsolvable within the cultural and institutional order of the pre-1966 Chinese state. The political impasse the socialist factory in China came to and the various attempts to find a way out of it eventuated in increasingly divisive rifts in 1975.

The January Storm was neither an ordinary wind of popular unrest, nor exactly a seizure of power by a part of the class of true proletarians intent on overthrowing the new bourgeoisie. We have discussed in chapter 7 how thorny an issue naming events was. Nonetheless, the January Storm was definitely not a counterrevolutionary or anticommunist movement, since the participants on both sides confidently believed themselves to be more "red" than their opponents. With all these paradoxes, and above all the insurmountable difficulty of setting it within an acquired conceptual framework, the January Storm was a crucial turning point in the changes looming before the contemporary Chinese state. In the following years, any effort at reorganization could not avoid dealing with the true root causes of that event. A pure and simple return to a previous situation was no longer possible.

The Maoists had begun promoting in the late sixties a series of political experiments in a number of factories, in Shanghai as well as in other industrialized areas like the regions in the northeast, aimed at reconfiguring the operational modes of the socialist factory. The emergence of independent workers' organizations in 1966–67 posed a challenge to ideology and organization. No one knew how to deal with them by applying conventional socialist political doctrine because those events had snapped a crucial link in the political and conceptual chain that connected the workers, the factories, and the state under socialism.

The formula of the classical socialist doctrine can be summarized as the conceptual chain worker–factory–class–party–state. In other words, the relations between worker and factory were politically and socially made possible through the concept of the working class organized by a party that headed a special form of state, which for its part fully acknowledged the political and social relations linking worker and factory. The circularity of the argument is as evident as it is symptomatic of the structural instability of the phenomenon.

In fact, from the Marxist point of view, the relationship between worker and factory has no stable place in the social relations of the age of "big capitalist industry." It is, on the contrary, a sort of empty point in sociality. Far from occupying the lowest place in society, the worker–factory tie is situated at the most precarious point in the social bond. The worker cannot be linked within any established "communitarian order," which as such is but an obstacle to the very logic of big capitalistic industry and to the concept of the free market.

The worker vis-à-vis the factory is necessarily unlinked to any customary community, even less so to a factory community. The latter is the most artificial and the most precarious community imaginable: the purely anarchic requirements of capital's self-valorization decide whether a given factory community is to exist or not. In short, the labor force has no consistent real sociocommunitarian existence. It must be "individualized," but only insofar as it circulates as just one of the various commodities that are equally exchangeable in the market. The link of worker to factory in Marx's view is no ordinary social tie; it can only be established through a special form of coercion, which he called "factory despotism."

Socialism promised to overturn the situation completely and to attribute a special political worth to the figure of the worker and his/her relationship with the factory. If the relationship between worker and factory under capitalism is poised over a void or gap in the social bond and subject to the "unconditional authority of the capitalist," the worker under socialism could acquire the value of a prominent political exponent, and the worker–factory relationship could become the major, consistent factor in the body of the state.

One could say that the immense task of twentieth-century socialism was to transform the worker–factory relationship, which per se is devoid of any intrinsic sociality, into a fully fledged sociopolitical relationship. In order to do so, it created a special form of sociality, such as the industrial danwei in China and the Soviet Union's kombinat, whose link was forged and secured by its inclusion in the organization of the state.

The entanglement between ideological and organizational factors, to quote Schurmann's formula once more, was particularly compact. The industrial danwei was a specific configuration founded on the highly elaborate conceptual network noted above, which linked the workers as a class to the factory through the leading role of the party in the state. Finally, the socialist factory was conceived as the embodiment of the historical conjunction between the working class and the party-state.

The party therefore fully represented the class interests of the proletariat. The very idea of workers forming autonomous organizations that could express their own political propositions outside the party was thus inconceivable. It was for this reason that the events in Shanghai during 1967 were so cataclysmic. As we have seen, even the right to strike was an issue that encountered doctrinal obstacles.

The socialist factory order was therefore a basic condition of the overall stability of the socialist state. But the factory order was in turn conditioned by the fact that the political role of the worker had to be internal to the party-state.

Therefore, the emergence in 1966-67 of new forms of political subjectivity among Chinese workers created a serious instability. The subjective issues at stake could not be dealt with by means of the conceptual chain worker-factory-class-party-state, nor could they have anything but a destabilizing effect on the factory order. The very concept of the working class was brought into question, resulting in a radical subjective and organizational crisis in the relationship between class and party-state. What could legitimize the Communist Party's authority as the leading apparatus of the socialist state machinery if its historical-political connection with the working class, its major social basis, was challenged on the very terrain of political organization?

Against this background, the process of the reorganization of the state and the experimentation with new political forms in factories were some of the most urgent and difficult tasks facing the Maoists in the following months and years. The tortuous development of the Cultural Revolution remains inexplicable without taking into account these issues. If masses of workers declared such a strong determination to create self-organized forms of political activity, how was the socialist factory to be managed? The whole organization of the industrial danwei was shaped by the presupposed stability of a working class that was fully embodied in the state machinery. The industrial danwei was a state institution, and the worker was to a certain extent a petty state official. In this sense, the industrial danwei shaped the stability of the working class and defined its limits.

The change that the political existence of workers' organizations outside the party wrought in the established ideological relationships formerly linking worker to factory, as well as to state and party, inevitably produced destabilizing effects on all the organizational planes, from the most elementary workshop relations to the implementation of the tasks assigned by the state plan. The very existence of a chain of command in the factory, the technical regulations, the production discipline, the job assignments, the peculiar forms of wages (only partly in money; much consisted of the various benefits that state workers enjoyed), and the sociality of the danwei itself became questions that could not be decided simply on the basis of the previous socialist factory order.

For the Maoists, a prerequisite for finding a new order was discovering how to remold the political role of the workers in the factories. The rhetoric of the "marble man,"[9] the socialist labor hero, the model worker, inspired by the Stakhanovism of the thirties in the USSR, was largely discredited by the events of 1966-67 that revealed its disciplinary and antipolitical nature. It was in fact used by the loyalists and the Shanghai party authorities to quash the independent workers' organizations. The canonical formula of the workers as "the masters of the state" would remain empty propaganda if new forms of relations between worker and factory were not experimented with by going beyond the terms of the ordinary running of the industrial danwei.

Experiments in the Factories and the Study of Theory

At least two such experiments were underway in several Chinese factories by 1975: "workers' universities" (工人大学 *gongren daxue*) and "workers' theoretical contingents" (工人理论队伍 *gongren lilun duiwu*). The former were first established in Shanghai in 1968 in the famous machine factory praised by Mao just before the last meeting with the Red Guard leaders in July of that year, and the scope of the experiment was extended to China's other main cities in 1973–74. Workers' universities were projects for reforming industrial organization in order to reduce the hierarchies based on the technical division of labor by interchanging jobs among levels. The aim was to train workers through study periods (courses) enabling them to master technical and management responsibilities and have technicians and managers cooperate and regularly participate with them in periods of productive tasks.[10]

The workers' theoretical contingents were organized during the pi Lin pi Kong movement in 1973. By 1975, their topics involved the study of the theory of the dictatorship of the proletariat. These groups were to combine "study theory" classes with their shop-floor duties. The very idea that theoretical work, including the study of philosophy, history, and economics, should be an activity inherent to the job of any ordinary worker was as unprecedented in the socialist as it would be in the capitalist workplace.

Both kinds of experiment were purposed to a political reinvention of the factory, and Mao and his group oriented much of their efforts to develop the "movement for the study of theory." The workers' theoretical contingents, which had already gained experience in the very tangled historical issues raised during the pi Lin pi Kong movement, were further developed to explore a set of highly abstract questions, such as those raised by Mao on the very nature of the dictatorship of the proletariat. It was a shift in focus that led in turn to the factories becoming key venues as forums for the debates over the nature of the factory itself under socialism.

The workers' universities, for their part, were attempts to lever up the skills of workers as a means of curbing the hierarchical structure of the division of labor, an issue that soon came to be related to another—how to "limit bourgeois right." All these experiments were seen by the Maoists as belonging to a socialist set of "new-born things" (新生事物 *xinsheng shiwu*) that had arisen during the Cultural Revolution and, hence, as even more suitable as think tanks for elaborating new political ideas.

Workers' universities were a project rooted in Marx's vision of the modern factory. "Big industry" for Marx was a singular historical phenomenon suspended between the most archaic forms of despotism and immense potentialities for liberation. The key issue was the division of labor: modern large-scale industry put an end to the premodern division of labor that was socially structured among the productive branches (the social division of labor typical of precapitalist forms) but introduced a more severe technical division concentrated in a factory that separated mental and manual functions within itself.

Every producer in the outmoded traditional form of social division was annexed for a lifetime to a single specialized activity of which he or she mastered both the mental and manual skills to the exclusion of all other specializations—*Sutor, ne ultra crepidam*. The advent of the modern technical division, on the other hand, removed the separation among the branches of production, and nearly everybody could do almost any job. However, it also removed the mental power of production that every worker had possessed. The worker in large-scale industry is annexed to machine systems, about which s/he knows only what is strictly necessary to his/her own particular job, a very tiny portion indeed of the technical and managerial system. The structure of the technical division of labor, having at its two extremes manual and mental labor, fashions de facto all the relations within the factory.

Most significantly, the technical division of labor establishes the rationale of the chain of command, since the mental powers of production expropriated from the workers are concentrated in the unconditional authority of the capitalist. This organization is, however, largely determined by ideological factors (in Marx's, not Schurmann's, sense). In this case, too, a phenomenon of fetishism is at work. For Marx the fetishism of technology transmits back to the people the image of their mutual relations as solely determined by technical relationships among machines, independently of any real personal and social difference. The fetishism of technology thus plays a major ideological role in creating the social consensus concerning the hierarchical and disciplinary order in the modern factory.

These Marxist analyses of the structure and function of the modern factory became widespread in 1975 China, referred to and quoted in hundreds of newspaper articles and essays. Subtle aspects of the "twofold nature of the commodity" were hotly debated, and not without some literary flair, the "Autobiography of a Commodity" published by the Maoist journal in Shanghai, 学习与批判 *Xuexi yu pipan* (Study and criticism) being an example. Its radical brother 北京大学学报 *Beijing daxue xuebao* (Journal of Beijing University) was in 1975–76 another major source of theoretical articles such as those analyzing the interchange between the "double fetishism," of commodity and technology.[11]

The fundamental point was that rather than solely concerning the capitalist system, Marxist references were seen in mid-seventies China as illuminating key features of the socialist factory itself. In the socialist system, the Maoists argued, crucial forms of the capitalist organization, including its fetishes, were still fully operative. Far from being defenders of the intrinsic superiority of socialist order, the Maoists were deeply concerned with the fact that socialism as such was, in some important respects, a direct continuation of the capitalist order.

The question of how to experiment with new forms of politics in the factories after the crisis of 1966–67 therefore involved two converging difficulties. Not only did the political activism of the workers exceed the limitations of the party-state in the socialist factory, thus requiring new forms of political organization, but even the technical organization of the socialist factory should not be fetishized and should be radically transformed in key points. The two planes were obviously interrelated because the technical and the political organizations in the industrial *danwei* were closely knitted, if not totally soldered together. Moreover, the Maoists argued that the technical division of labor on which the chain of command pivoted was basically cut from the same cloth as its capitalist counterpart, a view that radically departed from Stalin's formulas such as "technique decides everything, the cadres decide everything."

The factories were of particular import for the study theory movement. They now contained "new socialist things" like the workers' universities and the theoretical contingents that could play an active role in political study, and the issues being focused on concerned the destiny of the socialist factory itself in the end. In effect, they even concerned, for the reasons discussed above, the fate of the socialist form of the state. The most urgent political options and the most abstract conceptualizations were at play at the same time. Only through the study of theory, the Maoists believed, could those options be elucidated, and the factories were certainly considered by them as the beacons that would shine the light on both the basic concepts and the operational methods the tasks required.

The effects of this theoretical impulse on the existing political experiments were remarkable. The workers' universities, for instance, were analyzed anew from the new theoretical perspective. The policies for reducing the technical and hierarchical gap between workers and management were therefore considered forms of limitations of bourgeois right. The workers' theoretical contingents, which obviously echoed Mao's May 7 Directive, considered themselves the vanguard for reducing the gap between manual and intellectual labor on all social levels. In the wake of Marx's analyses, that gap was seen as the major source of inequality, even lying at the root of the "division among classes," and therefore as the very basis of bourgeois right. The whole set of "new-born things" was considered by the Maoists as a series of experiments embodying the search for the true political content of otherwise empty concepts. Only those experiments, the Maoists argued, could lead to forms of limitation of bourgeois right.

As is well known, Marx's analysis of the modern factory system included the prediction that the workers, if politically organized, would be able to spark unprecedented possibilities, starting with the transformation of the conditions of the division of labor. The question involved nothing less than the transition from "partial workers annexed for a lifetime to a social function of detail" to persons endowed with "omni-lateral" capacities.

Marx had called the political organization of workers capable of realizing this transition "the dictatorship of the proletariat." He considered this formula as embodying the essence of his political discovery. In 1975 China, however, it had become the designation for a peculiar form of the state whose political capabilities were dubious. What was unclear was how the dictatorship of the proletariat could be an institutional framework within which the potential of omni-lateral men and women could exist. Only new-born inventions, the Maoists said, could be the true organizational grounds for deploying the capabilities of the workers and to realize such a radical change in the political and technical relations in the factory. In other words, these 1975 experiments were conceived as the only way to reinvent the content of a set of fundamental political concepts that had by then become obscure.

Forms of Ownership and Authority

When Mao observed that what had changed was the form of ownership, clearly he meant that this was a radical discontinuity with respect to capitalism, but that in itself did not constitute any definitive guarantee. But in what way did the abolition of capitalist private property of the means of production constitute the prerequisite for the dictatorship of the proletariat? What has really changed on this terrain since the Cultural Revolution in China? And ultimately, what was Marx's theory about the dictatorship of the proletariat that Mao declared it was so urgent to reexamine?

Drawing a line of thought from Marx to Lenin and then Mao, the dictatorship of the proletariat designated a space of invention within which organized communists attempted to implement the goal of downsizing the state's bureaucratic-military machinery. Far from being a particular form of government—Marx was notably critical regarding the idea of a future state[12]—instead, the dictatorship of the proletariat indicated the set of political experiments aimed at dismantling—or "smashing," as Marx put it—the state apparatus as an entity separated from society, and dispersing its functions among the people.

When, in the early months of the Cultural Revolution, Mao told the Red Guards that all of them had "to be concerned about the affairs of the state" (关心国家大事 guanxin guojia dashi), he expressed the spirit of the dictatorship of the proletariat perfectly. One of the fundamental components of the original agenda of the Cultural Revolution was initiating a series of political inventions that would entrust the carrying out of state functions to the "concern" (guanxin) of the masses.

Yet putting the dictatorship of the proletariat into practice as a form of mass politics required a critical rethinking of what the socialist states, starting with the Soviet Union, had become. More specifically, the Cultural Revolution called into question the fact that in all the dictatorships of the proletariat of the twentieth century, state functions had become the prerogative of a special echelon of party officials instead of being dispersed among the common people.

Although the Cultural Revolution never managed to complete this exhaustive account and reinvention of the dictatorship of the proletariat as a historical enterprise, it articulated a set of questions that recast older problems in a new light, requiring further conceptual investigation and practical experimentation. A core issue among these was that of the relationship between the abolition of private ownership of the means of production and the prospect of the extinction of the state.

I suggest focusing on the issue of authority, in the elementary sociological sense of the ability to get obedience to a command. Viewing the state as a set of "apparatuses"[13] helps to shed light on its phenomenology but risks dimming its essential role as the crystallization of the general principle of authority in a given historical-social world. While Marx was surely right in pointing to different modes of production—slavery, feudalism, and capitalism—for a mode of production to function properly, subordinates must obey their superiors. Whatever the phenomenology of the "halls of power"—which varies depending on the society—obedience is achieved according to the specific general principle of authority, and the state, rather than a set of places, is the set of the forms of authority that are dominant within a society.

Authority has assumed a variety of dominant forms in human societies—personal, transcendent, charismatic, and so forth. Yet the relations of authority dominant in the modern world differ from previous others because they are based on a singular tenet of capitalism—the buying and selling of labor as a commodity. Labor as a commodity—and the consequent "freedom" of the capitalist to buy it or not depending on the self-valorizing demands of capital—is the foundation of the relationship between command and obedience in the modern world.

In this sense, private ownership of the means of production is first and foremost the exercise of an unconditional authority over the masses of wage earners. In other words, it is the decision-making power over the lives of those who are valued only as sellers of labor. In short, in the historical bourgeois society, the buying and selling of labor is the atom of authority's elementary structures of relations. The current trend toward an increasingly precarious workforce aims at restoring the unconditional authority over the remaining vestiges of the constraints that for more than a century the workers' politics had imposed on the domination of capital.

Given this modern form of authority, Marx argued that abolishing private ownership of the means of production would not only signal a break with capitalist society but would also play a preliminary role in the process of the dissolution of the state. Abolishing private ownership of the means of production entails not only an end to the commodification of labor, but also the disappearance of the general principle of authority in bourgeois society. Thus, if the state constitutes the set of powers needed to command obedience in given sociohistorical conditions, abolishing the commodification of labor deprives the state of an essential function by suppressing capital's unconditional authority.

In fact, the abolition of capitalist private property inherent in every proclamation of the dictatorship of the proletariat in the twentieth century bore the seeds of the process that, according to Marx, was supposed to smash the state and eviscerate a crucial pillar of authority of bourgeois society. Once deprived of the freedom to purchase labor power in the marketplace, that entire system of governance would be irreparably altered.

What are we supposed to think of the socialist exception to capitalism that lasted approximately two-thirds of the twentieth century, especially now that the rule of labor-power commodification has been fully reinstated globally? The current discourses of totalitarianism and despotism that dominate most of the historiography of socialism do their best to distort what socialism was in its aspirations, victories, and failures. The crux of the matter is how to assess the actual consequences produced by the dictatorships of the proletariat that appeared in the twentieth century—the abolition of private ownership and the ensuing end to the commodification of labor. Given that the very conceptual coordinates that supported this abolition have been undone, such a reassessment is no easy task.

Current opinions dismiss the entire enterprise as unrealistic, as a mere "ideological forcing," as it is often termed, and hence, destined to deliver only disastrous results. True, the results were more than equivocal. However, the abolition of private ownership for Marx and Lenin was underpinned by a detailed analysis of the real conditions of capitalism and informed by a probing logic that would lay the groundwork for political experimentation on a grand scale. The decision to do away with labor as a commodity was, in fact, a risky and challenging endeavor, the results of which should be assessed vis-à-vis the aims of the political project to which it belonged.

Abolishing the commodification of labor, of course, was not an end in itself—it was only the first step of a project aimed at drastically reducing the functions of the state. Indeed, without pursuing or extending experimentation that would limit the state's machinery, the results produced by that first step could not but turn into the opposite of what it aimed to accomplish. Yet this is a conclusion that can be drawn only ex post facto, and only if we take into account the experimental nature of these processes. In this context, our categories are still provisional.

The assumption that we can make, however, given the historical record of the dictatorships of the proletariat in the twentieth century, is that the evisceration of the state due to the abolition of private property released a kind of reactive energy that filled the very void left by this process. The "halved" state was in turn duplicated by the Communist Party, with the latter replacing the former principle of authority based on the commodification of labor with a new authority to command obedience as the party that represented the vanguard of the working class.

Installing industrial labor in the sphere of state administration was envisaged as a way to dissolve capitalist authority over wage slavery. Yet labor's very inclusion in that sphere, and the substitution of capitalist authority by that of the vanguard of the working class, ended up reconstituting the entire apparatus of the state that the abolition of private property was supposed to have smashed. Indeed, the new organism was even more inflexible than the previous one, since it had to fill the void that the abolition of commodified labor power had left in the general principle of authority.

Once we account for these peculiar circumstances, we have more elements to reassess the references to class (*jieji*) during the Cultural Revolution, as well as their reiteration in the current discourse of the Chinese authorities, which we will discuss in the next chapter. The persistent references to class during the Cultural Revolution can be taken as a symptom of the insurmountable impasse that had arisen between the working class and its vanguard in the socialist state. The obsession with the concept symptomatically masked the questioning of its real political value by the people who were supposedly its subjects. The proletariat—which, along with its dictatorship, was supposed to be the political subject leading to the dissolution of the state—had become an integral part of a process of reconstructing the state's bureaucratic machine.

It is remarkable that during this revolutionary decade the issue of the working class was approached from the perspective of a critical reappraisal of the very organization of industrial labor. One of the most significant political questions posed during the Cultural Revolution was what made the socialist factory different from a capitalist one. True, authority was no longer vested in the commodification of the labor force. Yet the question that Mao and the Maoists had raised ever since the late 1950s—the 1960 Constitution of Anshan Iron and Steel Company[14] being one example—was that the workers themselves should be able to devise new forms of political experimentation, otherwise the industrial danwei would simply end up reiterating subordinate workplace relations just like those of the capitalist factory.

At stake was precisely what Marx had argued at length in his anatomy of the organization of the modern workplace: how to subvert the technical division of labor whereby the factory command subsumes the intellectual powers of production expropriated from the workers, who are then relegated to mere accessories to the array of machine tools,[15] with the added complication that the fundamental structure of authority in the industrial danwei relied on the ambiguities in the relations between the working class and its vanguard.

As a result of these unresolved tensions, the political import of the issue came explosively to the fore in late 1966 in Shanghai. While the January Storm still calls for much research, it was undoubtedly the episode that smashed the preceding principle of authority under which the Communist Party was the only political organization possible. At that point, the industrial danwei could not continue to operate as before—it had lost its ability to command obedience.

How to deal with the decline of authority from that moment on became a crucial issue that marked the entire revolutionary decade. For the Maoists, the way forward was to organize a series of experiments aimed at a political rethinking of the socialist factory, an agenda that included the need for a thorough transformation of its technical organization. Wherever they were strong and well organized—as in Shanghai and the Northeast—they actively promoted political experiments aiming, as we have seen, at creating a new worker intellectuality.

The party apparatus responded to these experiments with lukewarm detachment that soon turned into passive resistance. The executive cadres of the industrial danwei no longer possessed the stature needed to assert their unconditional authority, and were at a loss as to what to do. Any pretense of reestablishing the former order was impracticable, and a new order had yet to be invented. Lacking a clear principle of authority in the factories, the political system wobbled on unstable foundations.

We will see in the next chapter that the central goal of Deng's strategy was to find a new principle of authority. To evaluate the effectiveness of Deng's solutions, however, it will be necessary to consider the key steps of his contention with the Maoists during the last two years of the Cultural Revolution.

10

Foundations of Deng Xiaoping's Strategy

The Chinese government today is usually considered the heir to the "reform policies" initiated in the late 1970s. It is also generally acknowledged that the chief strategist of those policies and the course they laid out, which the current government in large measure continues to follow, was Deng Xiaoping.

Indeed, it would be more exact to say this was the post–Cultural Revolution Deng, since his first moves in devising and implementing that strategy stemmed from a fierce controversy with Mao Zedong in 1975–76. While recent research adds new insights for a better understanding of this key turning point, the most singular feature of their dispute was its nature—at once political and theoretical—and it is deserving of further exploration.[1] Deng's project and its subsequent development were largely shaped by the hotly contested nature of that controversy. The years 1975–76 were as decisive for the immediate success of Deng and his allies over the Maoists as they were for Deng's subsequent long-term strategy.

Deng Xiaoping after the Cultural Revolution

Charting the source and course of Deng's strategy requires close periodization. The point of departure was provided by Mao's theses concerning the study of theory. They were circulated first among the party leadership in December 1974 and published in newspapers in early February. Deng was appointed vice-premier during the Fourth People's Congress in January 1975. For some years he had remained in the countryside away from Beijing, along with most of the other leaders of the party-state, following his and their "fall" in 1966–67; he had held minor posts between 1973 and 1974 that paved the way for his full rehabilitation.[2] The new position in the government gave Deng a breadth of resources and a remarkable freedom of maneuver. However, none of what Deng had done in the preceding two years anticipated his moves in 1975, the year the point turned.[3]

There were no signs prior to that date indicating that Deng and those who would later be his closest associates at the top of the party leadership had a definite program. One might assume that they had carefully avoided revealing their intentions before reaching positions of authority in the government at the Fourth National People's Congress. It is, however, far more likely that they neither had an effective plan nor constituted a cohesive coalition.

Many cadre leaders of the CCP at every level were animated by a strong desire for revenge, both political and personal, resulting from the setbacks they had endured in 1966. They were also aware that any effective strategy could not simply be based on the continuation with previous structures, but they did not know what form the necessary dividing line should take. Even for those who harbored the bitterest resentment against the Cultural Revolution, a new governmental order could not be a simple reassertion of "orthodoxy," whatever its formula. While many wanted to settle scores with those whose challenges had led to the loss of their positions in the state hierarchy, none of them could seriously think of restoring the status quo ante. Deng alone managed to identify exactly the point needed to make a clean break with the past, and on it he built his program.

There are two politically distinct Dengs, one before and the other after the Cultural Revolution. The latter Deng was undoubtedly the more original and important, and he formed that persona principally during the political struggles in the crucial year of 1975.[4] He acted not to "restore" a "socialist" state system, nor even, as is often repeated, to put in order a country in disarray or a collapsing economic system. China in 1975 was anything but chaotic, and its economy was in good health even according to the most conventional "economist" measures.

The key point in Deng's strategy was, as per his renowned canonical formula, the chedi fouding (彻底否定), the "thorough negation," of the Cultural Revolution. Yet this negation was in no way truly thorough, nor could it ever have been. Indeed, it would have been altogether ineffective had Deng not succeeded in incorporating into his strategy of negation something essential that the Cultural Revolution itself had proved to be inconsistent with respect to the previous governmental order. Deng clearly did not return to pre-1966 socialism. Less obvious, however, is what Deng owed to the Cultural Revolution while so vigorously denying it. For it was the Cultural Revolution that showed him what of the pre-1966 order could no longer be resurrected.

The details of the compromise that led to Deng's rehabilitation in 1972–73 are not fully known. It is very likely that the main condition for his return to government was the declaration that he would "never reverse the verdict" (永不翻案 *yong bu fan'an*) on the Cultural Revolution. In 1975–76, Deng was blamed for, among other things, not keeping his word. However, besides the fact that Deng's statement was not made public at the time, the issue of how to evaluate the Cultural Revolution, a radical matter per se, had been reopened by the theoretical questions posed by Mao in late 1974.

The 1975 movement for the study of theory, which was conceived of as a prerequisite for a political reconsideration of the revolutionary decade, and more in general for rethinking the entire communist experience, became in fact an essential condition in the formation of Deng's program. Deng managed to leverage this movement, albeit his intent was completely opposed to Mao's. For Mao, the issue was how to gain new theoretical insight, as well as the criteria attaching thereto, in support of a political assessment of the Cultural Revolution and to acknowledge and rectify its mistakes. For Deng, on the other hand, the issue was how to deny it, even if he could not but incorporate some key issues concerning the inconsistencies of the former order.

Deng's strategy took shape through a series of moves instantiated when Mao himself called the reassessment of the Cultural Revolution into play again with his theses. As noted in the previous chapter, the question marks that punctuated the theoretical issues he raised provided the key to the situation: Why Lenin? Why did Lenin speak of "special government"? And with him, Marx, Engels, and all the others? What did they really mean? What was the difference in principle between socialism and capitalism? No communist political leader at that time would ever have put a question mark, other than a rhetorical one, after a quotation from Lenin.

Although Deng initially seemed to be occupied with other matters— "putting in order everything in every field," as he put it—what guided all his work in 1975 was the problem of how to handle these issues and the political activism they stirred up. Since questions concerning the dictatorship of the proletariat could not but be strongly felt among workers in the China of 1975, the factories became one of the explicit targets Deng's plans kept in sight.

During that year, we can distinguish three main tactical steps Deng deployed. First, he hedged his bet, refraining from discussing or even mentioning Mao's theses. This was as much an elusive move as a very clear stand. Yet the ground was shifting due to developing circumstances. Within a few months, the political activism those issues were stimulating meant he could no longer avoid mentioning Mao's theses. His next move was thus to formulate a set of opposing arguments summarized in a "General Program." In the third and what turned out to be the decisive step, he made a seemingly passive move, almost a renunciation of support for his own line. While it did cause his second political downfall, that was short-lived, and actually cemented his already strong position, which then led him to complete victory. Let us look at these three stages in detail.

"Everything Must Be Put in Order in Every Field"

For several months, Deng at first showed indifference to Mao's theoretical arguments and spoke almost exclusively about the need to restore order (整顿 zhengdun), which was the key expression in all his statements of 1975. In Ezra Vogel's recent, voluminous biography of Deng, Mao's theses and the following "movement for the study of the theory of the dictatorship of the proletariat" do not play any significant role in the circumstances of 1975. The scene he portrays is fully occupied by the struggle between a Mao "mercurial" as well as "paranoid" and a Deng firmly committed to "restoring order."[5] However, as discussed below, denying that Mao's theoretical theses had any value, or merely paying them lip service, was part of Deng's deliberate political response to the circumstances. In the event, Deng's allegedly pragmatic lack of interest in ideological issues should not be taken too literally. Indeed, Deng would have never been able to build a strategy to accomplish his aims without paying close attention to Mao's theses and executing a series of specific maneuvers in response to them.

Mao's theses had been discussed within the central organs of the party since December, and national and local media relaunched them daily in hundreds of articles and essays from early February. In addition to the theoretical novelty they contained and the subjective urgency they manifested, the importance of these theses was heightened by the fact that for several years no important statements by Mao had been published.

That the main thesis was a crucial question without any definitive answer increased the attention and the degree of subjective anxiety those theses raised. Exploring them in the detail they called for required a very personal, theoretical effort, but no one, including Mao himself, had any predetermined plan for mustering it. In short, the appeal that "it is necessary for the whole country to be informed" came to be taken very literally, and the issues soon became the subject of a public debate that was engaged in party meetings at all cadre levels and in the industrial danwei, the factories being at the forefront of these workplaces.

Deng at first never cited Mao's formulations for the study of theory and refrained especially from intervening in their content. His lack of interest in theoretical matters and issues of principle has become proverbial, as in the famous motto of the "color of the cat." Mao would sometimes say that Deng was "deaf," meaning that he was deaf to political theory. Deng himself was duly disturbed by the very existence of ideological debates, which he considered a waste of time—time stolen from the effective management of state command.

However, Deng's careful avoidance of any reference to studying theory was in itself a precise sign of intention, although at the time he was in no position to declare his intent openly. In all his speeches in 1975, or at least in those later collected in his *Selected Works*, Deng spoke in particular of 整顿 zhengdun, a term in the Chinese political idiom meaning "to correct a disorder" in an unmistakably disciplinary sense.[6] "Discipline" (纪律 *jilü*), and "more severe rules" (规章制度严一些 *guizhang zhidu yan yixie*), Deng continually repeated, were indispensable for combating the main evil of the moment: "disorder" (乱 *luan*), and more specifically "factionalism" (派性 *paixing*).

Before examining the issue of "put in order" versus "disorder/factionalism," it should be noted that, unlike Mao's calls to study theory that were basically aimed at everyone, the appeals made by Deng in 1975, which were no less urgent and full of subjective pathos, had very definite targets. They were primarily meant for the ruling cadres at all levels of the party-state, and especially for those in top-tier positions leading the industrial danwei.

The other major topic of his statements was what Deng called "put the word *dare* in the first place" (把'敢'字当头 *ba "gan" zi dang tou*). The formula echoed the slogan of the early months of the Cultural Revolution, "dare to rebel against reactionaries." (In fact, it was a slogan with a long revolutionary pedigree, going back at least to Saint-Just.) This time, though, the significance of the call was quite the opposite: "dare" to give the "rebels" a lesson.

Deng was chiefly addressing his remarks to a sprawling *nomenklatura* that had been hotly contested during the Cultural Revolution: leading cadres at all levels, from the danwei up to the provincial and central governments who, like Deng himself, had been overthrown (被打倒 *bei dadao*) in 1966–67. Almost all of them had returned to their posts by 1972, but only after having publicly acknowledged that they had committed political mistakes in their bureaucratic responsibilities in having opposed the mass movements at the beginning of the Cultural Revolution.

The problem now was, as Deng said, that many of these leaders continued to be "afraid of being overthrown," even of being criticized, and had therefore "put the word 'fear' in the first place" (把'怕'字当头 ba "pa" zi dang tou), thereby tolerating the disorder brought about by factionalism everywhere. If they continued to be afraid, he warned, they would be swept away definitively. Deng stated that personally he was "not afraid," and did not care who criticized his "put-in-order" policies as a program of restoration. He, indeed, pressed for an increase in severity: orders, rigid rules, ironhanded discipline, and so on were the only remedies to a situation that Deng depicted as being on the edge of the abyss.[7] The alternatives Deng posed were between a total engagement in his put-in-order policies by the party-state cadres or their catastrophic overthrow, this time definitively.

The nature, real extent, and true causes of the overthrow that Deng declared he wanted to avoid are issues that deserve consideration that goes beyond his version of the facts. The strong subjective pathos of the appeal was undoubtedly a key component in the success of his strategy. Deng's alarm about the menace of destruction of the entire structure of hierarchical ranks in the system of state control created a coalition with an extraordinary ideological and operational unity within the ranks of the senior cadres of the Chinese party-state.

Deng's appeal to the leaders of the CCP consisted in proclaiming that the risk was absolute, and that the only chance they had not to be toppled forever was not to be afraid of being overthrown *at that precise moment*. The timeliness and subjective tension of the appeal was essential: it was certainly an appeal to courage. However, if we try to analyze China in 1975, the picture Deng portrayed of the situation should be reviewed in detail, not because a fundamental crisis was not actually involved (the persuasiveness of Deng's appeal to the leaders of the CCP did not rest on purely imaginary elements), but because the perspective Deng applied was the result of the very solution that he prescribed as the only possible one, not the analytical objective premise he claimed it to be.

In other words, it was because Deng was unable to conceive of anything but the command of state order that he saw disorder everywhere. What Deng called disorder was actually a series of political experiments—embryonic to be sure, but far from chaotic—in search, particularly in factories, of new forms of emancipation and equality in the organization of the collective existence of ordinary people. The main problem was that those experiments were being conducted within the horizon of an irreversible crisis casting its shadow over a certain institutional state order and a constituent space of political culture.

Deng and his supporters in 1975 greatly exaggerated the actual extent of the disorder, which they depicted as a matter of public security, as well as overemphasizing, retrospectively, the effectiveness of the real "put in order" at the time. The official biographies of Deng show, moreover, that the policies of zhengdun lasted only a few months, in particular between March and May.[8] Even less convincing are the data regarding the miraculous effects of the policies of zhengdun on production. To show how effective the put-in-order policies had been in 1975, Deng's biographers cite a GDP growth of 11.9 percent compared to 1974 and 15.1 percent in industry.[9] Besides the question of the reliability of official government statistics, which especially for those years are controversial, it is unlikely that this extraordinary economic performance was the result of immediate policies, which in a few months were supposed to have wiped out the almost endemic anarchy Deng and his team portrayed in speeches and documents in the spring of 1975.

Assuming that the data on growth in 1975 are accurate, the economic performance they portray would have been impossible without a solid structural ground and a high degree of organizational stability. In this connection, one cannot but observe that, purely in terms of the 1975 GDP growth rate, there are no great differences between that and the past four decades of the Chinese "economic miracle." Although the point is seldom mentioned, the average GDP growth rate for the years 1967–76 is estimated at 7.1 percent.[10] The question was thus not a fall in production, and the "reform policy" Deng pursued was in no way a remedy for any economic crisis.

Moreover, after 1968 serious turmoil was a rare occurrence for the maintenance of public order by China's law-enforcement authorities, and a conspicuous rise in production capacity had been achieved, as is shown by the statistics cited to prove Deng's miracles in 1975. Considering the extent of mass movements in the preceding years and the complexity of the disputes underway, the situation in Chinese factories in the mid-seventies was quite orderly.

The fact that so many workers were politically engaged created a sense of responsibility, self-discipline, and personal attachment to the factory, which was a major organizational factor, should not be underestimated. On the other hand, the political activism of the workers at that time made the reinvention of organizational criteria unavoidable. The problem was one not of public order but of how to create an organization of collective life in the factory that might match the workers' political activism, with the added complication that this politicization had outstripped the previously established relationship between the working class and the industrial danwei.

As for the equivalence between "disorder" and "factionalism," Deng's key topic at the time, the situation in the mid-seventies was quite different from what it had been in 1967–68, as discussed in the previous chapters. What Deng treated as factionalism in the factories in 1975 was a phenomenon that was in no way comparable either in magnitude or mass to the clashes between factions in the core years of the Cultural Revolution. Deng correctly pointed to the phenomenon in the industrial danwei. Yet what he portrayed as pure chaos that must be restored to order was, in actual fact, a crucial political issue: What was the desired relationship between the workers' experiments and the reorganization of the leading organs in factories? Given the depth of the rupture the events of the Cultural Revolution had caused in the previous forms of organization, a reorganization of the managing groups of the industrial danwei, along with all cadre levels of the party-state, was certainly a highly tangled web of issues.

The January Storm and its aftermath led to new forms of organization. Called "triple combines" (三结合 *san jiehe*), they were purposed to involve the cadres of the party-state, technicians, and the new activists who had emerged from the ranks of the "rebel" workers during the Cultural Revolution in the production management teams. Many of these people had gained their political experience in organizations that were independent of the party and had later been brought into it. The Maoists were seeking to strike a balance between the party-state and the new forms of political activism that had emerged during the Cultural Revolution. For example, during the Tenth Congress of the party in 1973, much emphasis was placed on the designation of Wang Hongwen, one of the main leaders of the Shanghai rebels, as vice-president of the CCP. All these attempts were inevitably caught between the strain to renew the political profile of the party-state, as the Maoists hoped, and the reabsorption of tensions in the bureaucratic infighting usual among officials.

By the mid-seventies, membership in the CCP had almost doubled compared to 1966, and many new members were recruited among the activists of the late sixties. In the factories, it was the younger, politicized workers who were most involved in experiments like the workers' universities and the study-theory groups. Most of the previous cadres were probably less enthusiastic, or at least more skeptical about the "new things" that diminished their hierarchic prestige and implied considerable theoretical effort. For Deng Xiaoping this situation was simply a clash between factionalism and order. Only those who were members of the party before the Cultural Revolution were to be considered reliable, whereas the new members were, as Deng said, "fans of the rebel leaders."[11] The latter were therefore seen as a factor of disorder that needed to be reined in by more forceful regulations.[12]

While Deng continued to deal with the situation only as a disciplinary matter throughout the first half of 1975, the development of the study-theory movement was gaining momentum. The forms of political experimentation it engendered had spread to the factories, spurring the subjective personal and intellectual growth of many workers and, hence, revealing that the issues at stake were far more politically significant than any lack of regulations. The question was what role the political activism of the workers should play in the experimentation with a new political idea of the factory. It is likely that these experiments were stronger or weaker depending on the factory. The politicized groups of workers in factories whose preexisting cadres were less inclined to be involved in the search for new paths were more polemical vis-à-vis their management teams. It was a situation that clearly fueled disputes in and among workers and cadres.

Needless to say, at stake too was the new composition of the managerial groups in Chinese factories. As in any form of state organization, it inevitably involved bureaucratic rivalries. However, there was a fundamental difference between resolving such disputes by enforcing restraint through regulations versus by reconsidering the theoretical and practical relationships between workers and the socialist factory. Moreover, as already noted, neither had a significant problem of social disorder arisen during those months nor had the initial circumstances remained the same. Quite the contrary. The political momentum of the study-theory movement had given Chinese society a peculiar dynamic stability. It had focused people's attention on theoretical issues that, though certainly very abstract, directly addressed specific concerns in the organization of collective life, particularly in the industrial danwei.

The Three Directives as the Axis

While the study-theory movement was developing in mid-1975, Deng realized he could no longer so blatantly ignore the theoretical and political issues at stake. No real political influence could be exerted by merely invoking a restoration of order and imposing regulations as disciplinary measures in attempts to oppose these issues. Indeed, Deng knew that such tactics would expose him to a direct confrontation with Mao's theories. This was a second turning point that came to define his strategy. Since February 1975 he had simply argued that it was necessary to put everything in order, without any reference to the theoretical issues under discussion. A few months later, however, he could not help but also put in order Mao's theoretical arguments.

All things considered, the main source of disorder was the theoretical issues themselves. They called into question concepts that were fundamental to an order that was both ideological and institutional. Putting the core political issue of the dictatorship of the proletariat up for theoretical probing was radically destabilizing. It was so because not only was it such a fundamental pillar of the entire edifice of the socialist state, but it was Mao himself who had raised it, and without indicating any prescribed answer. He appealed to "the whole country" to find a new rational basis for it.

Deng Xiaoping had no inclination to compete directly in a theoretical and political dispute of that sort or magnitude. Since it needed to be addressed on a considerable level of abstraction—where he did not feel at ease—he resorted to "professional" ideologists. In the spring of 1975, he organized his own think tank, the State Council Political Research Office (国务院政治研究室 *Guowuyuan zhengzhi yanjiushi*), a working group composed of some of the most prestigious CCP theorists of the years preceding the Cultural Revolution. By summer they set about drafting a blueprint that laid out a series of ideological countermoves to adapt Deng's policies to the theoretical level of the political situation at the time.

Noteworthy in this connection is that the Political Research Office ideologists labeled Mao's theses as "metaphysical," thereby casting a cloud of suspicion over them and a clear ray of light on Deng's opposing "put-in-order" line. Let's pause a moment here before dismissing the term as a mere rhetorical device of cultural bureaucrats. "Metaphysics" had a peculiar meaning in revolutionary culture. As noted in the *Hai Rui* dispute, it was the opposing corollary of "dialectics." However, such a charge was rooted in a typical antimetaphysical tradition of modern philosophy.

Metaphysics is, in a technical philosophical sense, always a synonym of disorder. It is the radical indeterminacy of a basic component of a certain system of knowledge, and more essentially an indeterminacy regarding the "essence of being." Alain Badiou has reevaluated a modern current of "dialectical metaphysics"—an unacceptable oxymoron in Stalinist philosophy—which takes such "indeterminacy" not as an unprovable dogma of faith (say, God in theology) but as a starting point for a new process of thinking. Dialectical metaphysics, Badiou argues, puts a basic concept as indeterminate in order to attain a new determinacy for it, thereby making indeterminacy an indispensable step toward new knowledge.[13] Badiou cites Hegel, Marx, and Freud as major instances. Of course, their respective positions are among the most controversial of modern thought, and have often aroused the same suspicion as metaphysics in the name of positive knowledge based on a fully determined set of concepts.

Mao too could be added to this trio of great "dialectical metaphysicians" for his last theoretical theses. He appealed for a "clarification" (*yao gao qingchu*), a new rational determination of the basic concept of the edifice of political thought organizing the socialist state, the dictatorship of the proletariat. Without such a clarification, the probable defeat became almost inevitable. However, Mao's first step was a question without an answer—Why did Lenin say dictatorship over the bourgeoisie?—and it raised the concept to radical indeterminacy. The suspicion of metaphysics as a source of disorder, which Deng's ideologists leveled against those theses in an attempt to put them in order, was in line with a long antimetaphysical modern tradition. In rough approximation, it was the same positivist argument that Comte, for example, had opposed to the metaphysics of the French Revolution. Deng, of course, was no Comte, but his political position after the Cultural Revolution was after all a vision conceived in terms of order and progress.

By late summer, the Political Research Office had drawn up three main documents reflecting Deng's policies in the preceding months, setting them in an ideological framework that, at least formally, addressed the theoretical topics raised by Mao. Completed in October, the most important document was the "General Program of Activities of the Party and the Whole Country."[14] Immediately after the publication of the General Program, Mao, who in the preceding months had maintained a neutral position toward Deng and the steps he was taking, began to reply very critically.

The General Program released by Deng's Political Research Office took aim at Mao's statements on studying theory. While it did not actually discuss the content of Mao's theses, it did finally cite them, whereas Deng had simply ignored them for several months. The main point was that "Mao's directive on the study of theory," as the Program called it, was surely "very important" but "could not be separated in any way" (implying an error the Deng ideologists labeled as "metaphysical") from the other two "directives of Chairman Mao" in earlier months. One had called for "stability and unity" (安定团结 *anding tuanjie*), and the other had encouraged "further development of the national economy" (把国民经济搞上去 *ba goumin jingji gao shangqu*).

The Deng think tank then came up with the formula of "taking the three directives as the axis" (以三项指示为纲 *yi san xiang zhishi wei gang*), stating that it should become the nub of the General Program. The slogan served two purposes. It was primarily aimed at Mao's central disturbing questions about a potential epochal turning point of the socialist form of state, the main theoretical issue at stake in those months. It first sought to place this directive and the two general assertions about the advisability of social cohesion and economic growth, statements that Mao could have made at various other times, on the same level. It then countered the metaphysical argument with that of order and progress. The think tank's mission was to stifle the issues that were animating the study-theory movement within a liturgy that deprived them of any political value.

The Urgency of a Political Assessment and Its Ban

For much of 1975, Mao did not raise any objection to Deng's policies of zhengdun and left him largely to his own devices. In early October, however, facing the distortion of his own position, which had even been presented as the key point in the General Program, Mao intervened, issuing a statement that repudiated in no uncertain terms such a "creative" interpretation (as it is still presented by Deng's official biographers). The tone was one of notable impatience: "What 'three directives as the axis'! [什么 "以三项指示为纲" *Shenme "yi san xiang zhishi wei gang"*].... 'Stability and unity' do not mean there is no class struggle. Class struggle is the main thread in the net. The rest is just the mesh."[15]

Mao's intervention became a turning point in his relationship with Deng but did not reach the point of a definitive break. Nor could it have done so, for Mao was asserting that addressing the problems of China at the time, including social cohesion, should be given priority in politics ("class struggle" obviously being its main synonym). Then, too, a series of theoretical issues he had raised in December reopened the question of what exactly the actual content of politics itself was after the Cultural Revolution—dictatorship of the proletariat was another synonym for politics under socialism. Moreover, he also reopened the problem of what assessment should be given to the political events of the preceding decade. It was precisely on this point that Mao's dispute with Deng focused in the following weeks.

Deng maintained a very uncompromising stance in this crucial transition, whereas Mao showed a remarkable willingness to come to an agreement. Deng Rong, Deng's daughter, wrote in her memoirs that Mao's attitude toward her father was at the time one of "utmost tolerance and patience" (仁至义尽 *renzhi yijin*).[16] In October, when Mao criticized the formula of the three directives as the axis, he was not seeking outright confrontation with Deng. Rather, he immediately made Deng an offer to tackle the key point, namely the assessment of the Cultural Revolution.

Mao proposed starting a broad public debate in order to thoroughly reappraise all aspects of the preceding decade, starting with the negative ones, and asked Deng to lead a national discussion. The proposal was obviously very difficult: it was as divisive as it was generous, and Mao repeatedly tried to persuade Deng to accept it. Mao's verdict on the Cultural Revolution was definitely positive, though with a critical reserve. He was convinced that the Cultural Revolution had opened up new possibilities for egalitarian mass activism, but he was also aware that it had led to destructive and self-destructive reactions that had led to grave injustices.

Using a "classical" percentage, he said it had been "70 percent positive," but it had been 30 percent "inadequate" (有所不足 *you suo bu zu*). Of those events, he said, there were "very different points of view" (看法不见得一致 *kanfa bu jiande yizhi*). Then too, among those not in favor of the endeavor were some who were simply "dissatisfied" (不满意 *bu manyi*) because they had been treated unfairly, and others, on the other hand, who wished "to settle [old] scores" (算帐 *suan zhang*) with the Cultural Revolution. It was time to submit the evaluation of the Cultural Revolution to mass-scale "research" (研究 *yanjiu*, the same term used when talking about research as scholarly study) in order to understand precisely what had gone wrong or had been short of the mark.[17] In other words, Mao argued that it was time to explore primarily what had not worked in the Cultural Revolution.[18] Only an open debate and research that extended across the entire country, he argued, could clarify the issues.

Mao then proposed that Deng should assume the task of leading a working group created within the Central Committee to launch a national campaign of "research" into this crucial issue. Clearly, such a campaign would have been impossible without the involvement of Deng, who was in fact already acting as premier given the serious illness of Zhou Enlai, who passed away in January 1976. Mao received a very clear rejection, which Deng reiterated on several occasions during the autumn of 1975. Deng replied that he was not the right person for the job because he was not aware of events in which he had not participated after 1967.

This turned out to be a pretext, although it did put him in a difficult position indeed. By refusing to assume the political leadership of research into the Cultural Revolution, Deng actually even renounced exerting any national political role, particularly when Mao had so clearly distanced himself from Deng's General Program and from its formula of the three directives as the axis. Deng's choice, however, was only an apparent retreat. His rejection of Mao's proposal in October 1975 resulted in a substantial limitation of his direct command for about a year. Although Deng remained indirectly very influential in all the events of 1976, his intransigence on this point in fact became the main element of his following success.

One can only wonder what sort of mass debate about the Cultural Revolution, launched by Mao and directed by Deng, might have ensued in China at the end of 1975. We can only speculate that such a campaign on what had not worked would have likely been a large-scale movement involving high subjective tension. It was time to criticize political injustices and to acknowledge the reasons why those unfairly accused had suffered. Yet to distinguish between those who complained about unfair treatment and those who just wanted to settle old scores would not have been an easy task.

A mass debate of that kind would have reopened innumerable individual cases, often very painful wounds, and should have reexamined difficult and uncomfortable truths involving the accountability of many people from all the factions: rebels, loyalists, cadres at all levels, the army, and so on. Finally, such a debate would inevitably have entailed even a reexamination of a number of Mao's political decisions. The reassessment required thoroughgoing collective criticism and self-criticism in order to discern right from wrong, new roads for which the mass activism had paved the way, and which mistakes should not be repeated. Just as necessary, if not more so, was a thorough critical rethinking of the concept of the dictatorship of the proletariat as a prerequisite for the assessment of the inadequacies of the revolutionary decade.

The autumn of 1975 was undoubtedly a crucial turning point. It was a window showing the extent of and the alternatives in play in the Chinese political situation at the time, at least from Mao's perspective. That Mao offered a deal that would have put Deng in a tight spot, and that the latter had to refuse, should not be taken for granted. It was, if anything, a risky offer. Mao repeated his invitation several times in October, and Deng's official biographers, including his daughter, all reveal a certain surprise when reporting how resolutely Deng rejected it.

Clearly, here were two completely divergent perspectives. For Mao, the priority was to promote a mass rethinking of egalitarian politics; for Deng, the priority was to restore governmental order, and any mass initiative would bring more disorder. Mao's aim was to promote a political self-assessment using an indefinitely multiple set of egalitarian subjectivities, which he considered capable of "educat[ing] themselves by themselves" and "liberat[ing] themselves"—the implication being even from their own mistakes. In contrast, Deng aimed at reconstructing well-defined hierarchies that would be able to free themselves from any egalitarian initiatives of the masses, which he considered inherently anarchic.

Deng was certainly among those who wanted to settle old scores with the Cultural Revolution. Yet many other leaders of the CCP wanted to do the same but did not know how to go about it. The sense of Deng's move—his stubbornness, and in particular its effectiveness—should be seen in the context of the entire political situation in 1975. Deng could have exerted enormous influence as chairperson of a commission of the Central Committee to lead a movement of national study on the mistakes and shortcomings of the Cultural Revolution.

Deng, however, was in no way interested in a political rethinking of the Cultural Revolution. Rather, given his subsequent strategy, it becomes clear that thwarting any attempt at a political reappraisal of the Cultural Revolution was for Deng the fundamental condition for restoring governmental order. What he aimed at, even running the risk of immediate failure, was to clear the way for what became the thorough negation. This third step of Deng's in October 1975 was thus essential for charting his future strategy. Deng's position immediately became weaker, and in the last months of the year every previous step he had undertaken, including the Political Research Office, lost momentum altogether. Deng was "ousted" again the following spring, but this second fall was brief. In October 1976, exactly one month after Mao's death and following a short "Thermidor" during which the Maoist leaders on the Central Committee were arrested, the process that led to the thorough negation of the Cultural Revolution began. It became the basic formula on which the "new Chinese order" was built.[19]

"The Bourgeoisie Is in the Communist Party"

Deng's categorical refusal of Mao's offer quashed any chance of generating a mass movement for a critical reappraisal of the Cultural Revolution. In the end, Mao's proposal was an effort for a critical and self-critical reappraisal of and by the party itself. Indeed, Deng's resolute intransigence underscored, insofar as the highest cadres were concerned, that the CCP had no intention whatsoever of endorsing a mass political movement of any kind. The Cultural Revolution and the outcomes it eventuated constituted an unbridgeable divide between Mao's view of what revolutionary politics should be and what the most powerful party leaders intended they would be.

After Deng's and clearly the entire party leadership's unshakable opposition to a critical reflection on the revolutionary decade, Mao himself formulated a general assessment of events. A few months before having to accept "the invitation of Marx and Lenin to go and meet them" (as he had told the Albanians ten years before), his last political thesis, pronounced from a position of almost total isolation, completed the series of predictions of the previous twenty years that it was still to be seen whether socialism or capitalism would win. Indeed, given the insurmountable obstacles that Deng's coalition posed to critically rethinking the Cultural Revolution, and with it the entire historical experience of socialism, the capitalist road was completely open.

Once again, Mao opened with a question, but this time he also provided an answer. "You make the socialist revolution and you don't know where the bourgeoisie is. The bourgeoisie is in the Communist Party" (搞社会主义革命，不知道资产阶级在哪里，资产阶级就在共产党内 *gao shehuizhuyi geming, bu zhidao zichanjieji zai nali, zichanjieji jiu zai gongchandang nei*).[20] If taken literally, Mao's words can merely be seen as a reiteration of a Stalinist line—the "class enemy" has infiltrated the core leadership of the proletariat's political organization. Yet his assertion was far more than any such Stalinist reductionism. It encapsulated the consequences of a long-lived political experiment that had forged a path well beyond the cultural boundaries of revolutionary politics itself.

I suggest that in Mao's statement, "bourgeoisie" is to be taken not as a social class or as the product of a certain economic base as represented by infiltrators within the Communist Party. Even less is it meant as a given stage in a presumed historical teleology of economic and state designs. "Bourgeoisie" is rather the generic designation of the dominant subjectivity in the governing circumstances of the sociohistorical condition of capitalism. As a command mode of labor, that condition is what Marx and Engels analyzed in unsurpassed clarity and detail. Mao's thesis that the bourgeoisie is precisely in the Communist Party points to a dual meaning: that the party per se tends to occupy the same place as the dominant governing subjectivity of the bourgeois social world. And, as Mao had striven so strenuously to promote in his final political efforts, this condition could only be countered by new political inventions brought forth via a mass movement for the study of theory.

As we have noted, in Mao's theses of 1975 "there are no big differences" between the socialist and capitalist forms of the state except for the form of ownership (所有制) of the means of production—a crucial difference to be sure, but not sufficient by itself to ensure the almost certain triumph of an egalitarian political vision. Socialism was an exception to the rule of the modern governing condition. By that very token, it had to be kept revitalized by mass political inventions, for a failure to do so would make it "very easy to make capitalism."

A closer reading of Mao's theses shows that in no way do they fit the currently common depiction of Mao as despotic paladin of an ideal model of socialism. Quite the contrary. Despite assumed appearances, he argued that the structure of the command of labor in China, as well as in all socialist states, was intrinsically compatible with capitalism. The real difference, the form of ownership, was no warranty of stability. By the mid-seventies China was already "nearly capitalist" and the Communist Party was ready to transform into a variant of the governing subjectivity typical of the modern sociohistorical condition. By removing from the scene any form of mass political experimentation, it would have been very easy to fully deploy that bourgeois subjectivity.

The Original Stages of Deng's Strategy

On his part, Deng was aware that he could not simply restore the previous system of command and would have to create a new one in its stead. He also had to be able to map out a long-term strategy for effectively establishing "order," the byword for reestablishing authority over the factory workers. By considering the whole process of reform, it is possible to identify at least three basic moves carried out consistently: the suppression of the Maoist experiments in the factories, the full commodification of labor, and the maintenance in the government discourse of the ideological reference to the working class and its historical connection to its class vanguard, the Communist Party.

The first obstacle to overcome was the set of experiments that had called into question the formal and political order of the industrial danwei, and the related rediscussion of key theoretical issues. This prerequisite was achieved very early. The coup of October 1976 quickly shut down these experiments, declaring them to be mere "conspiracies" by a small gang of usurpers. The new government also dealt summarily with the appeals to set up a movement for the study of theory. It immediately proclaimed these steps to be "nonsense" aimed at "defaming the dictatorship of the proletariat" and ultimately at overthrowing it.

The commodification of labor came next as a crucial step for any reordering but was inevitably implemented more gradually. Once the historical-political command structure of the industrial danwei had been discredited, only the full commodification of labor could bring the conjoint authority of the "technical division of labor" and "factory despotism" fully to bear. The process started in the late 1970s. It began first with the generalization of piecework wage, praised as the highest achievement of the Marxist principle "to each according to his work" (按劳分配 *an lao fenpei*).[21] In the 1990s, following the bloody suppression of the Tian'anmen Square movement, the commodification of labor was fully established, with millions of internal migrant workers moving to form a workforce as massive as it was precarious.[22]

In fact, the main condition that allowed the complete commodification of the workforce was the availability of an immense quantity of cheap labor obtained thanks to the suppression of the agricultural people's communes at the beginning of the 1980s. At this point, which was decisive in affirming

Deng's strategy, we again find the questions we examined at the beginning of this volume, or rather the fact that they did not find any effective resolution during the revolutionary decade. The problem of what could be a political role for the peasants under socialism, which had been the essence of Lushan's 1959 clash and which had been at the center of the historical-theatrical prologue, was never really the object of great attempts at reinvention, as it was in the factories.

During the Cultural Revolution there were certainly initiatives to limit city–country differences, with the extension of education and public health to the countryside. The flag of a famous model commune, Dazhai, was constantly displayed by the Maoists, but that did not inspire mass peasant political movements in the countryside that aimed to rethink their political role directly, comparable to those that had arisen among the factory workers.

The problem of a new peasant politics remained unsolved for the whole decade, except for the confirmation of the superiority of the people's communes. But even there, without political reinvention those forms of agricultural cooperative had no intrinsic stability. Indeed, precisely because the communes were not properly within the state structure, as were the industrial danwei, it was a relatively simple matter to suppress them.

The Maoists had argued, as we saw in the article by Yao Wenyuan that had opened the prologue, that the abolition of the popular agricultural communes would entail the return of the great landowners. So far, this has not happened, and even if it is not clear what the fate will be of land ownership in China, certainly that was not the immediate consequence of the end of agricultural cooperatives. The first deliberately pursued result was to open a huge reservoir of cheap labor for industry. Once it became clear that the government no longer intended to promote any political intervention in the countryside, and the prospect was mere individual survival, but that it was possible to find jobs in industry, hundreds of millions of peasants poured into the cities. Although precarious, underpaid, and not sharing any of the rights of city dwellers, these hundreds of millions of nomadic migrant workers constitute an immense "reserve industrial army," which forms the foundation of China's economic miracle of the last decades.

Mummifying the Working Class

The new modes for disciplining labor are not just a restoration of the previous socialist measures. The conditions of wage labor in China are a paradigm of despotic capitalist command in the workplace, and the labor market is among the most flexible in the world. A strictly Taylorist organization prevails in factories, and a fast turnover of staff is an organizational strongpoint at Foxconn. The Chinese working class of today has nothing in common with that of the earlier industrial danwei. The organization of work at Foxconn, a "model factory" in contemporary China that Pun Ngai's research analyzes in the most disturbing detail, essentially amounts to that of the capitalist factory analyzed by Marx.[23]

However, such a definitive reordering was achieved by a further key element, which was ultimately vital to the policy of reform. Mao had predicted that "it would be easy to make capitalism in China." However, in order to do so in a China where the political role of workers had been so hotly debated (during and even before the Cultural Revolution), it was also essential to prevent any side effects, specifically by removing any chance the workers might have of organizing themselves politically.[24] After all, such a chance had occurred in late 1966.

The new rulers clearly perceived the danger, and all of them had in mind Marx's dictum: "The bourgeoisie creates its own gravediggers." Repressive measures would have been ineffective and hazardous, although when necessary the Chinese government has given ample proof of its readiness to deploy them, especially against workers.[25] Preemptive measures based on a governmental discourse that leaves no doubt as to the state's intention to wield an iron fist against those who violate the rules have hitherto been more successful. These measures form part of an apparently contradictory but actually consistent strategy in which the upholding of the icon of the working class among the insignia of power paralleled and definitely supported the emptying of its political value.

Nonetheless, the new ruling elites in China have felt that it was necessary to maintain certain key terms from the previous hierarchical rituals, namely the affirmation of a special relationship between the Communist Party and the working class in Chinese governmental discourse. In the most recent CCP constitution, for instance, the first sentence proclaims, as in all the previous versions, that the party is "the vanguard of the working class" (工人阶级的先锋队 *gongren jieji de xianfengdui*).[26] Is this a flashy anachronism? For reform policies that have received much praise for their "pragmatism" and for having rejected what Deng called "ideological chitchat," it is hard to believe that the formula is merely a residue of a past still performing the function of an obsolete liturgy.

The Chinese government is so eager to affirm technocratic values in labor relations that one may wonder why it has not adopted a more postsocialist language. After all, the CCP must have acquired more up-to-date expertise in political propaganda. The reason why the CCP claims to be the vanguard of the working class cannot merely be attributed to the long pedigree of the formula or the fact that in the past it was most often an effective way of maintaining authority over the workers in socialist states. China's rulers realize full well they can no longer rely on outdated clichés since the workers themselves had eschewed the disciplinary working-class rituals during the Cultural Revolution.

Thus, being a nod neither to nostalgia nor to liturgy, the assertion that the CCP is the vanguard of the working class must satisfy a critical need, which ultimately must be the prohibition of all forms of autonomous workers' organizations. All the above-mentioned steps in the sterilization of political value of the reference to the working class were conceived with this purpose in mind. Yet a major concern of the new Chinese elites seems to be that without a clear-cut and definitive declaration, their intent would be ineffective or misunderstood. The insistence on pairing the Chinese Communist Party with the working class through the concept of a political avant-garde, which is the equivalent of political organization, says loud and clear to every single worker and to everybody else in China, "I am the Chinese Communist Party, and thou shalt have no other political organizations before me."

If, for example, a young female worker (打工妹 *dagongmei*) at Foxconn, or one of her male fellow workers (打工仔 *dagongzai*) were to object that, after all, such a vanguard is nothing more than a peculiar organization of the capitalist command, she or he would be informed with plenty of doctrinal details that the laws of historical development today require capitalism. In official Chinese governmental discourse, capitalism is a condition of the historical progress that will lead to advanced stages of socialism, until the day the very development of productive forces will also bring about communism. The first paragraph of the CCP constitution ends with the assertion that the "highest ideal" and the "ultimate goal" of the party is to "realize Communism" (实现共产主义 *shixian gongchanzhuyi*).

It is perfectly understood by all in China—both by those who write and by those who must read these formulas—that they mean only one thing: independent political organizations are unacceptable, especially for workers, who are under special surveillance in contemporary China. Anyone violating this principle knows full well what the consequences of doing so are. Far from being an ideological remnant, such formulas continue to have a very real and powerful impact today.

For four decades, Deng's turning point ensured China a stability of institutions far exceeding that of many other state systems, not to mention those socialist countries and communist parties around the world that have collapsed. One of the factors behind China's stability was certainly Deng's ability to anticipate an epochal change in contemporary governing circumstances.

However, the decisive factor in his success was the elimination from the scene of the political figure of the worker through the annihilation of that singular political moment of 1975 in China, while retaining at the same time the designation "worker" in first place in the state insignia.

The "new order in China" has in no way restored the former principle of authority that the Cultural Revolution had smashed. Deng's strategic acuity was to grasp immediately that such a restoration was impossible and that new approaches had to be found in order to command obedience. In truth, the means employed were anything but new. In the end, capitalism's main principle of authority was revived: the command of commodified labor.

What was new about the "Chinese miracle," alongside the exercise of capitalist authority, was the fact that the CCP maintained its claim to being the vanguard of the working class. Obviously, no one believes it, least of all those who say it. Yet the category working class is still an essential component of the government's discourse, albeit shorn of its political value. It is clearly retained as a cautionary principle of interdiction, a warning prohibiting any incipient form of independent political existence for workers.

I even risk a prediction that the stability of the Chinese government is assured as long as the dualism holds: on one side, the capitalist principle of authority regulates the lives of wage earners; on the other, the "vanguard of the working class" acts as a preemptive censor to prevent the emergence of any political organization independent of the party. The former is, to a certain extent, a given in that it reiterates the basic rule governing the modern global social condition. The latter, however, is a fiction that can retain its grip only with subsequent emendations of more or less esoteric formulas that amplify its hold—such as the "three represents" (三个代表 *san ge daibiao*), "scientific development" (科学发展 *kexue fazhan*), "harmonious society" (和谐社会 *hexie shehui*), and the latest, "Chinese dream" (中国梦 *Zhongguo meng*).

In this book I have argued that the study of the Cultural Revolution is not only unavoidable for a new assessment of egalitarian politics; it is also indispensable for understanding the present and the possible destinies of China. Current opinion favors the image of a miraculous continuity between the supposed internal stability of the multi-millennium imperial regime and that of contemporary Marxo-Confucianism. Between these two there have presumably been a series of historical "accidents" concerning at most national identity, which today the new government is able to uphold firmly.

Actually, the assessment of the Cultural Revolution lies at the crossroads of understanding China's present as much as its modern history. Without considering the events of the 1960s and 1970s, not only do the conditions of the current governmental stability of this immense country remain opaque, but also the entire political and intellectual path of modern China becomes unintelligible. To imagine that a twentieth-century China existed without the Cultural Revolution, which instead was an integral part of it, amounts to zeroing its political value.

And yet China, which was an epicenter of that epochal transition, is still governed by a huge communist party that continues to proclaim itself the representative of the working class. This paradox requires a global review of the consequences of that political decade. It effectively closed with the annihilation of every political value of the worker figure, whose worldwide herald was the postrevolutionary Chinese government, despite having kept the name "worker" among the government rituals. The mass parties of the twentieth century, the communist ones and the parliamentary ones alike, were swept away by that passage, which called into question their own original reason for being. Nevertheless, the Chinese Communist Party managed to ride out that passage because it was able not only to annihilate the workers' political experiments, but to maintain the simulacrum of the working class as a guarantee that new political experiments cannot exist.[27]

For a new politics to emerge in China, waged laborers themselves will have to invent original forms of independent organization and critically reappraise the political value of the entire history of modern labor politics. If the main barrier against the political existence of ordinary people is the reference to a mummified working class enshrined in official discourse, nothing that is politically novel will be able to come into being without an explicit, conscious effort to keep this fiction at bay.

NOTES

Introduction

1. 毛泽东 Mao Zedong, 关于理论问题的谈话要点, 1974年, 12月 "Guanyu lilun wenti de tanhua yaodian, 1974 nian, 12 yue" [Main points of the talk on the theoretical problems, December 1974], in 建国以来毛泽东文稿 *Jianguo yilai Mao Zedong wengao* [Manuscripts of Mao Zedong after 1949] (Beijing: Zhongyang wenxian chubanshe, 1998), vol. 13, 413–15.
2. 张春桥 Zhang Chunqiao, 在法庭上的讲话 "Zai fating shang de jianghua" [Speech in court], 1981, accessed April 2019, https://blog.boxun.com/hero/201308/zgzj/15_1.shtml. In Chinese, the statement is 按照这个世界的规则, 我早就想好了有这么一天. "Anzhao zhege shijie de guize, wo zao jiu xianghaole you zheme yi tian."
3. An exhaustive synthesis can be found in Roderick MacFarquar and Michael Schoenals, *Mao's Last Revolution* (Cambridge MA: Harvard University Press, 2006).

Chapter 1: Afterlives of an "Upright Official"

1. Marie Claire Bergère, *La république populaire de Chine de 1949 à nos jours* (Paris: Armand Colin, 1987), 174–75.
2. The two main monographic studies are James R. Pusey, *Wu Han: Attacking the Present through the Past* (Cambridge, MA: Harvard University Press, 1969); and 张湛彬 Zhang Zhanbin, 文革第一文字狱 *Wenge diyi wenziyu* [The first literary inquisition of the Cultural Revolution] (Xianggang: Taiping shiji chubanshe, 1998). Both works are intensely apologetic for the figure of Wu Han, although with opposing arguments: a champion of "anti-totalitarianism" for the former, a champion of "fidelity to the party" for the latter.
3. Marc Bloch, *Apologie de l'histoire ou métier d'historien* ([1949], Paris: Armand Colin, 2018). English translation: *The Historian's Craft* (Manchester, UK: Manchester University Press, 1992).

4. For a large and accurate collection of documents concerning the dispute about *Hai Rui ba guan* and its antecedents, see 丁望主编 Ding Wang, ed., 吴晗与《海瑞罢官》事件 *Wu Han yu "Hai Rui ba guan" shijian* [Wu Han and the affair of *Hai Rui Dismissed from Office*], in 中共文化大革命资料汇编, 第四卷 *Zhonggong wenhua da geming ziliao huibian, disi juan* [Collected materials on the great Cultural Revolution of the Chinese Communist Party, vol. 4] (Xiang Gang: Mingbao yuekan she, 1968).
5. Mary G. Mazur, *Wu Han, Historian: Son of China's Times* (Plymouth, UK: Lexington, 2009).
6. See Mazur, *Wu Han*, chapter 3, "Commitment to Ming History," 73–115.
7. A selection of articles and comments on *Hai Rui ba guan* published in the early sixties was reprinted in the *Wenhui bao* in various issues in December 1965. The drama was staged only for some months in 1961, a sign that from the beginning it had probably met with some significant political criticism, or was not considered particularly successful in Chinese theatrical circles.
8. One paradox of the play is that the theme of "dismissal," albeit in the forefront in the title, was in fact absent in the plot. We will discuss this and other aspects of the drama per se in chapter 3.
9. As Clive M. Ansley remarked in *The Heresy of Wu Han: His Play "Hai Rui's Dismissal" and Its Role in China's Cultural Revolution* (Toronto: Toronto University Press, 1971).
10. The term for upright official is 青天 *qingtian*, literally "Blue Sky." Though the expression became idiomatic, its literal sense still obtains. The sky obviously held a crucial place in Chinese culture. That upright officials represented its crystal purity was a cardinal point of imperial ideology.
11. 吴晗 Wu Han, 海瑞罢官 *Hai Rui ba guan* [Hai Rui dismissed from office], 1961 (Beijing: Beijing chubanshe, 1979), act 6, lines 47–56. For the English version, see Wu Han, *Hai Jui Dismissed from Office*, translated by C. C. Huang, *Asian Studies at Hawaii* 7 (1972): 104–20.
12. Other important Chinese historians wrote "new historical dramas" (新历史剧 *xin lishi ju*) in those years. Wu Han had been active in the discussion about the use of the theater to spread historical knowledge. Cf. 吴晗 Wu Han, 论历史剧 "Lun lishi ju" [On historical drama], in 文学评论 *Wenxue pinglun* [Literary critique] 3 (1961), reproduced in Ding Wang, ed., *Wu Han yu "Hai Rui ba guan" shijian*, 150–54. See also Wu Han, 论历史知识的普及 "Lun lishi zhishi de puji" [On the popularization of historical knowledge], 文汇报 *Wenhui bao*, March 27, 1962, reproduced in 吴晗选集 *Wu Han xuanji* [Selected works of Wu Han] (Tianjin: Tianjin renmin chubanshe, 1988), 392–407. There is some helpful information on the new historical dramas of the early sixties in Tom Fisher, "'The Play's the Thing': Wu Han and Hai Rui Revisited," in *Using the Past to Serve the Present*, ed. Jonathan Unger (Armonk, NY: M. E. Sharpe, 1992), 9–45. Fisher promises to take the issue back "from the context to the text," but actually he clarifies some elements of the political-cultural context without any particular analysis of the play.
13. In the preface Wu Han said that professionals of the Beijing opera helped him in the revision. See also Mazur, *Wu Han*, 408–11.
14. I owe this clarification to the late Edoarda Masi, who was then a student at Beida.

15 Étienne Balazs, "Théorie politique et réalité administrative dans la Chine traditionnelle," in *La bureaucratie céleste: Recherches sur l'économie et la société de la Chine traditionnelle* (Paris: Gallimard, 1968); original edition, *Chinese Civilization and Bureaucracy* (New Haven, CT: Yale University Press, 1967). I quote from the Italian version, *La burocrazia celeste* (Milano: Il Saggiatore, 1971), 175. It should be noted that the faction of scholar-officials here quoted by Balasz, the Donglin Party, was an explicit reference in the early sixties used by a group of high cadres of the party apparatus of propaganda, to which Wu Han belonged.

16 Yao's text was about the length of an average scholarly essay. See 姚文元 Yao Wenyuan, 评新编历史剧《海瑞罢官》 "Ping xin bian lishi ju 'Hai Rui ba guan'" [On the new historical play *Hai Rui Dismissed from Office*], 文汇报 *Wenhui bao*, November 11, 1965, reprinted in 人民日报 *Renmin ribao*, November 30, 1965, 5.

17 Yao Wenyuan, "Ping xin bian lishi ju 'Hai Rui ba guan.'" I quote, with minor changes, the English version published in *Chinese Studies in History and Philosophy* 2, no. 1 (1968): 13-43 (quotation on 16-19).

18 Most of the archival research was done by a brilliant specialist of Ming history, 朱永嘉 Zhu Yongjia, who later played an important role in the revolutionary events in Shanghai as a member of the group of radical intellectuals who first joined the rebel workers in late 1966.

19 Even the most official versions of the episode admit now that Yao's criticism concerning documentary issues was accurate. See Zhang Zhanbin, *Wenge diyi wenziyu*, 80.

20 Michel Cartier, *Une réforme locale en Chine au XVI siècle: Hai Rui à Chun'an 1558-1562* (Paris: Mouton, 1972), 86.

21 Cartier, *Une réforme locale en Chine au XVI siècle*, 36, 40.

22 Incidentally, the full privatization of land is still a hot and unresolved issue in contemporary China, even though conditions are altogether of a different nature.

23 The people's communes were abolished at the end of the 1970s.

24 The United States had imposed a strict embargo on China by 1949, and from the early sixties the USSR had unilaterally broken all the agreements concerning economic cooperation, and had withdrawn en bloc over 10,000 engineers and technicians, thus depriving the Chinese government of a significant number of resources needed for economic reorganization. The CPSU attributed the entire fault for the rupture to the CCP, blaming it for developments in an ideological disagreement that had begun with the CCP in 1956 and had become particularly heated by the early 1960s. At the time, nearly all the communist parties in the world had fallen completely in line with the views of the CPSU.

Chapter 2: Political and Historical Dilemmas

1 Mao Zedong, 在杭州的会议上的讲话 "Zai Hangzhou de huiyi shang de jianghua" [Talk at the Hangzhou Meeting], December 21, 1965, reproduced in several unofficial collections of Mao's speeches published by different Red Guard organizations. I quote here from a version that seems to me more complete and is included in a selection of Mao's texts published under the generic title 资料选编 *Ziliao Xuanbian* [Collection of materials], n.p., February 1967, 319. An English version of this

speech, from a different source, can be found in in S. Schram, ed., *Mao Tse-tung Unrehearsed: Talks and Letters 1956–1971* (London: Penguin, 1974).

2 Since his youth, Mao Zedong had cultivated systematic historical scholarship, with a special interest in Chinese history, as is evident from the innumerable historical references in his writings and speeches. See 王子今 Wang Zijin, 历史学者毛泽东 *Lishi xuezhe Mao Zedong* [Mao Zedong as a history scholar] (Beijing: 西苑出版社 Xiyuan chubanshe, 2013); 张贻玖 Zhang Yijiu, 毛泽东读史 *Mao Zedong du shi* [Mao Zedong studying history] (Beijing: 当代中国出版社 Dangdai Zhongguo chubanshe, 2005). For Mao's attitude to the history of the Ming Dynasty, see also 胡长明 Hu Changming, 毛泽东：《明史》我看了最生气 "Mao Zedong: 'Ming shi' shi wo kanle zui shengqi" [Mao Zedong: The "History of the Ming" is what most irritates me], accessed September 12, 2016, http://news.xinhuanet.com/politics/2008-06/01/content_8292979_1.htm.

3 Marie Claire Bergère, *La repubblica popolare cinese* [The People's Republic of China] (Bologna: Il Mulino, 2000), 134.

4 李锐 Li Rui is also the author of a well-known biography of the young Mao, 毛泽东早期革命活动 *Mao Zedong zaoqi geming huodong* (Changsha: Hunan jiaoyu chubanshe, 1983). English translation: Li Jui, *The Early Revolutionary Activities of Comrade Mao Tse-tung* (White Plains, NY: M. E. Sharpe, 1977).

5 李锐 Li Rui, 庐山会议实录 *Lushan huiyi shilu* [The authentic documents of the Lushan Conference] (Changsha: 湖南教育出版社 Hunan jiaoyu chubanshe, 1989). Besides being driven by strong personal resentment toward Mao, Li was intent on saving his own and Peng Dehuai's honor in all his comments, since he was one of the few who shared the fate of the minister of defense. Yet, despite this, the wealth of detail he reports contains enough documentation to enable one to formulate a very different opinion from his and from that of the current government. What Li probably wanted to demonstrate implicitly is that at the time of the conference, apart from himself and a few others, Peng received no support from the same leaders who after the Cultural Revolution decreed his sanctification. This would explain why only provincial publishing houses, and not the more official central ones, published his work. Li's diary recalls in some aspects a famous work of ancient Chinese historiography, the *Discourses over Salt and Iron* (盐铁论 *Yan tie lun*), dating to 81 BC, wherein a political clash concerning basic orientations of the state between Legalists and Confucians in the Han Age was accurately recorded. Huan Kuan, *Discourses on Salt and Iron: A Debate on State Control of Commerce and Industry in Ancient China*, trans. Esson McDowell Gale (Leyden: E. J. Brill, 1931). See also Georges Walter, *Chine, An-81: Dispute sur le sel et le fer; un prodigieux document sur l'art de gouverner* (Paris: Seghers, 1978). This book, which was written by the Confucian party to hand down its point of view, also records statements by both contending sides and enables the reader to grasp the precise political terms of the dispute.

6 A number of texts by Mao concerning the Lushan Conference are collected in volume 8 of 建国以来毛泽东文稿 *Jianguo yilai Mao Zedong wengao* [Mao's manuscripts after 1949] (Beijing: 中央文献出版社 Zhongyang wenxian chubanshe, 1993). This volume collects the texts of 1959.

7 See Daniel F. Vukovich, *China and Orientalism: Western Knowledge Production and the PRC* (London: Routledge, 2012), 66–86; Mobo Gao, *Constructing China: Clashing Views of the People's Republic* (London: Pluto, 2018), 158–92.
8 As Mobo Gao has observed, "every level of leadership looked to the level above for a performance index, but wouldn't look to the level below for an idea of what would be wrong on the ground. Furthermore, the decentralization let loose by Mao led the local authorities to interpret their own policy priorities. On the one hand everyone seemed to guess what was wanted from a level above in the government hierarchy, and on the other hand, people were motivated to outperform the other to do what they thought was the correct understanding of the situation." Mobo Gao, *Constructing China*, 164.
9 Franz Schurmann, *Ideology and Organization in Communist China* (Berkeley: University of California Press, 1966).
10 The film by Andrzej Wajda, *The Marble Man* (1978), the bitter story of a Polish "work hero," came out at the dawn of the independent trade union Solidarność.
11 The item of study for party cadres at various levels was at the top of the agenda drawn up by Mao to be discussed at Lushan. See 庐山会议讨论问题 "Lushan huiyi taolun wenti" [Problems to discuss at the Conference of Lushan], in *Jianguo yilai Mao Zedong wengao*, vol. 8, 331–33.
12 For an English translation of Mao's "Reading Notes" to the *Manual of Soviet Political Economy* (about 1960), see Mao Zedong, *A Critique of Soviet Economics* (New York: Monthly Review, 1977).
13 One is struck by the almost idyllic atmosphere of the first days. The most important leaders were even exchanging poems written for the occasion, not all of which were particularly original. Indeed, they were rather stereotypical verses but were in any case a sign of a (too) relaxed atmosphere. Some of their poems are reported at the beginning of Li Rui's book, *Lushan huiyi shilu*. Immediately before the conference, Mao wrote "Ascending the Lushan," which is the most intensely contemplative of those composed in those days. As at other politically critical moments, Mao had sought to reflect on political issues, or rather to weigh up his own disquiet, from a poetic distance. However, as can be deduced from the texts and the preparatory speeches, Mao was also optimistic and had worked carefully to achieve a positive outcome.
14 Peng Dehuai's version is in 彭德怀自述 *Peng Dehuai zishu* [Autobiography of Peng Dehuai] (Beijing: Renmin chubanshe, 1981), 281–87.
15 Peng Dehuai's letter is in the appendix to *Peng Dehuai zishu*, 284. See also Li Rui, *Lushan huiyi shilu*, 132. Peng Dehuai refers to the Taiwan Strait crises of 1954 and 1958 and to the Lhasa revolt in spring 1959.
16 Li Rui, *Lushan huiyi shilu*, 134.
17 Li Rui, *Lushan huiyi shilu*, 197–201.
18 Alain Badiou, *Logiques des mondes* (Paris: Seuil, 2006).
19 Mao Zedong, "Inquiry into the Peasant Movement in Hunan" (1927); English translation in *Selected Works* (Beijing: Foreign Languages Press), vol. 1.
20 See Mao Zedong, "On the Ten Major Relationships" (1956), https://www.marxists.org/reference/archive/mao/selected-works/volume-5/mswv5_51.htm.

21 Of use is the brief presentation to the whole drafted by the editorial board of 新建设 *Xin Jianshe* [New construction]: 当代史学界对中国农民战争史几个问题的讨论 "Dangdai shixue jie dui Zhongguo nongmin zhangzheng shi jige wenti de taolun" [The current discussion among Chinese historians on some questions concerning the history of peasant wars in China], *Xin Jianshe* 2 (1962): 23-25. In the terminology used at the time in China, the discussion was between "historicists" and "classists." In fact, however, the difference was that the former rejected, on the basis of an analysis of class, the antifeudal view of peasant revolts, while the latter seconded it, on the basis of equally classist arguments they used in the opposite sense. On the main interventions that negated for class reasons the antifeudal nature of those wars, see 蔡美彪 Cai Meibiao, 在论中国农民战争史的几个问题 "Zai lun Zongguo nongmin zhanzheng shi de jige wenti" [More on some questions of the history of peasant wars in China], *Xin jianshe* 11 (1962): 32-41; 孙柞 Sun Zuomin, 在中国农民战争史研究中运用历史主义和阶级观点 "Zai zhongguo nongmin zhanzheng shi yanjiu yunyong lishizhuyi he jieji guandian" [Historicism and the point of view of class in the study of the history of peasants' wars in China], *Renmin ribao*, February 27, 1964, 3. Among those that supported the political value of peasants' revolts in terms of class, see 林杰 Lin Jie, 用什么观点和方法研究农民战争 "Yong shenme guandian he fangfa yanjiu nongmin zhanzheng" [From which viewpoint and with which method to study peasants' wars], *Xin Jianshe* 4 (1964): 40-51. I am grateful to the late Edoarda Masi for letting me read her unpublished notes on the debate in the early sixties on the peasant revolts in imperial China, originally prepared for a course on Chinese history at the Istituto Orientale di Napoli in 1973. She gives a list of about sixty essays published in the most important Chinese political and scholarly journals between 1961 and 1965, with her commentaries on the most important ones.

22 *A Concise History of China* (Beijing: Foreign Languages Press, 1964).

23 翦伯贊 Jian Bozan, 历史问题论丛 *Lishi wenti luncong* [Collected discussions on historical problems] (Beijing: Renmin chubanshe, 1962); 翦伯贊历史论文选集 *Jian Bozan lishi lunwen xuanji* [Jian Bozan's selected historical essays] (Beijing: Renmin chubanshe, 1980).

24 Jian Bozan, 对处理若干历史问题的初步意见 "Dui chuli ruogan lishi wenti de chubu yijian" [Preliminary opinions on how to deal with some historical problems], *Guangming ribao*, December 22, 1963, reprinted in *Jian Bozan lishi lunwen xuanji*, 59-73. The expression recurs in passing in the first part of the essay 如何处理历史上的阶级关系 "Ruhe chuli lishi shang de jieji guanxi" [How to deal with class relationships in history], 60. Presentations of Jian Bozan's historiographical theories appear in Wang Xuedian, "Jian Bozan's Theoretical Contribution to China's Historical Science," *Social Sciences in China* 3 (1991): 144-62; Clifford Edmunds, "The Politics of Historiography: Jian Bozan's Historicism," in *China's Intellectuals and the State: In Search of a New Relationship*, ed. Merle Goldman, Timothy Cheek, and Carol Lee Hamrin (Cambridge, MA: Harvard University Press, 1987), 65-106. Neither of the two essays, unfortunately, discusses the theory of the policies of concessions.

25 See 戚本禹 Qi Benyu, 林杰 Lin Jie, and 阎长贵 Yan Changgui, 翦伯贊同志的历史观点应当批判 "Jian Bozan tongzhi de lishi guandian yinggai pipan" [Comrade Jian

Bozan's conception of history must be criticized], *Renmin ribao*, March 25, 1966. Qi Benyu had also been the author of another famous article criticizing Jian Bozan, published in December 1965, though without mentioning his name explicitly. See 为革命而研究历史 "Wei geming er yanjiu lishi" [Studying history for the revolution], 红旗 *Hongqi* 13 (1965): 14–22. The first article criticizing the hegemony of the theory of concessions in the historiography of peasant revolts had been written in September 1965 by a young historian, 孙达人 Sun Daren, 应该怎样估价 "让步政策" "Yinggai zenyang gujia 'rangbu zhengce'" [How is the "politics of concessions" to be evaluated?], 光明日报 *Guangming ribao*, September 9, 1965, 4.

26 His essay 论中国古代的农民战争 "Lun Zhongguo gudai de nongmin zhangzheng" [On the peasant wars in Chinese antiquity] was first published in 1951. It is reprinted in both the above-quoted collections of Jian Bozan's texts.

27 The thesis is contained in Lenin's *What Is to Be Done?*, chapter 2. "The Spontaneity of the Masses and the Consciousness of the Social-Democrats," section A, "The Beginning of the Spontaneous Upsurge" (the workers *were not, and could not be* conscious of . . .). See https://www.marxists.org/archive/lenin/works/1901/witbd/.

28 Qi Benyu, Lin Jie, and Yan Changgui, "Jian Bozan tongzhi de lishi guandian yingdang pipan."

29 Omnipresent since the prologue of events, historical materialism had its own pedigree, dating back to Stalin, quite different from the "materialistic conception of history" of Marx and Engels. The "creative contribution" of Stalin was to proclaim, in the late 1930s, the twofold concepts of "dialectical materialism and historical materialism." Dialectical materialism was the "worldview of the Marxist-Leninist party," while historical materialism was its "application to the phenomena of society and history." Joseph Stalin, *Dialectical and Historical Materialism*, 1938, https://www.marxists.org/reference/archive/stalin/works/1938/09.htm. The difference between Stalin and Marx is not just a variation in terminology. Marx's materialist conception of history was not a philosophy of history, but the cornerstone of a political vision whose mainstay issue was the end of social classes and the state. The axis of Stalin's historical materialism, its raison d'être, was instead the "cultural" stability of the socialist state, guaranteed by a philosophical worldview. Dialectical materialism was understood as a device of state order. Historical materialism, even more than its application to historical-social phenomena, was the nucleus of the ideology that defined not only the culture, but also the organizational horizon of the socialist states, phrased moreover in strongly disciplinary terms.

Chapter 3: An Unresolved Controversy

1 批判彭真 "Pipan Peng Zhen" [Criticizing Peng Zhen], in 毛泽东思想万岁 *Mao Zedong sixiang wansui* [Long live Mao Zedong thought] (1969), 641. This is a well-known collection of Mao's texts after 1949 not included in the official edition of his *Selected Works*. The volume was published by an unspecified organization of Red Guards, with no indication of place.

2 Marie Claire Bergère, *La repubblica popolare cinese* (Bologna: Il Mulino, 2000), 174.

3   邓小平 Deng Xiaoping, 对起草 "关于建国以来党的若干历史的决议的意见" "Dui qicao 'Guanyu jianguo yilai dang de ruogan lishi de jueyi' de yijian" [Opinions on the successive drafts of the "Resolution on some issues of the history of our party from the foundation of the PRC"], March 1980–June 1981, in 邓小平文选 *Deng Xiaoping wenxuan* [Deng Xiaoping selected writings] (Beijing: Renmin chubanshe, 1983), 273. Deng's statement is quoted by, among others, 王年一 Wang Nianyi, 大动乱的年代 *Da dongluan de niandai* [The years of the great disorder] (Zhengzhou: Henan renmin chubanshe, 1988), 12; and by 席宣 Xi Xuan and 金春明 Jin Chunming, "文化大革命"简史 *"Wenhua da geming" jianshi* [The "Great Cultural Revolution": A brief history] (Beijing: Zhonggong dang shi chubanshe, 1996), 84. Deng also spoke about his own responsibility and that of the other central leaders in a mode somewhat more self-critical than that single phrase cited by Chinese historians, and he said he wanted "to draw a lesson," without further elaborating. The entire passage says: "It is true that on some issues we [the central leaders at the moment] did not oppose [Mao Zedong], therefore we have some responsibilities. Naturally, in those circumstances, given the real situation, it was difficult to oppose. However, it cannot be avoided to speak about 'us,' and it is not bad if we accept our part of responsibility because we can draw a lesson from it."

4   The other Shanghai newspaper, the 解放日报 *Jiefang ribao* [Liberation Daily], was a party organ.

5   Cited by 薄一波 Bo Yibo, 若干重大决策与事件的回顾 *Ruogan zhongda juece yu shijian de huigu* [A retrospective on some important political decisions and events] (Beijing: Yinshua gongye chubanshe, 1997), 1885.

6   The Group of Five was established in 1964 under the leadership of Peng Zhen as an organ of the Central Committee in charge of what was called the "Cultural Revolution" (*wenhua geming*). The name referred in general to political activities in the cultural sphere and did not correspond to what was later named the "Great Proletarian Cultural Revolution" [*wuchanjieji wenhua da geming*]. Ironically, the first decision of the Great Proletarian Cultural Revolution was to disband the Group of Five.

7   These are two statements made by Zhang Chunqiao in December 1965 and May 1966, quoted by 张湛彬 Zhang Zhanbin, 文革第一文字狱 *Wenge diyi wenziyu*, 131.

8   The bulletin was first entitled 文汇情况 *Wenhui qingkuang* [Review of the cultural situation] and then 记者简报 *Jizhe jianbao* [Journalists' briefing].

9   Zhang Zhanbin, *Wenge diyi wenziyu*, 128–30.

10 Other similar collections of materials reproducing opinions on specific topics prepared by editorial boards of newspapers were distributed to the leading organs of the party-state. In those months there was at least another one edited by the *Guangming ribao* that reported opinions in the academic sphere on issues related to *Hai Rui Dismissed from Office*.

11 Zhang Chunqiao gave this figure in his speech at the Central Committee in May, as quoted by Wang Nianyi, *Da dongluan de niandai*, 11. Given the tight control

exerted by cultural authorities, even if only a selection of the articles and letters on *Hai Rui* actually appeared in print, they were accorded prime coverage in the Chinese press. A list compiled in 1968 that was restricted to the main articles published in the national press and the most important local papers names over five hundred titles from December 1965 to May 1966; see 中共报纸批判吴晗资料索引 "Zhonggong baozhi pipan Wu Han ziliao suoyin" [Index of the articles criticizing Wu Han in the CCP newspapers], in 丁望主编 Ding Wang, ed., 吴晗与《海瑞罢官》事件 *Wu Han yu "Hai Rui ba guan" shijian*, 717–48.

12 Zhang Zhanbin, *Wenge diyi wenziyu*, 91.
13 *Renmin ribao*, November 29, 1965.
14 A collection of the editorial notes that accompanied the reprint of Yao Wenyuan's article in the various newspapers appears in 《海瑞罢官》问题的讨论逐步展开 "Hai Rui ba guan wenti de taolun zhubu zhankai" [The discussion on the problem of *Hai Rui Dismissed from Office* gradually unfolds], *Wenhui bao*, December 6, 1965, 1.
15 赵少荃 Zhao Shaoquan, 陈匡时 Chen Kuangshi, 李春元 Li Chunyuan, and 韩国劲 Han Guojin, 复旦大学历史系四位同志的来信 "Fudan daxue lishixi siwei tongzhi de laixin" [Letter from four comrades in the History Department of Fudan University], *Wenhui bao*, November 29, 1965, 2; English translation, *Chinese Studies in History and Philosophy* 2, no. 1 (1968): 44–48. On the same day and on the same page, the *Wenhui bao* also published three other letters on the issue. One of them, quite favorable to Wu Han, was 范民声 Fan Minsheng, 盛郁 Sheng Yu, and 马圣贵 Ma Shenggui, 上海戏剧学院三位同志的来信 "Shanghai xiju xueyuan sanwei tongzhi de laixin" [Letter from three comrades of the Shanghai Institute of Theater], *Wenhui bao*, November 29, 1965, 2. The other letters reported a variety of opinions similar to that of Fudan but less detailed. See 陆嘉亮 Lu Jialiang and 倪墨炎 Ni Moyan, 中华书局上海编辑所两位同志的来信 "Zhonghua shuju Shanghai bianjisuo liangwei tongzhi de laixin" [Letter from two comrades of the Shanghai Editorial Board of Zhonghua Book Company], *Wenhui bao*, November 29, 1965, 2; 王彦坦 Wang Yantan, 蒋景源 Jiang Jingyuan, and 王家范 Wang Jiafan, 华东师范大学历史系三位同志的来信 "Huadong shifan daxue lishixi sanwei tongzhi de laixin" [Letter from three comrades of East China Normal College], *Wenhui bao*, November 29, 1965, 2.
16 The *Wenhui bao* was the newspaper that published most texts concerning the dispute: between late November 1965 and May 1966, almost two hundred articles, letters, and minutes of discussions were related to the issues raised by Yao. Early in December it also reprinted the script of *Hai Rui ba guan*, the reviews in the press of the premiere, all extremely favorable, and earlier essays by the author on the relationships between history and historical theater. The *Wenhui bao* published all these texts in a special section under the title 关于《海瑞罢官》的讨论 "Guanyu 'Hai Rui ba guan' de taolun" [Discussion about *Hai Rui Dismissed from Office*]. In the *Renmin ribao*, the articles on the dispute were published in the section 学术研究 "Xueshu yanjiu" [Scholarly research].

17 The following analysis is limited to the above-quoted *Renmin ribao*, the central organ of the CCP; the Shanghai *Wenhui bao* that first published Yao Wenyuan's article; the *Guangming ribao*, the newspaper more oriented toward intellectual issues; and the *Beijing ribao*, organ of the Beijing Party Committee.
18 See 马捷 Ma Jie, 也谈《海瑞罢官》 "Ye tan 'Hai Rui ba guan'" [More on *Hai Rui Dismissed from Office*], *Wenhui bao*, November 30, 1965, 4.
19 蔡成和 Cai Chenghe, 怎样更好地评价历史人物和历史剧—评《评新编历史剧〈海瑞罢官〉》 "Zenyang genghao de pingjia lishi renwu he lishiju—ping 'Ping xinbian lishiju "Hai Rui ba guan"'" [How to better evaluate historical personages and historical plays: Criticism of the "Criticism of the historical drama recently composed *Hai Rui Dismissed from Office*"], *Wenhui bao*, December 1, 1965, 4.
20 See 李华 Li Hua and 实夫 Shi Fu, 海瑞有值得学习的地方 "Hai Rui you zhide xuexi de difang" [There are aspects of Hai Rui that deserve to be studied], *Wenhui bao*, December 23, 1965, 4; 王鸿德 Wang Hongde, 不要锄掉《海瑞罢官》这朵花 "Bu yao chudiao 'Hai Rui ba guan' zhei duo hua" [*Hai Rui Dismissed from Office*: A flower that should not be uprooted], *Wenhui bao*, December 25, 1965, 4; 亦鸣 Yi Ming, 评新编历史剧《海瑞罢官》读后 "Ping xin bian lishiju 'Hai Rui ba guan' du hou" [After reading "Criticism of the recently composed historical drama *Hai Rui Dismissed from Office*"], *Renmin ribao*, December 25, 1965, 5; 朱相黑 Zhu Xianghei, 海瑞让步使人民得益 "Hai Rui rangbu shi renmin deyi" [Hai Rui's concessions brought benefit to the people], *Wenhui bao*, December 28, 1965, 4; 戴不凡 Dai Bufan, 《海瑞罢官》的主题思想 "'Hai Rui ba guan' de zhuti sixiang" [The main theme of *Hai Rui Dismissed from Office*], *Wenhui bao*, December 28, 1965, 4; 李传勇 Li Chuanyong and 马鸿生 Ma Hongsheng, 海瑞推动了历史前进 "Hai Rui tuidong le lishi qianjin" [Hai Rui has promoted historical progress], *Wenhui bao*, December 28, 1965, 4.
21 See 刘元高 Liu Yuangao, 《海瑞罢官》必须批判 "'Hai Rui ba guan' bixu pipan" [*Hai Rui Dismissed from Office* should be criticized], *Wenhui bao*, December 15, 1965, 4; 方克立 Fang Keli, 《海瑞罢官》歪曲了历史真实 "'Hai Rui ba guan' waiqu le lishi zhenshi" [*Hai Rui Dismissed from Office* distorts historical reality], *Beijing ribao*, December 16, 1965, 2; 杨金亭 Yang Jinting, 《海瑞罢官》是阶级调和论的传声筒 "Hai Rui ba guan' shi jieji tiaohelun de chuanshengtong" [*Hai Rui Dismissed from Office* is the mouthpiece of the theory of class conciliation], *Beijing Ribao*, December 25, 1965, 3; 杨金龙 Yang Jinlong, 对农民形象的歪曲 "Dui nongmin xingxiang de waiqu" [A deformation of the image of the peasants], *Renmin ribao*, December 25, 1965, 5.
22 胡守钧 Hu Shoujun, 《海瑞罢官》为封建王法唱颂歌 "'Hai Rui ba guan' wei fengjian wangfa chang songge" [*Hai Rui Dismissed from Office* is a hymn to feudal law], *Wenhui bao*, December 17, 1965, 4; 张益 Zhang Yi, 揭穿《海瑞罢官》的错误实质 "Jiechuan 'Hai Rui ba guan' de cuowu shizhi" [Expose the wrong essence of *Hai Rui Dismissed from Office*], *Wenhui bao*, December 20, 1965, 4; 郭庠林 Guo Xianglin, 陈绍闻 Chen Shaowen, 《海瑞罢官》为谁服务 "'Hai Rui ba guan' wei shui fuwu?" [*Hai Rui Dismissed from Office* is at the service of whom?], *Wenhui bao*, December 23, 1965, 4; 王宏业 Wang Hongye, 向海瑞学习的目的何在？ "Xiang Hai Rui xuexi de mudi hezai?" [What is the purpose of learning from *Hai Rui Dismissed from Office*?], *Wenhui bao*, December 23, 1965, 4; 徐连达 Xu Lianda, 陈匡时 Chen Kuangshi, and

李春元 Li Chunyuan, "'青天大老爷'真能'为民做主'吗？" "'Qingtian dalaoye' zhen neng 'wei min zuozhu' ma?" [Could "The great lord Blue Sky" really "decide in favor of the people"?], *Wenhui bao*, December 25, 1965, 4; 师文伍 Shi Wenwu, 用封建"王法"掩盖了阶级矛盾 "Yong fengjian 'wangfa' yangai le jieji maodun" [Cover class contradictions with "imperial law"], *Renmin ribao*, December 25, 1965, 5.

23. 刘大杰 Liu Dajie, 《海瑞罢官》的本质 "'Hai Rui ba guan' de benzhi" [The essence of *Hai Rui Dismissed from Office*], *Wenhui bao*, December 23, 1965, 4.

24. These arguments, with various shades of emphasis, are in 林丙义 Lin Bingyi, 海瑞与《海瑞罢官》 "Hai Rui yu 'Hai Rui ba guan'" [Hai Rui and *Hai Rui Dismissed from Office*], *Wenhui bao*, December 3, 1965, 4; 唐真 Tang Zhen, 《海瑞罢官》的主题是什么 "'Hai Rui ba guan' de zhuti shi shenme?" [What is the theme of *Hai Rui Dismissed from Office*?], *Wenhui bao*, December 15, 1965, 4; 郝昺衡 Hao Bingheng, 试论海瑞和《海瑞罢官》 "Shilun Hai Rui he 'Hai Rui ba guan'" [Examine Hai Rui and *Hai Rui Dismissed from Office*], *Wenhui bao*, December 20, 1965, 4; 王金祥 Wang Jinxiang, 几个疑问 "Jige yiwen" [Some questions], *Wenhui bao*, December 28, 1965, 4.

25. 樵子 Qiao Zi, 也谈海瑞和《海瑞罢官》 "Yetan Hai Rui he 'Hai Rui ba guan'" [More about Hai Rui and *Hai Rui Dismissed from Office*], *Renmin ribao*, December 1965, 5.

26. 李振宇 Li Zhenyu, 《海瑞罢官是》一出较好的历史剧 "Hai Rui ba guan shi yi chu jiao hao de lishi ju" [*Hai Rui Dismissed from Office* is a good historical play], *Beijing ribao*, December 9, 1966, 3.

27. 姚全兴 Yao Quanxing, 不能用形而上学代替辩证法。评 评新编历史《海瑞罢官》 "Bu neng yong xing'ershangxue daiti bianzhengfa. Ping 'Ping xinbian lishiju Hai Rui ba guan'" [It is not possible to replace dialectics with metaphysics. A criticism of the "Criticism of the recently written historical play *Hai Rui Dismissed from Office*"], *Guangming ribao*, December 15, 1965, 3.

28. 羽白 Yu Bai, 《海瑞罢官》基本上应该肯定 "'Hai Rui ba guan' jibenshang yinggai kending" [*Hai Rui Dismissed from Office* should be given a basically positive evaluation], *Wenhui bao*, December 17, 1965, 4.

29. 燕人 Yan Ren, 对历史剧《海瑞罢官》的几点看法—与姚文元同志商榷 "Dui lishiju 'Hai Rui ba guan' de jidian kanfa—yu Yao Wenyuan tongzhi shangque" [Some views on the historical play *Hai Rui Dismissed from Office*: A discussion with comrade Yao Wenyuan], 文汇报 *Wenhui bao*, December 2, 1965, 4; English translation, *Chinese Studies in History and Philosophy* 2, no. 1 (1968): 56–67. From the first days of the dispute, other contributions discussed *Hai Rui ba guan* from the perspective of the theory of concessions. See 严北溟 Yan Beiming, 对"让步政策"也要"一分为二" "Dui 'rangbu zhengce' ye yao 'yi fen wei er'" [Also with regard to the "politics of concessions" we must apply the principle "one divides into two"], *Wenhui bao*, December 16, 1965, 4; 康健 Kang Jian, 关于"让步政策"的浅见 "Guanyu 'rangbu zhengce' de qianjian" [A modest opinion on the "policies of concessions"], *Wenhui bao*, December 18, 1965, 4; 王连升 Wang Liansheng and 杨燕起 Yang Yanqi, 海瑞与"清官" "Hai Rui yu 'qingguan'" [Hai Rui and the "honest officials"], *Beijing ribao*, December 18, 1965, 3.

30. 人民日报编者 Renmin ribao bianzhe [*People's Daily* Editorial Board], 关于《海瑞罢官》问题各种意见的简介 "Guanyu 'Hai Rui ba guan' wenti gezhong yijian de

jianjie" [A summary of views on *Hai Rui Dismissed from Office*], *Renmin ribao*, December 15, 1965, 5.

31 The pseudonym sounded like "a student [生 *sheng*] looking toward the sun [向阳 *xiang yang*]," likely an allusion to the author's loyalty to a higher principle.

32 Liao Mosha (1907–1990) was a well-known writer and journalist who after 1949 held important positions in the state cultural apparatuses. He was a deputy head of the Propaganda Department of the Beijing Municipal Party Committee, head of the Education Department and of the United Front Work Department affiliated with the Committee, vice-chairman of the Beijing People's Political Consultative Conference, and a member of the Chinese People's Political Consultative Conference (CPPCC).

33 向阳生 Xiang Yangsheng [邓拓 Deng Tuo], 从《海瑞罢官》谈到道德继承论, "Cong 'Hai Rui ba guan' tandao daode jicheng lun" [Discussing the theory of moral heritage from *Hai Rui Dismissed from Office*], *Beijing ribao*, December 12, 1965, 2–3. Deng's criticism of the unforgivable doctrinal mistakes of Wu Han was reinforced by the same newspaper in a summary of various articles published on the topic of "moral heritage" in the previous years. See 岳华 Yue Hua, 关于道德的阶级性和继承性问题的讨论介绍 "Guanyu daode de jiejixing he jichengxing wenti de taolun jieshao" [Presentation of the discussion of the class character of morals], *Beijing ribao*, December 18, 1965, 3. In the only monograph on Deng Tuo in English, the article, published under the name Xiang Yangsheng, has not attracted much attention; see Timothy Cheek, *Propaganda and Culture in Mao Zedong's China: Deng Tuo and the Intelligentsia* (Oxford: Clarendon, 1997).

34 方求 Fang Qiu, 《海瑞罢官》代表一种什么社会思潮？ "'Hai Rui ba guan' daibiao yizhong shenme shehui sichao?" [Which kind of social current of thought does *Hai Rui Dismissed from Office* represent?] *Renmin ribao*, December 29, 1965, 7.

35 For reactions in China to Fang Qiu's article, see Zhang Zhanbin, *Wenge diyi wenziyu*, 140–41.

36 James Pusey, *Wu Han: Attacking the Present through the Past*, 64.

37 吴晗 Wu Han, 关于《海瑞罢官》的自我批评 "Guanyu 'Hai Rui ba guan' de ziwo piping" ["A self-criticism of *Hai Rui Dismissed from Office*], *Beijing ribao*, December 29, 1965, 3; reprinted in *Renmin ribao*, December 30, 1965, 5. I quote with minor changes from the English translation in *Chinese Studies in History and Philosophy* 2, no. 1 (1968): 68–107.

38 See Zhang Zhanbin, *Wenge diyi wenziyu*, 137.

39 In mid-January Wu published a second self-criticism on the question of "moral inheritance," although it did not add much to the first. See 吴晗 Wu Han, 是革命，还是继承 "Shi geming, haishi jicheng" [Revolutionizing or inheriting?], *Beijing ribao*, January 12, 1966, 3.

40 After his dismissal in 1959 Peng was never directly named in the press except by this formula.

41 吴晗 Wu Han, 论海瑞 "Lun Hai Rui," *Renmin ribao*, September 17, 1959, reprinted in 吴晗选集 *Wu Han xuanji* [Selected works of Wu Han] (Tianjin: Tianjin renmin chubanshe, 1988), 347–70.

42 Since the rehabilitation of Peng following the Cultural Revolution, that paragraph has been considered "unfair." See Zhang Zhanbin, *Wenge diyi wenziyu*. It is remarkable how many subjective dilemmas are scattered throughout Chinese historiography on the subject.
43 Cited in 逢先知 Feng Xianzhi and 金冲及主编 Jin Chongji, 毛泽东传 *Mao Zedong zhuan* [Biography of Mao Zedong] (Beijing: Zhongyang wenxian chubanshe, 2003), vol. 2, 941. See also Li Rui, *Lushan huiyi shilu*, 125.
44 Hu Qiaomu became a key figure in the return to power of Deng Xiaoping in the mid-seventies.
45 Mary G. Mazur, *Wu Han, Historian: Son of China's Times* (Plymouth, UK: Lexington, 2009), 407. The author quotes testimony by a secretary of Hu Qiaomu.
46 吴晗 Wu Han, 海瑞骂皇帝 "Hai Rui ma huangdi," in 人民日报 *Renmin ribao*, June 16, 1959, 8.
47 The essential passages in the memorandum are translated in Theodore De Bary and Richard Lufrano, eds., *Sources of Chinese Tradition* (New York: Columbia University Press, 2000), vol. 2, 472–73. In a slightly modernized translation, this passage reads: "The most urgent problems today are the absurdity of imperial policies and the lack of official responsibilities."
48 See 戚本禹 Qi Benyu, 《海瑞骂皇帝》和《海瑞罢官》的反动实质 "'Hai Rui ma Huangdi' he 'Hai Rui ba guan' de fandong shizhi" [The reactionary nature of "Hai Rui scolds the Emperor" and *Hai Rui dismissed from Office*], *Renmin ribao*, April 2, 1966, 5; 关锋 Guan Feng and 林杰 Lin Jie, 《海瑞骂皇帝》和《海瑞罢官》是反党反社会主义的两株大毒草 "'Hai Rui ma huangdi' he 'Hai Rui ba guan' shi fandang fan shehuizhuyi de liangzhu da ducao" ["Hai Rui scolds the Emperor" and *Hai Rui dismissed from Office* are two antiparty and antisocialist poisonous weeds], *Renmin ribao*, April 5, 1966, 5.
49 Zhang Zhanbin, *Wenge diyi wenziyu*, 31.
50 On this point Tom Fisher quotes sources from Red Guard publications. See "'The Play's the Thing': Wu Han and Hai Rui Revisited," 28.
51 Li Rui, *Lushan huiyi shilu*, 347.
52 上海学术界部分人士座谈吴晗的《关于〈海瑞罢官〉的自我批评》"Shanghai xueshujie bufen renshi zuotan Wu Han de 'Guanyu "Hai Rui ba guan" de ziwo piping'" [A discussion among some members of Shanghai academic circles on Wu Han's "Self-criticism of *Hai Rui Dismissed from Office*"], *Wenhui bao*, January 7, 1966, 4; English translation in *Chinese Studies in History and Philosophy* 2, no. 3 (1968): 42–59.
53 周予同 Zhou Yutong, cited in "Shanghai xueshujie bufen renshi zuotan Wu Han."
54 魏建猷 Wei Jianyou (historian, Shanghai Teachers College), cited in "Shanghai xueshujie bufen renshi zuotan Wu Han."
55 谭其骧 Tan Qixiang (Fudan University), cited in "Shanghai xueshujie bufen renshi zuotan Wu Han."
56 刘大杰 Liu Dajie, cited in "Shanghai xueshujie bufen renshi zuotan Wu Han." As quoted above, Liu Dajie had published on December 23 a critical article in the

Wenhui bao. For other articles of criticism of Wu Han's "Self-Criticism," see 徐德政 Xu Dezheng, 张锡厚 Zhang Xihou, and 栾贵明 Luan Guiming, 评吴晗同志《关于〈海瑞罢官〉的自我批评》 "Ping Wu Han tongzhi 'Guanyu *Hai Rui ba guan* de ziwo piping'" [Discussing Comrade Wu Han's "Self-criticism about *Hai Rui Dismissed from Office*"], *Beijing ribao*, December 31, 1965; 戈锋 Ge Feng,《论海瑞》的错误仅仅是思想方法上的片面性吗? "'Lun Hai Rui' de cuowu jinjin shi sixiang fangfa shang de pianmianxing ma?" [Are the errors of "On Hai Rui" only a one-sided ideological method?], *Beijing ribao*, December 31, 1965, 3; 李东石 Li Dongshi, 评吴晗同志的历史观 "Ping Wu Han tongzhi de lishiguan" [Discussing Comrade Wu Han's vision of history], *Beijing ribao*, January 8, 1966, 3; 蔡尚思 Cai Shangsi, 这是什么样的"自我批评" "Zheshi shenmeyang de 'ziwo piping'" [What self-criticism is this?], *Wenhui bao*, January 25, 1966, 4. Wu Han's second self-criticism was also the object of criticism. See 严问 Yan Wen, 评吴晗同志关于道德问题的"自我批评" "Ping Wu Han tongzhi guanyu daode wenti de 'ziwo piping,'" [Discussing Comrade Wu Han's self-criticism on morals], *Beijing ribao*, January 14, 1966, 3.

57 李俊民 Li Junmin (editor-in-chief at Shanghai Zhonghua Press, a scholarly publishing house), cited in "Shanghai xueshujie bufen renshi zuotan Wu Han."
58 束世澄 Shu Shicheng (historian, East China Teachers College), cited in "Shanghai xueshujie bufen renshi zuotan Wu Han."
59 杨宽 Yang Kuan (historian, Shanghai Academy of Social Sciences), cited in "Shanghai xueshujie bufen renshi zuotan Wu Han."
60 Liu Dajie and Shu Shizheng, cited in "Shanghai xueshujie bufen renshi zuotan Wu Han."
61 Chen Xiangping, cited in "Shanghai xueshujie bufen renshi zuotan Wu Han."
62 史绍宾 Shi Shaobin, 评《关于〈海瑞罢官〉的自我批评》的几个问题 "Ping 'Guanyu *Hai Rui ba guan* de ziwo piping' de jige wenti" [Comment on some problems of "Self-criticism on *Hai Rui Dismissed from Office*"], in *Guangming ribao*, January 9, 1966; English translation in *Chinese Studies in History and Philosophy* 2, no. 3 (1968): 32–41.
63 史文群整理 Shi Wenqun, ed., 武汉学术界展开《海瑞罢官》的讨论 "Wuhan xueshujie zhankai *Hai Rui ba guan* de taolun" [Wuhan academic circles open a discussion on *Hai Rui Dismissed from Office*], in 羊城晚报 *Yangcheng Wanbao* [Yangcheng Evening News], January 15, 1966; reprinted in Ding Wang, ed., *Wu Han yu "Hai Rui ba guan" shijian*, 442–46; English translation in *Chinese Studies in History and Philosophy* 2, no. 3 (1968): 4–10.
64 Shi Wenqun, "Wuhan xueshujie zhankai *Hai Rui ba guan* de taolun."
65 Shi Wenqun, "Wuhan xueshujie zhankai *Hai Rui ba guan* de taolun." Several articles in January were quite favorable to the theory of concessions, arguing that they were "class policies of the new ruling groups" who nevertheless were "by-products" (副产品 *fuchanpin*) of peasant revolts. See 徐德嶙 Xu Delin, 对"让步政策"的几点看法 "Dui 'rangbu zhengce de jidian kanfa'" [Some opinions on the "policy of concessions"], *Wenhui bao*, January 13, 1966, 4; 杨国宜 Yang Guoyi and 张海鹏 Zhang Haipeng, 究竟怎样认识"让步政策" "Jiujing zenyang renshi 'rangbu zhengce'" [Finally, how to understand the "policy of concessions"?], *Wenhui bao*, January 17, 1966, 4; 张延举 Zhang Yanju, 海瑞实行了让步的改良 "Hai Rui shixing le rangbu de gailiang" [Hai

Rui implemented the policy of concessions], *Beijing ribao*, January 26, 1966; 姚铎铭 Yao Duoming, 全面地理解"让步政策" "Quanmian de lijie 'rangbu zhengce'" [Thoroughly understand the "policy of concessions"], *Wenhui bao*, January 27, 1966, 4.

66 Shi Wenqun, "Wuhan xueshujie zhankai *Hai Rui ba guan* de taolun." For other critical opinions on the theory of the policy of concessions in January, see 肖镞 Xiao Zu, 从"教训"谈到"让步政策"—同严北溟等先生商榷 "Cong 'jiaoxun' tandao 'rangbu zhengce'—tong Yan Beiming deng xiansheng shangque" [Let us talk about the "policy of concessions" starting from their "lessons": A discussion with Mr. Yan Beiming and others], *Wenhui bao*, January 13, 1966, 4; 谭慧中 Tan Huizhong, "让步政策"保存了农民战争的胜利果实吗？—与严北溟同志商榷 "'Rangbu zhengce' baocun le nongmin zhanzheng de shengli guoshi ma?—Yu Yan Beiming tongzhi shangque" [Did the "policy of concessions" retain the victorious result of the peasant wars? A discussion with Mr. Yan Beiming], *Wenhui bao*, January 27, 1966, 4.

67 See 习中文 Xi Zhongwen, 应该一分为二的看"清官"和"贪官" "Yinggai yifenweier de kan 'qingguan' he 'tanguan'" [We must apply the principle of one divides into two in assessing the "honest officials" and "corrupt officials"], *Wenhui bao*, January 6, 1966, 4; 华山 Hua Shan, 论肯定与赞扬 "Lun kending yu zanyang" [On positively assessing and praising], *Wenhui bao*, January 11, 1966, 4; 吴君伟 Wu Junwei, 清官和贪官有别 "Qingguan he tanguan youbie" [There were differences between corrupt and honest officials], *Wenhui bao*, January 14, 1966, 4; 沈志 Shen Zhi, 对海瑞应当又批判又肯定 "Dui Hai Rui yingdang you pipan you kending" [We must both criticize and positively assess Hai Rui], *Wenhui bao*, January 14, 1966, 4; 华山 Hua Shan, 为什么要肯定"清官"、"好官"？ "Weishenme yao kending 'qingguan,' 'haoguan'?" [Why we must positively assess the honest officials and the good officials?], *Wenhui bao*, January 17, 1966, 4; 计红绪 Ji Hongxu, 要以阶级观点看待"清官" "Yao yi jieji guandian kandai 'qingguan'" [We must look at the honest officials from the class viewpoint], *Wenhui bao*, January 28, 1966, 4; 刘序琦 Liu Xuqi, 给海瑞以公正的评价 "Gei Hai Rui yi gong zheng de pingjia" [Give a fair assessment of Hai Rui], *Wenhui bao*, February 4, 1966, 4.

68 See 朱理章 Zhu Lizhang, 拨开迷雾看"清官" "Bokai miwu kan 'qingguan'" [Dissolve the curtain of fog around the "honest officials"], *Wenhui bao*, January 6, 1966, 4; 袁良义 Yuan Liangyi, 论"清"官不清 "Lun 'qing' guan bu qing" [On the dishonesty of "honest officials"], *Wenhui bao*, January 11, 1966, 4; 商鸿逵 Shang Hongkui, 由假海瑞谈到真海瑞 "You jia Hai Rui tandao zhen Hai Rui" [From the false Hai Rui let's talk about the real Hai Rui], *Wenhui bao*, January 11, 1966, 4; 史军 Shi Jun, "颠倒了历史的《海瑞罢官》" "Diandao le lishi de '*Hai Rui ba guan*'" [*Hai Rui Dismissed from Office* turns history upside down], *Renmin ribao*, January 19, 1966, 5; 韩国劲 Han Guojin and 周胜昌 Zhou Shengchang, 海瑞"清官"生活真相 "Hai Rui 'qingguan' shenghuo zhenxiang" [The real facts of life of Hai Rui "honest official"], *Wenhui bao*, February 1, 1966, 4; 韦格明 Wei Geming, 海瑞"刚直不阿"的反动性 "Hai Rui 'gangzhibue' de fandongxing" [The reactionary nature of the "outright and outspoken" Hai Rui], *Wenhui bao*, February 8, 1966, 4.

69 See 唐长孺 Tang Changru, 历史唯物论，还是阶级调和论 "Lishi weiwulun, haishi jieji tiaohelun" [Historical materialism or theory of class conciliation?], *Wenhui bao*,

January 14, 1966, 4; 史哲 Shi Zhe, 告状难道是农民革命斗争吗？ "Gaozhuang nandao shi nongmin geming douzheng ma?" [Were the complaints really the revolutionary struggle of peasants?], *Wenhui bao*, January 18, 1966, 4; 黄喜蔚 Huang Xiwei, 这是阶级的分歧 "Zheshi jieji de fenqi" [This is a class divergence], *Wenhui bao*, January 18, 1966, 4; 瞿林东 Qu Lindong and 冯祖贻 Feng Zuyi, 阶级斗争的事实是抹煞不了的——评吴晗同志关于海瑞"退田"的辩解 "Jieji douzheng de shishi shi mosha buliao de—Ping Wu Han tongzhi guanyu Hai Rui 'tuitian' de bianjie" [The reality of the class struggle cannot be obliterated: Discussing the explanation of Wu Han about "surrendering land"], *Beijing ribao*, January 26, 1966; 牛子明 Niu Ziming, 哪个阶级的立场？ "Nage jieji de lichang?" [Which class position?], *Wenhui bao*, January 28, 1966, 4.

70 平实 Ping Shi, 谈《海瑞罢官》中人物的阶级关系—与姚文元等同志商榷 "Tan 'Hai Rui ba guan' zhong renwu de jieji guanxi—yu Yao Wenyuan deng tongzhi shangque" [On the class relationships among the characters of *Hai Rui Dismissed from Office*: A discussion with Comrade Yao Wenyuan and others], *Beijing ribao*, December 31, 1965, 3; 张彬 Zhang Bin, 并没有原则分歧 "Bing meiyou yuanze fenqi" [There are no divergences of principle], *Wenhui bao*, January 18, 1966, 4.

71 Shi Wenqun, "Wuhan xueshujie zhankai *Hai Rui ba guan* de taolun."

72 广州学术界对《海瑞罢官》的一些看法 "Guangzhou xueshu jie dui *Hai Rui ba guan* de yixie kanfa" [Some opinions on *Hai Rui Dismissed from Office* in Guangzhou academic circles], *Yangcheng Wanbao*, January 15, 1966; English translation in *Chinese Studies in History and Philosophy* 2, no. 3 (1968): 11–19.

73 For other discussions on the nature of law in the imperial regime, see 张晋藩 Zhang Jinfan, 海瑞执行的王法究竟是什么样的法？ "Hai Rui zhixing de wangfa jiujing shi shenmeyang de fa?" [What law was the imperial law that Hai Rui applied?], *Wenhui bao*, February 4, 1966, 4.

74 The Shanghai Party Committee spread Mao Zedong's view about the "dismissal" as early as in December. However, on a national level the official guidelines of the debates formally excluded this interpretation. See the Chronology, appendix B of the Circular of 16 May 一九六五年九月到一九六六年五月文化战线上两条道路斗争大事记 in 中发 [66] 267 号附件二, reprinted in Song Yongyi, ed., *Chinese Cultural Revolution Database* (Hong Kong: University Center for China Studies, 2002), part I.

75 Shi Shaobin, "Ping 'Guanyu *Hai Rui ba guan* de ziwo piping' de jige wenti." See also 澄宇 Cheng Yu, 《海瑞罢官》为谁唱赞歌？ "'Hai Rui ba guan' wei shui chang zange?" [For whom does *Hai Rui Dismissed from Office* sing?], *Beijing ribao*, January 18, 1966, 3.

76 思彤 Si Tong, 接受吴晗同志的挑战 "Jieshou Wu Han tongzhi de tiaozhan" [To accept the challenge of comrade Wu Han], *Renmin ribao*, January 13, 1966, 5.

77 赵衍孙 Zhao Yansun, 吴晗同志是和无产阶级进行较量 "Wu Han tongzhi shi he wuchanjieji jinxing jiaoliang" [Comrade Wu Han is competing with the proletariat], *Beijing ribao*, January 14, 1966, 3; 王希曾 Wang Xizeng and 杨寿堪 Yang Shoukan, 为什么要歌颂"海瑞骂皇帝" "Weishenme yao gesong 'Hai Rui ma Huangdi'" [Why praise "Hai Rui scolds the emperor"?], *Beijing ribao*, January 14, 1966, 3.

78 马泽民 Ma Zemin and 王锐生 Wang Ruisheng, 《海瑞》是吴晗同志反党反社会主义的政治工具 "'Hai Rui' shi Wu Han tongzhi fan dang fan shehuizhuyi zhengzhi gongju" ["Hai Rui" is an antiparty and antisocialist political tool of Comrade Wu

Han], *Guangming ribao*, January 29, 1966, 3; 罗思鼎 Luo Siding, 拆穿"退田"的西洋镜 "Chaichuan 'tuitian' de xiyangjing" [Reveal the deception of the "return of land"], *Wenhui bao*, February 8, 1966, 4.

79 For example, the pen name Shi Shaobin could be read, through assonances, as "Mao Zedong's Soldier in History." Su Tong was the pen name of Wang Ruoshui, who after the Cultural Revolution became quite famous for having converted to the issue of "alienation."

80 Ironically, the official name of the Group of Five was almost the same as the political event that led to its disbanding. In fact, it became the first apparatus of the party-state to be overthrown by the Cultural Revolution.

81 The Group of Five's members were Peng Zhen; 陆定一 Lu Dingyi, who was the head of the Propaganda Department (宣传部 *Xuanchuan bu*); 周扬 Zhou Yang, a senior cultural official whom we have already met as Fang Qiu; 吴冷西 Wu Lengxi, the editor of the *Guangming ribao*, the most authoritative cultural newspaper; and 康生 Kang Sheng, who represented the Maoist "minority."

82 中共中央批转文化革命五人小组关于当前学术讨论的汇报提纲 "Zhonggong zhongyang pizhuan wenhua geming wuren xiaozu guanyu dangqian xueshu taolun de huibao tigang" [Issued with instructions from the CCPCC: Outline report by the five-member Cultural Revolution small group concerning the current academic discussion], February 12, 1966, reprinted in Song Yongyi, *Chinese Cultural Revolution Database*, part 1; English translation in J. Myers, J. Domes, and E. von Groeling, eds., *Chinese Politics: Documents and Analysis* (Columbia: University of South Carolina Press, 1986), vol. 1, 194–97.

83 See the Chronology, appendix B of the Circular of 16 May, in Song Yongyi, ed., *Chinese Cultural Revolution Database*, part 1.

84 "After Yao Wenyuan's essay was published," explains a dictionary of the Cultural Revolution in the entry "February Outline," "in every sphere of Chinese society, and especially in the academic and educational arenas, the most indignant reactions were expressed against Yao's arbitrary and domineering criticism." See 巢峰 Chao Feng, ed., "文化大革命" 词典 *"Wenhua da geming" cidian* [A dictionary of the "Great Cultural Revolution"] (Xianggang: Ganglong chubanshe, 1993), 289.

85 See Zhang Zhanbin, *Wenge diyi wenziyu*, 154.

Chapter 4: A Probable Defeat and Revisionism

1 I have examined this subject in some essays since the beginning of my research on the Cultural Revolution—recently, in "Egalitarian Inventions and Political Symptoms: A Reassessment of Mao's Statements on the 'Probable Defeat,'" *Crisis & Critique* 3, no. 1 (2016): 259–78. An earlier discussion can be found in "The Probable Defeat: Preliminary Notes on the Chinese Cultural Revolution," *positions* 6, no. 1 (1998): 179–202.

2 Quoted in 逢先知 Feng Xianzhi and 金冲及 Jin Chongji, eds., 毛泽东传 *Mao Zedong zhuan, 1949-1976* [Biography of Mao Zedong, 1949–1976] (Beijing: Zhongyang wenxian chubanshe, 2003), 1410. The meetings Mao mentioned were of the Central Committee, which was about to issue the Circular of 16 May 1966 (see chapter 5).

3 给江青的信 "Gei Jiang Qing de xin" [Letter to Jiang Qing], in *Jianguo yilai Mao Zedong wengao* [Manuscripts of Mao Zedong after 1949] (Beijing: Wenxian chubanshe, 1998), vol. 12, 71–77.
4 和卡博, 巴庐库同志的谈话 "He Kabo, Baluku tongzhi de tanhua" [Conversation with the comrades Kabo and Baluku], February 3, 1967, in 毛泽东思想万岁 *Mao Zedong sixiang wansui* [Long live Mao Zedong thought] (Beijing: n.p., 1969), 663.
5 对阿尔巴尼亚军事代表团的讲话 "Dui Aerbanya junshi daibiaotuan de jianghua" [Speech to an Albanian military delegation], May 1, 1966, in *Mao Zedong sixiang wansui*, 673.
6 We should not consider the issue as completely outdated. A few years ago an influential essay in the journal of the Chinese Academy of Social Sciences assured us that we are now witnessing a "great victory." See Wang Weiguang, "The Great Victory of Marxism in China," *Social Sciences in China* 32, no. 4 (2011): 3–18.
7 Joseph Stalin, "On the Draft Constitution of the USSR" (1936), https://www.marxists.org/reference/archive/stalin/works/1936/11/25.htm.
8 Mao Zedong, "On the Correct Handling of Contradictions among the People" (1957), https://www.marxists.org/reference/archive/mao/selected-works/volume-5/mswv5_58.htm.
9 在扩大的中央工作会议的讲话 "Zai kuoda zhongyang gongzuo huiyi de jianghua" [Speech at the Enlarged Working Conference], January 30, 1962, in *Mao Zedong sixiang wansui*, 407.
10 *Mao Zedong sixiang wansui*, 422.
11 在八届十中全会上的讲话 "Zai ba jie shi zhongquanhui shang de jianghua" [Speech at the Tenth Plenary Session of the Eighth Congress], September 24, 1962, in *Mao Zedong sixiang wansui*, 431.
12 In *Jianguo yilai Mao Zedong wengao*, vol. 6, 60.
13 苏联 "政治经济学" 读书笔记 "Sulian 'Zhengzhi jingjixue' dushu biji," in *Mao Zedong sixiang wansui*, 337–40.
14 谈谦虚戒骄 "Tan qianxu jiejiao" [Being modest and watchful against arrogance], December 13, 1963, in *Mao Zedong sixiang wansui*, 447–48.
15 *Mao Zedong sixiang wansui*, 494.
16 *Mao Zedong sixiang wansui*, 490, 494.
17 For a discussion of this topic, see my "Notes on the Critique of Revisionism: Lenin, Mao and Us," *Crisis & Critique* 4, no. 2 (2017): 362–75.
18 Lenin, *State and Revolution* (1917), https://www.marxists.org/archive/lenin/works/1917/staterev/.

Chapter 5: Shrinking the Cultural Superego

1 Hong Yung Lee, *The Politics of the Chinese Cultural Revolution: A Case Study* (Berkeley: University of California Press, 1978), 34.
2 王年一 Wang Nianyi, 大动乱的年代 *Da dongluan de niandai*, 38; 张湛彬 Zhang Zhanbin, 文革第一文字狱 *Wenge diyi wenziyu*, 60.
3 André Malraux, *Antimemorie* (Milan: Bompiani, 1968), 494.

4 His writings on education during the period of the New Culture Movement are collected in Mao Zedong, *Inventare una scuola: Scritti giovanili sull'educazione*, ed. Fabio Lanza and Alessandro Russo (Rome: Manifestolibri, 1996).
5 Cf. Zhang Zhanbin, *Wenge diyi wenziyu*, 134.
6 Mao lived far from Beijing from September 1965 to July 1966, moving around various places in southern China; it was one of the longest periods he ever spent away from the capital after 1949.
7 Zhang Zhanbin, *Wenge diyi wenziyu*, 38; Wang Nianyi, *Da dongluan de niandai*, 76.
8 逄先知 Feng Xianzhi and 金冲及 Jin Chongji, eds., 毛泽东传 *Mao Zedong zhuan, 1949-1976* [Biography of Mao Zedong, 1949-1976] (Beijing: Zhongyang wenxian chubanshe, 2003), 1406.
9 高皋 Gao Gao and 严家其 Yan Jiaqi, "文化大革命"十年史 *"Wen hua da geming" shi nian shi* [History of ten years of the "Great Cultural Revolution"] (Tianjin: Tianjin renmin chubanshe, 1986), 72.
10 In 1966, Peng Dehuai was in Sichuan as head of an important project for the military and economic reinforcement in the inland regions called the "third front" (*di san xian*).
11 Zhang Zhanbin, *Wenge diyi wenziyu*, 137.
12 Mao Zedong, 在政治局扩大会议上的讲话 "Zai zhengzhi ju kuoda huiyi shang de jianghua" [Speeches to the Enlarged Meeting of the Political Bureau], March 17 and 20, 1966, in *Mao Zedong sixiang wansui* [Long live Mao Zedong thought] (Beijing: n.p., 1969), 634-40. In the second of these interventions, of which there is a detailed transcription, Mao also spoke about academic and educational problems, the situation of the Chinese industrial system, the decision not to take part in the CPSU's Twenty-Third Congress, and about continuing to maintain independence from the USSR.
13 Mao Zedong, "Zai zhengzhi ju kuoda huiyi shang de jianghua," 640.
14 Zhang Zhanbin, *Wenge diyi wenziyu*, 179.
15 Zhang Zhanbin, *Wenge diyi wenziyu*.
16 Among those attending were Kang Sheng, Jiang Qing, and Zhang Chunqiao.
17 打到阎王, 解放小鬼: 与康生同志的谈话 "Dadao yanwang, jiefang xiaogui: Yu Kang Sheng tongzhi de hua" [Down with the Prince of Hell, set free the imps: A conversation with Comrade Kang Sheng], in *Mao Zedong sixiang wansui*, 640-41.
18 Miyazaki Ichisada, *China's Examination Hell: The Civil Service Examinations of Imperial China*, trans. Conrad Schirokauer (New York: Weatherhill, 1976). I have edited and introduced an Italian version of this book, *L'inferno degli esami* (Torino: Bollati Boringhieri, 1986). According to the "testimony" of an ample satirical literature, to which the Japanese historian had abundant recourse in his witty description of this huge bureaucratic rite, the aspiring mandarins, who were isolated for days in narrow cells compiling their abstruse compositions according to the most surreal rules, were tormented by phantoms of every type. In the course of the examinations, these phantoms, typical characters in popular Chinese stories, all servants of the King of Hell, punished candidates for their past bad deeds, above all for licentious conduct, with the result that they were excluded, by means of cruel

tricks and terrifying apparitions, from the highly limited list of winners and future imperial officials. At times the phantoms even made them die of fright.

19 Without, however, any direct participation on the part of Mao. He had been away from Beijing for many months and was to return only the following July.

20 Some of the topics of those meetings are still classified, probably because they concerned sensitive issues of PRC foreign policy. Apart from the clash over the Outline, disagreements about key military issues were presumably on the agenda and, as we shall see, converged in the final decisions. Highly controversial items, such as relations with the USSR and other communist parties, as well as the developments of and posture to strike vis-à-vis US military escalation in Vietnam, were additional issues that influenced the decisions and political atmosphere in those months.

21 师 东兵 Shi Dongbing, 最初的抗争: 彭真在"文化大革命"前夕 *Zui chu de kangzheng: Peng Zhen zai "wen hua da geming" qianxi* (Beijing: 中共中央党校出版社Zhonggong zhongyang dangxiao chubanshe, 1993). The author's name is certainly a pseudonym.

22 Zhang Zhanbin, *Wenge diyi wenziyu*, 181–82. Zhang Chunqiao's text is frequently quoted but unfortunately known only indirectly.

23 Shi Dongbing, *Zui chu de kangzheng*, 265.

24 Shi Dongbing, *Zui chu de kangzheng*, 274.

25 Deng Tuo committed suicide a few weeks later. Although the motives for such a tragic gesture are never self-evident, an aggravating factor was likely the strong pressure exerted by those who not only attacked him but also wanted to "help" him.

26 Wang Nianyi, *Da dongluan de niandai*, 12.

27 Mao Zedong, 批判彭真 "Pipan Peng Zhen" [Criticizing Peng Zhen], April 28, 1966, in *Mao Zedong sixiang wansui*, 641 (after the Circular had been drawn up). In an earlier intervention (in *Mao Zedong sixiang wansui*, 640–41) he had said: "Peng Zhen, the Party Committee in Beijing and the Central Ministry of Propaganda continue to protect the bad elements [*huai ren*]. The Party Committee in Beijing, the Central Ministry of Propaganda, and the Group of Five must be disbanded. In September last year I asked some comrades: if revisionism appears in the Center, what is to be done? This is probable [很可能的 *hen kenengde*] and it is also the most dangerous thing. We must protect the left, form the lines of the left during the course of the Cultural Revolution."

28 *Jianguo yilai Mao Zedong wengao* [Manuscripts of Mao Zedong after 1949] (Beijing: Wenxian chubanshe, 1998), vol. 12, 31.

29 中国共产党中央委员会通知及原件附件二 "Zhongguo Gongchandang zhongyang weiyuanwei tongzhi ji yuanjian fujian er" [China Communist Party Central Committeee, Circular with the original appendix 2] (May 16, 1966), in 中国文化大革命文库 *Zhongguo wenhua dageming wenku* [Chinese Cultural Revolution Database] part 1.

30 Mao's additions to the Circular are in *Jianguo yilai Mao Zedong wengao*, vol. 12, 38–45.

31 A proverbial expression with a notable literary background dating to Tang poetry and originally indicating the illusory and the absurd.

32 Alain Badiou has run very much against the tide in his enterprise to reorganize philosophically the issue of "truths." See *L'immanence des Vérités* (Paris: Fayard, 2018), the last volume of his trilogy *Being and Event*.

33 关于哲学问题的讲话 "Guanyu zhexue wenti de jianghua" [Speech on philosophical problems], August 18, 1964, in *Mao Zedong sixiang wansui*, 548–61.
34 Wang Nianyi, *Da dongluan de niandai*, 10.
35 Wang Nianyi, *Da dongluan de niandai*, 15.
36 Of the four top leaders that the CCP Central Committee dismissed in May 1966, only two were directly involved in the *Hai Rui* dispute—Peng Zhen and Lu Dingyi, the head of the Central Department of Propaganda, the highest authority in the King of Hell's Palace. However, the dismissal of the other two, Luo Ruiqing and Yang Shangkun, was unrelated to the events of the previous months and had already been decided in December as a result of other divergences within the central leadership. Nonetheless, these dismissals were officially associated with the criticism of the "Peng-Luo-Lu-Yang antiparty clique," a formula that obfuscated the singular stakes at play in the previous months. The conflict with Peng and Luo presumably concerned military policy, then particularly controversial in light of US escalation in Vietnam. Luo Ruiqing had been chief of the Joint Staff Department of the Central Military Commission and was replaced in late 1965 by Lin Biao. Yang Shangkun, another veteran of the Long March, was charged with an obscure case of espionage against Mao. Apart from the opacity of political divisions, the ousting of Luo and Yang was an affair internal to the Celestial Palace and apparently unrelated to the release of any imps.
37 林彪 Lin Biao, 在扩大工作会议上的讲话 "Zai kuoda gongzuo huiyi shang de jianghua" [Speech at an enlarged working session of the Politburo], May 18, 1966, reproduced in Song Yongyi, ed., *Chinese Cultural Revolution Database* (Hong Kong: University Center for China Studies, 2002), part 3.
38 Mao agreed to publish Lin Biao's speech with restrictions. It was printed as an "internal" party document and, hence, did not appear in the press. It had wide circulation and profound influence in shaping the opinion of the revolutionaries at the time. Yet that it did not appear in the dailies likely restricted its relevance, perhaps even indicating a disagreement over Lin's position.
39 It also explains the above-mentioned ousting of pro-professionalism Chief of Staff Luo Ruiqing.
40 See my discussion of Durkheim's concept of school in "Schools as Subjective Singularities: The Inventions of Schools in Durkheim's *L'évolution Pédagogique en France*," *Journal of Historical Sociology* 19, no. 3 (2006): 308–37.
41 Wang Nianyi, *Da dongluan de niandai*, 26. While the conciseness of classical Chinese (因势利导 *yin shi li dao* is an ancient motto that has become proverbial in modern Chinese) contains various nuances, its meaning is quite clear. Politics (class struggle was the name for politics) can be "conducted" (*dao*) "efficiently" (*li*), solely "on the basis of" (*yin*) the "circumstances" (*shi*, which are also the tendencies, the forces in play, and their developments). The quotation, taken from a text of a few years earlier, conveyed one of Mao's firm convictions, which had typically been an object of orthodox criticism since the 1920s in the name of the "historical laws" of "class struggle," a critique that in the end Wang subscribes to.
42 Louis Althusser, "Ideology and State Ideological Apparatuses" (1970), https://www.marxists.org/reference/archive/althusser/1970/ideology.htm.

Chapter 6: Testing the Organization

1 This was the text of a famous revolutionary song of the 1940s.
2 An initial formulation of this perspective can be found in my "The Probable Defeat: Preliminary Notes on the Cultural Revolution," *positions* 6, no. 1 (1998): 179–202. A recent reassessment appears in "Mummifying the Working Class: The Cultural Revolution and the Fates of the Political Parties of the 20th Century," *China Quarterly* 227 (2016): 653–73.
3 Max Weber, "Politics as Vocation" (1919), in *Weber's Rationalism and Modern Society*, trans. and ed. Tony Waters and Dagmar Waters (New York: Palgrave Macmillan, 2015).
4 I proposed a broader discussion of the "governmental drive" in "The Sixties and Us," in *The Idea of Communism 3: The Seoul Conference*, ed. Alex Taek-Gwang Lee and Slavoj Žižek (London: Verso, 2016), 136–78.
5 Saint-Just specifically states that there is no legitimate power, only the "theory of what is Good." For him the "Good" is a fundamental political category. "L'esprit de l'égalité n'est point que l'homme puisse dire à l'homme: je suis aussi puissant que toi. Il n'y a point de puissance légitime; ni les lois ni Dieu même ne sont des puissances, mais seulement la théorie de ce qui est bien. L'esprit de l'égalité est que chaque individu soit une portion égale de la souveraineté." Louis Antoine Léon de Saint-Just, *L'esprit de la révolution et de la constitution de la France* (1791) (Paris: Editions 10/18, 2003), 25.
6 The existence of myriad independent organizations, even in Europe, was the characteristic of political situations from the end of the 1960s. In Italy, for example, there was a vast proliferation of nonparliamentary groups and, in general, independent forums that sprang up in diverse areas, from schools to factories, even in the field of psychiatry. The parliamentary parties called these organizations "*gruppuscoli extraparlamentari*" (extraparliamentary splinter groups), obviously in a derogatory sense.
7 The number of these independent newspapers, that is, those not subject to prior government control, may be considered an indication of the extent of the phenomenon. In the Beijing University Library alone, there are about 10,000 periodicals of this type. Even if one ignores those that lasted for a very short time, there were still thousands of organizations throughout China.
8 Nie Yuanzi participated in the anti-Japanese resistance in 1937 and became a party member in 1938. She was a political cadre in the province of Heilongjang starting in 1946, and in 1964 she became the secretary of the party branch at the Philosophy Department of Peking University. While she was an experienced party member, in writing this dazibao and signing it together with that group of teachers and students, she acted deliberately outside the party organization. After the Cultural Revolution, she was imprisoned for some years. She has since published her memoirs. See 聂元梓 Nie Yuanzi, 回忆录 *Huiyilu* [Memoirs] (Hong Kong: Time International, 2005).
9 Ying Hongbiao has demonstrated that this dazibao was the result of an independent initiative of the group of teachers and students. His painstakingly wide-ranging research included interviews with the dazibao's authors and other wit-

nesses. Based on the array of convincing information collected, the author came to the conclusion that the dazibao was written without external interference, despite Nie Yuanzi in her interview having stated the contrary. See 印红标 Yin Hongbiao, 文革的 第一张马列主义大字报 "Wenge de 'di yi zhang maliezhuyi dazibao'" ["The first Marxist-Leninist dazibao" of the Cultural Revolution], in 文化大革命: 事实与研究 Wenhua da geming: shishi yu yanjiu [The Cultural Revolution: Facts and analysis] (Hong Kong: Chinese University Press, 1996), 3–16.

10 Reproduced in Song Yongyi, ed., *Chinese Cultural Revolution Database* (Hong Kong: University Center for China Studies, 2002), part VI.

11 On the work teams, see 高皋、严家其 Gao Gao and Yan Jiaqi, "文化大革命"十年史 *"Wenhua da geming" shi nian shi*, 18–38; Hong Yung Lee, *The Politics of the Chinese Cultural Revolution: A Case Study*, 26–63.

12 Hung Yong Lee, *The Politics of the Chinese Cultural Revolution*; Gao Gao and Yan Jiaqi, *"Wenhua da geming" shi nian shi*.

13 At a later date, when the work teams were withdrawn, one of the key points in the student organizations' ferment was a request to the government to obliterate completely the police dossiers fabricated against them. These dossiers were finally eliminated toward the end of 1966.

14 In Mao's dazibao of August 5, 1966, entitled "Bombard the General Headquarters." See 炮打司令部. 我的一张大字报 "Paoda silingbu: Wode yi zhang dazibao" [Bombard the General Headquarters], in *Jianguo yilai Mao Zedong wengao* [Manuscripts of Mao Zedong after 1949] (Beijing: Wenxian chubanshe, 1998), vol. 12, 90–92.

15 Gao Gao and Yan Jiaqi give a detailed account of how Liu conducted the operation and of his personal dislike of students such as Kuai Dafu. *"Wenhua da geming" shi nian shi*, 23–35.

16 中国共产党中央委员会关于无产阶级文化大革命的决定 "Zhongguo gongchandang zhongyang weiyuanhui guanyu wuchanjieji wenhua da geming de jueding", [Decision of the Central Committee of the Chinese Communist Party Concerning the Great Proletarian Cultural Revolution], (Adopted on August 8, 1966) in 中国文化大革命文库 *Zhongguo wenhua da geming wenku* [Chinese Cultural Revolution Database], part I. See also 人民日报社论 Renmin ribao shelun, 学习十六条, 熟悉十六条, 运用十六条 "Xuexi shiliu tiao, shuxi shiliu tiao, yunyong shiliu tiao" [Study the 16 Articles, get familiar with the 16 Articles, use the 16 Articles], *Renmin ribao*, August 13, 1966.

17 Some of these organizations were then called "conservative" (保守派 *baoshoupai*), others "old Red Guards" (老红卫兵 *lao hongweibing*). Despite a few differences, these organizations were fixated on determining class limits for the admission of new members in common. The new organizations that appeared from August through September qualified themselves as "rebels" (造反派 *zaofanpai*).

18 The change that Jiang Qing proposed was, in Chinese: 父母革命儿接班, 父母反动儿背叛 *fu mu geming er jieban, fu mu fandong er beipan*. See 江青、王任重、康生对北京中学生的讲话 "Jiang Qing, Wang Renzhong, Kang Sheng dui Beijing zhongxuesheng de jiang hua" [Speeches by Jiang Qing, Wang Renzhong, and Kang Sheng to junior high school students in Beijing], August 6, 1966, reproduced in 江青文稿

Jiang Qing wengao [Texts by Jiang Qing], vol. 1, 387–94 (quote at 388). This is a three-volume collection of texts and speeches by Jiang Qing from the 1930s, edited and published by Utopia Bookshop in Beijing. The work was purchased by the present author in 2007.

19 The most aberrant was the case of Yu Luoke, a middle-school student who in 1966 wrote a famous pamphlet that played a decisive role in discrediting the bloodline theory, but in the following years was subject to prosecution under false charges for being involved in a "counterrevolutionary plot" and finally sentenced in 1970. On this case, see Yiching Wu, *The Cultural Revolution at the Margins: Chinese Socialism in Crisis* (Cambridge, MA: Harvard University Press, 2014), 67–92.

20 Cf. Hong Yung Lee, *The Politics of the Chinese Cultural Revolution*; Gao Gao and Yan Jiaqi, *"Wen hua da geming" shi nian shi*.

21 Hong Yung Lee (*The Politics of the Chinese Cultural Revolution*) points out that the whole "destroy the four old things" movement was not a spontaneous result of the student movement, but was largely manipulated by the center of the party. Gao Gao and Yan Jiaqi (*"Wen hua da geming" shi nian shi*) confirm this analysis. Qi Benyu, then a member of the "Group in Charge of the Cultural Revolution" (CRSG), wrote in his memoirs that the *Renmin ribao* June 1, 1966, editorial, which initiated the movement (横扫一切牛鬼蛇神 "Hengsao yiqie niugui sheshen" [Destroy all ox-ghosts and snake demons]) was written without consulting either Mao or the CRSG, and in any case did not correspond to the political intentions of the Maoists at that time. See 戚本禹回忆录 *Qi Benyu huiyilu* [Qi Benyu's memoirs], chapter 6, section 3, accessed April 2019, https://www.marxists.org/chinese/reference-books/qibenyu/3-06.htm. However, the movement to "destroy the four olds," which was widely hegemonized by the first groups of "conservative" Red Guards, at that time met with broad support among the students for some weeks. The situation was extremely ambiguous. The difficulty of the Maoists was how to avoid opposing the mass movement while not sharing their methods and objectives. Barbara Mittler offers a rather multifaceted picture of the situation, recalling that Qi Benyu himself was committed to coordinating the rescue of works of art and ancient books by museums and libraries. See Barbara Mittler, "'Enjoying the Four Olds!' Oral Histories from a 'Cultural Desert,'" *Transcultural Studies* 1 (2013): 177–215.

22 *Jianguo yilai Mao Zedong wengao*, vol. 12, 99.

23 The formula was quoted by Zhou Enlai in August 1966 and highlighted when published by the *Renmin ribao* on September 18, 1966. Cf. *Jianguo yilai Mao Zedong wengao*, vol. 12, 108.

24 "Sur le marc d'argent" (April 1791), in Maximilien Robespierre, *Pour le bonheur et la liberté: Discours* (Paris: La Fabrique, 2000), 72–93.

25 In a conversation with an Albanian delegation on February 8, 1967. This passage was officially cited in the *Renmin ribao* and is reproduced in *Jianguo yilai Mao Zedong wengao*, vol. 12, 220. Note that the date was exactly at the watershed between the two phases of the pluralization process. Mao Zedong was rather optimistic but not triumphalist. During the same conversation he insisted, as he often did at this time, on the probable defeat of the Cultural Revolution. For the full text, see 毛

泽东思想万岁 *Mao Zedong sixiang wansui* [Long live Mao Zedong thought] (Beijing: n.p., 1969), 663–67 (where it is dated February 3, 1967).
26 Émile Durkheim, *The Rules of Sociological Method* (1895), ed. Steven Lukes (New York: Free Press, 1982).
27 Stanley Rosen, *Red Guard Factionalism and the Cultural Revolution in Guangzhou* (Boulder, CO: Westview, 1982).
28 Elizabeth Perry and Li Xun show it for the leaders of ardently opposing worker organizations in Shanghai. See *Proletarian Power: Shanghai in the Cultural Revolution* (New York: Routledge, 1997).
29 See Lynn T. White III, *Policies of Chaos: The Organizational Causes of Violence in China's Cultural Revolution* (Princeton, NJ: Princeton University Press, 1989). See also his synthesis "The Cultural Revolution as an Unintended Result of Administrative Policies," in Joseph C. W. Wong and David Zweig, eds., *New Perspectives on the Cultural Revolution* (Cambridge, MA: Harvard University Press, 1989), 83–104.
30 Andrew Walder, *Fractured Rebellion: The Beijing Red Guard Movement* (Cambridge, MA: Harvard University Press, 2009).
31 Walder, *Fractured Rebellion*, 205.
32 Walder, *Fractured Rebellion*, 219.
33 Walder, *Fractured Rebellion*, chapter 4.
34 Walder, *Fractured Rebellion*, chapter 8.
35 Walder, *Fractured Rebellion*, 205.
36 See Joel Andreas, *The Rise of the Red Engineers: The Cultural Revolution and the Origins of China's New Class* (Stanford, CA: Stanford University Press, 2009).
37 Andreas, *The Rise of the Red Engineers*, 128.
38 Andreas, *The Rise of the Red Engineers*, 9.
39 Andrew Walder, *Agents of Disorder: Inside China's Cultural Revolution* (Cambridge, MA: Harvard University Press, 2019.

Chapter 7: A Subjective Split in the Working Class

1 I have analyzed these processes in "Destinies of University," *Polygraph* 21 (2009): 41–75, and more recently in "Parlomurs: A Dialogue on Corruption in Education," in *What Is Education?*, ed. Adam Bartlett and Justin Clemens (Edinburgh: Edinburgh University Press, 2017), 185–238.
2 陈伯达在上海安亭火车站的工人的电报 "Chen Boda zai Shanghai Anting huochezhan de gongren dianbao" [Chen Boda's telegram to Shanghai workers in Anting train station], reproduced in 陈伯达言论集 *Chen Boda yanlunji* [Chen Boda speeches and remarks], vol. 1, 214 (a three-volume collection published by Beijing Utopia Bookstore and purchased by the present author in 2007).
3 See 李逊 Li Xun, 革命造反年代：上海文革运动史稿 *Geming zaofan niandai: Shanghai wenge yundong shigao* [The age of revolutionary rebellion: A history of the Cultural Revolution movement in Shanghai] (Hong Kong: Oxford University Press, 2015), vol. 1, 318. On the episode, see also Jiang Hongsheng, "The Paris Commune in Shanghai: The Masses, the State, and Dynamics of 'Continuous Revolution'" (PhD dissertation, Duke University, 2010), 261, accessed April 2018, https://dukespace.lib.duke

.edu/dspace/bitstream/handle/10161/2356/D_Jiang_Hongsheng_a_201005.pdf. Both works discuss in detail the Shanghai events based on ample documentation, though from opposite points of view. Jiang's is a generous attempt to reaffirm the political value of the events. Li writes in the framework of the governmental judgment.

4 Walder, *Agents of Disorder*, 40.

5 A firsthand account giving a lively picture of the events and grasping some of the main issues at stake is that by Neal Hunter, who was at that time an English-language instructor at the Shanghai Language Institute. See *Shanghai Journal* (New York: Praeger, 1969).

6 This was, in fact, one answer that an old "loyalist" worker who participated in the events gave me during an interview in a Guangzhou factory in 1989.

7 Franz Schurmann, *Ideology and Organization in Communist China* (Berkeley: University of California Press, 1966).

8 David Bray has analyzed in detail the tortuous and complex process that led to the establishment of the danwei system. *Social Space and Governance in Urban China: The Danwei System from Origins to Reform* (Stanford, CA: Stanford University Press, 2005). While some of its antecedents trace back to forms of governance of the Guomindang period and even to traditional Confucian "familism," its starting point was in the Yan'an period. Its generalization from the early fifties was not linear, even less the implementation of a preestablished plan. Yet one can assume that the main thrust to the organizational stabilization of the danwei system was the peculiar ideological relation between factory workers and the Communist Party. On the other hand, the thrust to the transformation of the danwei system in the economic reform lies in the crisis that relation underwent during the Cultural Revolution.

9 In fact, one of the earliest scholarly analyses of the danwei was done in a hospital. See Gail E. Henderson and Myron S. Cohen, *The Chinese Hospital: A Socialist Work Unit* (New Haven, CT: Yale University Press, 1984). See also the seminal essay by 路风 Lu Feng, 单位，一种特殊的社会组织形式 "Danwei: Yizhong teshude shehui zuzhi xingshi" [Danwei: A special form of social organization], 中国社会科学 *Zhongguo shehui kexue* 1 (1989): 3–18. In a worker survey conducted in Guangzhou, I have examined some aspects of the transformation of the danwei system in the early decade of economic reform. See my *Ouvrier et danwei: Note de recherche sur une enquete d'anthropologie ouvrière menée dans deux usines de Guangzhou en avril-mai 1989* (Paris: Université de Paris VIII, 1990).

10 The two statements of the rebels, 告全市人民书 "Gao quanshi renmin shu" and 紧急通告 "Jinji tonggao," appeared, respectively, in the *Wenhui bao* on January 4 and jointly in the *Wenhui bao* and *Jiefang ribao* on January 9. They were the most mature result of the workers' activism after the Anting incident. Besides the WGH, which strengthened the leading role acquired in the previous two months, ten other organizations cosigned the first and thirty-one the second, a sign of the rapid expansion of the pluralization and political growth that the independent organizations had experienced in the course of the struggle.

11 See Andrew G. Walder, *Chang Ch'un-ch'iao and Shanghai's January Revolution* (Ann Arbor: Center for Chinese Studies, University of Michigan, 1978). Not all urban

residents were included in the danwei system. In the Shanghai factories there were numerous contract workers who did not share the same conditions of the danwei fixed employees. According to Yiching Wu, the second largest rebel organization in Shanghai was constituted by non-danwei workers. See *The Cultural Revolution at the Margins: Chinese Socialism in Crisis* (Cambridge, MA: Harvard University Press, 2014), 93–141. The number of contract workers had increased in the early sixties. Later, during the early seventies, there was a considerable effort to give them stable positions.

12 In his study on economism in the January Storm, Yiching Wu, while acknowledging that the intentions of the SPC were to counter the rebel organizations, maintains that the criticism of economism makes sense in capitalism but not in socialism, and therefore the economic demands had a political value in that situation. However, this distinction, which in any case was not relevant for the rebel organizations, requires further exploration.

13 《红旗》评论员 "Hongqi" pinglunyuan [*Hongqi* commentator], 无产阶级革命派联合起来 "Wuchanjieji gemingpai liaheqilai" [Proletarian revolutionaries, unite!], *Hongqi* 2 (1967), reprinted in *Renmin ribao*, January 16, 1967.

14 无产阶级革命派大联合，夺走资本主义道路当权派的权 "Wuchanjieji gemingpai da lianhe, duo zou zibenzhuyi daolu dangquanpai de quan" [Proletarian revolutionaries form a great alliance to seize power from those in authority who are taking the capitalist road], *Renmin ribao*, January 22, 1967.

15 论无产阶级革命派的夺权斗争 "Lun wuchanjijeji gemingpai de duoquan douzheng" [On the Proletarian Revolutionaries' Struggle for Power], *Hongqi* 3 (1967); *Renmin ribao*, January 31, 1967.

16 In his study on the Shanghai Commune, Jiang Hongsheng argues that Mao was then urging the CGCR to draft the articles discussed above proclaiming the centrality of the seizure of power in order to counteract the reservations regarding the active role of the independent organizations after the collapse of party authority expressed by the Central Group. He writes that such influential members as Chen Boda and Zhou Enlai doubted the ability of rebel workers to cope with the situation after having undermined the SPC's authority. Chen Boda even worried about a "secret plan" to let the rebels "take power" to prove they were not up to it.

17 张春桥, 姚文元在在上海群众大会上的讲话 "Zhang Chunqiao, Yao Wenyuan zai Shanghai qunzhong dahui shang de janghua" [Speeches by Zhang Chunqiao and Yao Wenyuan at a mass meeting in Shanghai], February 24, 1967, in 张春桥文集 *Zhang Chunqiao wenji* [Zhang Chunqiao collected works], vol. 1, 203–53. This three-volume collection is an unofficial edition published by Utopia Bookstore in Beijing, purchased by the present author in 2008.

18 The study by Jiang Hongsheng on the Shanghai Commune and the discussion that Alain Badiou engaged in with him have the merit of reopening a window on theoretical questions. In his foreword to the French version of Jiang's study, Badiou argues, as in his earlier reading of those events, that the Commune was the highest communist novelty of the Cultural Revolution and that the subsequent Revolutionary Committee was a retreat to the traditional forms of the party-state. For

Jiang Hongsheng, conversely, the decision was not a return to the previous governmental organization but was intended to make all the political novelties that had emerged in Shanghai a point of reference for situations where the political initiative of the rebel organizations was less mature and original. See Jiang Hongsheng, *La Commune de Shanghai et la Commune de Paris* (Paris: La Fabrique, 2014).

19 对上海文化大革命的指示 "Dui Shanghai wenhua da geming de zhishi" [Directives on the Cultural Revolution in Shanghai], in *Mao Zedong sixiang wansui* [Long live Mao Zedong thought] (Beijing: n.p., 1969), 667–72.

20 金大陆 Jin Dalu, 非常与正常, 上海文革时期的社会生活 *Feichang yu zhengchang: Shanghai wenge shiqi de shehui shenghuo* [Abnormal and normal: Social life in Shanghai during the Cultural Revolution] (Shanghai: Cishu chubanshe, 2008).

21 "Zhang Chunqiao, Yao Wenyuan zai shanghai qunzhong dahui shang de janghua," 210.

22 It is nothing short of an outrage that there is no scholarly study of this foremost political figure of twentieth-century China, who even today, and in his own country, is pilloried by vulgar insults. This also holds true for the other Maoist leaders then active in Shanghai.

23 I do not analyze here the complex formation of the Revolutionary Committees, which lasted throughout the country for almost a year and a half from February 1967. The stabilization process was very controversial and in fact paralleled the factional involution of independent organizations. Only in late 1968, when the Red Guards were disbanded, did the Revolutionary Committees fully establish themselves. For a description of the process, see Wang Peijie, *Revolutionary Committees in the Cultural Revolution Era of China* (London: Palgrave Macmillan, 2017).

24 During the Wuhan incidents in summer 1967, among the most serious in those months, Mao did everything within his power to resolve a very tangled situation, even going personally to Wuhan despite the serious risks he ran in doing so. There is, unfortunately, no mention of any public stance he may have taken in these events, and even his journey and presence there had been kept secret until a few years ago.

25 One last clarification. I suggested in chapter 4 a "symptomatic reading" of the "probable defeat." Obviously, there are symptoms of a different nature. In the case of probable defeat, that symptom opened a void in the revolutionary culture that led to radical experimentation. The seizure of power concept played a substantially opposite role: filling a conceptual and organizational void that had opened up, by bringing experimentation back into the framework of previous political knowledge.

Chapter 8: Facing a Self-Defeat

1 Part of what follows is from the translation and analysis of this document in my essay "The Conclusive Scene: Mao and the Red Guards in July 1968," *positions*, 13, no. 3 (2005): 535–74.

2 It was performed to acclaim by the Teatro dei Dispersi troupe in my Italian translation and directed by Gianfranco Rimondi at Bologna in 2003.

3 According to William Hinton, author of a book of inquiry written a few years after the events, thirty thousand workers took part in the demonstration in an

organized way, and at least as many joined spontaneously. See William Hinton, *Hundred Day War: The Cultural Revolution at Tsinghua University* (New York: Monthly Review, 1972).

4   The transcript was published under the title 召见首都红代会负责人的谈话 "Zhaojian shoudu hong dai hui fuzeren de tanhua" [Talk with the responsible persons of the conference of the Red Guards of the capital], hereafter cited as "Tanhua," in *Mao Zedong sixiang wansui* [Long live Mao Zedong thought] (Beijing: n.p., 1969), 687–716. Concerning the reliability of this collection, which is one of the main sources of Mao's "unofficial" texts, doubts could be raised about the editorial interventions of the anonymous curators. Although nothing guarantees the fidelity of the meeting transcript, I personally believe that the editing has been limited to putting it in a "theatrical" form. This is not the place for a philological analysis of the text, but other available versions do not deviate significantly from it.

5   It is almost superfluous to recall that the relationships between Mao and the Red Guards are unanimously considered by historians to possess an exclusive imaginary nature: "a curious alliance between an old leader and fanatical teenagers that adored him like a God." Marie-Claire Bergère, *La république populaire de Chine de 1949 à nos jours* (Paris: Colin, 1989).

6   "Tanhua," 687. In the present chapter, all the quotations are taken from the above-quoted volume, *Mao Zedong sixiang wansui*; all translations are mine.

7   三宝殿 *Sanbaodian*, from the name of a Buddhist "trinity"—the three jewels: the Buddha, the Law, and the Community of monks.

8   The faction of Nie Yuanzi majority at Beida, called "New Beida (Commune)," was affiliated with the Sky faction. Therefore, it was in principle allied with Kuai Dafu's and Han Aijing's group; whereas the Beida faction opposed to Nie (stemming from a division of the same New Beida faction), called "New Beida (Jinggangshan)," or only "Jinggangshan," was affiliated with the Earth faction. However, Jinggangshan was also the name of the majority faction at Qinghua led by Kuai Dafu, who was in principle an ally of Nie and therefore an enemy of the Jinggangshan faction of Beida. In fact, Nie pretended to be in a superior position (an Old Buddha) in regard to the network of alliances. Moreover, the faction opposed to Kuai at Qinghua was called "Jinggangshan (April 14th)," or simply April 14th; it resulted from the 1967 split of the original Jinggangshan of Kuai Dafu, now called "Jinggangshan (Headquarters)." There were obviously various contradictions within each of the two main factions as well. With the name "Jinggangshan" (the mountains of the first "red bases," created by Mao in 1929) caught in a tug-of-war between Sky and Earth, one of the great revolutionary modern Chinese names became politically exhausted.

9   Hinton, *Hundred Day War*.

10 "Tanhua," 697–98.

11 "Tanhua," 688.

12 "Tanhua," 688–89.

13 See *Mao Zedong sixiang wansui*, 648.

14 Bergère, *La république populaire de Chine*. For a memoir of an old Red Guard, see Hua Linshan, *Les années rouges* (Paris: Seuil, 1987).

15 "Tanhua," 689.
16 "Tanhua," 707–9.
17 "Tanhua," 689.
18 "Tanhua," 690.
19 "Tanhua," 690.
20 This is another historical reference, which here seems to have only a proverbial meaning, to the military revolts that marked the fall of the Han Dynasty between the second and the third centuries BC.
21 "Tanhua," 700–702.
22 Tan Houlan seemed not to have any special reason to oppose Jiang Qing, who during the meeting recalls an episode in which she had helped her. However, because of Tan's association with the Earth faction, she was allied with the Beida Jinggangshan (those who wanted to "fry" Jiang Qing), which was hostile to the Central Group (as was also the case of Qinghua April 14th). According to Jiang Qing's words, the opponents of Tan at the Normal University (those whom Tan had imprisoned in the dark without food and drink) seem to have also been hostile to the Central Group. The confused tangle of unprincipled alliances and enmities among factions was proportional to their political exhaustion.
23 The insistence with which the Central Group kept its distance from involvement in fights between Red Guard organizations can be explained as a reaction to tendencies manifested in the previous months inside the same organization. In September 1967, three of its members, Qi Benyu, Guang Feng, and Wang Li, had been removed, accused of stirring up hostilities between the factions to strengthen their own position inside the Central Group. The episode marked a critical passage, but during this meeting it was only marginally recalled.
24 As is well known, during the summer of 1967, the "Wuhan incident" showed the possibility of serious clashes between local military commands and the central military machine.
25 "Tanhua," 699–700.
26 In fact, Guangxi's factional armed struggle—one of the most self-destructive episodes of the Cultural Revolution—was dealt with in a very different way than that on Beijing's campuses. The clashes were closed off not by disarmed workers, like those who entered Qinghua, but by the People's Liberation Army and the armed militia, which treated students much more brutally. In the above-quoted memoir, *Les années rouges*, Hua Linshan, who was a member of a Red Guard organization in Guangxi, gives a different version than that offered here by Mao and Lin Biao, and insists on the purely military form of suppression. He confirms, however, and not without nostalgia, the heroic-militaristic imaginary vision of politics that dominated among the Guangxi student factions in 1968.
27 "Tanhua," 699.
28 "Tanhua," 704.
29 Hinton, *Hundred Day War*.

30 "Tanhua," 711.
31 "Tanhua," 700-701. Here Mao quotes almost verbatim a view expressed by Lenin in *"Left-Wing" Communism, an Infantile Disorder*: "Anarchism was not infrequently a sort of punishment for the opportunist sins of the working-class movement." For the online English version, see http://www.marx2mao.com/Lenin/LWC20.html, accessed June 2018.
32 The criticism of the theory as a "docile tool" was in those months one of the main polemical arguments against 刘少奇 Liu Shaoqi's most famous work, 论共产党员修养 *Lun gonchandagyuan xiuyang* [On the cultivation of a member of the Communist Party], translated into English with the title *How to Be a Good Communist*. In the early 1960s, this book became a fundamental ideological-moral breviary in the political pedagogy of the CCP.
33 A vivid narration of the disciplinary atmosphere in the Chinese schools in the early 1960s, especially the most prestigious ones, may be found in Rae Yang's memoir *Spider Eaters* (Berkeley: University of California Press, 1997).
34 "Tanhua," 693.
35 Gao Yubao was the author of a memoir translated into several languages by the Foreign Languages Press.
36 "Tanhua," 693.
37 Together with Claudia Pozzana, I have translated into Italian and commented on the works of these authors in two anthologies: *Nuovi poeti cinesi* (Torino: Einaudi, 1995) and "Un'altra Cina: Poeti e narratori degli anni Novanta," *In forma di Parole* 19, no. 1 (1999).
38 See Mao Zedong, *Inventare una scuola: Scritti giovanili sull'educazione*, ed. Fabio Lanza and Alessandro Russo (Rome: Manifestolibri, 1996). In this collection of writings by the young Mao on education in the May Fourth years, those on the Hunan self-study university are the most remarkable. Chinese texts are collected in 毛泽东早期文稿 *Mao Zedong zaoqi wengao* (Changsha: Hunan chubanshe, 1990). For an English version, see Stuart R. Schram, ed., *Mao's Road to Power: Revolutionary Writings 1912-1949* (Armonk, NY: M. E. Sharpe, 1992), vol. 1.
39 I have analyzed the inventiveness of educational policies from May Fourth to the Yan'an period in Chapters 5-8 of my book *Le rovine del mandato: La modernizzazione politica dell'educazione e della cultura cinesi* (Milan: Franco Angeli, 1985).
40 Jiang was cited here in the sarcastic sense of 反面教员 *fanmian jiaoyuan*, or "teacher in negative," which was one of the favorite expressions of the Maoists in those years.
41 *Tanhua*, 705-6.
42 "Mao zhuxi guanyu zhizhi wudou wenti de zhishi jingshen yaodian" [Basic points of the directives of Chairman Mao on the cessation of the armed struggle], reproduced in *"Wenhua da geming" yanjiu ziliao* [Material for the study of the "Great Cultural Revolution"] (Beijing: Guofang daxue, 1988), vol. 2, 153-54. The document that summarizes the main passages of the above-cited exchanges of Mao and Lin Biao was written under the supervision of a member of the Central Group, Xie

Fuzhi, and was signed by all five leaders of the Red Guards. On this episode, see 王年一 Wang Nianyi, 大动乱的年代 *Da dongluan de niandai*, 302–3.

43 Some interviews by William Hinton with the workers who attended the demonstration are remarkable.

44 A key decision taken in the following months that stemmed from this meeting (foreshadowed, as we've seen, by Mao's "some of you go North, others South. That way you can't see or attack each other") was the program that transferred all university students to the countryside, the so-called movement of educated youth to the countryside. A similar decision and destination was adopted for state functionaries called the "7 May cadre schools." Many students were initially enthusiastic, a conviction born perhaps as a way out of factionalism's political and existential impasse and even as a good firsthand experience of the real life of peasants. Michel Bonnin, who meticulously researched the phenomenon and came to a negative conclusion, notes, however, that many who participated had no regrets whatsoever even decades later, even evincing a certain nostalgia about the experience. See *The Lost Generation: The Rustication of China's Educated Youth, 1968–1980* (Hong Kong: Chinese University of Hong Kong Press, 2013). It seems to me that, at least initially, the experience was conceived by the participants themselves as a way out of the deadlock of the Red Guards and to gain direct knowledge of the Chinese countryside, and not as a disciplinary or punitive measure. However, the farther away in time it was removed from the propulsive political thrust of 1966–68, that is, when the independent organizations were at the height of their vitality, the more that resettlement program looks like a bureaucratically inspired enterprise. Somewhat similar remarks can be appended to the experiences of nearly all the state functionaries transferred to the countryside for rather lengthy periods of time after 1968.

45 Yang Guobin, *The Red Guard Generation and Political Activism in China* (New York: Columbia University Press, 2016).

46 From "Adieu Tomb: A Hazy Path Has Led Me amongst You." See Pozzana and Russo, eds., *Nuovi poeti cinesi*, 77. Gu Cheng's written interview is in the appendix, "Risposte a un questionario."

Chapter 9: Intellectual Conditions for a Political Assessment

1 Much in evidence, for example, was the emphasis given to the Han-period *Discourses on Salt and Iron* (盐铁论 *Yan tie lun*, 81 CE). Here the two schools faced off in an extraordinary duel over the major issues of Han economic policy.

2 These efforts brought to light spectacular finds, foremost among them the terracotta army in Xi'an, the Qin legal codes mentioned above, and earlier versions of classics of Chinese philosophy, like the *Daodejing*.

3 Zhang Chunqiao, in presenting the 1975 constitution, had specified that the issue of the freedom to strike was "added as Chairman Mao's proposal": see 张春桥 Zhang Chunqiao, 关于修改宪法的报告 "Guanyu xiugai xianfa de baogao" [Report on the revision of the constitution], 红旗 *Hongqi* 2 (1975): 15–19. Mao had been

very active in the development of the first constitution of the People's Republic of China in 1954.

4   The right to strike was abolished in the constitution of 1982, the first that the era of the Deng "reforms" ushered in, never again to reappear in China's legal system.

5   For the full text of Mao's theses on the study of theory, see Mao Zedong, 关于理论问题的谈话要点, 1974年, 12 月 "Guanyu lilun wenti de tanhua yaodian, 1974 nian, 12 yue" [Main points of the talk on the theoretical problems, December 1974], in 建国以来毛泽东文稿 *Jianguo yilai Mao Zedong wengao* [Manuscripts of Mao Zedong after 1949] (Beijing: Zhongyang wenxian chubanshe, 1998), vol. 13, 413-15. These theses had initially been set forth by Mao in December 1974 in a "theoretical seminar" held in the presence of Zhou Enlai, presumably as part of the preparatory meetings for the Fourth National Congress. Meetings for theoretical study at the top of the party were part of a tradition that dates back to the years of the War of Liberation and to some extent still remain today. Zhou Enlai personally arranged the circulation of the transcript of the interview, first in the central structures of the party and then in the press. Mao's choice of Zhou Enlai as the first interlocutor of those theoretical issues is a sign of the close relationship between the two, which lasted until the end. However, after late 1973 and throughout 1974 Mao had various disagreements with Zhou Enlai with regard to foreign policy, which cannot be dealt with here.

6   Mao Zedong, 对 '关于无产阶级专政的历史经验' 稿的批语和修改, 1956 年, 4月, 2 日, 4 日 "Dui 'Guanyu wuchanjieji zhuanzheng de lishi jingyan' gao de piyu he xiugai" [Comments on and revisions to the draft of "On the historical experience of the dictatorship of the proletariat," April 2-4, 1956], in *Jianguo yilai Mao Zedong wengao*, vol. 6, 59-67.

7   Zhang Chunqiao, 论对资产阶级全面专政 "Lun dui zichanjieji quanmian zhuanzheng" [The complete dictatorship over the bourgeoisie], *Hongqi* 4 (1975): 3-12.

8   The article that launched the campaign and published Mao's theses for the first time was an editorial in the *People's Daily*. See 人民日报社论 Renmin ribao shelun [*People's Daily* editorial], 学好无产阶级专政的理论 "Xuehao wuchanjieji zhuanzheng de lilun" [Carefully study the theory of the dictatorship of the proletariat], *Renmin ribao*, February 9, 1975, 1. Mao, who was very active in leading this theoretical movement, closely monitored the publication of a series of texts that relaunched his positions. Among them was an essay by 姚文远 Yao Wenyuan, 林彪反党集团的社会基础 "Lin Biao fan dang jituan de shehui jichu" [The social bases of Lin Biao's antiparty clique], *Hongqi* 3 (1975): 20-29; and another by Zhang Chunqiao, "论对资产阶级全面专政 "Lun dui zichanjieji quanmian zhuanzheng" [The complete dictatorship over the bourgeoisie], *Hongqi* 4 (1975): 3-12. Great emphasis was also placed on the publication of a selection of excerpts from texts by Marx, Engels, and Lenin, which summed up the "classical" references. See 人民日报, 红旗杂志编者 Renmin ribao, Hongqi zazhi bianzhe [Editorial board of *People's Daily* and *Red Flag*], 马克思, 恩格斯, 列宁, 论无产阶级专政 "Makesi, Engesi, Liening

lun wuchanjieji zhuanzheng" [Marx, Engels, and Lenin on the dictatorship of the proletariat], *Hongqi* 3 (1975): 3–19. In this selection, Stalin is evidently missing.

9 Andrzej Wajda's 1977 film *Man of Marble* was a profound questioning of the role of workers in Polish socialism and anticipated the Solidarity movement.

10 In her PhD dissertation, "The Workers University in the Chinese Cultural Revolution" (São Paulo University, 2018), Andrea Piazzaroli Longobardi has done the first large scholarly study on the issue, with particular reference to the Shanghai Machine Tool Factory, where the experiment originated. See www.teses.usp.br/teses/disponiveis/8/ . . . /2018_AndreaPiazzaroliLongobardi_VOrig.pdf (accessed April 2019).

11 See, for example, 马彦文 Ma Yanwen, 马克思主义的重大发展。学习毛主席重要指示的一点体会 "Makesizhuyi de zhongda fazhan. Xuexi Mao Zhuxi zhongyao zhishi yi dian tihui" [Major development of Marxism. Some experience of studying Chairman Mao's important instructions], in 北京大学学报 *Beijing daxue xuebao* 2 (1976): 23–29 (with two sequels in issue no. 3: 15–21, 22–29); 景池 Jing Chi, 商品自述 "Shanpin zishu" [Autobiography of the Commodity], 学习与批判 *Xuexi yu pipan*, no. 5 (1975): 19–24, with sequels in issues no. 6: 22–26, and no. 7: 15–27. The series was also published as a book at Shanghai Renmin Chubanshe, 1975.

12 Karl Marx, *Critique of the Gotha Program* (1875), https://www.marxists.org/archive/marx/works/1875/gotha/.

13 See Louis Althusser, "Ideology and Ideological State Apparatuses" (1970), reprinted in *On Ideology* (London: Verso, 2008).

14 The original remark by Mao, dated March 22, 1960, in 建国以来毛泽东文稿 *Jianguo yilai Mao Zedong wengao*, vol. 9, 89–92; English translation at https://www.marxists.org/reference/archive/mao/selected-works/volume-8/mswv8_49.htm.

15 The issue is discussed in several of Marx's works, including specific passages in *Das Kapital*, chapter 14, "The Division of Labor and Manufacture," and chapter 15, "Machinery and Modern Industry."

Chapter 10: Foundations of Deng Xiaoping's Strategy

1 See 程中原 Cheng Zhongyuan and 夏杏珍 Xia Xingzhen, 历史转折的前奏。邓小平在一九七五 历史转折的前奏。邓小平在一九七五 *Lishi zhuanzhe de qianzou: Deng Xiaoping zai yijiuqiwu* [The prelude to the historical turning point: Deng Xiaoping in 1975] (Beijing: Qingnian chunashe, 2004). See also Fredrick Teiwes and Warren Sun, *The End of the Maoist Era: Chinese Politics during the Twilight of the Cultural Revolution, 1972–1976* (Armonk, NY: M. E. Sharpe, 2007). The biographies of the main protagonists give other interesting elements, though strictly following the judgment of the Chinese government on the events. See 逄先知 Feng Xianzhi and 金冲及 Jin Chongji, eds., 毛泽东传 1949–1976 *Mao Zedong zhuan, 1949–1976* (Biography of Mao Zedong, 1949–1976) (Beijing: Zhongyang wenxian chubanshe, 2003); 毛毛 [邓榕] Mao Mao [Deng Rong], 我的父亲邓小平. '文革'岁月 *Wo de fuqin Deng Xiaoping: "Wen'ge" suiye* [Deng Xiaoping, my father: The years of the "Cultural Revolution"] (Beijing: Zhongyang wenxian chubanshe, 2000); 刘武生 Liu Wusheng, 周恩来的晚年岁月 *Zhou Enlai de wannian suiyue* [Zhou Enlai: The late years] (Beijing: Renmin

Chubanshe, 2006). The biography by Ezra Vogel, *Deng Xiaoping and the Transformation of China* (Cambridge, MA: Belknap Press of Harvard University Press, 2011), in the chapters concerning 1975, follows Cheng Zhongyuan and Xia Xingzhen, *Lishi zhuanzhe de qianzou*, and Mao Mao, *Wo de fuqin Deng Xiaoping*.

2 The memoir published by his daughter, Deng Rong, shows that after 1966 Deng Xiaoping was not particularly oppressed, nor jailed; on the contrary, he was carefully protected by both Mao and Zhou Enlai in view of a possible return to government. After 1967 Mao himself suggested this possibility. From 1969 to 1972, Deng was sent to an agricultural district in Jiangxi, where he lived with his family and took part in manual work in a factory. His living conditions were quite proportionate to his rank. From this village he kept up relationships with the government and with the party center.

3 In 1973 his main task was participating in a UN session where he gave a speech that confirmed the key positions of Chinese foreign policy in those years, namely the theory of the "three worlds" and China's membership in the Third World.

4 It is meaningful that the official publication of the writings of Deng Xiaoping in the eighties started with a volume covering the years from 1975 to 1981: 邓小平文选 1975-1982 *Deng Xiaoping wenxuan. 1975-1982* [Selected works of Deng Xiaoping, 1975-1982] (Beijing: Renmin chubanshe, 1983). The volume covering the years before 1966 appeared only later. The aforementioned voluminous monograph by Ezra Vogel treats the biography of Deng before 1966 in about thirty pages. For a larger biography of the years before the Cultural Revolution, see Alexander V. Pantsov with Steven I. Levine, *Deng Xiaoping: A Revolutionary Life* (Oxford: Oxford University Press, 2015).

5 Vogel, *Deng Xiaoping and the Transformation of China,* chapter 3.

6 Zhengdun appears in the titles of five of the eight 1975 essays. See 邓小平 Deng Xiaoping, 军队要整顿 "Jundui yao zhengdun" [The army must be put in order], January 25, in *Deng Xiaoping wenxuan*, 1-3; and Deng Xiaoping, 各方面都要整顿 "Ge fangmian dou yao zhengdun" [Everything must be put in order in every field], September 27 and October 4, in *Deng Xiaoping wenxuan*, 32-34. These texts come from speeches at meetings and conferences held in the central bodies of the army, the party, and the government. Vogel renders zhengdun as "consolidation," which obliterates the disciplinary connotation of the term.

7 全党讲大局, 把国民经济搞上去 *Quandang jiang daju, ba guomin jingji gao shan qu* [The whole party must take into consideration the overall situation and raise the national economy], May 3, in *Deng Xiaoping wenxuan*, 4-7; 当前钢铁工业必须解决的几个问题 "Dangqian gangtie gongye bixu jiejuede jige wenti" [Some present problems to solve in the iron and steel industry], May 29, in *Deng Xiaoping wenxuan*, 8-11.

8 In actual fact, they were focused on the specific situation of an important railway junction. Although these reconstructions remain vague in the detailed description of the event, it seems that the disorganization in that area was also the result of overlapping authorities at different government levels—neighboring provinces, the Ministry of Transport, local authorities, and so forth—and were not generically "disorders."

9 These data are cited in Cheng Zhongyuan and Xia Xingzhen, *Lishi zhuanzhe de qianzou*, 590. The data referring to 1975 economic growth are quite different but equally positive in Feng Xianzhi and Jin Chongji, eds., *Mao Zedong zhuan*, 1752: GDP 8.7 percent; industry, 15.1 percent, agriculture, 3.1 percent.

10 I am grateful to Cui Zhiyuan, professor of public policy and management at Qinghua University, for discussing these data with me.

11 Cited in Cheng Zhongyuan and Xia Xingzhen, *Lishi zhuanzhe de qianzou*, 539. Many new members were admitted into the party in 1974.

12 Deng was particularly tough with the "heads of factions" (头头 *toutou*). They had to be isolated by "cutting off their internal and external links" and "moved to other units." If they refused to leave, they had to have "their salary suspended": "If your job is to create factional unrest, why do you come to us to get a salary?" See Deng Xiaoping, 全党讲大局, 把国民经济搞上去 "Quandang jiang daju, ba goumin jingji gao shangqu" [The whole party must take into consideration the overall situation and raise the national economy], May 3, in *Deng Xiaoping wenxuan*, 6.

13 Alain Badiou, "Metaphysics and the Critique of Metaphysics," *Pli* 10 (2000): 174–90, accessed April 2019, https://plijournal.com/files/Pli_10_9_Badiou.pdf.

14 论全党全国各项工作的总纲 "Lun quandang quanguo ge xiang gongzuo de zonggang," October 7, 1975; reprinted in 中国人民解放军, 国防大学, 党史政工教研室 Zhongguo renmin jiefangjun, Guofang daxue, Dangshi zhenggong jiaoyanshi, "文化大革命"研究资料 *"Wenhua da geming" yanjiu ziliao* [Research materials on the "Great Cultural Revolution"], vol., 2 (1988): 507–17. Two other documents, which I cannot discuss here, were on industry and scientific research: 关于加快工业发展的若干问题。讨论稿 "Guanyu jiakuai gongye fazhan de ruogan wenti. Taolun gao" [Some problems concerning the acceleration of industrial development: Draft for discussion], September 2, 1975, *"Wenhua da geming" yanjiu ziliao*, 487–97; and 关于科技工作的几个问题 "Guanyu keji gongzuo de jige wenti" [Some problems on scientific and technological work], August 11, 1975, *"Wenhua da geming" yanjiu ziliao*, 528–31. At the time none of these programs was officially published in the press, due to the fact that Deng's political initiative ended in October 1975. In the following weeks, however, there were widespread editions for "internal use" (i.e., not directly available in the official press or in bookshops but distributed only within the danwei), and these were later reprinted in early 1976 as appendixes to three separate volumes of criticism on Deng Xiaoping's three programs.

15 毛主席重要指示 "Mao zhuxi zhongyao zhishi 1975–76" [Important directives of Chairman Mao, 1975–76], in *Jianguo yilai Mao Zedong wengao* (Manuscripts of Mao Zedong after 1949) (Beijing: Wenxian chubanshe, 1998), vol. 13, 486.

16 Mao Mao, *Wo de fuqin Deng Xiaoping*, 426.

17 "Mao zhuxi zhongyao zhishi 1975–76," vol. 13, 487–88.

18 Vogel narrates this crucial moment as the result of Mao's determination to force Deng into giving a positive evaluation of the Cultural Revolution. This certainly fits the current image, but the available documents show rather that Mao was interested in a critical reflection on the mistakes of the Cultural Revolution, whereas Deng was definitely hostile to it. It is true, however, as Vogel notes, that if

Deng had accepted the challenge, even as a critical exercise vis-à-vis the Cultural Revolution, his following strategy based on thorough negation would have been vitiated even before its conception was completed.

19 Though stemming from the 1976 coup, the term appears officially only later in 关于建国以来党的若干历史问题的决议 "Guanyu jianguo yilai dang de ruogan lishi wenti de jueyi" [On some questions concerning the history of the party since the founding of the PRC], *Renmin ribao*, July 1, 1981, 1–7. The official campaign to totally negate the Cultural Revolution took place in earnest between 1984 and 1986, with dozens of editorials appearing in official newspapers calling for the total eradication of so-called leftist elements formerly associated with the Cultural Revolution.

20 "Mao zhuxi zhongyao zhishi 1975–76," vol. 13, 487.

21 In the meantime, the Chinese media were engaged in a widespread campaign of defamation against the workers, whom they portrayed as being dependent on the "iron rice bowl" (铁饭碗 *tiefanwan*); that is, they were models of laziness and parasites of public resources. I have examined the issue in *Ouvrier et "danwei": Note de recherche sur une enquête d'anthropologie ouvrière menée à Canton en avril 1989* (Paris: Université de Paris VIII, 1990).

22 The suppression of the Tian'anmen movement was one prerequisite for imparting an even more strictly neoliberal drive to the "reforms" in the months that followed. On this key passage of economic policies in the 1990s, see Wang Hui, *China's New Order* (Cambridge, MA: Harvard University Press, 2003).

23 Pun Ngai and Jenny Chan, "Global Capital, the State, and Chinese Workers: The Foxconn Experience," *Modern China* 38 (2012): 383–410. See also the extensive study by Pun Ngai, Jenny Chan, and Mark Selden, *Morire per un i-Phone*, ed. Ferruccio Gambino and Devi Sacchetto (Milan: Jaca Book, 2015).

24 As is well known, forms of resistance by workers, such as strikes, demonstrations, and riots, are prevalent throughout China today. In his study on the protests of workers laid off from state-owned enterprises, William Hurst documents that local authorities have a range of responses for dealing with such protests, from the most stringent to the most compromising, depending on the circumstances. See William Hurst, *The Chinese Worker after Socialism* (New York: Cambridge University Press, 2009), 108–31. However, while grievances and claims concerning wages and welfare are, to varying degrees, tolerated, it is strictly unacceptable for any form of worker organization to claim a political role that positions itself in opposition to the class vanguard, the CCP. For updated documentation on workers' struggles, see the website of the Students and Scholars against Corporate Misbehaviour, http://sacom.hk, and insightful analyses of the Chinese workers' life in *Made in China: A Quarterly on Chinese Labour, Civil Society, and Rights*, http://www.chinoiresie.info/madeinchina/.

25 The spur behind the order for military intervention at Tian'anmen Square in 1989, which came after the disbanding of the student movement, was the nascent formation of autonomous workers' organizations. For elements of analysis of the tragic episode, see Claudia Pozzana and Alessandro Russo, "China's New Order and Past Disorders: A Dialogue Starting from Wang Hui's Analyses," *Critical Asian Studies* 3 (2006): 329–51.

26 *Zhongguo Gongchandang zhangcheng* [Constitution of the Chinese Communist Party] (Beijing: Renmin chubanshe, 2017), 1.
27 I have proposed a larger discussion of the topic in "The Sixties and Us," in *The Idea of Communism 3: The Seoul Conference* (London: Verso, 2016), 137–78, and in "Mummifying the Working Class: The Cultural Revolution and the Fates of the Political Parties of the 20th Century," *China Quarterly* 227 (2016): 653–73.

BIBLIOGRAPHY

Althusser, Louis. "Ideology and State Ideological Apparatuses." In *"Lenin and Philosophy" and Other Essays*, translated by Ben Brewster, 123–73. London: New Left, 1971. Reprinted in *On Ideology*. London: Verso, 2008.
Althusser, Louis, and Etienne Balibar. *Lire le Capital*. Paris: Maspero, 1968.
Andreas, Joel. *The Rise of the Red Engineers: The Cultural Revolution and the Origins of China's New Class*. Stanford, CA: Stanford University Press, 2009.
Ansley, Clive M. *The Heresy of Wu Han: His Play "Hai Rui's Dismissal" and Its Role in China's Cultural Revolution*. Toronto: Toronto University Press, 1971.
Badiou, Alain. "Metaphysics and the Critique of Metaphysics," *Pli* 10 (2000): 174–90. Accessed April 2019. https://plijournal.com/files/Pli_10_9_Badiou.pdf.
Badiou, Alain. "The Cultural Revolution. The Last Revolution?". *positions* 13, no. 3 (2005): 481–514.
Badiou, Alain. *Logiques des mondes*. Paris: Seuil, 2006.
Badiou, Alain. *L'immanence des vérités*. Paris: Fayard, 2018.
Balazs, Étienne. "Théorie politique et réalité administrative dans la Chine traditionnelle." In *La bureaucratie céleste: Recherches sur l'économie et la société de la Chine traditionnelle*. Paris: Gallimard, 1968. English edition, *Chinese Civilization and Bureaucracy*. New Haven, CT: Yale University Press, 1967.
Bergère, Marie Claire. *La repubblica popolare cinese* [The People's Republic of China]. Bologna: Il Mulino, 2000. Original edition, *La république populaire de Chine de 1949 à nos jours*. Paris: Colin, 1989.
Bloch, Marc. *Apologie de l'histoire ou métier d'historien*. [1949]. Paris: Colin, 2018. English translation: *The Historian's Craft*. Manchester, UK: Manchester University Press, 1992.
Bonnin, Michel. *The Lost Generation: The Rustication of China's Educated Youth: 1968-1980*. Hong Kong: Chinese University of Hong Kong Press, 2013.

Bray, David. *Social Space and Governance in Urban China: The Danwei System from the Origins to Reform.* Stanford, CA: Stanford University Press, 2005.

Cartier, Michel. *Une réforme locale en Chine au XVI siècle: Hai Rui à Chun'an 1558-1562.* Paris: Mouton, 1972.

Cheek, Timothy. *Propaganda and Culture in Mao Zedong's China: Deng Tuo and the Intelligentsia.* Oxford: Clarendon, 1997.

De Bary, Theodore, and Richard Lufrano, eds. *Sources of Chinese Tradition.* New York: Columbia University Press, 2000.

Durkheim, Émile. *The Rules of Sociological Method.* Edited by Steven Lukes. New York: Free Press, [1895]. 1982.

Edmunds, Clifford. "The Politics of Historiography in Jian Bozan's Historicism." In *China's Intellectuals and the State: In Search of a New Relationship*, edited by Merle Goldman, Timothy Cheek, and Carol Lee Hamrin, 65-106. Cambridge, MA: Harvard University Press, 1987.

Fisher, Tom. "'The Play's the Thing': Wu Han and Hai Rui Revisited." In *Using the Past to Serve the Present*, edited by Jonathan Unger, 9-45. Armonk, NY: M. E. Sharpe, 1992.

Gao Mobo. *The Battle for China's Past: Mao and the Cultural Revolution.* London: Pluto, 2008.

Gao Mobo. *Constructing China: Clashing Views of the People's Republic.* London: Pluto, 2018.

Henderson, Gail E., and Myron S. Cohen. *The Chinese Hospital: A Socialist Work Unit.* New Haven, CT: Yale University Press, 1984.

Hinton, William. *Hundred Day War: The Cultural Revolution at Tsinghua University.* New York: Monthly Review, 1972.

Hong Yung Lee. *The Politics of the Chinese Cultural Revolution: A Case Study.* Berkeley: University of California Press, 1978.

Huan Kuan. *Discourses on Salt and Iron: A Debate on State Control of Commerce and Industry in Ancient China.* Translated by Esson McDowell Gale. Leyden: E. J. Brill, 1931.

Hunter, Neal. *Shanghai Journal.* New York: Praeger, 1969.

Hurst, William. *The Chinese Worker after Socialism.* New York: Cambridge University Press, 2009.

Jian Bozan et al. *A Concise History of China.* Beijing: Foreign Languages Press, 1964.

Jiang Hongsheng. *La Commune de Shanghai et la Commune de Paris.* Préface de Alain Badiou. Paris: La Fabrique, 2014.

Jiang Hongsheng. "The Paris Commune in Shanghai: The Masses, the State, and Dynamics of 'Continuous Revolution.'" PhD dissertation, Duke University, 2010. Accessed April 2018. https://dukespace.lib.duke.edu/dspace/bitstream/handle/10161/2356/D_Jiang_Hongsheng_a_201005.pdf.

Lenin, V. I. *"Left-Wing" Communism, an Infantile Disorder.* [1920]. Peking: Foreign Languages Press, 1970. Accessed June 2018. http://www.marx2mao.com/Lenin/LWC20.html.

Lenin, V. I. *State and Revolution.* [1917]. In *Collected Works*, vol. 25, 381-492. Moscow: Progress, 1964. https://www.marxists.org/archive/lenin/works/1917/staterev/.

Lenin, V. I. *What Is to Be Done?* [1902]. In *Collected Works*, vol. 5, 347-530. Moscow: Foreign Languages Publishing, 1961. https://www.marxists.org/archive/lenin/works/1901/witbd/.

MacFarquar, Roderick, and Michael Schoenals. *Mao's Last Revolution*. Cambridge, MA: Harvard University Press, 2006.

Malraux, André. *Antimemorie*. Milan: Bompiani, 1968.

Mao Zedong. *A Critique of Soviet Economics*. [1960]. New York: Monthly Review, 1977.

Mao Zedong. "Inquiry into the Peasant Movement in Hunan." [1927]. In *Selected Works*, vol. 1. Beijing: Foreign Languages Press, 1965.

Mao Zedong. *Inventare una scuola: Scritti giovanili sull'educazione*. Edited by Fabio Lanza and Alessandro Russo. Rome: Manifestolibri, 1996.

Mao Zedong. *Mao's Road to Power: Revolutionary Writings 1912-1949*. Edited by Stuart R. Schram. Armonk, NY: M. E. Sharpe, 1992.

Mao Zedong. "On the Correct Handling of Contradictions among the People." [1957]. https://www.marxists.org/reference/archive/mao/selected-works/volume-5/mswv5_58.htm.

Mao Zedong. "On the Ten Major Relationships." [1956]. https://www.marxists.org/reference/archive/mao/selected-works/volume-5/mswv5_51.htm.

Marx, Karl. *The Capital. A Critique of Political Economy*, vol. 1. [1867]. https://www.marxists.org/archive/marx/works/download/pdf/Capital-Volume-I.pdf.

Marx, Karl. *Critique of the Gotha Program*. [1875]. https://www.marxists.org/archive/marx/works/download/Marx_Critque_of_the_Gotha_Programme.pdf.

Mazur, Mary G. *Wu Han, Historian: Son of China's Times*. Plymouth, UK: Lexington, 2009.

Mittler, Barbara. "'Enjoying the Four Olds!' Oral Histories from a 'Cultural Desert.'" *Transcultural Studies* 1 (2013): 177-215.

Miyazaki, Ichisada. *China's Examination Hell: The Civil Service Examinations of Imperial China*. Translated by Conrad Schirokauer. New York: Weatherhill, 1976.

Myers, James T., Jurgen Domes, and Erik Von Groeling, eds. *Chinese Politics: Documents and Analysis*, vol. 1: *Cultural Revolution to 1969*. Columbia: University of South Carolina Press. 1986.

Pantsov, Alexander V., and Steven I. Levine. *Deng Xiaoping: A Revolutionary Life*. Oxford: Oxford University Press, 2015.

Perry, Elizabeth, and Li Xun. *Proletarian Power: Shanghai in the Cultural Revolution*. New York: Routledge, 1997.

Piazzaroli Longobardi, Andrea. "The Workers University in the Chinese Cultural Revolution," PhD thesis, São Paulo University and Bologna University, 2019. Accessed April 2019. www.teses.usp.br/teses/disponiveis/8/ . . . /2018_AndreaPiazzaroliLongobardi_VOrig.pdf.

Pozzana, Claudia. "Althusser and Mao: A Political Test for Dialectics." In *The Idea of Communism 3: The Seoul Conference,* ed. Alex Taek-Gwang Lee and Slavoj Žižek, 98-109. London: Verso, 2016.

Pozzana, Claudia, "Distances of Poetry: An Introduction to Bei Dao." *positions* 15 (2007): 91-111.

Pozzana, Claudia. *La poesia pensante: Inchieste sulla poesia cinese contemporanea*. Macerata, Italy: Quodlibet, 2010.

Pozzana, Claudia. "Spring, Temporality, and History in Li Dazhao." *positions* 3 (1995): 283–305.

Pozzana, Claudia, and Alessandro Russo. "China's New Order and Past Disorders: A Dialogue Starting from Wang Hui's Analyses." *Critical Asian Studies* 3 (2006): 329–51.

Pozzana, Claudia, and Alessandro Russo, eds. *Nuovi poeti cinesi*. Torino: Einaudi, 1996.

Pozzana, Claudia, and Alessandro Russo, eds. "Un'altra Cina: Poeti e narratori degli anni Novanta." *In forma di Parole* 19, no. 1 (1999).

Pun Ngai, and Jenny Chan. "Global Capital, the State, and Chinese Workers: The Foxconn Experience." *Modern China* 38 (2012): 383–410.

Pun Ngai, Jenny Chan, and Mark Selden. *Morire per un i-Phone*. Edited by Ferruccio Gambino and Devi Sacchetto. Milan: Jaca Book, 2015.

Pusey, James R. *Wu Han: Attacking the Present through the Past*. Cambridge, MA: Harvard University Press, 1969.

Robespierre, Maximilien. *Pour le bonheur et la liberté: Discours*. Paris: La Fabrique, 2000.

Rosen, Stanley. *Red Guard Factionalism and the Cultural Revolution in Guangzhou*. Boulder, CO: Westview, 1982.

Russo, Alessandro. "The Conclusive Scene: Mao and the Red Guards in July 1968." *positions* 13, no. 3 (2005): 535–74.

Russo, Alessandro. "Destinies of University." *Polygraph* 21 (2009): 41–75.

Russo, Alessandro. "Egalitarian Inventions and Political Symptoms: A Reassessment of Mao's Statements on the 'Probable Defeat.'" *Crisis and Critique* 3, no. 1 (2016): 259–78.

Russo, Alessandro. "Mummifying the Working Class: The Cultural Revolution and the Fates of the Political Parties of the 20th Century." *China Quarterly* 227 (2016): 653–73.

Russo, Alessandro. "Notes on the Critique of Revisionism: Lenin, Mao and Us." *Crisis and Critique* 4, no. 2 (2017): 362–75.

Russo, Alessandro. *Ouvrier et "danwei": Note de recherche sur une enquête d'anthropologie ouvrière menée à Canton en avril 1989*. Paris: Université de Paris, 1990.

Russo, Alessandro. "Parlomurs: A Dialogue on Corruption in Education." In *What Is Education?*, edited by Adam Bartlett and Justin Clemens, 185–238. Edinburgh: Edinburgh University Press, 2017.

Russo, Alessandro. "The Probable Defeat: Preliminary Notes on the Cultural Revolution." *positions* 6, no. 1 (1998): 179–202.

Russo, Alessandro. *Le rovine del mandato: La modernizzazione politica dell'educazione e della cultura cinesi*. Milan: Franco Angeli, 1985.

Russo, Alessandro. "Schools as Subjective Singularities: The Inventions of Schools in Durkheim's *L'évolution Pédagogique en France*. *Journal of Historical Sociology* 19, no. 3 (2006): 308–37.

Russo, Alessandro. "The Sixties and Us." In *The Idea of Communism 3: The Seoul Conference*, edited by Alex Taek-Gwang Lee and Slavoj Žižek, 137–78. London: Verso, 2016.

Saint-Just, Louis Antoine Léon de. *L'esprit de la révolution et de la constitution de la France.* [1791]. Paris: Editions 10/18, 2003.

Schram, Stuart, ed. *Mao Tse-tung Unrehearsed: Talks and Letters 1956-1971.* London: Penguin, 1974.

Schurmann, Franz. *Ideology and Organization in Communist China.* Berkeley: University of California Press, 1966.

Stalin, Joseph. *Dialectical and Historical Materialism.* [1938]. https://www.marxists.org/reference/archive/stalin/works/1938/09.htm.

Stalin, Joseph. "On the Draft Constitution of the U.S.S.R." Report Delivered at the Extraordinary Eighth Congress of Soviets of the U.S.S.R (November 25, 1936). https://www.marxists.org/reference/archive/stalin/works/1936/11/25.htm.

Teiwes, Fredrick, and Sun Warren. *The End of the Maoist Era: Chinese Politics during the Twilight of the Cultural Revolution, 1972-1976.* Armonk, NY: M. E. Sharpe, 2007.

Vogel, Ezra. *Deng Xiaoping and the Transformation of China.* Cambridge, MA: Belknap Press of Harvard University Press, 2011.

Vukovich, Daniel F. *China and Orientalism: Western Knowledge Production and the PRC.* London: Routledge, 2012.

Walder, Andrew G. *Agents of Disorder. Inside China's Cultural Revolution*, Cambridge, MA: Harvard University Press, 2019.

Walder, Andrew G. *Chang Ch'un-ch'iao and Shanghai's January Revolution.* Ann Arbor: Center for Chinese Studies, University of Michigan, 1978.

Walder, Andrew G. *Fractured Rebellion. The Beijing Red Guard Movement.* Cambridge, MA: Harvard University Press, 2009.

Walter, Georges. *Chine, An-81: Dispute sur le sel et le fer; un prodigieux document sur l'art de gouverner.* Paris: Seghers, 1978.

Wang Hui. *China's New Order.* Cambridge, MA: Harvard University Press, 2003.

Wang Peijie. *Revolutionary Committees in the Cultural Revolution Era of China.* London: Palgrave Macmillan, 2017.

Wang Weiguang. "The Great Victory of Marxism in China." *Social Sciences in China* 32, no. 4 (2011): 3-18.

Wang Xuedian. "Jian Bozan's Theoretical Contribution to China's Historical Science." *Social Sciences in China* 3 (1991): 144-62.

Weber, Max. "Politics as Vocation." [1919]. In *Weber's Rationalism and Modern Society*, translated and edited by Tony Waters and Dagmar Waters. New York: Palgrave Macmillan, 2015.

White, Lynn T., III. "The Cultural Revolution as an Unintended Result of Administrative Policies." In *New Perspectives on the Cultural Revolution*, edited by Joseph C. W. Wong and David Zweig, 83-104. Cambridge, MA: Harvard University Press, 1989.

White, Lynn T., III. *Policies of Chaos: The Organizational Causes of Violence in China's Cultural Revolution.* Princeton, NJ: Princeton University Press, 1989.

Wu Yiching. *The Cultural Revolution at the Margins: Chinese Socialism in Crisis.* Cambridge, MA: Harvard University Press, 2014.

Yang Guobin. *The Red Guard Generation and Political Activism in China*. New York: Columbia University Press, 2016.

Yang Rae. *Spider Eaters*. Berkeley: University of California Press, 1997.

Works in Chinese

薄一波 Bo Yibo. 若干重大决策与事件的回顾 *Ruogan zhongda juece yu shijian de huigu* [A retrospective on some important political decisions and events]. Beijing: Yinshua gongye chubanshe, 1997.

蔡成和 Cai Chenghe. 怎样更好地评价历史人物和历史剧—评《评新编历史剧〈海瑞罢官〉》"Zenyang genghao de pingjia lishi renwu he lishiju—ping 'Ping xinbian lishiju "Hai Rui ba guan"'" [How to better evaluate historical personages and historical plays: Criticism of the "Criticism of the historical drama recently composed *Hai Rui Dismissed from Office*"]. *Wenhui bao*, December 1, 1965, 4.

蔡美彪 Cai Meibiao. 在论中国农民战争史的几个问题 "Zai lun Zongguo nongmin zhanzheng shi de jige wenti" [More on some questions of the history of peasant wars in China]. *Xin jianshe* 11 (1962): 32–41.

蔡尚思 Cai Shangsi. 这是什么样的"自我批评" "Zheshi shenmeyang de 'ziwo piping'" [What self-criticism is this?]. *Wenhui bao*, January 25, 1966, 4.

巢峰 Chao Feng, ed. "文化大革命"词典 *"Wenhua da geming" cidian* [A dictionary of the "Great Cultural Revolution"]. Xianggang: Ganglong chubanshe, 1993.

陈伯达 Chen Boda. 在上海安亭火车站的工人的电报 "Zai Shanghai Anting huochezhan de gongren dianbao" [Chen Boda's telegram to Shanghai workers in Anting train station]. In 陈伯达言论集 *Chen Boda yanlunji* [Chen Boda speeches and remarks], vol. 1, 214. Beijing: Utopia Bookstore, n.d.

澄宇 Cheng Yu. 《海瑞罢官》为谁唱赞歌？"'Hai Rui ba guan' wei shui chang zange?" [For whom does *Hai Rui Dismissed from Office* sing?]. *Beijing ribao*, January 18, 1966, 3.

程中原 Cheng Zhongyuan and 夏杏珍 Xia Xingzhen. 历史转折的前奏. 邓小平在一九七五 历史转折的前奏. 邓小平在一九七五 *Lishi zhuanzhe de qianzou: Deng Xiaoping zai yijiuqiwu* [The prelude to the historical turning point: Deng Xiaoping in 1975]. Beijing: Qingnian chubanshe, 2004.

戴不凡 Dai Bufan. 《海瑞罢官》的主题思想 "'Hai Rui ba guan' de zhuti sixiang" [The main theme of *Hai Rui Dismissed from Office*]. *Wenhui bao*, December 28, 1965, 4.

邓小平 Deng Xiaoping 文选 *Wenxuan 1975-1982* [Selected works, 1975-1982]. Beijing: Renmin chubanshe, 1983.

邓小平 Deng Xiaoping. 军队要整顿 "Jundui yao zhengdun" [The army must be put in order] (January 25, 1975). In 邓小平文选 *Deng Xiaoping wenxuan 1975-1982* [Selected works of Deng Xiaoping, 1975-1982]. Beijing: Renmin chubanshe, 1983, 1–3.

邓小平 Deng Xiaoping. 全党讲大局, 把国民经济搞上去 "Quandang jiang daju, ba guomin jingji gao shan qu" [The whole party must take into consideration the overall situation and raise the national economy]. May 3, 1975. In *Deng Xiaoping wenxuan*, 4–7.

邓小平 Deng Xiaoping. 当前钢铁工业必须解决的几个问题 "Dangqian gantie gongye bixu jiejuede jige wenti" [Some present problems to solve in the iron and steel industry]. May 29, 1975. In *Deng Xiaoping wenxuan*, 8–11.

邓小平 Deng Xiaoping. 各方面都要整顿 "Ge fangmian dou yao zhengdun" [Everything must be put in order in every field]. September 27–October 4, 1975. In 邓小平文选 *Deng Xiaoping wenxuan*, 32–34.

邓小平 Deng Xiaoping. 对起草 "关于建国以来党的若干历史的决议的意见" "Dui qicao 'Guanyu jianguo yilai dang de ruogan lishi de jueyi' de yijian" [Opinions on the successive drafts of the "Resolution on some issues of the history of our party from the foundation of the RPC"]. March 1980–June 1981. *Deng Xiaoping wenxuan*, 255–74.

丁望主编 Ding Wang, ed. 吴晗与《海瑞罢官》事件 *Wu Han yu "Hai Rui ba guan" shijian* [Wu Han and the Affair of *Hai Rui Dismissed from Office*]. In 中共文化大革命资料汇编, 第四卷 *Zhonggong wenhua da geming ziliao huibian, disi juan* [Collected materials on the Great Cultural Revolution of the Chinese Communist Party, vol. 4]. Xianggang: Mingbao yuekan she, 1968.

范民声 Fan Minsheng, 盛郁 Sheng Yu, and 马圣贵 Ma Shenggui. 上海戏剧学院三位同志的来信 "Shanghai xiju xueyuan sanwei tongzhi de laixin" [Letter from three comrades of the Shanghai Institute of Theater]. *Wenhui bao*, November 29, 1965, 2.

方克立 Fang Keli. 《海瑞罢官》歪曲了历史真实 "'Hai Rui ba guan' waiqu le lishi zhenshi" [*Hai Rui Dismissed from Office* distorts historical reality]. *Beijing ribao*, December 16, 1965, 2.

方求 Fang Qiu. 《海瑞罢官》代表一种什么社会思潮？ "'Hai Rui ba guan' daibiao yizhong shenme shehui sichao?" [Which kind of social current of thought does *Hai Rui Dismissed from Office* represent?] *Renmin ribao*, December 29, 1965, 7.

逄先知 Feng Xianzhi and 金冲及 Jin Chongji, eds. 毛泽东传 *Mao Zedong zhuan, 1949-1976* [Biography of Mao Zedong, 1949-1976]. Beijing: Zhongyang wenxian chubanshe, 2003.

高皋 Gao Gao and 严家其 Yan Jiaqi. "文化大革命"十年史 *"Wen hua da geming" shi nian shi* [History of ten years of the "Great Cultural Revolution"]. Tianjin: Tianjin renmin chubanshe, 1986.

戈锋 Ge Feng. 《论海瑞》的错误仅仅是思想方法上的片面性吗？ "'Lun Hai Rui' de cuowu jinjin shi sixiang fangfa shang de pianmianxing ma?" [Are the errors of "On Hai Rui" only a one-sided ideological method?] *Beijing ribao*, December 31, 1965, 3.

关锋 Guan Feng and 林杰 Lin Jie. 《海瑞骂皇帝》和《海瑞罢官》是反党反社会主义的两株大毒草 "'Hai Rui ma huangdi' he 'Hai Rui ba guan' shi fandang fan shehuizhuyi de liangzhu da ducao" ["Hai Rui scolds the emperor" and *Hai Rui dismissed from Office* are two antiparty and antisocialist poisonous weeds]. *Renmin ribao*, April 5, 1966, 5.

广州学术界对《海瑞罢官》的一些看法 "Guangzhou xueshu jie dui *Hai Rui ba guan* de yixie kanfa" [Some opinions on *Hai Rui Dismissed from Office* in Guangzhou academic circles]. *Yangcheng Wanbao* [Yangcheng Evening News], January 15, 1966. English translation in *Chinese Studies in History and Philosophy* 2, no. 3 (1968): 11–19.

郭庠林 Guo Xianglin and 陈绍闻 Chen Shaowen. 《海瑞罢官》为谁服务 "*Hai Rui ba guan* wei shui fuwu?" [*Hai Rui Dismissed from Office* is at the service of whom?] *Wenhui bao*, December 23, 1965, 4.

国务院政治研究室 Guowuyuan zhengzhi yanjiu shi [State Council Political Research Office]. 论全党全国各项工作的总纲 "Lun quandang quanguo ge xiang gongzuo de zonggang," October 7, 1975. Reprinted in 中国人民解放军, 国防大学, 党史政工教研室 Zhongguo renmin jiefangjun, Guofang daxue, Dangshi zhenggong jiaoyanshi. [Chinese People's Liberation Army, National Defense University, Political Work on Party History, Teaching and Research Office] "文化大革命"研究资料 *"Wenhua da geming" yanjiu ziliao* [Research materials on the "Great Cultural Revolution"] 2 (1988): 507-17.

韩国劲 Han Guojin and 周胜昌 Zhou Shengchang. 海瑞"清官"生活真相 "Hai Rui 'qingguan' shenghuo zhenxiang" [The real facts of life of Hai Rui "honest official"]. *Wenhui bao*, February 1, 1966, 4.

郝昺衡 Hao Bingheng. 试论海瑞和《海瑞罢官》 "Shilun Hai Rui he 'Hai Rui ba guan'" [Examine Hai Rui and *Hai Rui Dismissed from Office*]. *Wenhui bao*, December 20, 1965, 4.

红旗评论员 "Hongqi" pinglunyuan [Hongqi commentator]. 无产阶级革命派联合起来 "Wuchanjieji gemingpai liaheqilai" [Proletarian revolutionaries, unite!]. *Hongqi* 2 (1967). Reprinted in *Renmin ribao*, January 16, 1967.

胡长明 Hu Changming. 毛泽东：《明史》是我看了最生气 "Mao Zedong: 'Ming shi' shi wo kanle zui shengqi" [Mao Zedong: "The 'History of the Ming' is what most irritates me"]. Accessed September 12, 2016. http://news.xinhuanet.com/politics/2008-06/01/content_8292979_1.htm.

胡钧 Hu Shoujun. 《海瑞罢官》为封建王法唱颂歌 "'Hai Rui ba guan' wei fengjian wangfa chang songge" [*Hai Rui Dismissed from Office* is a hymn to feudal law]. *Wenhui bao*, December 17, 1965, 4.

华山 Hua Shan. 论肯定与赞扬 "Lun kending yu zanyang" [On positively assessing and praising]. *Wenhui bao*, January 11, 1966, 4.

华山 Hua Shan. 为什么要肯定"清官"、"好官"？ "Weishenme yao kending 'qingguan,' 'haoguan'?" [Why we must positively assess the honest officials and the good officials?] *Wenhui bao*, January 7, 1966, 4.

黄喜蔚 Huang Xiwei. 这是阶级的分歧 "Zhe shi jieji de fenqi" [This is a class divergence]. *Wenhui bao*, January 18, 1966, 4.

计红绪 Ji Hongxu. 要以阶级观点看待"清官" "Yao yi jieji guandian kandai 'qingguan'" [We must look at the honest officials from the class viewpoint. *Wenhui bao*, January 28, 1966, 4.

翦伯赞 Jian Bozan. 历史问题论丛 *Lishi wenti luncong* [Collected discussions on historical problems]. Beijing: Renmin chubanshe, 1962.

翦伯赞 Jian Bozan. 对处理若干历史问题的初步意见 "Dui chuli ruogan lishi wenti de chubu yijian" [Preliminary opinions on how to deal with some historical problems]. *Guangming ribao*, December 22, 1963.

翦伯赞 Jian Bozan. 论中国古代的农民战争 "Lun Zhongguo gudai de nongmin zhangzheng" [On the peasant wars in Chinese antiquity]. In 翦伯赞历史论文选集 *Jian Bozan lishi lunwen xuanji* [Jian Bozan's selected historical essays]. Beijing, Renmin chubanshe, 1980.

翦伯赞 Jian Bozan. 历史论文选集 *Lishi lunwen xuanji* [Selected historical essays]. Beijing: Renmin chubanshe, 1980.

江青、王任重、康生对北京中学生的讲话 "Jiang Qing, Wang Renzhong, Kang Sheng dui Beijing zhongxuesheng de jiang hua" [Speeches by Jiang Qing, Wang Renzhong, and Kang Sheng to junior high school students in Beijing], August 6, 1966]. Reproduced in 江青文稿 *Jiang Qing wengao* [Texts by Jiang Qing], vol. 1, 387-94. Beijing: Utopia Bookshop, 2007.

金大陆 Jin Dalu. 非常与正常，上海文革时期的社会生活 *Feichang yu zhengchang: Shanghai wenge shiqi de shehui shenghuo* [Abnormal and normal: Social life in Shanghai during the Cultural Revolution]. Shanghai: Cishu chubanshe, 2008.

景池 Jing Chi 商品自述 "Shangpin zishu" [Autobiography of the Commodity]. 学习与批判 *Xuexi yu pipan* 5 (1975): 19-24 (with sequels in the issues 6: 22-26 and 7: 15-27).

康健 Kang Jian. 关于"让步政策"的浅见 "Guanyu 'rangbu zhengce' de qianjian" [A modest opinion on the "policies of concessions"]. *Wenhui bao*, December 18, 1965, 4.

李传勇 Li Chuanyong and 马鸿生 Ma Hongsheng. 海瑞推动了历史前进 "Hai Rui tuidong le lishi qianjin" [Hai Rui has promoted historical progress]. 文汇报 *Wenhui bao*, December 28, 1965, 4.

李东石 Li Dongshi. 评吴晗同志的历史观 "Ping Wu Han tongzhi de lishiguan" [Discussing Comrade Wu Han's vision of history]. *Beijing ribao*, January 8, 1966, 3.

李华 Li Hua and 实夫 Shi Fu. 海瑞有值得学习的地方 "Hai Rui you zhide xuexi de difang" [There are aspects of Hai Rui that deserve to be studied]. 文汇报 *Wenhui bao*, December 23, 1965, 4.

李锐 Li Rui. 毛泽东早期革命活动 *Mao Zedong zaoqi geming huodong*. Changsha: Hunan jiaoyu chubanshe 1983. English translation: Li Jui. *The Early Revolutionary Activities of Comrade Mao Tse-tung*. White Plains, NY: M. E. Sharpe, 1977.

李锐 Li Rui. 庐山会议实录 *Lushan huiyi shilu* [The authentic record of the Lushan Conference]. 长沙 Changsha: Hunan jiaoyu chubanshe, 1989 (enlarged edition, 郑州 Zhengzhou: Henan renmin chubanshe, 1999).

李逊 Li Xun. 革命造反年代．上海文革运动史稿 *Geming zaofan niandai: Shanghai wenge yundong shigao* [The age of revolutionary rebellion: A history of the Cultural Revolution movement in Shanghai]. Hong Kong: Oxford University Press, 2015.

李振宇 Li Zhenyu. 海瑞罢官是一出较好的历史剧 "*Hai Rui ba guan* shi yi chu jiao hao de lishi ju" [*Hai Rui Dismissed from Office* is a relatively good historical play]. *Beijing ribao*, December 9, 1966, 3.

林彪 Lin Biao. 在扩大工作会议上的讲话 "Zai kuoda gongzuo huiyi shang de jianghua" [Speech at an enlarged working session of the Politburo] (May 18, 1966). In 中国文化大革命文库 *Zhongguo wenhua dageming wenku* [Chinese Cultural Revolution Database, part 3]. Xianggang: Zhongwen daxue, 2002.

林丙义 Lin Bingyi. 海瑞与《海瑞罢官》"Hai Rui yu 'Hai Rui ba guan'" [Hai Rui and *Hai Rui Dismissed from Office*]. *Wenhui bao*, December 3, 1965, 4.

林杰 Lin Jie. 用什么观点和方法研究农民战争 "Yong shenme guandian he fangfa yanjiu nongmin zhanzheng" [From which viewpoint and with which method to study peasants' wars]. *Xin Jianshe* 4 (1964): 40-51.

刘大杰 Liu Dajie. 《海瑞罢官》的本质 "'*Hai Rui ba guan*' de benzhi" [The essence of *Hai Rui Dismissed from Office*]. *Wenhui bao*, December 23, 1965, 4.

刘少奇 Liu Shaoqi. 论共产党员修养 *Lun gonchandagyuan xiuyang* [On the cultivation of a member of the Communist Party]. 1939. https://www.marxists.org/chinese

/liushaoqi/1967/035.htm. English translation, *How to Be a Good Communist*. Beijing: Foreign Languages Press. https://www.marxists.org/reference/archive/liu-shaoqi/1939/how-to-be/index.htm.

刘武生 Liu Wusheng. 周恩来的晚年岁月 *Zhou Enlai de wannian suiyue* [Zhou Enlai: The late years]. Beijing: Renmin chubanshe, 2006.

刘序琦 Liu Xuqi. 给海瑞以公正的评价 "Gei Hai Rui yi gong zheng de pingjia" [Give a fair assessment of Hai Rui]. 文汇报 *Wenhui bao*, February 4, 1966, 4.

刘元高 Liu Yuangao. 《海瑞罢官》必须批判 "'Hai Rui ba guan' bixu pipan" [*Hai Rui Dismissed from Office* should be criticized]. *Wenhui bao,* December 15, 1965, 4.

路风 Lu Feng. 单位，一种特殊的社会组织形式 "Danwei: Yizhong teshude shehui zuzhi xingshi" [Danwei: A special form of social organization]. 中国社会科学 *Zhongguo shehui kexue* 1 (1989): 3-18.

陆嘉亮 Lu Jialiang and 倪墨炎 Ni Moyan. 中华书局上海编辑所两位同志的来信 "Zhonghua shuju Shanghai bianjisuo liangwei tongzhi de laixin" [Letter from two comrades of the Shanghai Editorial Board of Zhonghua Book Company]. *Wenhui bao,* November 29, 1965.

罗思鼎 Luo Siding. 拆穿"退田"的西洋镜 "Chaichuan 'tuitian' de xiyangjing" [Reveal the deception of the "return of land"]. *Wenhui bao*, February 8, 1966, 4.

马捷 Ma Jie. 也谈《海瑞罢官》"Ye tan 'Hai Rui ba guan'" [More on *Hai Rui Dismissed from Office*]. *Wenhui bao*, November 30, 1965, 4.

马彦文 Ma Yanwen. 马克思主义的重大发展。学习毛主席重要指示的一点体会 "Makesizhuyi de zhongda fazhan. Xuexi Mao Zhuxi zhongyao zhishi yi dian tihui" [Major development of Marxism. Some experience of studying Chairman Mao's important instructions]. In 北京大学学报 *Beijing daxue xuebao* 2 (1976): 23-29 (with two sequels in issue 3: 15-21, 22-29).

马泽民 Ma Zemin and 王锐生 Wang Ruisheng. 《海瑞》是吴晗同志反党反社会主义的政治工具 "'Hai Rui' shi Wu Han tongzhi fan dang fan shehuizhuyi zhengzhi gongju" ["Hai Rui" is an antiparty and antisocialist political tool of Comrade Wu Han]. *Guangming ribao*, January 29, 1966, 3.

毛毛 [邓榕] Mao Mao [Deng Rong]. 我的父亲邓小平. "文革"岁月 *Wo de fuqin Deng Xiaoping: "Wen'ge" suiye* [Deng Xiaoping, my father: The years of the "Cultural Revolution"]. Beijing: Zhongyang wenxian chubanshe, 2000.

毛泽东 Mao Zedong. 早期文稿 *Zaoqi wengao* [Early manuscripts]. Changsha: Hunan chubanshe, 1990. English version: Stuart R. Schram, ed., *Mao's Road to Power: Revolutionary Writings 1912-1949*, vol. 1. Armonk, NY: M. E. Sharpe, 1992.

毛泽东 Mao Zedong. 建国以来毛泽东文稿 *Jianguo yilai Mao Zedong Wengao* [Mao's manuscripts after 1949], 13 volumes. Beijing: Zhongyang wenxian chubanshe, 1987-1998.

毛泽东 Mao Zedong. 对'关于无产阶级专政的历史经验'稿的批语和修改, 1956 年, 4月, 2 日, 4 日 "Dui 'Guanyu wuchanjieji zhuanzheng de lishi jingyan' gao de piyu he xiugai" [Comments on and revisions to the draft of "On the historical experience of the dictatorship of the proletariat," April 2-4, 1956]. In *Jianguo yilai Mao Zedong wengao*, vol. 6: 59-67. Beijing: Wenxian chubanshe, 1992.

毛泽东 Mao Zedong. 庐山会议讨论问题 "Lushan huiyi taolun wenti" [Problems to discuss at the Conference of Lushan] [1959]. *Jianguo yilai Mao Zedong wengao*, vol. 8: 331-33. Beijing: Zhongyang wenxian chubanshe, 1993.

毛泽东 Mao Zedong. 苏联 "政治经济学" 读书笔记 "Sulian 'zhengzhi jingjixue' dushu biji" [Reading notes on the Soviet "Manual of Political Economy"] [1960]. In *Mao Zedong sixiang wansui*, 337-40. Beijing: n.p., 1969.

毛泽东 Mao Zedong. 在扩大的中央工作会议的讲话 "Zai kuoda zhongyang gongzuo huiyi de jianghua" [Speech at the Enlarged Working Conference], January 30, 1962. In 毛泽东思想万岁 *Mao Zedong sixiang wansui*, 399-423. Beijing: n.p., 1969.

毛泽东 Mao Zedong. 在八届十中全会上的讲话 "Zai ba jie shi zhongquanhui shang de jianghua" [Speech at the Tenth Plenary Session of the Eighth Congress], September 24, 1962. In *Mao Zedong sixiang wansui*, 430-36. Beijing: n.p., 1969.

毛泽东 Mao Zedong. 谈谦虚戒骄 "Tan qianxu jiejiao" [Being modest and watchful against arrogance], December 13, 1963. In *Mao Zedong sixiang wansui*, 446-54. Beijing: n.p., 1969.

毛泽东 Mao Zedong. 关于哲学问题的讲话 "Guanyu zhexue wenti de jianghua" [Speech on philosophical problems], August 18, 1964. In *Mao Zedong sixiang wansui*, 548-61. Beijing: n.p., 1969.

毛泽东 Mao Zedong. 在杭州的会议上的讲话 "Zai Hangzhou de huiyi shang de jianghua" [Talk at the Hangzhou Meeting], December 21, 1965. In 资料选编 *Ziliao Xuanbian* [Collection of materials], 318-21 n.p., February 1967.

毛泽东 Mao Zedong. 在政治局扩大会议上的讲话 "Zai zhengzhiju kuoda huiyi shang de jianghua" [Speeches to the Enlarged Meeting of the Political Bureau], March 17 and 20, 1966. In *Mao Zedong sixiang wansui*, 634-40. Beijing: n.p., 1969.

毛泽东 Mao Zedong. 打到阎王, 解放小鬼与康生同志的谈话 "Dadao yanwang, jiefang xiaogui: Yu Kang Sheng tongzhi de tanhua" [Down with the King of Hell, set free the imps: A conversation with Comrade Kang Sheng], April 1966. In *Mao Zedong sixiang wansui*, 640-41. Beijing: n.p., 1969.

毛泽东 Mao Zedong. 批判彭真 "Pipan Peng Zhen" [Criticizing Peng Zhen], April 1966. In 毛泽东思想万岁 *Mao Zedong sixiang wansui*, 641-42. Beijing: n.p., 1969.

毛泽东 Mao Zedong. 对阿尔巴尼亚军事代表团的讲话 "Dui Aerbanya Daibiaotuan de jianghua" [Speech to an Albanian military delegation], May 1, 1966. In *Mao Zedong sixiang wansui*, 673-79. Beijing: n.p., 1969.

毛泽东 Mao Zedong. 炮打司令部. 我的一张大字报 "Paoda silingbu: Wode yi zhang dazibao" [Bombard the General Headquarters. My dazibao], August 5, 1966. In *Jianguo yilai Mao Zedong wengao*, vol. 12, 90-92. Beijing: Zhongyang wenxian chubanshe, 1993.

毛泽东 Mao Zedong. 给江青的信 "Gei Jiang Qing de xin" [Letter to Jiang Qing], July 8, 1966. In *Jianguo yilai Mao Zedong wengao*, vol. 12, 71-75. Beijing: Zhongyang wenxian chubanshe, 1993.

毛泽东 Mao Zedong. 和卡博, 巴庐库同志的谈话 "He Kabo, Baluku tongzhi de tanhua" [Conversation with the Comrades Kabo and Baluku], February 3, 1967. In *Mao Zedong sixiang wansui*, 663-67. Beijing: n.p., 1969.

毛泽东 Mao Zedong. 对上海文化大革命的指示 "Dui Shanghai wenhua da geming de zhishi" [Directives on the Cultural Revolution in Shanghai], February 1967. In *Mao Zedong sixiang wansui*, 667–72. Beijing: n.p., 1969.

毛泽东 Mao Zedong. 召见首都红代会负责人的谈话 "Zhaojian shoudu hong dai hui fuzeren de tanhua" [Talk with the responsible persons of the Conference of the Red Guards of the Capital], July 28, 1968. In *Mao Zedong sixiang wansui*, 687–716. Beijing: n.p., 1969.

毛泽东 Mao Zedong. 毛主席关于制止武斗问题的指示精神要点 "Mao zhuxi guanyu zhizhi wudou wenti de zhishi jingshen yaodian" [Basic points of the directives of Chairman Mao on the cessation of the armed struggle], July 28, 1968. In *"Wenhua da geming" yanjiu ziliao* [Material for the study of the "Great Cultural Revolution"], vol. 2, 153–54. Beijing: Guofang Daxue, 1988.

毛泽东 Mao Zedong. 关于理论问题的谈话要点, 1974年, 12月 "Guanyu lilun wenti de tanhua yaodian, 1974 nian, 12 yue" [Main points of the talk on the theoretical problems, December 1974]. In *Jianguo yilai Mao Zedong wengao*, vol. 13, 413–15. Beijing: 中央文献出版社 Zhongyang wenxian chubanshe, 1998.

毛泽东 Mao Zedong. 毛主席重要指示 "Mao zhuxi zhongyao zhishi 1975–76" [Important directives of Chairman Mao, 1975–76]. In *Jianguo yilai Mao Zedong wengao* [Manuscripts of Mao Zedong after 1949], vol. 13, 486. Beijing: Wenxian chubanshe, 1998.

聂元梓 Nie Yuanzi. 回忆录 *Huiyilu* [Memoirs]. Hong Kong: Time International, 2005.

牛子明 Niu Ziming. 哪个阶级的立场？ "Nage jieji de lichang?" [Which class position?]. *Wenhui bao*, January 28, 1966, 4.

彭德怀 Peng Dehuai. 自述 *Zishu* [Autobiography]. Beijing: Renmin chubanshe, 1981.

平实 Ping Shi. 谈《海瑞罢官》中人物的阶级关系—与姚文元等同志商榷 "Tan 'Hai Rui ba Guan' zhong renwu de jieji guanxi—yu Yao Wenyuan deng tongzhi shangque" [On the class relationships among the characters of *Hai Rui Dismissed from Office*: A discussion with Comrade Yao Wenyuan and others]. *Beijing ribao*, December 31, 1965, 3.

戚本禹 Qi Benyu. 为革命而研究历史 "Wei geming er yanjiu lishi" [Studying history for the revolution]. 红旗 *Hongqi* 13 (1965): 14–22.

戚本禹 Qi Benyu, 林杰 Lin Jie, and 阎长贵 Yan Changgui. 翦伯赞同志的历史观点应当批判 "Jian Bozan tongzhi de lishi guandian yingdang pipan" [Comrade Jian Bozan's conception of history is to be criticized]. *Renmin ribao*, March 25, 1966.

戚本禹 Qi Benyu. 《海瑞骂皇帝》和《海瑞罢官》的反动实质 "'Hai Rui ma Huangdi' he 'Hai Rui ba guan' de fandong shizhi" [The reactionary nature of "Hai Rui scolds the emperor" and *Hai Rui Dismissed from Office*]. *Renmin ribao*, April 2, 1966, 5.

戚本禹 Qi Benyu. 回忆录 *Huiyilu* [Memoirs]. 2016. Accessed April 2019. https://www.marxists.org/chinese/reference-books/qibenyu/3-06.htm.

樵子 Qiao Zi. 也谈海瑞和《海瑞罢官》"Yetan Hai Rui he 'Hai Rui ba guan'" [More about Hai Rui and *Hai Rui Dismissed from Office*]. *Renmin ribao*, December 1965, 5.

瞿林东 Qu Lindong and 冯祖贻 Feng Zuyi. 阶级斗争的事实是抹煞不了的——评吴晗同志关于海瑞"退田"的辩解 "Jieji douzheng de shishi shi mosha buliao de—Ping Wu Han tongzhi guanyu HaiRui 'tuitian' de bianjie" [The reality of the class struggle cannot be obliterated: Discussing the explanation of Wu Han about "surrendering land"]. *Beijing ribao*, January 26, 1966, 3.

人民日报编者 Renmin ribao bianzhe [*People's Daily* editorial board]. 关于《海瑞罢官》问题各种意见的简介 "Guanyu 'Hai Rui ba guan' wenti gezhong yijian de jianjie" [A summary of views on *Hai Rui Dismissed from Office*]. *Renmin ribao*, December 15, 1965, 5.

人民日报社论 Renmin ribao shelun [*People's Daily* editorial]. 横扫一切牛鬼蛇神 "Hengsao yiqie niugui sheshen" [Destroy all ox-ghosts and snake demons]. *Renmin ribao*, June 1, 1966.

人民日报社论 Renmin ribao shelun [*People's Daily* editorial]. 学习十六条, 熟悉十六条, 运用十六条 "Xuexi shiliu tiao, shuxi shiliu tiao, yunyong shiliu tiao" [Study the 16 Articles, get familiar with the 16 Articles, use the 16 Articles]. *Renmin ribao*, August 13, 1966.

人民日报社论 Renmin ribao shelun [*People's Daily* editorial]. 无产阶级革命派大联合, 夺走资本主义道路当权派的权 "Wuchanjieji gemingpai da lianhe, duo zou zibenzhuyi daolu dangquanpai de quan" [Proletarian revolutionaries form a great alliance to seize power from those in authority who are taking the capitalist road]. *Renmin ribao*, January 22, 1967.

人民日报社论 Renmin ribao shelun [*People's Daily* editorial]. 论无产阶级革命派的夺权斗争 "Lun wuchanjijeji gemingpai de duoquan douzheng" [On the Proletarian Revolutionaries' Struggle for Power], *Hongqi* 3 (1967). *Renmin ribao*, January 31, 1967.

人民日报, 红旗杂志编者 Renmin ribao, Hongqi zazhi bianzhe [Editorial Board of *People's Daily* and *Red Flag*]. 马克思, 恩格斯, 列宁, 论无产阶级专政 "Makesi, Engesi, Liening lun wuchanjieji zhuanzheng" [Marx, Engels, and Lenin on the dictatorship of the proletariat]. *Hongqi* 3 (1975): 3–19.

人民日报社论 Renmin ribao shelun [*People's Daily* editorial]. 学好无产阶级专政的理论 "Xuehao wuchanjieji zhuanzheng de lilun" [Carefully study the theory of the dictatorship of the proletariat]. *Renmin ribao*, February 9, 1975, 1.

商鸿逵 Shang Hongkui. 由假海瑞谈到真海瑞 "You jia Hai Rui tandao zhen Hai Rui" [From the false Hai Rui let's talk about the real Hai Rui]. *Wenhui bao*, January 11, 1966, 4.

上海学术界部分人士座谈吴晗的《关于〈海瑞罢官〉的自我批评》 "Shanghai xueshujie bufen renshi zuotan Wu Han de 'Guanyu' Hai Rui ba guan 'de ziwo piping'" [A discussion among some members of Shanghai academic circles on Wu Han's "Self-criticism of *Hai Rui Dismissed from Office*"]. *Wenhui bao*, January 7, 1966, 4. English translation in *Chinese Studies in History and Philosophy* 2, no. 3 (1968): 42–59.

沈志 Shen Zhi. 对海瑞应当又批判又肯定 "Dui Hai Rui yingdang you pipan you kending" [We must both criticize and positively assess Hai Rui]. *Wenhu bao*, January 14, 1966, 4.

师东兵, Shi Dongbing 最初的抗争. 彭真在"文化大革命" 前夕 Zui chu de kangzheng. "Peng Zhen zai 'wen hua da geming' qianxi" [The Earliest Resistance: Peng Zhen on the Eve of the "Great Cultural Revolution"]. Beijing: 中共中央党校出版社 Zhonggong zhongyang dangxiao chubanshe, 1993.

师文伍 Shi Wenwu. 用封建"王法"掩盖了阶级矛盾 "Yong fengjian 'wangfa' yangai le jieji maodun" [Cover class contradictions with "imperial law"]. *Renmin ribao*, December 25, 1965, 5.

史军 Shi Jun. 颠倒了历史的《海瑞罢官》 "Diandao le lishi de 'Hai Rui ba guan'" [*Hai Rui Dismissed from Office* turns history upside down]. *Renmin ribao*, January 19, 1966, 5.

史绍宾 Shi Shaobin. 评《关于〈海瑞罢官〉的自我批评》的几个问题 "Ping 'Guanyu *Hai Rui ba guan* de ziwo piping' de jige wenti" [Comment on some problems of Wu Han's "Self-criticism on *Hai Rui Dismissed from Office*"]. *Guangming ribao*, January 9, 1966. English translation in *Chinese Studies in History and Philosophy* 2, no. 3 (1968): 32–41.

史文群整理 Shi Wenqun, ed. 武汉学术界展开《海瑞罢官》的讨论 "Wuhan xueshujie zhankai *Hai Rui ba guan* de taolun" [Wuhan academic circles open a discussion on *Hai Rui Dismissed from Office*]. In *Yangcheng Wanbao* [Yangcheng Evening News], January 15, 1966. English translation in *Chinese Studies in History and Philosophy* 2, no. 3 (1968): 4–10.

史哲 Shi Zhe. 告状难道是农民革命斗争吗 "Gaozhuang nandao shi nongmin geming douzheng ma?" [Were the complaints really the revolutionary struggle of peasants?] *Wenhui bao*, January 18, 1966, 4.

思彤 Si Tong. 接受吴晗同志的挑战 "Jieshou Wu Han tongzhi de tiaozhan" [To accept the challenge of comrade Wu Han]. *Renmin ribao*, January 13, 1966, 5.

孙达人 Sun Daren. 应该怎样估价"让步政策" "Yinggai zenyang gujia 'rangbu zhengce'" [How is the "politics of concessions" to be evaluated?]. 光明日报 *Guangming ribao*, September 22, 1965, 4.

孙柞 Sun Zuomin. 在中国农民战争史研究中运用历史主义和阶级观点 "Zai zhongguo nongmin zhanzheng shi yanjiu yunyong lishizhuyi he jieji guandian" [Historicism and the point of view of class in the study of the history of peasants' wars in China]. *Renmin ribao*, February 27, 1964, 3.

谭慧中 Tan Huizhong. "让步政策"保存了农民战争的胜利果实吗？—与严北溟同志商榷 "'Rangbu zhengce' baocun le nongmin zhanzheng de shengli guoshi ma?—Yu Yan Beiming tongzhi shangque" [Did the "policy of concessions" retain the victorious result of the peasant wars? A discussion with Comrade Yan Beiming]. *Wenhui bao*, January 27, 1966, 4.

唐长孺 Tang Changru. 历史唯物论, 还是阶级调和论 "Lishi weiwulun, haishi jieji tiaohelun" [Historical materialism or theory of class conciliation?]. *Wenhui bao*, January 14, 1966, 4.

唐真 Tang Zhen. 《海瑞罢官》的主题是什么 "'Hai Rui ba guan' de zhuti shi shenme?" [What is the theme of *Hai Rui Dismissed from Office*?] *Wenhui bao*, December 15, 1965, 4.

王鸿德 Wang Hongde. 不要锄掉《海瑞罢官》这朵花 "Bu yao chudiao 'Hai Rui ba guan' zhei duo hua" [*Hai Rui Dismissed from Office*: A flower that should not be uprooted]. *Wenhui bao*, December 25, 1965, 4.

王宏业 Wang Hongye. 向海瑞学习的目的何在？ "Xiang Hai Rui xuexi de mudi hezai?" [What is the purpose of learning from *Hai Rui Dismissed from Office*?] 文汇报 *Wenhui bao*, December 23, 1965, 4.

王金祥 Wang Jinxiang. 几个疑问 "Jige yiwen" [Some questions]. *Wenhui bao*, December 28, 1965, 4.

王连升 Wang Liansheng and 杨燕起 Yang Yanqi. 海瑞与"清官" "Hai Rui yu 'qingguan'" [Hai Rui and the honest officials]. *Beijing ribao*, December 18, 1965, 3.

王年一 Wang Nianyi. 大动乱的年代 *Da dongluan de niandai* [The years of the Great Disorder]. Zhengzhou: Henan renmin chubanshe, 1988.

王希曾 Wang Xizeng and 杨寿堪 Yang Shoukan. 为什么要歌颂"海瑞骂皇帝" "Weishenme yao gesong 'Hai Rui ma Huangdi'" [Why praise "Hai Rui scolds the emperor"?]. *Beijing ribao*, January 14, 1966, 3.

王彦坦 Wang Yantan, 蒋景源 Jiang Jingyuan, and 王家范 Wang Jiafan. 华东师范大学历史系三位同志的来信 "Huadong shifan daxue lishixi sanwei tongzhi de laixin" [Letter from three comrades of East China Normal College]. *Wenhui bao*, November 29, 1965, 2.

王子今 Wang Zijin. 历史学者毛泽东 *Lishi xuezhe Mao Zedong* [Mao Zedong as a history scholar]. Beijing: Xiyuan chubanshe, 2013.

韦格明 Wei Geming. 海瑞"刚直不阿"的反动性 "Hai Rui 'gangzhibue' de fandongxing" [The reactionary nature of the "outright and outspoken" Hai Rui]. *Wenhui bao*, February 8, 1966, 4.

文汇报编者 Wenhuibao bianzhe [Wenhuibao's editor]. "海瑞罢官" 问题的讨论逐步展开 "Hai Rui ba guan wenti de taolun zhubu zhankai" [The discussion on the problem of *Hai Rui Dismissed from Office* gradually unfolds]. *Wenhui bao*, December 6, 1965, 1.

吴晗 Wu Han. 海瑞骂皇帝 "Hai Rui ma huangdi." *Renmin ribao*, June 16, 1959, 8.

吴晗 Wu Han. 论海瑞 "Lun Hai Rui." *Renmin ribao*, September 17, 1959. Reprinted in 吴晗选集 *Wu Han xuanji*, 347-70. Tianjin: Tianjin renmin chubanshe, 1988.

吴晗 Wu Han. 海瑞罢官 *Hai Rui ba guan* [*Hai Rui dismissed from office*]. [1961]. Beijing: Beijing chubanshe, 1979. English version: Wu Han, *Hai Rui Dismissed from Office*, translated by C. C. Huang. *Asian Studies at Hawaii* 7 (1972): 104-20.

吴晗 Wu Han. 论历史剧 "Lun lishi ju" [On historical drama]. *Wenxue pinglun* [Literary critique] 3 (1961).

吴晗 Wu Han. 论历史知识的普及 "Lun lishi zhishi de puji" [On the popularization of historical knowledge]. [1962]. In 吴晗选集 *Wu Han xuanji* [Selected works of Wu Han], 392-407. Tianjin: Tianjin renmin chubanshe, 1988.

吴晗 Wu Han. 关于《海瑞罢官》的自我批评 "Guanyu 'Hai Rui ba guan' de ziwo piping" [A self-criticism of *Hai Rui Dismissed from Office*]. *Beijing ribao*, December 29, 1965, 3. English translation in *Chinese Studies in History and Philosophy* 2, no. 1 (1968): 68-107.

吴晗 Wu Han. 是革命, 还是继承 "Shi geming, haishi jicheng" [Revolutionizing or inheriting?]. *Beijing ribao*, January 12, 1966, 3.

吴君伟 Wu Junwei. 清官和贪官有别 "Qingguan he tanguan youbie" [There were differences between corrupt and honest officials]. *Wenhui bao*, January 14, 1966, 4.

习中文 Xi Zhongwen. 应该一分为二的看"清官"和"贪官" "Yinggai yifenweier de kan 'qingguan' he 'tanguan'" [We must apply the principle of one divides into two in assessing the "honest officials" and "corrupt officials"]. *Wenhui bao*, January 6, 1966, 4.

席宣 Xi Xuan and 金春明 Jin Chunming. "文化大革命"简史 *"Wenhua da geming" jianshi* [The "Great Cultural Revolution": A brief history]. Beijing: Zhonggong dang shi chubanshe, 1996.

向阳生 Xiang Yangsheng [邓拓 Deng Tuo]. 从《海瑞罢官》谈到道德继承论 "Cong 'Hai Rui ba guan' tandao daode jicheng lun" [Discussing the theory of moral heritage from *Hai Rui Dismissed from Office*]. *Beijing ribao*, December 12, 1965, 2–3.

肖镞 Xiao Zu. 从"教训"谈到"让步政策"—同严北溟等先生商榷 "Cong 'jiaoxun' tandao 'rangbu zhengce'—tong Yan Beiming deng xiansheng shangque" [Let us talk about the "policy of concessions" starting from their "lessons": A discussion with Mr. Yan Beiming and others]. *Wenhui bao*, January 13, 1966.

新建设变着 *Xin Jianshe* bianzhe [New Construction Editorial Board]. 当代史学界对中国农民战争史几个问题的讨论 "Dangdai shixue jie dui Zhongguo nongmin zhangzheng shi jige wenti de taolun" [The current discussion among Chinese historians on some questions concerning the history of peasant wars in China]. *Xin Jianshe* 2 (1962): 23–25.

徐德嶙 Xu Delin. 对"让步政策"的几点看法 "Dui 'rangbu zhengce de jidian kanfa'" [Some opinions on the "policy of concessions"]. *Wenhui bao*, January 13, 1966, 4.

徐德政 Xu Dezheng, 张锡厚 Zhang Xihou, and 栾贵明 Luan Guiming. 评吴晗同志《关于〈海瑞罢官〉的自我批评》"Ping Wu Han tongzhi 'Guanyu *Hai Rui ba guan* de ziwo piping'" [Discussing Comrade Wu Han's "Self-criticism about *Hai Rui Dismissed from Office*"]. *Beijing ribao*, December 31, 1965.

徐连达 Xu Lianda, 陈匡时 Chen Kuangshi, and 李春元 Li Chunyuan. "青天大老爷"真能"为民做主"吗？"'Qingtian dalaoye' zhen neng 'weimin zuozhu' ma?" [Could "The great lord Blue Sky" really "decide in favor of the people"?] *Wenhui bao*, December 25, 1965, 4.

严北溟 Yan Beiming. 对"让步政策"也要"一分为二" "Dui 'rangbu zhengce' ye yao 'yi fen wei er'" [Also with regard to the "politics of concessions" we must apply the principle "one divides into two"]. *Wenhui bao*, December 16, 1965, 4.

燕人 Yan Ren. 对历史剧《海瑞罢官》的几点看法—与姚文元同志商榷 "Dui lishiju 'Hai Rui ba guan' de jidian kanfa—yu Yao Wenyuan tongzhi shangque" [Some views on the historical play *Hai Rui Dismissed from Office*: A discussion with comrade Yao Wenyuan]. 文汇报 *Wenhui bao*, December 2, 1965, 4. English translation: *Chinese Studies in History and Philosophy* 2, no. 1 (1968): 56–67.

严问 Yan Wen. 评吴晗同志关于道德问题的"自我批评" "Ping Wu Han tongzhi guanyu daode wenti de 'ziwo piping'" [Discussing Comrade Wu Han's self-criticism on morals]. *Beijing ribao*, January 14, 1966, 3.

杨国宜 Yang Guoyi and 张海鹏 Zhang Haipeng. 究竟怎样认识"让步政策" "Jiujing zenyang renshi 'rangbu zhengce'" [Finally, how to understand the "policy of concessions"?]. *Wenhui bao*, January 17, 1966, 4.

杨金龙 Yang Jinlong. 对农民形象的歪曲 "Dui nongmin xingxiang de waiqu" [A deformation of the image of the peasants]. *Renmin ribao*, December 25, 1965, 5.

杨金亭 Yang Jinting. 《海瑞罢官》是阶级调和论的传声筒 "'Hai Rui ba guan' shi jieji tiaohelun de chuanshengtong" [*Hai Rui Dismissed from Office* is the mouthpiece of the theory of class conciliation]. *Beijing ribao*, December 25, 1965, 3.

姚铎铭 Yao Duoming. 全面地理解"让步政策" "Quanmian de lijie 'rangbu zhengce'" [Thoroughly understand the "policy of concessions"]. *Wenhui bao*, January 27, 1966, 4.

姚全兴 Yao Quanxing. 不能用形而上学代替辩证法。评"评新编历史《海瑞罢官》" "Bu neng yong xing'ershangxue daiti bianzhengfa: Ping 'Ping xinbian lishiju *Hai Rui ba guan*'" [It is not possible to replace dialectics with metaphysics: A criticism of the "Criticism of the recently written historical play *Hai Rui Dismissed from Office*"]. *Guangming ribao*, December 15, 1965, 3.

姚文元 Yao Wenyuan. 评新编历史剧《海瑞罢官》 "Ping xin bian lishi ju 'Hai Rui ba guan'" [On the new historical play *Hai Rui Dismissed from Office*]. 文汇报 *Wenhui bao*, November 10, 1965. Reprinted in 人民日报 *Renmin ribao*, November 30, 1965, 5. English version: *Chinese Studies in History and Philosophy* 2, no. 1 (1968): 13-43.

姚文远 Yao Wenyuan. "林彪反党集团的社会基础" "Lin Biao fan dang jituan de shehui jichu" [The social bases of Lin Biao's antiparty clique]. *Hongqi* 3 (1975): 20-29.

亦鸣 Yi Ming. 评新编历史剧《海瑞罢官》读后 "Ping xin bian lishiju 'Hai Rui ba guan' du hou" [After reading "Criticism of the recently composed historical drama *Hai Rui Dismissed from Office*"]. *Renmin ribao*, December 25, 1965, 5.

印红标 Yin Hongbiao. 文革 的 "第一张 马列主义大字报" Wenge de "di yi zhang maliezhuyi dazibao" [The first Marxist-Leninist dazibao of the Cultural Revolution]. In 文化大革命: 事实与研究 *Wenhua da geming: Shishi yu yanjiu* [The Cultural Revolution: Facts and analysis], 3-16. Hong Kong: Chinese University Press, 1996.

羽白 Yu Bai. 《海瑞罢官》基本上应该肯定 "'Hai Rui ba guan' jibenshang yinggai kending" [*Hai Rui Dismissed from Office* should be given a basically positive evaluation]. *Wenhui bao*, December 17, 1965, 4.

袁良义 Yuan Liangyi. 论"清"官不清 "Lun 'qing' guan bu qing" [On the dishonesty of "honest officials"]. *Wenhui bao*, January 11, 1966, 4.

岳华 Yue Hua. 关于道德的阶级性和继承性问题的讨论介绍 "Guanyu daode de jiejixing he jichengxing wenti de taolun jieshao" [Presentation of the discussion of the class character of morals]. *Beijing ribao*, December 18, 1965, 3.

张彬 Zhang Bin. 并没有原则分歧 "Bing meiyou yuanze fenqi" [There are no divergences of principle]. *Wenhui bao*, January 18, 1966, 4.

张春桥 Zhang Chunqiao. 关于修改宪法的报告 "Guanyu xiugai xianfa de baogao" [Report on the revision of the constitution]. *Hongqi* 2 (1975): 15-19.

张春桥 Zhang Chunqiao. 论对资产阶级全面专政 "Lun dui zichanjieji quanmian zhuanzheng" [The complete dictatorship over the bourgeoisie]. *Hongqi* 4 (1975): 3-12.

张春桥 Zhang Chunqiao. 在法庭上的讲话 "Zai fating shang de jianghua" [Speech in court], 1981. Accessed April 2019. https://blog.boxun.com/hero/201308/zgzj/15_1.shtml.

张春桥, 姚文元在上海群众大会上的讲话 "Zhang Chunqiao, Yao Wenyuan zai Shanghai qunzhong dahui shang de janghua" [Speeches by Zhang Chunqiao and Yao Wenyuan at a mass meeting in Shanghai], February 24, 1967. In 张春桥文集 *Zhang Chunqiao wenji* [Zhang Chunqiao collected works]. Beijing: Utopia Bookstore, n.d.

张晋藩 Zhang Jinfan. 海瑞执行的王法究竟是什么样的法？"Hai Rui zhixing de wangfa jiujing shi shenmeyang de fa?" [What law was the imperial law that Hai Rui applied?] *Wenhui bao*, February 4, 1966, 4.

赵少荃 Zhao Shaoquan, 陈匡时 Chen Kuangshi, 李春元 Li Chunyuan, and 韩国劲 Han Guojin. 复旦大学历史系四位同志的来信 "Fudan daxue lishixi siwei tongzhi de laixin" [Letter from four comrades in the History Department of Fudan University]. *Wenhui bao*, November 29, 1965, 2. English translation: *Chinese Studies in History and Philosophy* 2, no. 1 (1968): 44–48.

张延举 Zhang Yanju. 海瑞实行了让步的改良 "Hai Rui shixing le rangbu de gailiang" [Hai Rui implemented the policy of concessions]. *Beijing ribao*, January 26, 1966.

赵衍孙 Zhao Yansun. 吴晗同志是和无产阶级进行较量 "Wu Han tongzhi shi he wuchanjieji jinxing jiaoliang" [Comrade Wu Han is competing with the proletariat]. *Beijing ribao*, January 14, 1966, 3.

张益 Zhang Yi. 揭穿《海瑞罢官》的错误实质 "Jiechuan 'Hai Rui ba guan' de cuowu shizhi" [Expose the wrong essence of *Hai Rui Dismissed from Office*]. *Wenhui bao*, December 20, 1965, 4.

张贻玖 Zhang Yijiu. 毛泽东读史 *Mao Zedong du shi* [Mao Zedong studying history]. Beijing: Dangdai Zhongguo chubanshe, 2005.

张湛彬 Zhang Zhanbin. 文革第一文字狱 *Wenge diyi wenziyu* [The first literary inquisition of the Cultural Revolution]. Xianggang: Taiping shiji chubanshe, 1998.

中国共产党中央委员会关于无产阶级文化大革命的决定 "Zhongguo gongchandang zhongyang weiyuanhui guanyu wuchanjieji wenhua da geming de jueding", [Decision of the Central Committee of the Chinese Communist Party Concerning the Great Proletarian Cultural Revolution] (Adopted on August 8, 1966) in 中国文化大革命文库 *Zhongguo wenhua da geming wenku* [Chinese Cultural Revolution Database], part 1.

中国共产党第十一届中央委员会第二次全体会议 Zhongguo gongchandang di shi jie zhongyang weiyuanhui di er ci quanti hui [The Second Plenary Session of the Eleventh Central Committee of the Communist Party of China]. 关于建国以来党的若干历史问题的决议 "Guanyu jianguo yilai dang de ruogan lishi wenti de jueyi" [On some questions concerning the history of the party since the founding of the PRC]. *Renmin ribao*, July 1, 1981, 1–7.

中国共产党章程 *Zhongguo Gongchandang zhangcheng* [Constitution of the Chinese Communist Party]. Beijing: Renmin chubanshe, 2017.

中国共产党中央委员会通知及原件附件二 Zhongguo Gongchandang zhongyang weiyuanwei tongzhi ji yuanjian fujian er [China Communist Party Central Committeee, Circular with the original appendix 2], May 16, 1966. In 中国文化大革命文库 *Zhongguo wenhua da geming wenku* [Chinese Cultural Revolution Database], part 1.

中国人民解放军, 国防大学, 党史政工教研室 Zhongguo renmin jiefangjun, Guofang daxue, Dangshi zhenggong jiaoyanshi [Chinese People's Liberation Army, National Defense University, Teaching and Research Section on Party History and Political Work]. 文化大革命" 研究资料 *"Wenhua da geming" yanjiu ziliao* [Research materials on the "Great Cultural Revolution"], 2. Beijing: Guofang daxue, 1988.

中国文化大革命文库 *Zhongguo wenhua da geming wenku* [Chinese Cultural Revolution Database]. 主编, 宋永毅 Editor in chief, Song Yongyi. Xianggang: Zhongwen daxue, 2002.

中共中央批转文化革命五人小组关于当前学术讨论的汇报提纲 "Zhonggong zhongyang pizhuan wenhua geming wuren xiaozu guanyu dangqian xueshu taolun de huibao tigang" [Issued with instructions from the CCP CC: Outline report by the five-member Cultural Revolution small group concerning the current academic discussion], February 12, 1966. In 中国文化大革命文库 *Zhongguo wenhua dageming wenku* [Chinese Cultural Revolution Database], part 1. English translation: *Chinese Politics: Documents and Analysis*, vol. 1: *Cultural Revolution to 1969*, edited by J. Myers, J. Domes, and E. von Groeling, 194–97. Los Angeles: University of Southern California Press, 1986.

朱理章 Zhu Lizhang. 拨开迷雾看"清官" "Bokai miwu kan 'qingguan'" [Dissolve the curtain of fog around the "honest officials"]. *Wenhui bao*, January 6, 1966, 4.

朱相黑 Zhu Xianghei. 海瑞让步使人民得益 "Hai Rui rangbu shi renmin deyi" [Hai Rui's concessions brought benefit to the people]. 文汇报 *Wenhui bao*, December 28, 1965, 4.

INDEX

"Adieu Tomb" (Gu Cheng), 232–33
Agents of Disorder (Walder), 164
agricultural cooperatives, 77
agricultural production, 23–24, 29–30, 32
Albanian delegation, 91–92, 131, 141, 277
Albanian Workers' Party, 92
Althusser, Louis, 137, 202
Andreas, Joel, 162
années rouges, Les (Hua Linshan), 314n26
anti-Japanese resistance, 306n8
Anti-Memoirs (Malraux), 96
"Appeal to All Shanghai People" (WGH), 177–78, 180, 188, 191
April 14th faction, 163, 217, 224

Badiou, Alain, 37, 125, 272
Balasz, Étienne, 17
base/superstructure model, 40, 42–43, 243–44
Beida dazibao, 141, 144, 150, 185, 194, 208
Bei Dao, 227
Beijing daxue xuebao, 256
Beijing opera, 17, 49
Beijing Party Committee, 50, 61, 116–17, 294n17
Beijing ribao, 52, 60–62, 294n17

Beijing University (Beida), 39, 207–8, 229
Bergère, Marie Claire, 28, 47–48
Black Hand, 207–17, 224. *See also* Red Guards
Bloch, Marc, 12
bloodline theory, 156, 168, 308n19
Blue Sky figures, 64, 68, 73
Bolsheviks, 171, 210
Bourdieu, Pierre, 163
bourgeoisie: ideology of, 83, 112, 126; morals of, 62; relationship with, 125, 182–83, 187, 247; restoration of, 76, 95, 122, 277–80; rights of, 249, 257; society of, 63, 155, 259. *See also* class

Cao Cao, 216, 219
Cao Diqiu, 169, 199
capitalism, 84; alternatives to, 1–2, 4; conditions of, 174, 278; dominance of, 247, 256, 283; followers of, 184, 192; and private property, 257; restoration of, 95, 98, 127, 130, 235; and socialism, 83, 91, 102, 265
Cartier, Michel, 21
Celestial Palace, 120, 126, 305n36

censorship, 49–51, 53–54, 71, 81, 112–13, 153, 225
Central Committee of the CCP, 82–83, 107, 110, 116–17, 120, 127, 182, 189, 225, 275, 292n6, 292n11
Central Group of the Cultural Revolution (CGCR): positions of, 169–71; and the Red Guards, 204–25, 230, 314n22, 315n42; and the Shanghai Commune, 189, 200–201
Charlemagne, 134
chedi fouding (thorough negation), 264
Chen Boda, 115, 118, 169, 214, 240, 311n16
Cheng Zhongyuan, 318n1, 319nn9,11
Chen Pixian, 169
China: and the CPSU, 248; education system of, 105–6; history of, 243, 245; isolation of, 77; and the USSR, 143, 303n12, 304n20
Chinese Civil War, 199, 316–17n5. *See also* People's War
Chinese Communist Party (CCP): authority of, 253, 260; and capitalism, 2; Congresses of, 241, 270; and the CPSU, 94, 131–32, 143; foundation of, 80; leadership of, 30, 147, 150, 153, 241, 264, 268, 276; membership in, 270; and the peasants, 28, 45, 55, 73; and the people's communes, 31; principles of, 23, 34, 61, 120, 159–60, 216, 234; role of, 154, 192, 194; and the state bureaucratic apparatus, 151, 235; and the study of theory, 32–33, 272; and the USSR, 35, 95; and workers, 167–68, 281, 310n8
Chinese cultural identity, 20, 68
Chinese foreign policy, 304n20, 319n3
Chinese historiography, 74, 110–11, 135, 198
Chinese People's Political Consultative Conference (CPPCC), 296n32
Civil War in France (Marx), 100
class: analysis of, 25, 52; consciousness of, 43–44; in the Cultural Revolution, 261; distinctions of, 84; enemies based on, 146, 278; hierarchy of, 19, 21, 23, 46, 56, 247; and morality, 59, 61; and nature of truth, 124–25; reconciliation of, 77–78; and struggle, 40, 61, 63–66, 76–78, 80, 124, 151, 181, 187, 227. *See also* bourgeoisie; proletariat
Cold War, 35, 131, 151
collectivization, 23, 37
commodity exchange, 132, 157–58, 248–49
communism: as an economic ideal, 30; culture of, 246; experimental visions of, 173; international movement of, 95; official doctrines of, 187; reexamination of, 1–2; and socialism, 61, 96, 99, 282
Communist Manifesto (Marx and Engels), 1–2, 246
Communist Party of the Soviet Union (CPSU): and the CCP, 35, 94–95, 98, 131–32, 143; and China, 248; dissolution of, 194; ideology of, 101–2; and Stalin, 96; Twentieth Congress of, 95, 101; Twenty-Third Congress of, 303n12
Comte, Auguste, 273
Confucianism, 6, 21, 69–70, 73, 114, 241–43, 310n8. *See also* Legalism
Congress of the CCP: Nineteenth, 241; Tenth, 270
Constitution of Anshan Iron and Steel Company, 261
counterrevolutionary subversion, 129
countryside, 21, 24, 31, 34, 38, 280
coups d'état, 129–31, 241, 279
Criticize Confucius Campaign, 241–43, 245
"Criticizing Confucianism, Discussing Legalism." *See* Criticize Confucius Campaign
Cui Zhiyuan, 320n10
cultural apparatuses, 54, 105–6
Cultural Revolution: assessment of, 30, 139, 240, 245–46, 274–75, 277, 283; class in, 261; and the danwei system,

250–54; dismissal during, 145–46; early stages of, 47, 51, 53, 258; ending years of, 262; and the January Storm, 182; leadership of, 127; and likelihood of defeat, 91–103; Mao's concerns during, 103–5; mass phase of, 5, 154, 167–68, 204, 270; opposition to, 264; outcomes of, 6, 195, 264; and pluralization, 146–48; prologue to, 11–27, 67, 82, 119, 128, 136, 272; reassessment of, 265, 267; scholarship on, 3, 124, 135, 148–50; targets of, 13
cultural struggle, 217

Dante, 225
danwei system, 173–77, 250–54, 310n8
Daodejing, 316n2
Dazhai, 280
decentralization, 29, 289n8
Decision in 16 Points, 154, 169, 206, 230
defeat (probability of), 91–103, 196, 204–37
Deng Rong, 274, 318n2
Deng Tuo, 60–62, 65, 86, 108, 116–17, 123–24, 304n25
Deng Xiaoping: appointment of, 264; biographies of, 276; and factionalism, 268–70; leadership of, 107, 153, 212, 292n3; and Mao Zedong, 49–50, 240, 266, 271, 273–75, 318n2; and the mass study movements, 6; and Peng Dehuai, 38; and Peng Zhen, 115; and pluralization, 152; and political theory, 267; reforms of, 31, 316n4; rehabilitation of, 265, 297n44; *Selected Works* of, 267; strategy of, 27, 262–85; supporters of, 7, 268–69
Department of Propaganda, 50, 111, 113–14, 137, 305n36
"destroy the four old things" movement, 156–57, 308n21
dialectical materialism, 52
dialectical metaphysics, 272
dialectics, 58, 216, 272

dictatorship of the proletariat, 6, 98–99, 102, 127, 170, 182, 197, 246–50, 254, 257–58, 265, 272, 279
discipline, 30, 153, 267–68, 280–81
Discourses over Salt and Iron, 288n5
dismissal, 127–29, 145–48, 235–36, 286n8
disorder, 269
Donglin Party, 17
Durkheim, Émile, 134, 161

Earliest Resistance, The (Party School of the Central Committee), 114, 116–17
Earth faction, 159, 208–9, 221, 314n22. *See also* Sky faction
economics: and the ideal of communism, 30; inequalities of, 158
economism, 180, 311n12
education, 105–6, 131–35, 141, 143, 154, 168, 225–30
Emperor Jiaqing, 26–27, 69
Emperor Qin Shi Huangdi, 69
Engels, Fredrich, 1, 100, 265, 278, 291n29
equality, 19, 147, 249; and mass activism, 275; subjectivities of, 147; virtues of, 241

factionalism: dissolution of, 205–25, 315–16n44; explanations of, 161, 164–65, 204, 239; and revolutionary culture, 232–35; rise of, 150, 159, 187, 200; threat of, 267, 269; violence of, 206
factories, 174–76, 250–57
falsified statistics, 29–30, 32, 67
famine, 29
Fang Qiu. *See* Zhou Yang
February Outline: criticism of, 113; and the *Hai Rui* controversy, 112, 123, 136; publication of, 81–89, 110–11; reversal of, 114–18, 120, 143
Feng Xianzhi, 318n1, 319n9
fetishism of commodities, 248, 256
fetishism of technology, 255–56
feudalism, 42–43, 45, 56, 62–63, 78, 243, 245–46

First Literary Inquisition of the Cultural Revolution, The (Zhang Zhanbin), 51
five-year plan of 1953-58, 37
Fourth National People's Congress, 246-47, 264
Foxconn, 281-82
Fractured Rebellion (Walder), 162
France, 167
freedom: of political thought, 217; of the press, 148; of speech, 112-13, 119-20; to strike, 246, 252, 316n4
French Revolution, 1, 134-35, 157-58, 273
Freud, Sigmund, 272
Fudan letter, 54

Gang of Four, 3
Gao Gao, 110-11
Gao Mobo, 29, 289n8
Gao Yubao, 227
"General Program of Activities of the Party and the Whole Country" (Political Research Office), 266, 273
Great Leap Forward, 20, 27, 29-34, 61, 67-68, 95
great purges, 94
great school, 131-35, 226
"Great Union of the Popular Masses, The" (Mao Zedong), 184
Group of Five, 50, 62, 81-82, 87, 109-10, 113-18, 120, 136-37, 292n6, 301n80
Guan Feng, 314n23
Guangming ribao, 52, 294n17
Guangxi, 222, 314n26
Gu Cheng, 232-33
Guomindang, 36, 97, 194, 310n8

Hai Rui: critiques of, 11-25, 68-70; and Deng Tuo, 116; development of, 11-26, 38-39, 286n4; figure of, 11-26, 30, 56-58, 72, 78; influence of, 47-92, 123, 127, 136, 141, 143, 154, 243; and Mao Zedong, 30, 103, 106-12; theatrical rendition of, 5, 11-26, 38, 46-47, 51, 54, 56, 74, 79, 106, 293n16

Han Aijing, 207, 209, 215, 220-25
Han Dynasty, 69, 288n5
Han Feizi, 243
Han Shaogong, 227
Hegel, Georg Friedrich Wilhelm, 175, 272
Hinton, William, 224, 314n29
historical materialism, 5, 25, 42, 46, 56, 58, 61, 80, 87, 94-96, 125, 181, 241-46, 291n29. See also dialectical materialism
historiography, 24, 38-42, 47-51, 57, 74, 79, 108-11, 121, 124, 135, 198, 204-5, 212, 260, 288n5
Hongqi, 182-83, 188
How to Be a Good Communist (Liu Shaoqi), 315n32
Hua Linshan, 314n26
Huang Yongshen, 211
Huang Zouzhen, 208, 223-24
humanism, 94-95
Hunan self-study university, 228
Hu Qiaomu, 67-68, 71-72, 297n44
Hu Sheng, 111

ideology, 27, 137, 174, 243
independent organizations, 172, 177-78, 181, 186, 193, 250-51
industrial danwei, 173-77, 279
industrialization, 31, 37
intellectual class, 102
International communist movement, 95, 144
isolation of China, 77
Italy, 167

Jade Palace, 122, 126, 128
January Storm, 5, 150, 159, 166, 173, 176, 180, 187-89, 191-92, 198, 202, 232, 250-51, 261, 270, 311n12
Japanese invasion, 97
Jian Bozan, 39-41, 44-46, 58
Jiang Qing, 49, 51, 93, 106-7, 121, 130, 156, 207, 215, 219, 228, 242, 314n22
Jiefangjun bao, 52

Jiefang ribao, 19, 49
Jin Chongji, 318n1, 319n9
Jing Chi, 318n11
Jinggangshan, 163, 224
Journey to the West (Wu Cheng'en), 118

Kang Sheng, 107, 115, 219
Kapital, Das (Marx), 202, 248
Kautsky, Karl, 99–101
Khrushchev, Nikita, 35, 94, 127, 143, 196
King of Hell, 112–14, 118–19, 126, 128, 131, 136–37, 144–45, 303n18, 305n36
Kuai Dafu, 209, 212, 215, 217, 219, 223–24

labor: commodification of, 160, 259–69, 279–80, 283; division of, 174, 198, 255, 257; and heroism rhetoric, 32; relations of, 259
Legalism, 6, 69, 243–44, 288n5. *See also* Confucianism
Lenin, Vladimir, 19–20, 43–44, 99–101, 173, 180, 196–97, 228, 246–50, 258, 260, 265, 277, 291n27
Levin, Steven, 319n4
L'évolution pédagogique en France (Durkheim), 134
Liao Mosha, 116, 296n32
Liberation, the, 37–38
Lin Biao, 127, 129–33, 139, 211, 213, 215–16, 222–23, 226, 228, 241–42, 305n36, 315n42
Li Rui, 28, 34, 288n5, 289n13
literature, 12, 23, 205, 226–27
Little Generals, 205–25
Liu Bei, 216
Liu Dajie, 57, 75
Liu Shaoqi, 107, 115, 152–54, 212
Long March, 199, 305n36
L'Unità, 95
Luo Ruiqing, 305n36
Lushan (Mount Lu), 27, 240
Lushan Conference: controversy at, 26–27, 36, 41, 44, 47, 71, 76, 280; original agenda of, 28–31; outcomes of, 33, 77, 108–9; perceptions of, 28, 30, 289n13; preparation for, 67
Lushan huiyi shilu (Li Rui), 289n13

Machiavelli, Niccolò, 243
Malraux, André, 96–97, 105–6
Mang Ke, 227
Manifesto of the Shanghai Commune, 190–92
Manual of Soviet Political Economics, 33
Maoism: and cult of personality, 141; leaders of, 147, 204; politics of, 87, 243, 253, 261, 270; rhetoric of, 141
Mao Zedong: assassination attempt on, 239; attitude of, 31, 98, 120, 131, 160; authority of, 28, 116–17, 129–31, 240; compared to Qin Shi Huangdi, 245; and Deng Xiaoping, 274–75, 318n2; and the dictatorship of the proletariat, 254, 257; and dismissal, 300n75; on education, 226; and factionalism, 201, 239; and the February Outline, 82; and the Guangxi situation, 222; and the Hai Rui controversy, 12, 26, 47, 51, 67, 91, 104–9; historiographical view of, 193; influence of, 183; and the January Storm, 181–87, 202; and Lin Biao, 241–42, 315n42; and metaphysics, 272–73; opposition to, 27, 29, 49–50, 52, 110, 273; and other communist leaders, 258; and the peasants, 36; and Peng Dehuai, 33–35, 66–67, 71; and Peng Zhen, 109, 113, 115; personality cult of, 49, 142, 144, 157; and philosophy, 124, 225; politics of, 88, 92, 135–40, 261; and the Red Guards, 207–25, 230, 313n5; and revisionism, 99, 101–3; and seizure of power, 234; self-criticism of, 276; and the Shanghai Commune, 190, 192; and the study of theory, 263, 265–67, 271–72, 316n5; style of, 204; thinking of, 61, 83; and the USSR, 102, 248; and victory discourses, 97; writings of, 37–38, 68, 95, 98, 125, 184, 191, 289n13, 303n4

Marx, Karl, 1, 44, 92–93, 100–101, 158, 173, 197, 202, 228, 247–49, 255, 257–58, 260, 265, 272, 277–78, 281, 291n29
Marxism, 126, 132, 156, 173, 213, 227–28, 246, 251, 279
Marxism-Leninism, 6, 43, 58, 61, 83–84, 181, 212, 231, 249
Marxo-Confucianism, 39, 283
mass movements, 6, 30, 91–92, 98, 102
materialism, 130, 155
May 7 Directive, 137, 241, 257
May 16 Circular, 83, 114, 117–23, 127–29, 134–35, 143–44, 182, 204n30
Ma Yanwen, 318n11
May Fourth Movement, 184, 228
means of production, 258–59
mechanization, 37
Menshevik, 210
metaphysics, 58, 272
militarism, 36, 131–32
military-civilian interchange, 132
military policy, 205n36
military strategy, 216
Ming Dynasty, 11–12, 21–22, 27, 60, 71, 79
Miyazaki Ichisada, 114
modes of production, 258
Montesquieu, Charles-Louis de Secondat, 243
moral inheritance, 60, 108, 116
morality, 13–14, 22, 59, 61–62
movement for the study of the theory, 241, 250

New Beida (Commune), 208
New Beida (Jingangshan), 210, 218
New China News Agency, 107
New Culture Movement, 105–6, 303n4
Nie Yuanzi, 150, 207–8, 211–13, 218, 220
Niu Huilin, 220
Normal University (Beijing), 209, 219, 314n22

October Revolution, 1, 101–2
Office for Academic Criticism, 86

"On Hai Rui" (Wu Han), 63–64, 70–75
"On Some Questions Regarding the Historical Play" (Wu Han), 75
On the Correct Handling of Contradictions among the People (Mao Zedong), 95
"On the Historical Experience of the Dictatorship of the Proletariat" (*Renmin ribao* editorial), 98, 248
"On the Proletarian Revolutionaries' Struggle to Seize Power" (*Renmin ribao*), 183–84
On the Ten Major Relationships (Mao Zedong), 38
opportunism, 99
ownership (forms of), 43, 45, 64, 257–62, 287n22

Palatine School, 134
Pantsov, Alexander, 319n4
Paris Commune, 100–102, 185, 191, 195
Party Central Committee, 26–27
Party Committee of Beijing Municipality, 116
Party School of the Central Committee, 114
party-state apparatus, 57, 74, 161, 192, 205, 217, 253, 256, 270
peasants: conditions of, 14–15, 17, 19; perception of, 20, 22; political subjectivity of, 5, 19–20, 28, 30–31, 35–40, 42, 46, 73, 78, 280; revolts by, 39–40, 42, 45
Peng Dehuai, 26–29, 33–36, 38, 66, 70, 73, 108–9, 112, 240, 288n5, 297n42
Peng Zhen, 50–53, 59–60, 62–63, 80–82, 103, 106–13, 115, 117, 120–27, 131, 292n6
people's communes, 23–24, 27, 31, 87, 132, 280
People's Liberation Army (PLA), 36, 52–53, 131–32, 218, 222, 241, 314n26
People's War, 30, 33, 36–37, 41, 78, 96, 132, 218
periodization, 148–50, 186, 263
Piazzaroli Longobardi, Andrea, 317n10

pi Lin pi Kong movement. *See* Criticize Confucius Campaign
pluralization, 128, 131, 145–48, 154, 157–58, 165, 187, 200, 235
policy of concessions, 39–42, 58, 299n66
Politburo of the Central Committee, 50–51
politics: and activism, 36, 141–42, 155–56; culture of, 128, 240; and experimentation, 3, 29, 33, 61, 71, 98, 131, 149, 151, 161–62, 168, 197–99, 234, 236, 250–51, 254–57, 268; and morality, 22; and philosophy, 123–27; as a profession, 145–46, 181; and realism, 96–97; and sociology, 20; subjectivity of, 44, 67, 253, 280; and theater, 11–25
Pozzana, Claudia 315n37
Pravda, 95
PRC Constitution of 1975, 316n3
production statistics, 29–30, 32, 67
progress: of communism, 96; of history, 26, 44, 46, 56; visions of, 95
"Proletarian Revolutionaries Form a Great Alliance" (*Renmin ribao*), 183
proletariat, 80, 187. *See also* class; dictatorship of the proletariat
propaganda, 14, 30, 32, 57, 59, 61, 111, 113, 137, 224, 281
Propaganda Department of the Beijing Municipal Party Committee, 296n32
Pun Ngai, 281

Qianxian, 61
Qi Benyu, 45–46, 308n21, 314n23
Qing Dynasty, 13, 36
Qinghua University, 154, 162–63, 206
Quemoy, 33

Ranke, Leopold von, 46
Red Army, 37
Red Guards: activism of, 157, 225; and the Black Hand, 207–17; dissolution of, 158–61, 205–7, 223, 233, 239; in the early Cultural Revolution, 258; early organizations of, 152, 155; expansion of, 150–52, 156; and imaginary seizure of power, 235; leaders of, 204–6, 218; and Mao Zedong, 207–25, 313n5; politics of, 168, 230; rise of, 141, 143–44, 147, 165; and the Scarlet Guards, 186; violence of, 314n26
relations of production, 244
Renmin ribao, 53–54, 59, 98, 107, 182–83, 248, 294n17
Report of Investigation on the Peasant Movement in Hunan (Mao Zedong), 37
Repressive State Apparatuses (RSAs), 137
"Response to Guo Moruo" (Mao Zedong), 191
revisionism, 24, 91–103, 113, 126–28, 130, 132, 143, 157
revolutionary classism, 146
Revolutionary Committee, 5, 189, 192–93, 199. *See also* Shanghai Commune
revolutionary consciousness, 44
revolutionary culture, 6, 19–20, 95–96, 145, 160, 187, 191, 232, 234, 242–43
Revolutionary Rebel Workers, 163, 170–71
Robespierre, Maximilien, 157–58

Saint-Just, Louis Antoine Léon de, 147, 267
San jia cun ("The Village of the Three Families"), 61, 116
Scarlet Guards, 163, 171–73, 177–79, 186, 188, 192
Schurmann, Franz, 31, 174, 252, 255
Second Shanghai People's Commune, 190
seizure of power, 6, 162, 164, 180–92, 196, 199, 202–3
"Self-Criticism" (Wu Han), 63–66, 68, 74–76, 80, 86–87
Shanghai Commune, 5, 181–82, 189–92, 200. *See also* Revolutionary Committee

Shanghai Party Committee (SPC), 49, 109, 169–71, 176, 178–79, 186–87, 192, 253, 300n74
Shanghai political experimentation, 197–99
Shanghai Workers Revolutionary Rebel General Headquarters (WGH), 169–71, 177–80, 182, 188, 192, 200
Shi Shaobin, 80
Sima Yi, 216
Sky faction, 159, 208–9, 221. *See also* Earth faction
social inequalities, 155
socialism: and capitalism, 83, 91, 102, 265, 282; classical doctrine of, 251; and classifying of the people, 155; and communism, 61, 96, 98; enthusiasm for, 57; as the exception, 1–2, 91–96, 98–99, 247, 278; experiences of, 277; and peasants, 5; and the political role of workers, 184, 200; regimes of, 128, 246; structure of, 243
social value of workers, 43
sociology, 161–66
"Some Opinions about the Group of Five's Outline" (Zhang Chunqiao), 115
sovereignty, 147
Soviet planning theory, 32–33
Spider Eaters (Yang Rae), 315n33
Stakhanovism, 32, 179, 253
Stalin, Josef, 94, 96, 228, 256, 291n29
Stalinism, 125, 248, 272, 278
Standing Committee of the Political Bureau, 110
state apparatus, 29, 48–49, 268
State Council Political Research Office, 272
state cultural apparatus, 136, 141
student movements, 143, 152–54, 167–68, 214, 222
student organizations, 169, 307n13
study of theory, 254–57, 270
Sun, Warren, 318n1
Sun Quan, 216

Tan Houlan, 207, 209, 216, 219, 314n22
Taylorism, 281
Teacher Training College in Changsha, 133–34, 228
technocratic values, 281
Teiwes, Fredrick, 318n1
Tian'anmen movement of 1989, 194, 279, 321n22, 321n25
totalitarianism discourses, 259
triple combines, 270

United Nations, 319n3
United States: and China, 287n24; in Vietnam, 131, 304n20, 305n36
University of the Anti-Japanese Resistance, 228
"Urgent Notice" (WGH), 177–78, 180, 182, 188–89, 191
USSR: and bourgeois ideas, 84; capitalism in, 95; and China, 35, 143, 248, 303n12, 304n20; consolidation of, 94; and economic cooperation, 287n24; influence of, 32, 253; and Mao Zedong, 102; transformation of, 258

victory discourses, 93, 95–98, 196
Vietnam War, 132, 151, 304n20, 305n36; US aggression in, 131
Vogel, Ezra, 266
Vukovich, Daniel, 289n2

wage: labor, 175; slavery, 92
Wajda, Andrzej, 32
Walder, Andrew, 162–65
Wang Dabing, 207, 209, 213
Wang Guangmei, 154
Wang Hongwen, 170, 192, 270
Wang Li, 314n22
Wang Nianyi, 135, 292n11
War of Liberation, 199, 316–17n5
Weber, Max, 145–46, 154, 181, 187
Wenhui bao, 49–50, 54, 59, 74, 80, 107, 112, 286n7, 293n16, 294n17
What Is to Be Done? (Lenin), 43, 291n27

White, Lynn, 161
workers: and the CCP, 310n8; as a class, 167–203, 280–84; independent organizations of, 251; intellectual activity of, 198; mobilization of, 232; organization of, 168–73, 257; political activism of, 269; political subjectivity of, 179, 184, 187, 200, 253; precarity of, 259; and the relationship to the factory, 252; rights of, 246; study groups of, 245; and universities, 255. *See also* class
World War I, 100–101
World War II, 132
Wu Cheng'en, 118
Wu Han: and the *Hai Rui* controversy, 5, 11–26, 120; influence of, 39, 116, 268n12; opposition to, 53, 59, 62–63, 80–81, 105, 107, 296n33; and Peng Dehuai, 109; self-criticism of, 74–76; supporters of, 57, 77–78, 86–87
Wu Zhuanbin, 221

Xia Xingzhen, 318n1, 319nn9,11
Xiang Yangsheng. *See* Deng Tuo
Xie Fuzhi, 207, 213, 224, 315n42
Xinhua Shudian, 51–52
Xuexi yu pipan, 255
Xu Liqun, 111

Yan'an period, 49
Yang Guobin, 232

Yang Lian, 227
Yang Rae, 315n33
Yang Shangkun, 205n36
Yan Jiaqi, 110–11
Yao Wenyuan: and the *Hai Rui* controversy, 11–26, 39, 48, 51, 79, 85, 107, 293n14, 294n17; influence of, 81–83, 87, 122, 198, 280; and Mao Zedong, 104–5, 113, 182, 192–94, 214, 219; opposition to, 57, 128; and the Shanghai Commune, 189; support for, 54
Years of Great Disorder, The (Wang Nianyi), 135
Yiguandao, 194
Youth League, 152
Yu Luoke, 308n19

Zhang Chunqiao, 3, 49–51, 106, 112, 115, 127, 170–71, 182, 189, 192–94, 198–99, 249, 316n3
Zhang Zhanbin, 51
zhengdun politics, 267, 269, 274
Zhongnanhai meeting of July 1968, 205–32, 239
Zhou Enlai, 35, 51, 54, 107, 215, 219, 221, 224–28, 275, 311n16, 316–17n5, 318n2
Zhou Quanying, 217
Zhou Yang, 62–63
Zhou Yu, 215
Zhou Yutong, 75

www.ingramcontent.com/pod-product-compliance
Lightning Source LLC
Chambersburg PA
CBHW050200240426
43671CB00013B/2195